THE UNPOLITICAL

The Unpolitical

On the Radical Critique of Political Reason

Massimo Cacciari

Edited and with an Introduction by Alessandro Carrera
Translated by Massimo Verdicchio

FORDHAM UNIVERSITY PRESS

New York   2009

The editor wishes to acknowledge the financial support of
the University of Houston GEAR (Grants to Enhance and
Advance Research) in the editing process of this book, and
the financial support of the University of Houston Small
Grants Program in the publication of this book.

Library of Congress Cataloging-in-Publication Data
Cacciari, Massimo.
The unpolitical : on the radical critique of political reason /
Massimo Cacciari ; edited and with an introduction by
Alessandro Carrera ; translated by Massimo
Verdicchio.—1st ed.
p.   cm.
Includes bibliographical references and index.
ISBN 978-0-8232-3003-7 (cloth : alk. paper)
ISBN 978-0-8232-3004-4 (pbk. : alk. paper)
1. Political science—Philosophy.
I. Carrera, Alessandro, 1954–   II. Title.
JA71.C23   2009
320.01—dc22
2008047151

Printed in the United States of America
11 10 09   5 4 3 2 1
First edition

CONTENTS

THE UNPOLITICAL

On Massimo Cacciari's Disenchanted Activism

Alessandro Carrera

Negative Thought and the Autonomy of Politics

Massimo Cacciari's career is nothing short of impressive. Both an academic philosopher and a public figure who has devoted a significant part of his life to active politics, he is also one of the high-profile intellectuals in contemporary Italy. Born in Venice in 1944, Cacciari graduated in philosophy from the University of Padua with a dissertation on Kant's *Critique of Judgment*. When he was twenty years old, he and literary scholar Cesare De Michelis started *Angelus novus*, an innovative journal that lasted from 1964 to 1966. Between 1968 and 1971 Cacciari coedited another journal, *Contropiano: Materiali marxisti* (Counterplan: Marxist Materials) with Alberto Asor Rosa, later an influential scholar and a leading literary critic. Between 1967 and 1969 Cacciari was close to the radical leftist movement Potere Operaio (Workers' Power). In the early 1970s he abandoned his initial radicalism and in 1971 was appointed professor of history of architecture at the Architecture Institute of Venice; in 1985, he became professor of aesthetics in the same school. In 1976 he joined the Italian Communist Party and served as representative to the Italian Parliament from 1976 to 1983. In 1983 he abandoned his party militancy.

At the beginning of the 1980s, Cacciari began an intensive collaboration with two new journals, *Il centauro* (The Centaur, 1980–1985), and

Laboratorio Politico (Political Laboratory, 1980–1985). Without neglecting his scholarly production, which culminated in his massive theoretical oeuvre, *Dell'inizio* (On Beginning, 1990), Cacciari remained in the political arena. After 1989, the official left wing being still reluctant to accept the broad ideological changes made inevitable by the fall of the Berlin Wall, he decided to act at the grassroots level. For two electoral terms, from 1993 to 2000, Cacciari was elected mayor of Venice. During his mandate, he demonstrated that the philosopher could indeed rule the *polis*, winning the respect of the citizens and even of his political adversaries. In the meantime he founded another philosophical journal, *Paradosso* (Paradox), coedited with philosophers Sergio Givone, Carlo Sini, and Vincenzo Vitiello. In 1988, thinking that a federal reform of the Italian Constitution was the solution to the excessive centralization of the Italian government and bureaucracy, Cacciari coauthored a "Federalist Charter" that was supposed to anticipate and prevent the separatist tendencies of new political entities such as the Northern League and the Venetian League. He received little or no political support from the official left wing, where many career politicians were suspicious of his maverick position. With or without their endorsement, Cacciari became a major force in the so-called Movimento dei sindaci (Mayors' Movement), a loose organization, or better, a forum, of one hundred Italian mayors who set out to convince the reluctant central government to give more political and fiscal autonomy to city councils. The year 2000 was another turning point in Cacciari's career. He resigned from his position as a representative in the European Parliament in Strasbourg and, still championing his federalist agenda, became a member of the Regional Council for the Veneto Region. In 2002, his decision to give up active politics came as a surprise to many. He accepted the position of dean of philosophy at the new Università Vita-Salute—San Raffaele in Cesano Maderno near Milan, where his aim was to create a school of high politics and to provide the Italian and European political scene with a new breed of public intellectuals and political scientists. In 2004, giving in to pressures from several Venetians, he accepted to run for mayor again, and he is now in his third term. He remains on the board of directors at San Raffaele University.

This busy man's bibliography is enormous: more than forty authored and coauthored books (several of them translated into all major European languages), and literally hundreds of articles, essays, interviews and journalistic pieces. Cacciari's range of scholarship has always ignored the boundaries of academic specialization. He has written with impressive competence, often breaking new ground, on Hegel, Novalis, Kierkegaard,

Leopardi, Schopenhauer, Nietzsche, Simmel, Sombart, Wittgenstein, Hofmannsthal, Musil, Kafka, Kraus, Benjamin, Lukács, Heidegger, Michelstaedter, Weil, and Jabès. A fine scholar of the aesthetics of architecture and the arts, he has published seminal essays on Adolf Loos, Otto Wagner, Pavel Florensky, and Marcel Duchamp. His works on political theory, ranging from Austrian Marxism to Max Weber, and from Walther Rathenau to Carl Schmitt, have challenged and continue to challenge the commonplaces of the postcommunist European Left. In his most ambitious theoretical books, Cacciari shows a masterful command of classical antiquity, Neoplatonism and Christian theology. In the 1960s and 1970s, he developed a new critique of classical idealism, based on the notion of "negative thought," or antidialectic. During the 1980s, he investigated the nexus between philosophy, political theory, and theology, engaging the most prominent Catholic theologians to challenging debates. In the 1990s he laid the foundations for a new "geophilosophy" of Europe that has received much critical attention among professional philosophers, even though it failed to enter the political discussion the way it was intended. Many of Cacciari's works are far from being easily accessible to the reader who is not well learned in Greek and German literature and philosophy. Cacciari possesses a distinctive, polyglot, "musical," and very dense style. No introduction, no didacticism. Cacciari plunges into the heart of his subject from the very first line. His early articles, published in the 1960s in *Angelus novus* and *Contropiano*, do nothing to hide the impervious side of his writing, but they are also revealing about the future direction of his research. In "Sulla genesi del pensiero negativo" (On the Genesis of Negative Thought, 1969), Cacciari is already on the path that he will follow for the next ten years: a strong reevaluation of nondialectical thought in Schopenhauer, Kierkegaard, Nietzsche, Wittgenstein, and Heidegger.

As I have mentioned, in 1969 Cacciari was close to Potere Operaio. Although he was never a spokesperson for the group, Cacciari's coming of age as a philosopher and political thinker would not be understandable without some reference to the theoretical roots of that group. At the end of the ebullient 1960s, the movement attracted followers among the union workers at Venice's harbor, Porto Marghera, disillusioned by the official leftist organizations that had abandoned revolution and accepted small-time reforms in return. The radicalism of Potere Operaio wholly inherited the uncompromising legacy of the splinter Marxist theory known as Neomarxism. In order to understand the influence of Neomarxism in the history of the Italian Left, we need to go back to the beginning of the 1960s

in Turin, when philosopher Raniero Panzieri gathered a circle of young
Marxist intellectuals around his journal *Quaderni rossi* (Red Notebooks).[1]

At that time, Panzieri and the Neomarxists were trying to bring the
working class back to the center of the revolutionary process, only to find
that their claims fell on deaf ears once they reached the arena of the institutional left wing. In 1967, however, the members of Potere Operaio in
Venice (some of them attended Panzieri's informal meetings) were ambitious enough to put the Neomarxist theory to the test without waiting for
official sanction. When in the spring of 1968 the student riots broke out,
followed by the large-scale workers' strikes in the fall of 1969, it seemed
for a moment that Potere Operaio had a chance to propagate to the masses
its vision of worker's centrality (*centralità operaia*). The founders of Potere
Operaio (political philosopher Antonio Negri and Cacciari among them)
strived to transform Neomarxist principles into revolutionary practice.
But, as he was looking for political support among the Porto Marghera
chemical-plant workers, Cacciari was also investigating Schopenhauer's
and Nietzsche's philosophical systems. No one has ever accused Cacciari
of being a populist. He appreciated neither the metaphysics of freedom
nor the Sorelian aesthetics of revolt that Negri found so appealing. While
he was pursuing his Neomarxist agenda, Cacciari had already stumbled
upon the nondialectical contradiction between dialectical and antidialectical thought. In the end, Cacciari's philosophical determination was to
lead him away from romantic radicalism.

Before that happened, there was the new journal *Contropiano*, edited by
Cacciari and Asor Rosa amid the turmoil of 1968 and dedicated to investi-
gate the notion of "planning" in its economic and political implications.
The journal's goal was to oppose a revolutionary counterplan to the condition of permanent crisis that was now endemic to capitalism. *Contropiano*
was the most ambitious attempt to add a new chapter to Panzieri's legacy
of Neomarxism. Panzieri had stressed that capital, far from being anarchic
(anarchic and irrational capitalism was an article of faith for the traditional
labor movement), was *social* capital—capital, that is, having planning capability. Panzieri did not go as far as to deny the old Marxist tenet that the
laws of capitalistic accumulation were contradictory. Yet, he pointed out
that capitalist planning operates at every level, including the factory. Once
it was understood that the capitalist productive mechanism was objective
(that is, scientific and technological), and that it objectively affected the
forces of production (since nothing was left outside the capital's planning
capability), the dominant Marxist view that the only rational moving

forces of history were the workers and their parties was no longer tenable. Contrary to the old assumption that capitalism was essentially market capitalism, Panzieri identified capitalism with the organization of labor. It was a Copernican revolution in Marxian hermeneutics, but it left the traditional labor movement with no clear perspective about the direction to take. The official left wing had assumed that the working class was rational because of its close relationship with the intrinsic rationality of technology. After Panzieri's warning that capitalism was rational in its own way, what new strategy could be elaborated on the part of the Left? How could it outrationalize the rationality of capital?

Panzieri died in 1964, not having dealt with the complexity of the question. The young Neomarxists' answer to Panzieri's conundrum was a full-fledged flight forward (*fuga in avanti*) toward extremism. A new and radical antagonism between workers and capital was quickly theorized. If capitalism was organization of labor, then the revolutionary movement should declare war against labor. Qualifications and professionalism were vilified as mere capitalistic tools to divide the working class into skilled and unskilled workers. In his enormously influential *Operai e capitale* (Workers and Capital, 1966), Neomarxist philosopher Mario Tronti stressed that the factory, being the only place where the worker was in control of his own labor, was also the only place where true antagonism was possible. Maybe society was nothing other than market, but the factory was the temple of real conflict. Neomarxism grew into worker-centered Marxism (*operaismo*), and Potere Operaio followed. Although Tronti was not and never would be a hard-core extremist, his book provided the theoretical ground both to Potere Operaio and to Antonio Negri's subsequent and most extreme ideas, from the refusal to work to the sabotage and destruction of work tout court.

After 1969, the magical moment that had brought together the radical groups and the traditional workers was over. The workers' unions were exhausted after the long struggle to force the government to sign the Statuto dei Lavoratori (Statute of Laborers). Right-wing reaction was mounting against the labor movement (a neofascist bomb in a Milanese bank on December 12, 1969, signaled the beginning of the terrorist era in Italy), and the gap between students and workers widened again. But the revolutionaries who had had their glorious days were not backing out. The organization of what was left of the avant-garde movement was now their most pressing issue. To what extent could radical workers organize within the factory and be autonomous from their official representatives in the political arena? "Autonomy" is the word that holds the key to an understanding of Tronti, Negri, Cacciari, and the political mayhem of Italy in the 1970s. Tronti soon realized that the struggle of the working class at the grassroots level was not turning into permanent political gain. It was the political network that held together the economic foundation of society. The lack of a theory of the state being a persistent weakness of Marxism, Tronti cut the Gordian knot and broke off with the old assumption that the structural conflict was the only acceptable basis for the superstructural conflict. According to the "new" Tronti, who had incorporated John Maynard Keynes into his Marxism, the way to fight capitalism in its multiheaded articulations was to view politics as autonomous, independent of society.

Panzieri had initiated a Copernican revolution in Marxism. Tronti's autonomy of politics was now the beginning of a Machiavellian revolution. As Machiavelli separated politics from morals, Tronti put Marxist politics at a safe distance from the ups and downs of the working-class struggle. He argued that the political representatives of the working class had to be relatively free from their constituency in order to pursue purely political gains within Parliament and the state's institutions. When his *Sull'autonomia del politico* (On the Autonomy of the Political, 1977) was published, many observed, and not without malice, that Tronti was providing the theoretical legitimization for his own retreat into the official ranks of the Communist Party, at a time when extremism had become incendiary. It may have been partially true, but in the autonomy of politics there was more at stake than Tronti's career. Militancy, state repression, the energy crisis of the early 1970s, and the increasingly violent radicalism of many disaffected young militants were coming together in a way that needed drastic solutions. Tronti found his in the disengagement of politics from street politics. Cacciari's and Negri's responses were very different.

On a superficial level, Cacciari's decision to join the ranks of the Communist Party seemed to be catering to Tronti's Machiavellian realism. Cacciari, however, was consistent with the path he had already undertaken. After the great tides of 1968 and 1969 began to recede, *operaismo* needed a strong theory of counterplan in order to oppose capitalistic planning. It was at this point that Cacciari's critique of the romantic and populist side of *operaismo* clashed with Negri's intention to reformulate the autonomous role of productive forces in a new and even more revolutionary way. The rift between the two intellectuals became larger and larger after the first year of *Contropiano*, when it was clear that Cacciari wanted the journal to be a Trojan horse of Potere Operaio into the walls of the organized labor movement. A few years later, Cacciari's decision to leave the movement and "enter" the Communist Party created even more of a fuss than Tronti's retreat. Even the old term *entrismo* ("entryism" or "entrism"), once used to describe Trotsky's 1934 "French turn" (when he suggested that his French followers dissolve their Communist League and join the Socialist Party), was revitalized for the occasion.

Unmoved by Cacciari's defection, Antonio Negri participated actively, between 1973 and 1977, in the creation of Autonomia Operaia (Workers' Autonomy), a new movement whose base was the faculty of political science at the University of Padua, where Negri was now professor. Much more radical than Potere Operaio, Autonomia Operaia expanded the notion of the worker far beyond the gates of the factory. In a way, Negri was just pushing Trontian autonomy to its extremes. If official politics was autonomous from society—so his argument went—society was autonomous from official politics, too. In the past, the pivotal figure of the institutional left wing was the *operaio di mestiere* (skilled worker). With the advent of mass capitalism the *operaio di mestiere* had been replaced by the *operaio massa* (unskilled mass worker), who in 1968 had stricken fear into the middle class with its spontaneous revolt. Now, according to Negri, the time was ripe for the third phase, from the *operaio massa* to the *operaio sociale* (socialized worker). The factory was no longer the center of class struggle. Given the capitalist tendency to proletarianize and marginalize large segments of white-collar workers, only people at the margins of society were now ready to be turned into revolutionary forces.

It should not come as a surprise that hardly one blue-collar worker could be found among the militants of Negri's Autonomia Operaia. And, although falling short of endorsing the terrorism of the Red Brigades, Autonomia openly advocated the use of revolutionary violence to sabotage capitalism. On April 7, 1979, Negri was arrested in Padua, along with fifty other militants of Autonomia Operaia, mostly academics, writers, and journalists. One of the charges was armed insurrection against the state. Pietro Calogero, the magistrate who signed the arrest warrant, convinced the judges that Autonomia Operaia was more or less the political branch of the Red Brigades. Negri was sentenced as the spiritual father of left-wing terrorism, and it is still in question today whether there was any legal basis for putting him in prison or whether the whole trial was a blatant violation of freedom of speech. It is interesting to note that judge Pietro Calogero was close to the Communist Party. In fact, the "April 7 Trial," as it was known, was tacitly endorsed by the official left wing and used to decapitate the intellectual leadership of the extreme left-wing movements. Occurring one year after the kidnapping and killing of Prime Minister Aldo Moro by the Red Brigades, the attack on Negri was supposed to mark the distance between respectable leftists and the extremists, and to that extent it achieved its objective. It would take many twists and turns before Negri would become the successful author of the antiglobalization bestsellers *Empire* (2001) and *Multitude* (2004). Suffice it to say that Cacciari's political writings of the 1970s could be hardly appreciated without knowing that at times they must be understood as answers to Negri's most provocative statements.[2]

In 1976, as I said, Cacciari "entered" the Communist Party. Given his expertise in the issues of the chemical plant in Porto Marghera, the party selected Cacciari to sit on the parliamentary Industry Committee (Chemicals Subcommittee). For Cacciari, 1976 was a breakthrough year in many respects. After several articles and a few books that had already established his reputation as a provocative critical Marxist, the publication of *Krisis* signaled the presence of a new, strong voice on the Italian philosophical scene. It would be difficult to underestimate the impact that *Krisis* had on a generation of young intellectuals who, had they been not warned by Cacciari's uncompromising style and approach, were on their way to becoming the latter-day incarnation of existentialist, idealist, historicist, structuralist, Lukácsian, or Frankfurt School Marxists. *Krisis* was hard to digest for the well-meaning, stubborn, humanistic, and utopian intellectuals of the historical Left. With *Krisis*, Cacciari made clear that negative thought, or antidialectical thought, was more effective in guiding capitalism through its crises than dialectics was in its endless shaping and reshaping of Marxism. Far from falling into the Lukácsian categories of "irrationalism" and "destruction of reason," the criticism of dialectics elaborated by Schopenhauer, Kierkegaard, Nietzsche, Max Weber, Wittgenstein, and ultimately Heidegger, was extremely rational in its core. As anyone who had eyes could see, negative thought had served its purpose well, namely, in providing the theoretical legitimacy of capitalism as a crisis-based system.

This was *Krisis* in a nutshell, but Cacciari's scope was wider than that. The entire turn-of-the-century Vienna in all its artistic and cultural glory, from Wittgenstein to Freud, from Mahler to Schönberg, from Kandinsky to Kokoschka, from Otto Wagner to Adolf Loos, was summoned in Cacciari's negative thought trilogy: *Krisis* (Crisis, 1976); *Pensiero negativo e razionalizzazione* (Negative Thought and Rationalization, 1977); and *Dallo Steinhof*, 1980 (English translation, *Posthumous Men*, 1996). The purpose was to show not only the historical effectiveness of negative thought, but also its intrinsic rationality.[3]

Marxists who grew up in the 1950s and the 1960s reading Lukács and Adorno were outraged. Even worse, they felt bypassed. The respected poet and essayist Franco Fortini went as far as to call Cacciari and some other young philosophers the "last Cains," eager to prostrate before the violence of history in order to solve their Oedipal problems with their own bourgeois upbringing.[4] Actually, the accusation could make some sense with reference to Antonio Negri and his romantic-Sorelian students of political science at the University of Padua (a.k.a. "autonomous workers"), but it was off the mark when aimed at Cacciari.

But when did it all begin? How did a former *operaista* like Cacciari turn into the pied piper who would lead so many unsuspecting young minds into the territory of counterdialectics? To find an answer, we must go back to Cacciari's 1969 essay "Sulla genesi del pensiero negativo."

The Politics of Renunciation

Not unusually for Cacciari, his philosophical analysis begins with an exercise in literary hermeneutics. Heinrich von Kleist's theater is his focus here. According to Cacciari, Kleist's *Penthesilea* (1808) constituted the first blow to dialectical thought. There is no romantic aura in Kleist, where the form of the tragedy nullifies reason and grows entirely separate from dialectics. Kleist dissolves romanticism as much as E. T. A. Hoffmann dissolves the "I" of his characters. Throughout Kleist's nullification of reason, however, "form" (the form of tragedy) is still saved. Or better, what is saved is the opposition between form and life. But form is authentic only to the extent that it withdraws from life, and there is no dialectical solution to this contradiction, which remains mired in its "negative" moment. Schopenhauer, in Cacciari's view, is the first philosopher who addresses negative thought in all its ramifications, including a strong criticism of bourgeois society and its acceptance of Hegelian dialectics. And yet, just by showing the limits of dialectics, negative thought is still functional to the society that it criticizes. As much as capitalism abandons its dreams of dialectical reconciliation among the different forces of society, negative thought turns into an essential tool for the capitalist *esprit fort*. Neither Lukács nor Löwith, as it seems, have understood that negative thought was not just the bourgeoisie's reaction to the revolutionary potentiality of dialectics. When Schopenhauer affirms that the contradiction between subject and object will *not* be resolved, from his "reactionary" point of view he denounces liberalism as the latest incarnation of the

Schillerian "beautiful soul." This is capitalism's modernity, from Kant to negative thought, bypassing Hegel. The subject remains absolute, but it is not going to be integrated into its object—be it life, or history.

Negative thought, however, strives to develop a system that aims to be more consistent than dialectics. As long as it exposes the contradiction instead of overcoming it, Schopenhauer's will is the "form" of this new, post-Kantian schematism. Contradiction, therefore, ceases to be an anomaly, or an aporia. It can be denied only ideologically, by overlooking life's violent aspect. As in post-Ricardian (non-Marxist) economy, where value is determined negatively, in Schopenhauer the value of bourgeois society is determined in the same negative way—as the opposite of reconciliation. The synthesis is possible only within life, and not in the realm of form. But what is the value of this synthesis, when we know that in Schopenhauer life results in self-denial? It takes Kierkegaard to demonstrate that Schopenhauer, as long as he is still convinced that it is possible to achieve freedom from the evils of life, is still an optimistic bourgeois. The Kierkegaardian man has no intention to free the world from evil. That would be an impossible abstraction. The contradiction must be lived through, and not overcome. The life of the Kierkegaardian "individual" is always given in specific circumstances—in the leap from one situation to another. Only religious faith realizes dialectics, not by reconciliation but by annihilating one of its opposites. This is how bourgeois reason is truly voided. And yet Kierkegaard cannot annihilate society entirely. After all, he still maintains (especially in his last phase, after 1849) that faith must have practical consequences in personal and collective life. Faith makes life repeat itself. As Job's life begins again, even the defender of faith can still get married and live a middle-class existence. After the conversion, his "difference" is over. But dialectical form has not been broken. It still possesses value.

Negative thought achieves fulfillment only in Nietzsche, where dialectical synthesis, once devoid of any moralistic or metaphysical value, is reduced to pure immanence without justification. In so doing, Nietzsche is the true interpreter of the spirit of his time. After 1870, capitalism enters a new phase in which mastering the negative *qua* negative is more important than overcoming it. That explains why there is no irrationalism in Nietzsche. He negates precisely those values that now get in the way of capitalistic domination. His criticism of the bourgeoisie rebuilds the system in a more effective way. Tragedy, in Nietzsche, is the blueprint of a world in which contradiction is accepted and considered unredeemable. Schopenhauer was deluded, and Wagner in his last years was also deluded, when they thought that grief and pain could be transcended.

The real free spirit knows that tragedy is only pessimism—overcome without redemption.

Total acceptance of destiny is not an ideal for the masses. Only the free spirit is ready for that. But Nietzsche's free spirit only anticipates Max Weber's disenchanted intellectual. The Weberian intellectual accepts the spirit of the world with no hope, or even desire, to redeem it with an injection of *Kultur*. This is the only decision he can make. As a matter of fact, it is not even the intellectual's decision—but he is aware of that, he has decided to accept that he cannot decide. It is not the single philosopher, but the capitalist system itself that periodically gets rid of the old and obsolete values. And the Nietzschean-Weberian system wants only power; it is the will to power incarnate. Weber fully integrates Nietzsche and empowers his vision, or so it seems, but a difference remains. Nietzsche's *Übermensch* is not directly involved with the system. He still keeps an aristocratic distance. That distance is annihilated in Weber, who demands an active role for his intellectual and/or politician. Furthermore, Nietzsche's "superman" cannot be separated from his subjectivity. This is not so in Weber, where the intellectual is merely functional. And yet, Weber unveils Nietzsche's real project, because the secret of Nietzschean subjectivity lies in the unavoidable dissolution of subjectivity itself. The ruler of the Weberian "administered world" has no time for the systems of values that are not functional to the stage reached by the capitalistic organization. The Protestant phase of capitalism is over, and the system is on the way to becoming a pure manifestation of power. Nietzsche knew that already. No transcendence is left outside the system. As a matter of fact, there is no outside. The situation is unprecedented, but it captures perfectly the tragedy of capitalism's mature phase. The will to power is the new substance, the new perfect form. Life is not synthesis, but will— toward domination and incorporation. And, since will to power embodies the essence of life, it will never be overcome. This is the meaning of Nietzsche's eternal return: the capitalistic system has now taken the place of the ancient tragic destiny.

And yet, as Cacciari observes, this is still a dialectical synthesis. Apparently, every contradiction has disappeared. Being and becoming have been reduced to identity. Negativity "comprehends" itself in a way that is not altogether different from the way the Hegelian absolute spirit coincides with its wholeness.

Cacciari brings his essay to this brilliant conclusion, which nonetheless does not dissolve some perplexities. On one hand, Cacciari's account of the history of negative thought is strongly deterministic, and in the most

Marxist sense of the word. Each thinker matches almost perfectly the corresponding historical phase of capitalistic development, with little "autonomy" left to the mind. On the other hand, Cacciari's interpretation of
antidialectics is even more deterministic than any Marxism could bear,
because it annihilates the very possibility of theoretical and social antagonism. If dialectics is not effective, and all nondialectical critiques of the
bourgeoisie end up reinforcing the same society that they criticize, then
what is the possible alternative to capitalism? With its strictly rationalistic
and deductive approach, Cacciari's critique unveils the rationalistic side
of Nietzsche's thinking. The downside, however, is that no rationalistic
criticism of capitalism (including Cacciari's) will be able to outline a different political scenario.

Cacciari struggled with this aporia for the next ten years, from 1969
to 1978, and only in his late 1970s works he was able to overcome the
deterministic side of his political philosophy. First of all, he investigated
the crucial category of *Entsagung* (renunciation) from Goethe to Schopenhauer and Thomas Mann. How does the capitalistic system maintain itself
open, avoiding the rigidity that seems to be implied in its own perfection?
Something must be sacrificed to make the system work, and what is sacrificed is the capitalist's enjoyment. Like Goethe's Faust and the tormented
couples in *Elective Affinities*, like Schopenhauer's will desiring its own van-
ishing, or the ascetic old merchants in Mann's *Buddenbrooks*, the heroic
capitalist is the one who gives up pleasure, postponing it indefinitely in
order to keep the system in motion. Max Weber and the ghost of his
Protestantism dominate these observations, but Cacciari would point out
that the ascetic solution springs directly from the theoretical obligations
of negative thought, regardless of Protestant ethics. From his essay *"Entsagung"* (1971) to *Pensiero negativo e razionalizzazione* (1977), Cacciari insists
that the capability of capitalism to postpone its fulfillment is one of its
strongest assets, if not *the* strongest. Why not bring the same ascetic
asset—which is also highly strategic—into the socialist camp? Cacciari has
always despised revolutionary-schizophrenic *jouissance*, whether it came
from Negri or Deleuze. In his essay "'Razionalità' e 'Irrazionalità' nella
critica del Politico in Deleuze e Foucault" ("Rationality" and "Irrationality" in Deleuze's and Foucault's Critique of Politics, 1977), Cacciari had
very harsh words against the "bad literature" that occasionally affected
Foucault, Deleuze, and Guattari, and he accused them of intellectual "in-
decency" on the account of their claim to an immediacy of thought. Cacciari learned from Wittgenstein that when you discard a set of rules, you
just start playing with new rules. Every set is limited, but there is no game

outside the game, no privileged position from which one can look at the whole system and decide to change it without being affected by the change. Of course, while he criticized Deleuze and Foucault, Cacciari's not-so-hidden polemical objective was Negri's "total autonomy" of the revolutionary subject—which Cacciari discarded as mere mythology. (Cacciari, however, overlooked both the Nietzschean side of Foucault and the Spinozian side of Deleuze—which did not escape Negri.)

In 1976, when *Krisis* reached the bookstores, Fortini and other Frankfurt School critics were not the only ones to cry foul. Gianni Vattimo scolded Cacciari for choosing speculative abstraction at the expense of revolutionary praxis, while Negri himself wrote a scathing review in which he accused Cacciari of mysticism pure and simple.[5] Cacciari's refurbished *operaismo* was mystical, according to Negri, because it was based on an assumption of naturalness about the economic datum. It celebrated the organization of labor as a pure game devoid of any values, but forgot to explain how the capitalistic division between value and labor was determined in the first place. Cacciari, in Negri's opinion, was turning into one of those negative thinkers he was writing about—a negative theologian of bourgeois humanism, ready to brush aside the question of labor because he was fearful of its revolutionary power. Cacciari could understand the power of labor only negatively, as authoritarianism or terrorism. By separating class-consciousness from the revolutionary subject, he had turned the autonomy of politics into pure theory, alienated from the reality of the class struggle. In the widening gap between political strategy and labor movement, negative revolutionaries like Cacciari would rather choose political conventionalism instead of a real confrontation with the masses and the urgency of their needs. Negri felt that all Cacciari wanted was an opportunistic revolution from above, inured to failure by its very absence of foundation.

Putting aside for a moment the issue of Negri's really being in touch with "the masses," Negri's remarks were not entirely unfounded. But no one more than Cacciari was aware that the autonomy of politics could not escape its lack of foundation. If politics (revolutionary politics) detaches itself from society, what legitimacy can it claim? If revolution is removed from the revolutionary masses, where is the difference between revolutionary power and the capitalist system? After all, Marxism conceived revolution as discontinuity and utopia. How can revolutionary politics find the same élan when revolution is reduced to administration? Was not the bureaucratization of politics what killed the socialist states of Eastern Europe? It was not enough to suggest, as Tronti did, that politics was more

powerful when it was reduced to technique. Capitalism always acknowledged that. If the labor movement was to become the heir of bourgeois
politics in the age of technology, then one had to admit that the labor
movement had much to learn, since it never conceived its struggle in terms
of "high politics."

As we see from the major points of this debate, ten years after 1968 the
autonomy of politics was already an empty shell. The next move was
toward the centrality of politics. It was a conscientiously cynical move,
since it acknowledged that the working class had lost its ethical centrality
and, very much like Weber's intellectual, was now merely functional to the
political battle. In *"Sinisteritas,"* a 1982 essay not included in this volume,
Cacciari went so far as to claim "grand opportunism" as the only possible
substitute for "grand politics," when grand politics was no longer viable.

But the crucial year, both for Cacciari and the Italian Left, came in
1978. Again, we need to take a step back in order to place the historical
facts in the right perspective. In 1972, a splinter faction of sociology students at the University of Trento (one of the most politicized universities
in post-1968 Italy) established the left-wing terrorist group known as the
Red Brigades. When compared with what was about to follow in the next
few years, the actions of the so-called *nucleo storico* (historical cell) of the
Red Brigades were mostly propagandistic. In the mid-1970s, however,
after the police arrested or killed the Red Brigades' first leaders, the new
generation openly turned to armed violence. In the meantime, after Augusto Pinochet overthrew Salvador Allende's socialist government of
Chile in the 1973 coup d'état, Enrico Berlinguer, then secretary of the
Italian Communist Party, decided that Italy was not going to risk a similar
civil war and proposed a *compromesso storico* (historic compromise) between
the Christian Democrats (the majority party since 1948) and the Communist Party (the second strongest party). Among the Christian Democratic
leaders, Aldo Moro was the one to pick up the olive branch. A moderate
Catholic known for his extremely cautious behavior, tortuous speech, and
Byzantine writing style, Moro had already brought the Socialist Party into
a joint government with the Christian Democrats in 1962. In the 1970s
he did not dislike the idea of repeating his gambit with the Communists.
Either because he wanted to ease tensions within Italian society, or because he preferred to keep his friends close and his enemies closer, Moro
worked for five years to build up the appropriate conditions for the historical compromise. In early March 1978, when he was secretary of the Christian Democrats, Moro felt that the moment had come.

On March 16, Moro was on his way to Parliament, where he and Berlinguer were going to formalize a loose governmental alliance that for the first time since 1948 would see the two major Italian political parties on the same side. But before Moro could reach the Chamber of Deputies a commando of the Red Brigades kidnapped him after killing his five bodyguards. Fifty-five days later, on May 10, Moro was found dead in the trunk of a Renault car, left by the Red Brigades in Via Caetani, a street in Rome that was halfway between the headquarters of the Christian Democrats and the Communist Party. The historical compromise, loathed by the radical groups for fear that this bipartisan regime would kill the revolutionary potential of the masses, was over. But Moro's killing was also the beginning of the end for the Red Brigades. The nation was shocked by their brutality, and their network of sympathizers thinned out considerably. By 1982, the Red Brigades militants were mostly in exile, arrested, *pentiti* (repentant), or in jail. Right-wing terrorism made a comeback with the deadliest attack in Italian history (a bomb at the Bologna train station killed eighty-six people on August 2, 1980), but after reaching this peak, it too was on the wane. In the meantime, Cacciari had a seat in Parliament, and Antonio Negri, who thanks to his temporary election as a representative of the Radical Party had been released from prison, became a political exile in France, where he obtained a teaching position at the Sorbonne.

Up to 1978, with the exception of two earlier papers, the antidialectical Cacciari had never confronted the very ghost of dialectics. With *Dialettica e critica del Politico. Saggio su Hegel* (Dialectics and the Critique of Politics: Essay on Hegel, 1978), Cacciari added a significant chapter to his bibliography. It was one of his most brilliant essays, and it provided some much-needed answers to the dead end of revolutionary politics. In his analysis of Hegel's *Philosophy of Right* (1821), Cacciari was obviously looking for traces of antidialectics. It would have been easier to find them in the realm of international law, since Hegel himself admitted that states recognized no laws and therefore no dialectical reconciliation above themselves (the rise and fall of international law is one of Carl Schmitt's great topics, and Schmitt's presence, which I will discuss later, is tangible in *Dialettica e critica del Politico*). Cacciari, however, chose to deconstruct Hegel's philosophy of politics at the level of contradiction between subjective interest and civil society—an opposition that cannot be overcome in the classical dialectical sense, because it presents itself again immediately after being resolved.

Long before Marx, Hegel had already tried to redeem society from its lapse into bad infinity. By putting the ethical state as the redemptive figure of the economic system, he pointed at the contradiction between civil society and the state. Paralyzed by the rules of economics, a wholly secularized state reduces itself to the mere satisfaction of the needs and desires of civil society (it is no more than the business committee of the bourgeoisie, as Marx would have it). By giving up its ethical-political essence, the state ends up being nothing more than the servant of subjective interests. And, as Hobbes and Mandeville already knew, subjective interests are essentially anarchic, opposed to the very idea of state. The Hegelian state rationalizes subjective anarchy and tempers the spread of needs and desires within civil society, but it cannot achieve more than that. Subjective interests haunt civil society to such an extent that the state will never control them. The endless development and transformation of production puts the state in a dilemma: either to direct the development in an authoritarian fashion, which would amount to the repression of civil society, or to subsume "dialectically" the development itself, at the risk of dissolving the state's ethical form in the anarchy of conflicting subjectivities.

In both cases, the state is condemned to impotence. In the first scenario, no amount of tolerable repression will put the anarchy of civil society under control; in the second one, the ideology of laissez faire would only be pretending that no anomaly exists. Since there is no way out from this contradiction, so argues Cacciari, Hegel chooses to remain in the contradiction without resolving it. The state appears as the culminating phase of the entire process not because it dissolves the contradiction between itself and civil society but because it remains *separated* from civil society. This separateness, according to Cacciari, must be understood as autonomy. It represents autonomous strength and autonomous *language* on the part of the state.

As we can see, Cacciari found in Hegel the common ground between Tronti's autonomy of politics and his own obsession with the autonomy of different languages (one of the key concepts in his "negative thought" trilogy maintains that the languages of different artistic disciplines, different social classes, and different political realities are not translatable into one another).

But, if the state is no longer the guardian of good economic behavior, then what is left to politics? Since it is no longer possible, at the end of the twentieth century, to resurrect the ghost of the ethical state, the only political ethics left is that of *Entsagung*, renunciation. Politics that renounces to resolve the contradiction of civil society into some superior harmony is grand politics. But such a renunciation is decision, which means that grand politics decides to separate itself (etymologically, deci-sion means separation) from the possibility of representing the whole. Grand politics does not harmonize conflicts. Grand politics *produces* the conflict, and gives up the dream of a reconciled society. Here is where Hegel meets Carl Schmitt. Social harmony is no less a myth than "just peace." It takes a "just war" to reach "just peace," but "just war" is an-other name for an endless state of war, where the enemy loses the right to be an enemy and is degraded to the status of a criminal.[6]

Socialism has never attained grand politics because it has always tried to reconcile, harmonize, and disalienate the various segments of society in the hope of leading them into universal consensus. Socialism strives to liberate politics from politics itself, and this is where it fails. There is no liberation from politics, and no liberation can be reached through politics. Negri is wrong because his reversal of classical political theory is a mere mirror effect. When Negri posits the revolutionary subject as absolute otherness from capital, asserting therefore the rationality of insurrection, he puts his faith in an authoritarian resolution of social conflict. Once revolution is over, social conflict is supposed to disappear, but the end of revolution is no less a myth than the war to end all wars. Politics, as Cacci-ari tirelessly repeats, produces and manages conflict; it does not strive to end it. The masses participate in the process of democratization and the inevitable depoliticization of the secularized state, but they do not provide the foundation for the state.

Cacciari's conclusions were a major blow to the core concepts of Marx-ism, at least in their popular fashion. On one hand, Cacciari anticipated by ten years the fall of socialist utopia. His personal Berlin Wall came down between 1978 and 1982. On the other, in various conversations and interviews given in those years, he repeatedly stressed that Marxism had indeed realized many of its goals, not in Eastern Europe but in the West-ern world. The best legacy of Marxism was alive in the West's democratic institutions, namely, that every segment of society must have its own polit-ical representation. What politics (including Marxist politics) cannot and must not attempt to represent, is society as a whole, and the state as a common good. Cacciari was and is aware that politics cannot refrain from behaving as if the representation of the good would be possible. Insofar as it strives for the impossible, politics coincides also with inoperativeness, endless scholarship, *otium* and *scholé* (Jean Luc Nancy's "inoperative com-munity" comes to mind). But, according to Cacciari, it would be a waste of time to look for conventional political theory in order to find a theoriza-tion of this unsurpassable or, we could say, "sublime" limitation of poli-tics. Thinkers who have remained on the margins of politics have a better

chance of understanding its limits. From their marginality they have per-
fected a unique, "unpolitical" point of view. "Unpolitical" does not mean
apolitical or antipolitical. On the contrary, it means suprapolitical, over-
political. The autonomy of politics was just a myth, maybe one that was
effective to a certain extent, but not different from other political myths.
The unpolitical gaze, however, looks at politics with perfect awareness
that the political reconciliation of the opposites is and will always be impossible. That does negate the effectiveness of politics. Instead, it stresses
the real power of politics. The unpolitical is the only point of view from
which politics can be seen both as vocation (in the Weberian sense of the
word) and technique. Under the unpolitical gaze, politics ceases to be
praxis alone and reveals itself also as *techné*.

The Unpolitical Gaze

With two exceptions, the essays collected in this volume were written between 1978 and 1982, the crucial years when Cacciari calls into question
the legacy of Marxism and political activism. The essays did not offer easy
solutions, because there were none, and because Cacciari was still struggling with the multiplicity of languages in his own philosophy. Marxism
and Neomarxism, the jargon of *operaismo*, Hegelian dialectics, negative
thought, Nietzsche's unpolitical dimension, Benjamin's complex theory of
political allegory (based on German baroque drama and applied by Cacciari to Hofmannsthal's plays), Weber's criticism of socialism, the deconstruction of key terms of political philosophy such as power, catastrophe
(read "revolution"), and project (read "plan" and "counterplan"): all these
conflicting legacies coexisted together in Cacciari's pages with no hope of
being translated into a new political and philosophical Esperanto. In fact,
in other essays of the same period, such as "Trasformazioni dello Stato e
progetto politico" (Transformations of the State and Political Project,
1978), not included in the present collection, Cacciari's style reached a
level of conceptual and semantic density that even the most benevolent
reader might have felt as overwhelming. Cacciari was not saying it openly
(because there was not just one language to say it), but he was hinting that
the whole arsenal of the postwar political lexicon was now obsolete. The
essays collected here, however, are less hermetic than the one just mentioned. Each one is a rite of passage, a transit from the harsh old world of
Cold War to the brave new world of Global Conflict. They bear witness

to five years of relentless intellectual challenge. After them, Cacciari was a different thinker.

In 1985 he published *Icone della legge* (Icons of Law), one of his most accomplished books and one in which philosophy, literature, and the arts truly seem to be translatable one into another. In 1986 he achieved commercial success with *L'angelo necessario* (*The Necessary Angel* in the 1994 English translation—the title being a nod to Wallace Stevens's eponymous poem), an erudite book on the semiotics of angelic communication (and/ or the nonsemiotics of angelic ineffability) from Dante to Paul Klee. In 1990 he completed *Dell'inizio*, in which he addressed Western philosophical and theological tradition from the circular and nondialectical point of view of Neoplatonism.

His 1980s trilogy *Icone*, *L'angelo*, and *Dell'inizio* would require a long discussion, exceeding the limits of this introduction. The same can be said for *Della cosa ultima* (2004), which completes *Dell'inizio*. "Impracticable Utopias," however (Chapter 1 of this volume) is a good starting point to gain access to Cacciari's mature thought. The text works at different levels. At first sight, it is the book-length postscript to a new Italian translation of Hofmannsthal's tormented drama *The Tower* (1901–1927). As an erudite essay on Hofmannsthal and his source (Calderón de la Barca's *La vida es sueño*), "Impracticable Utopias" includes a discussion of Lukács's reflections on tragedy, Benjamin's theory of Baroque drama, theater as political allegory, and the impossibility of tragedy in the modern world. At another level, "Impracticable Utopias" is exactly what the title suggests: a serious meditation on the failure of political utopias and the problematic impracticability of the very concept of utopia. The original Italian title, "Intransitabili utopie," comes from the first speech of King Basilius in Act II: "Die Mauern wanken von den Grundfesten aus und unser Weg ist ins Nicht-mehr-gangbare geraten," which in the English translation reads, "The walls are shaken at their foundation, and our path has strayed into impassable wastes." The Italian translation, somewhat closer to the original German, reads: "Le mura vacillano dalle fondamenta, e la nostra strada è finita nell'Intransitabile." "Intransitabile" is a road that is in ruin and that cannot be taken. More metaphorically, it is also something that cannot be carried on, for instance from one river's shore to the other. The translator's choice, "Impracticable Utopias," suggests that utopias are both impassable roads and unpractical burdens.[7]

Cacciari goes through the different stages of Hofmannsthal's drama to show how, one draft after another, the author progressively has reduced and, in the end, annihilated every hope of political reconciliation.

Through the various passages of his work, Hofmannsthal struggled with this inevitable, all-political conclusion. Not only Sigismund, the dreaming Prince, has been defeated (which is not surprising), but also no order has resulted from the revolution that dethroned him. And the sinister Olivier, the new tyrant, is also disillusioned. Although he has won, he knows all too well that his revolution has brought about conflict, not peace.

Is this a modern tragedy? Can we call it a tragedy? After Walter Benjamin, who in his *The Origin of German Baroque Drama* (1925) separated Baroque *Trauerspiel* (Mournful Drama) from Tragedy, the possibility of modern tragedy (still entertained by Georg Simmel and the young Lukács) has been largely dismissed. Hofmannsthal, who was familiar with Benjamin's work, could no longer accept a formal or aesthetic reconciliation of utopia's political dissolution. At the conclusion of *The Tower* the allegory remains open. After the Christlike Sigismund has disappeared, politics is left by itself, without any hope of finding a transcendental foundation for its power. God is hidden, does not reveal His face, and His being impenetrable is what marks the difference between *Trauerspiel* and tragedy, where God's will is after all manifested. Cacciari points out that if final peace is impossible, or just the allegory of an unending conflict, then decision will be the only political category left. Quoting from *Politische Theologie* (Political Theology, 1922), one of Carl Schmitt's most influential essays, Cacciari stresses that whoever makes the decision in an exceptional situation holds the power. And, in an unending conflict, an exceptional state is an everyday occurrence.[8] However, contrary to what Schmitt argues in *Die Diktatur* (Dictatorship, 1921), Cacciari emphasizes that decision is not dictatorship. Dictatorship aims at reconstructing form and order, thus bringing decision to an end. But decision knows its limitations—which is, inevitably, the next decision.

In the last scenes of *The Tower*, Sigismund and Olivier confront each other. One character represents pure utopia; the other stands for pure politics. Olivier needs Sigismund, because Sigismund possesses the only thing that Olivier cannot have—popular consensus. But Sigismund refuses to become a figurehead for Olivier's politics and chooses to die. The death of Utopia, as I said, leaves politics unfounded. Hofmannsthal offers no solution to this dilemma—and neither does Cacciari. After ten years of debate about the autonomy of politics, "Impracticable Utopias" made clear that the chasm between politics and society was so wide that no force, no idea, no decision was able to bridge the gap.

To a certain extent, Cacciari's conclusion harks back to Neomarxism's radicalism. In 1968 the word was that if capitalism is rational, we will fight its rationality. In 1978 it was that if politics has no foundation, we will learn how to inhabit its void. In "Impracticable Utopias," there is no trace of a theory of social mediation. After all, consensus can be won and lost, and common sense holds that democracy's legitimacy comes from representativeness. Modern democracies do not live in the Imperial Spain of Sigismund and Olivier. But Cacciari's views on democracy have little regard for common sense and bear the marks of his philosophical obsessions, namely, autonomy and groundlessness. Every instance of political representativeness is a mournful drama, if not a tragedy, because politics, as we have seen, cannot represent the common good. In this respect, democracy fares no better than totalitarianism. As Cacciari explains in "Misura e dismisura della democrazia" (Moderation and Excess in Democracy, 1984), not included in this collection, the modern state is established neither by natural consensus nor by nonmediated power. Democracy must therefore demonstrate its legitimacy, and it does so by injecting belief and faith in the juridical substance of its laws.

But juridical substance does not mean legitimacy. When the source of the law is the result of a revolutionary act (which interrupts existing laws), the jurist must accept the new legislative subject as a presupposition or revelation, because he has no other means to provide the new law with the same aura as the old. Political theology (in Schmittian terms: how politics represents values) gives way to negative theology (the source of the law is compared to a God the theologian-jurist can say nothing about). As the ultimate secularization of political theology, democracy radicalizes the conventionalism of juridical action. The outcome is paradoxical, and yet absolutely logical. New political subjects start revolutions only to see their subjectivity disappear in the new judicial system that owes its very existence to them. But the groundlessness of democracy is not pathological. On the contrary, Cacciari insists on its physiological nature. There is an excess, a desire for infinitude that is intrinsic to the democratic project, which is not limited by God or natural law. No representation of such boundlessness is possible (nothing will be the symbol incarnate of democracy), but there is responsibility that comes with it and, again, it is the responsibility of renunciation. Only by giving up any claim to finding a historical or anthropological foundation, can democracy become fully responsible for itself and to its subjects.

The cornerstones of Cacciari's political thought are conventionalism, formalism, functionalism, and the strong belief that every attempt to translate the languages of subjectivity into politics is doomed to fail. No longer a practicing Marxist, Cacciari has not embraced liberalism lightly, or at least he has done it with a good dose of skepticism. Cacciari is a philosopher-politician in the classical, pessimistic, and Platonic sense of the term. His philosophy is the lifelong education of the man engaged in public activities, equally divided between public duties, study, and meditation. It does not come as a total surprise that one right-wing historian and political commentator has provocatively called Cacciari an aristocratic conservative.[9]

Cacciari, however, knows modernity enough to be aware that real conservatives are not allowed in our times. The heart of his speculative enterprise lies in his cold and disenchanted gaze at the relationship between power and representativeness. In Cacciari there is no room for political sentimentality. We may concede that this is his aristocratic side. But his investigation about the limits of politics stems from what he views as the nature of power itself. If there are no limits there is no power. And, since utopias are impracticable, to what extent is politics practicable?

Cacciari's 1978 essays on the "unpolitical" Nietzsche and the "all-political" Max Weber must be viewed as a two-sided answer to the same question. In "Nietzsche and the Unpolitical" (Chapter 2 of this collection), Cacciari addresses Thomas Mann's *Reflections of a Nonpolitical Man* (1918) and challenges Mann's definition of Nietzsche as an unpolitical thinker.[10] Cacciari points out that, in order to rescue Nietzsche from his reactionary readers, Mann assigned Nietzsche's legacy to a bourgeois hatred of politics that was totally foreign to him. Nietzsche is unpolitical not because he represents German spirit and culture against the decadence of politics, but because he criticizes every politics that pretends to represent values. Nietzsche's "unpoliticalness" is the most radical criticism of politics. It is, ultimately, a call for grand politics, which is another name for total disenchantment, accepting nihilism and groundlessness as unavoidable features. Grand politics does not strive to free human nature from alienation. The myth of disalienation is a superstitious, theological idea that has affected negatively both democracy and socialism. In the Nietzschean, unpolitical view, democracy does not create values; rather, it dissolves them into the autonomous multiplication of the political subjects. The unpolitical view coldly acknowledges that socialism and democracy hasten the completion of politics, which will coincide with its final entropy and disappearance.

Nietzsche knows that there is no going back. Grand politics is when different subjects recognize themselves as separate and yet united by the common ground of their juxtaposition. As if prescient of the late-capitalistic shift from class struggle to civil and individual rights, Nietzsche points out that the socialist emphasis on the notion of working class is, at best, a waste of time. At the end of the political education promoted by socialism there is only the *individuum*—the single worker, now separated from the value of his labor (from his class ethics) and bearer of individual requests to society. As if he had foreseen—we might say—the unending conflicts of identity politics, Nietzsche warns that the "fools for the state" should beware: their worship of politics will bring such an amount of individual politicization in society that the state itself will forfeit its function.[11]

If Nietzsche maintains an unpolitical aloofness from both democracy and socialism, Max Weber's case is different. As Cacciari's essay "Weber and the Critique of Socialist Reason" (Chapter 3 of this volume) argues, Weber wants to prove that socialism is logically and politically inconsistent, but in order to do so he must question the very essence of capitalism. Weber views socialism as an antipolitical movement, aiming to replace politics with a technocratic bureaucracy. In Cacciari's words, Weber understands that socialism is a political movement that denies the autonomous role of politics. The socialist indictment of capitalism as being anarchic (the same accusation that Panzieri would refute sixty years later) is moralistic and useless. Capitalism can quantify its economic process without moralistic justifications. Marginal economics needs neither psychology nor morals. It only assumes that human beings satisfy some of their needs through the consumption of goods. By being rational, they will also treasure their experience and plan the future direction of their activities. Here Weber follows a neo-Kantian pattern. Neither empathy nor natural feelings are allowed in his disenchanted system. Socialism, on the contrary, in addition to being guilty of such sins, is also nostalgic of a mythical general interest, vainly opposed to the so-called capitalist anarchy.

Weber is aware, however, that socialism is not just an ideology. Once the utopia has been logically refuted, the reality of the political movement remains. And how is it possible to defend democracy against socialism if democracy too is undergoing a huge process of bureaucratization? Socialism and democracy are both the offspring of the secularization of politics. Apologias of democracy will not stop socialism. Only the strongest political competition, led by the strongest political leaders, will slow down the impending bureaucratization of democracy and will put a stop to the end of politics. Only if political leadership proves to be capable of effective decision, and only if this competition implies that the socialist movement wins its appropriate seat in Parliament, the socialist quest for representativeness will be satisfied. Socialism will become a parliamentary force— and the socialist threat will either be transformed or defeated.

The reader may ask whether Cacciari's précis explains Max Weber or sums up Italy in the 1970s. Is this the Weimar Republic rolling to its doom, or Aldo Moro and Enrico Berlinguer agreeing on the historical compromise that will bring the Communists into the government—only to neutralize them? Maybe both. There is often an allegorical side to Cacciari's essays, even when he is dealing with topics apparently remote from the Italian political situation. Comparisons between the Weimar Republic and the chaotic situation of Italy were common in the 1970s, and the analogy does not need be stressed any further.

Cacciari, however, points out that Weber's parliamentary solution to the socialist issue remains merely formal. It is based on the assumption that Parliament possesses the capability to formalize the real conflicts produced by democratic life. But this formalization inevitably leads to an increased bureaucratization, if the politician accepts to be led by "formalized" experts. It may also lead to a spoil system, if the politician rebels to the bureaucrats and replaces them with loyal party men. Deprived of competent bureaucrats, politics will no longer be autonomous; democracy will quickly lose authority and will be reduced to a mere tactical response to the demands of socialism.

Thanks to Weber's insights, Cacciari was somewhat prescient about the Italian situation. The latter scenario is exactly what happened in Italy in the 1980s. The historic compromise was no longer an option after Moro's death, leading the Communists to remain outside coalition governments. In the void that followed, under the new and "decisionist" leadership of Bettino Craxi the relatively small Socialist Party acquired an unprecedented role in Italian politics, shared power with the Christian Democrats for the next ten years, and established such a pervasive spoil system that Italy was led to the brink of collapse when the vast network of political corruption was unveiled in 1992 (the year the *Tangentopoli* scandal broke out—*Tangentopoli* meaning "Bribeville").

Twenty years after the fall of the Communist regimes in Eastern Europe, Cacciari's hairsplitting discussion on Max Weber's strategy to stifle socialism may seem largely academic. But the unresolved issue was, and still is, alienation. Essentially, socialism is a theory of alienation. The Weberian intellectual may endlessly argue that alienation is just a mythical construct, but he will never be able to prove it to the disenfranchised. Cacciari, however, is equally at odds when he affirms that socialism, far from being the dream of a nonalienated world, is much more effective as a political analysis, and immanent criticism, than the present capitalistic alienation.

Indeed, socialism may still find windows of opportunity for political intervention and prevent the bureaucratized segments of society from taking over the totality of the system—but, undoubtedly, this is a weak conclusion. Rather an exception in Cacciari, and yet a significant exception, because it captures him in that delicate moment between two paradigms, reluctant to abandon the old one and not quite sure of what the new one will be. At this crossroad, in this aporia, Cacciari finds no better solution than a theory of opportunism (he will expand it to "grand opportunism" a few years later). It is the same noble opportunism adopted by Ulrich, the "man without qualities" of Robert Musil's novel, every time he cannot decide between nihilism and activism. What is socialism, after all? Is it messianic waiting for the advent of disalienation, feebly masked as criticism of capitalistic reason, or productive transformation of society's many languages without losing sight of the final hope? Maybe now one thing, now another, depending on the different situations. The active nihilist is suspicious of decisions that are too strong to be revoked. Here is where Musil's relativism, mercifully, tempers Schmitt's unmerciful decisionism.[12] Even the most impatient activist, as Musil writes, is a dreamer who wants to dream God's dreams. And maybe, Cacciari concludes, it takes someone who knows the ways of the world to dream God's dreams. Active nihilism (we may also call it inoperative activism, once again echoing Jean-Luc Nancy), where politics meets the unpolitical, and where decision meets nonaction (one can be reminded of the Chinese concept of *wu-wei*), is the "sublime" of Cacciari's political thinking, the threshold where the political project faces its own catastrophe. The final hope may not be represented, but this impossibility of representation belongs to its very essence. And yet, the catastrophe of representation does not annihilate hope. It allows concrete situations to be mundanely possible, and gives the different languages of society the possibility of transforming themselves.

The paradoxical structure of the sublime (failure of imagination and empowerment of reason) is the kernel of Kant's *Critique of Judgment* (1790), on which Cacciari wrote his dissertation. However, there is a passage from the *Critique of Practical Reason* (1788) that may serve our purpose as well. It occurs in Book Two, Section "Dialectic" II, IX, where Kant observes that our cognitive faculties are somewhat made to measure for our moral scope and our desire to do God's will. But we could have asked for more. As a matter of fact, nature was as stingy as a cruel mother when it gave us less cognitive faculties than were needed to stay firmly in God's path. And yet, Kant concludes, the impenetrable wisdom that made us what we are is no less worthy of admiration for what it denied us.

In Cacciari's secularized political theology, the impossibility of representing the common good is no less worthy of admiration for what it forbids us. But forbid us, it does. "Thou shalt make no image" (viewed by Kant as the most sublime line in the Bible) hides a political agenda that questions the very foundations of politics and undermines the power of decision. Why decide, if no one can see what is decided for? Cacciari's fascination with Neoplatonism (culminating in *Dell'inizio*) maybe originates here. Neoplatonism, after all, is a gigantic theory of indecision. He who decides—*against* Neoplatonism—is Augustine. And while Cacciari has often been "Augustinian" in his politics (the second and third sections of *Dell'inizio* could be considered a phenomenology of tragic action), he has also been attracted by the arcane, intangible, perfectly circular indifference of the Neoplatonic order of the universe. Cacciari's style, as the reader may have guessed, has always been thoroughly logical-deductive. First he summarizes the thesis he is about to refute. After that, he proceeds to single out all the thesis's internal contradictions, logical flaws, and hidden inconsistencies. The conclusion is invariably a two-headed monster. Cacciari never loses sight of the text he is glossing, and yet the moment always comes when Cacciari speaks with the voice of its author, or forces the author to speak with Cacciari's voice. Cacciari the scholar (not the politician) is morbidly attracted by enormously complex metaphysical architectures (from Neomarxism to Neoplatonism), where the deductive-deconstructive game has so much material to deal with that it can virtually go on forever. However, there is another reason.

Dell'inizio, Cacciari's most significant work to date, whose "untimely" nature was nothing but welcomed in the less-than-ambitious academic landscape of the 1980s, is a search for the foundation of being and thinking—for the simultaneous beginning of being and speculation. In its highly "scholastic" approach, *Dell'inizio* teaches how to live with the awareness that the beginning is radically separated from what begins. In his inquiry, Cacciari questions every rivulet of the Western philosophical and theological tradition—with the exception, however, of the practice in which he operates. His search for the beginning takes for granted that there is a tradition, called "philosophy," which builds up so-called objects of thought such as the *arché*, or "the beginning of speculation." But speculation on beginnings does not disclose the beginning *qua* beginning. It only reveals the nature of the speculation itself and the "sense" of its movement. Cacciari is aware of that. And yet, regardless of his deep understanding of Nietzsche, he is not a genealogical thinker. A hard-working Kantian to the core—his philosophy is not Kantian, but his work ethics is, and maybe with a tinge of what Slavoj Žižek would call "heroism of alienation"[13]—Cacciari lines up problem after problem, question after question, demonstration after demonstration, refutation after refutation, but rarely takes a step back from the all-consuming job of critical philosophy just to ask: "What am I doing?" "What am I writing?" "Do the objects of my research have a reality outside the writing practice in which I conjure them up?" There are philosophers who write one thousand pages of commentary on few lines from a master of the past, while others would rather write a few brilliant lines on one thousand pages by the same master. Cacciari belongs to the first breed, and we will not hold his preferences against him. His books are fascinating labyrinths. Often the reader gets happily lost, sometimes in the company of the author himself.

To a certain extent, "Project" and "Catastrophes" (Chapters 4 and 5 of this volume), both written in 1981, are exercises in deconstruction, but not in the Derridian, grammatological sense. In Cacciari's opinion, Derrida's linguistic therapy is not altogether different from the extreme rationalization pursued by the joint forces of hard sciences and human sciences (we hear the echo of the dilemma Cacciari encountered in his early essay on negative thought: every rational criticism of capitalism reinforces capitalism). On the contrary, the notion of project must be understood in its political relevance. *Pro-ject* means to cut away from the presupposition, from the unchangeable order of the revelation. The project is therefore a modern problem, and there is no greater project than the modern state, with its claims to be entirely atheological and demythologized. However, insofar as it is not fully realized and needs the future to be completed, the modern state reintroduces myth and the politics of myth. Utopia is essential to the project of modernity. Freedom from presupposition and totalitarianism of the goal coexist in the myth of Utopia. But what holds Utopia together is not politics, but science. There is no politics in Francis Bacon's New Atlantis. The emphasis on morals and frugality relocates the egoism of the individual in the grandiosity of the technological project. In time, every desire will be satisfied, because in Utopia there is postponement, but not renunciation.

Max Weber has described the detheologization of the state as secularization. Schmitt called it depoliticization. And the politics of today, Cacciari argues, react to depoliticization with an ad hoc ideology: the politician claims to be open to the unpredictability of technology, but at the same time he would rather reduce the exceptionality of technological change to the bourgeois routine of ordinary administration. The bourgeois wants the change, but not the risks associated with it. (Cacciari refers here to the

European middle class. The American situation would require a different analysis.) In the age of globalization, however (in 1981, Cacciari calls it "political-economical planetary relationships"), this negative project will never find a remote island in which to grow undisturbed.

In "Catastrophes," Cacciari refers to René Thom's distinction between crisis and catastrophe. Contrary to common belief, catastrophe brings (new) order, not anarchy. It is the ongoing anarchy of crisis that suits restorative political projects perfectly, but at the price of a contradiction. Crisis-based conservatism is legitimized only if the crisis endures and is preserved as long as possible. Yet the present state of crisis (1981), argues Cacciari, will not last for long. The de-Westernization of politics and the resistance of the non-Western world to Western politics will usher in the "catastrophe" of the West. Not because the West will be defeated by hordes of foreigners, but because it will reach its catastrophic point, where a new unpredictable order will take the place of the comfortable, permanent crisis. Cacciari is not thinking in terms of Huntington's "clash of civilizations," because his analysis remains political. He simply points out that the West does not seem theoretically prepared for the transition from crisis to catastrophe.

In "The Language of Power in Canetti" (Chapter 6 of this volume), Cacciari praises Elias Canetti for being compelling and original in his description of the growth and behavior of the masses and because he refuses to subscribe to the so-called psychology of the masses that Gustave Le Bon turned into a commonplace. His refusal to extend Freud's individual psychology to the study of the masses puts Canetti in the same good company with Hans Kelsen and Hermann Broch. Canetti, however, does not produce a satisfying theory of counterpower. Democracy should be the best prevention against the formation of the masses, yet without the masses there would be no democracy. Better be aware, Cacciari warns, that the relationship between the masses and democracy is essential, but also precarious and contingent.

"Law and Justice" (Chapter 7) one of the most engaging essays in this collection, addresses Max Weber's distinction between mysticism and innerworldly asceticism. According to Weber, if the latter combines a religious attitude with social and political activism, the former merely rejects the world. On the contrary, Cacciari argues that mysticism is one of the major forces in modern politics, and one whose nature is not theological. Schmitt's political theology has nothing to do with mysticism; it remains entirely on the Weberian side, as an antecedent to secularization. And secularization is the issue here, because the modern state has not inherited the self-legitimizing political form of the Middle-Ages *respublica christiana*. Since the Leviathan cannot represent itself (cannot present itself as the new God), the new legitimacy belongs to Utopia alone and is derived entirely from Utopia.

Up to this point, Cacciari has made large use of Schmitt's *Politische Theologie*. His point, however, is different from Schmitt's. According to Cacciari, mysticism represents the absolute otherness to the thread that connects theology, politics, and the violence of the law. Uninterested in the mythical process that extracts the judicial system from archaic violence, mysticism has a strong affinity with justice, not with the law. Simone Weil, for instance, has been adamantly clear about obligation and law as being the wrong words to describe man's relationship to God. Mysticism is the language of the "just word," which cannot be confused with mundane communication. It is not by chance that Wittgenstein, in his *Tractatus Logico-Philosophicus* (1922), equated *das Mystische* with the mute language that can only point at the world without trying to voice it. Mysticism refuses the idolatry of history and the theological-political belief that one day the city of man and the city of God will be one and the same under the sun. Not at all indifferent to history, mysticism does provide the strongest critique of political eschatology. Being opposed to dialectics and progression, its affinity lies with the instant, the leap and, ultimately, the decision. It has nothing in common with quietism or resignation. In Kierkegaard, mysticism coincides with the absolute responsibility of the individual toward his calling. The individual decides, *cuts away*, breaks off with time and space. He has no home in this world and his redemption will not occur in history. But history, Cacciari emphasizes, is crucial to the understanding of Kierkegaard's critique of historical eschatology. The failed revolutions of 1848 proved to Kierkegaard, *within history*, that salvation would not come from historical developments unless they were revived by the nonhistorical strength of decision. Only decision makes mysticism a political factor and sometimes a revolutionary force. The writings of Bauer, Tocqueville, Stirner, Marx, and Kierkegaard after 1848 must be understood as responses to that historical catastrophe.

But if mysticism is decisionist, then decisionism must be aware of its mystic nature. Grand politics making grand decisions is deeply mystic at heart. Of course, mysticism can also decide not to decide at all. It can reject decision and ask for the justice of "what it is." This is Simone Weil's Gnostic attitude, which shuns from invoking redemption. But Weil's Gnostic dimension is political too, because it recognizes that, given time (*historical* time), every mystic decision faces its unavoidable secularization.

Weil understands the paradoxical nature of political mysticism, where a miraculous exception against history wants to remain indefinitely as a permanent historical force. In Cacciari's opinion, neither Weber nor Schmitt has penetrated the nature of decision deeply enough to answer Weil's paradox. Only Heidegger's solution looks radically different. In *Being and Time* (1927), Heidegger subtracts decision from the mystic/political arena and makes it one of the structures of existence—of *Dasein*. Decision is *Dasein* calling to itself—waking it up to the call that wants to get out from the inauthentic existence. This plea has no words; it happens in silence, and is totally unpolitical. It makes only one decision possible: the being-toward-death, and the acceptance of angst as the essential dimension of *Dasein*.

It was 1927 and six years before Heidegger betrayed his own unpoliticalness and "decided" to embrace Nazism and the *Rektorat*. Unless, of course, it was not a betrayal. Heidegger's unpoliticalness was deeply different from Nietzsche's. Unlike Nietzsche, Heidegger *despised* politics. That was, we may say, his petit-bourgeois side. His move toward Nazism, as Hannah Arendt amply demonstrated, began with his total dismissal of the political dimension. Cacciari, however, asks a different question. If the only way to clear decision from its mystical and political aporias, as Heidegger has shown, is to reduce it to the unpolitical, then what is the destiny of other key political terms, such as commitment, responsibility, or representation? The question is left unanswered, but it hints at the scary possibility that Heidegger's antipolitical unpoliticalness will find other followers.

"*Sinisteritas*," a brief essay not included in this volume, is nonetheless worth mentioning. It was originally delivered as a paper at the symposium "Il concetto di sinistra" (The Idea of the Left), organized in 1982 by the Cultural Office of Rome's City Hall. Although his etymological analysis of the word *sinistra* shows Derridian brilliance, Cacciari's argument owes more to Émile Benveniste than to Derrida, and the substance of the paper is not playful. Its real topic is the "catastrophic antagonism" that has characterized society since the collapse of the Weimar Republic. In 1982 Italy, when inflation had reached South American numbers (only to drop dramatically in the next two years, but at that time no one could foresee that outcome), the comparison with the Weimar Republic (as we have already mentioned) was taken at face value. Cacciari, however, is also referring to other transformations occurring in the world, such as the 1979 Iranian Revolution and the Solidarity movement in Poland. Obviously, these are no longer exceptions in an otherwise predictable world, and the political organizations should stop considering catastrophic occurrences as an enemy. Catastrophes should be seen as *occasions* in the highly philosophical sense of the word (the reference here is to Geulincx's and Malebranche's occasionalism). However, Cacciari admits that even an oxymoronic theory of contingency, or catastrophic occasionalism, would not be free from the Hamleticism of modern politics. Hamlet, as Schmitt pointed out in various essays, does not decide. Hamlet is the liberal who fears decision more than his enemies, condemning himself and his political faction to certain defeat.

Correcting Schmitt to a certain extent, Cacciari observes that Hamlet does not decide, but he does not avoid conflict either. Unfortunately, neither Hamletic sophistication nor catastrophic occasionalism has the power to modify the symmetry of the political spectrum. As long as someone claims to be on the Right, there will always be someone claiming to be on the Left, and vice versa. In disagreement with Mario Tronti, who in the same symposium was defending the mythical quality of the word *left*, Cacciari points out that a myth ceases to be effective at the very moment it is declared as such. With a nod to Machiavelli, Cacciari also adds that the Prince may be an atheist, but he will not announce it during Mass. Marxism had a politics of myth as long as its myths were not believed to be myths. And, against the now untenable politics of myth, Cacciari proposes a mixture of minimalist conventionalism and grand opportunism. The Left will cease to believe in its ontological difference from the rest of society ("We are different" was an old mantra of Italian Communists), and at the same time it will remain open to the occasions of a catastrophic time. Many of these good advices were either ignored or quickly forgotten, and especially after 9/11 they retain the smell of a simpler world gone by.

Can Venice (or Our Civilization) Be Saved from Itself?

As of today, Massimo Cacciari is mayor of Venice for the third time. Although his political career includes eight years as a representative in the Italian Parliament and three years in the European Parliament in Strasbourg, his most enduring political legacy will probably reside in his appointments as a mayor of his native city. The presence of Venice in Cacciari's political philosophy looms large. Much more than an obvious biographical background, Venice is a driving theoretical force that has shaped, to a certain extent, the direction of his thought. Beginning with "The Geophilosophy of Europe" (Chapter 8 of this volume), the 1992 essay that was revised for the eponymous volume (*Geo-filosofia dell'Europa*, 1994), Cacciari has progressed from political to geopolitical, articulating his *pensée de la différence* in a way that owes little to the deconstructionist debate. Differences, or "crises," that matter to him are those between East and West, "us" and "them," friend and foe, nation and federation. As a geopolitical philosopher, Cacciari may have been influenced by the peculiar geography of Venice. Sometimes in an overt manner, other times in a subtler way, Venice plays a role both in *Geo-filosofia dell'Europa* and its follow up, *L'arcipelago* (1997). The history and location of the "city of islands" have given Cacciari the basis for the geopolitical model he has tried to apply in several instances, from a federalist revision of the Italian Constitution (which he attempted in 1988) to a renewed idea of Europe in the arena of today's world. Also, Venice has been the theoretical tool he needed in order to incorporate Carl Schmitt in his political philosophy while at the same time keeping his distance from Schmitt's tendency to mythological reconstructions of the European political space.

Cacciari's political philosophy is, among many other things, a post-Marxist response to the challenges posed by Schmitt's political and juridical thought. The nature of enmity, the logic of decision, and the sharp distinction between the law of the land and the lawlessness of the sea are three of Schmitt's ideas that Cacciari has repeatedly belabored. In *Der Nomos der Erde* (The Law of the Earth, 1950), Schmitt outlines a fascinating but rather fictitious morphology of European history based on the juridical opposition between the *jus publicum Europaeum*, which applies only on firm soil, and the sea, where piracy and total absence of law were considered legal from the onset of modernity through the eighteenth century. One may say that lawlessness at sea provided an outlet for the same aggression and enmity that were regulated on land by the so-called *guerre en forme* (as opposed to the war of destruction). With due difference, a similar argument can be made for the colonies, which were not included in the territory of the *jus Europaeum* (Schmitt does not devote much attention to colonialism, even though his theories might prove very useful in the understanding of the colonial age). In all his major works, Schmitt has constantly lamented the decline of the *jus publicum Europaeum*, blaming Western societies for the erosion of international law and the failure in providing a new "law of the earth" after World War I. My point here is that Cacciari's political philosophy, with its emphasis on the nature of decision and its sobering assessment of the shortcomings of both extreme decisionism and quietist antidecisionism, is a Mediterranean response to the Nordic loss of the "law of the earth" mourned by Schmitt.

A Mediterranean response—or, to be precise, a Venetian one. No suspicion of decadence here, and little sentimentality as well. The very presence of Venice undermines the rigid distinction between land and sea. Venice does not fit into the category of "thalattocracy," or sea empire, that Schmitt reserves for the great maritime empires of the classical antiquity and the modern era. Venice has never been a land that could stretch the arm of its law out over the sea. On the contrary, Venice has always been both land *and* sea, a living contradiction in the heart of Europe. Cacciari is never too explicit about it, but from his writings on Venice one can surmise that the shape of the city on the water may hint at an alternative to the Schmittian rigid dichotomy of land and sea.

Venice is a tale of two cities, Venezia and Mestre, which are one and the same, one on water and the other on land. Usually, travelers on their road to Venice give just a distant look at Mestre's huge oil refinery. Venetians, of course, cannot afford that luxury. They know that the delicate Venetian architecture is counterbalanced by the brutal oil plant metal structure, which nonetheless looks very Venetian at night, when it is illuminated by thousands of lamps. Many citizens of Mestre are former inhabitants of Venice and maintain strong ties with the mother city. The two cities, as they know, need each other and share the same destiny. There have been attempts to divide Venice and Mestre and create two separate entities, but in the end the citizens have rejected the separation. Mestre is still a neighborhood of Venice and elects a deputy mayor.[14]

Even before he started teaching at the Architecture Institute of Venice, Cacciari was very close to historians of architecture such as Francesco Dal Co and Manfredo Tafuri (Dal Co was also one of the cofounders of Potere Operaio). In their work they combined theories of urban planning with a philosophical idea of the Metropolis, and they were getting their ideas not only from the history of architecture but also from literature and poetry. Cacciari's active interest in urbanism produced *De la vanguardia a la metrópoli* (written with Dal Co and Tafuri and published in Spain in 1972), *Metropolis* (1973), *Oikos* (1975), and the essay "Eupalinos o l'architettura" (1978).[15]

Urban planning and ideas of the city are inseparable from Cacciari's political philosophy. The notion of "unrepresentability," which is crucial to his understanding of modern political power, is already at work in *Metropolis*, which analyzes how German and Austrian authors interpreted the transition from city to metropolis between the nineteenth and the twentieth centuries. His point is that the city-metropolis is unrepresentable within the framework of nineteenth-century sociology. Only the literary essay, in its refusal of systematization, comes close to the experience of the new city. As Sombart, Simmel, and young Lukács understood—and Benjamin after them—the essay is a linguistic probe into modern life's complexity. It is not a refusal of form. Rather, the essay creates and destroys itself—it is form that establishes its own limits and criticizes itself in the process.

However, Cacciari points out that Simmel did not give up easily his nostalgia for the lost synthesis of life and form. In his essays on urbanism he was still trying to hold together nature and spirit, inner harmony and exteriority. Simmel found "his" city in San Gimignano, in Tuscany, which spoke to him the language of community and homeland. The harmonious image he had developed in San Gimignano, however, crumbled when he came to the city on the water. Venice could not be assimilated to romantic or nostalgic harmony, because Venice is not a utopia from the past. Venice is essentially *tragic*. It is a linguistic game á la Wittgenstein, exercising power only within defined limits. The essence of Venice lies in the Carnival, where the mask is a substance in itself and does not imply hidden meanings. Simmel's bewilderment with Venice's lack of "homelandishness" parallels Venice's discovery by Andreas, the protagonist of Hofmannsthal's unfinished novel, *Andreas or the Rejoined* (1912–1929). No education, no bildungsroman is possible for Andreas, because Venice is the city of adventure, labyrinths, alleys and channels where he gets lost, meeting mysterious women who are never what they seem and old wise men who understand the city only to the extent that they have given up any attempt to make sense of it.

Venice cannot be reduced to an essay because it is neither form nor life. It is *difference*, inscribed in language. Only poetry or aphorism may hope to capture it. Not with the poetry of memory, as in Rilke, but in the all-impressionistic *Venedig*, the short poem that Nietzsche included in *Ecce homo* (1888), here in my translation:

I was standing on the bridge, now,
in the dark night.
From afar came a song:
drops of gold were scattered
on the trembling vastness.
Gondolas, lights, music—
floating drunk in the twilight.
My soul—a string
plucked by the Invisible,

was singing to herself, in secret,
a gondolier song,
trembling in speckled bliss.
Has anybody ever heard it?

In Nietzsche, Venice is in the present tense (no past, memory, or nostalgia) and it is totally reduced to changing lights, sounds, and music. Definitely closer to Debussy than he is to Wagner, Nietzsche understands Venice as the pure joy of an instant—aware of its uniqueness. We may also refer to Cacciari's 1981 essay, "Sull'inesistenza dell'estetica nietzscheana" (On the Nonexistence of Nietzschean Aesthetics), in which Cacciari maintains that Nietzsche really broke away from art as sublimation, Platonic Idea, or theophany. The new poetry that Nietzsche envisioned grasps the instant in its absolute reality, without pretending to be eternal. But Nietzsche's utopian vision of art is closer to music than it is to other arts, says Cacciari, because music is invisible, a pure combination of sounds, and nothing else but a combinatory practice. Even more than language, music's "linguistic game" shows that nihilism cannot be overcome. Linguistic games stay where they are and stand effective where they are. In music, however, the impossibility of overcoming nihilism can at least be *heard*. It remains invisible and intangible, but it makes itself audible—it is *possible* to hear it. Cacciari's conclusion is not just poetic. His emphasis on possibility is just the beginning of a new phase in his philosophy that will find its expression ten years later, in *Dell'inizio*.

Possibility means chance, and chance is infinite only before it is realized. But the infinity of possibilities is not just an illusion, because the "game" is not over when one of the options has developed into actuality. In time, other options will make themselves available, case by case, now one thing, then another. In 1981, while searching for the Leibnizian notion of compossibility in Musil's *Man Without Qualities*, Cacciari begins an intense collaboration with Venetian composer Luigi Nono. When Nono points out that the third act of Wagner's *Tristan und Isolde* requires "pure" listening, entirely free from expectation on the part of the listener, Cacciari understands it as a new formulation of the classic Leibnizian problem: why being instead of nothing, or the next sound instead of no sound? The Aristotelian concept of possibility or potentiality gravitates always toward reality as the necessary outcome of possibility. But what about possibility *qua* possibility? This possibility is *necessarily* possible. It is necessitated by its own possibility, and its deepest essence resides in what cannot be brought into reality. Eventually, in *Dell'inizio* Cacciari will define possibility as indifferent in itself—indifferent to its resolution as reality or impossibility. In the early 1980s, he finds the contemporary presence of the possible and the necessary in Musil's prose and Nono's music.[16]

Cacciari's and Nono's collaboration culminated in 1984 with *Prometeo: Tragedia dell'ascolto* (Prometheus: A Tragedy of Listening), the last of Nono's large operas. Cacciari wrote the libretto, which was a montage of quotes adapted from Hesiod, Aeschylus, Hölderlin, and Benjamin. The word "opera," of course, is not the best description of Nono's work.[17] It could be better described as a "tragic (in)action." Prometheus brings *techné* to man. He is the god who sacrifices himself for humankind, holding together the world of gods and the world of men. His tragedy is that this reconciliation is impossible. But it is impossible only if we look at it from the point of view of actuality. From the point of view of possibility, Prometheus's impossibility is the "pure possible." In Aeschylus, Prometheus is still chained to the rock and as long as his trial is not over, he is the only link between the two worlds. This suspended possibility cannot be represented, because every representation would inevitably "decide" between different conclusions of the myth. It is possible, however, to listen to it. In *Prometeo* there are no scenes to watch and no action to follow. The original performance was conceived for the San Lorenzo church in Venice, for which Renzo Piano created a wooden structure that resembled the interior of a violin box. With the composer-director on the pedestal in the center of the church, overlooking the mixing console and the electronic instrumentation, players and singers were located on the shelves of the wooden framework. The audience was sitting halfway between the composer and the players, and the whole performance took place in half-light. There was nothing to look at, and one was supposed to apply all listening capabilities to the point of hearing the microintervals produced by the live interaction of voices, instruments, and electronics.

That is why *Prometeo* is "a tragedy of listening." It is also the tragedy of decision, because the intense listening experience required by the listener is the musical equivalent of the Heideggerian *Dasein* listening to the silent call of authenticity—the call bringing decision toward being-toward-death. But *Prometeo* is also the tragedy of indecision, because the pure possibility of Prometheus tied to the Caucasian rock, awaiting his judgment, makes decision impossible without plunging into what Jacques Lacan would call the impossibility of the real, or the impossible real (which is impossible precisely because, by being real, it is no longer possible). With its intrinsic indecision, Nono's and Cacciari's *Prometeo* realizes an immanent criticism of decision that had remained unspoken in Cacciari's essays of the early 1980s. Only in *Prometeo* the compossibility of decision and indecision "holds" the contradiction between law and lawlessness, land and sea, *logos* and absence of *logos*, without solving it once and for all.

Prometeo is indeed many things, including a meditation on geopolitical utopia. The work is divided into seven "islands." The reference is to Hölderlin's hymn *Der Archipelagus* (1800), in which the Greek system of islands functions as a metaphor for plurality and compossibility. In the context of Nono's and Cacciari's work, however, the obvious subtext of the Greek archipelago is Venice, albeit with one crucial difference. The Greek archipelago is natural, while Venice is almost entirely artificial. As Nono said in a conversation with Cacciari, "Venice is a complex system, offering precisely that multi-dimensional experience of listening we were discussing. . . . The sounds of the bells are diffused in various directions: some of them overlap, are carried along by the water, or transmitted by the channels. . . . Others fade away almost completely; others still are connected in several ways to different signals from the lagoon or the city. As an acoustic multiverse, Venice is totally opposed to the hegemonic sound-transmission and sound-hearing we have for centuries been accustomed to."[18]

Venice is a metaphor of localism and globalism at the same time. Every island has a meaning in itself; it is singular and yet connected to the system. The mysticism of decision-indecision "holds" itself by wandering through the Venetian archipelago, as the meaning of *Prometeo* lies in the listener's wandering through the seven islands of Nono's composition. Like a federalist state, the lagoon separates the islands and at the same time connects and protects them. In addition to being a living refutation of Schmitt's sharp separation of land and sea, Venice is also the Southern answer to the nomadic-rhizomatic utopia proposed by Deleuze and Guattari in *Mille Plateaux* (1980). Neither an "icy monster" (Nietzsche's definition of the state) nor a deflagration of egos, the federation of the islands promises neither melting pot nor dissolution of identity. Conflicts and occasional hegemony are in the nature of politics, and the archipelago is not the solution to the European crisis. Yet the issues of centralism versus federalism, or globalization versus local politics, acquire a new perspective in the light of archipelago politics. Not only is no man an island, but also no island is an island. Islands need to flourish as islands if they want to maintain their identity, but they cannot isolate themselves, they must remain open to trade and the arrival of foreigners.

And what if the foreigners are enemies? "The Geophilosophy of Europe" does not avoid the issue. Drawing extensively from Santo Mazzarino's historical research on the ancient world, Cacciari goes back to the archaic Mediterranean geopolitics, at the time when the geographical and cultural divisions between Europe and Asia were still unheard of. In the Homeric sea there were only cities and harbors, passages from one island to another island. Of course there was neither peace nor harmony, but the political distinction between East and West—between "us" and "them"— had yet to be born. Achaeans and Trojans shared the same civilization. They were enemies, but not each other's "other." Only the Greek-Persian wars forced the archipelago to know the enemy, to *name* it, and to know itself in order to defend itself. The result of this epistemological change was the *polis*—which the East never knew—and the birth of politics. Aeschylus's *The Persians* captured perfectly this epochal moment in the history of the West. Queen Atossa dreams of Europe and Asia as two women who are divided, and yet she is aware that they are blood sisters—that their beginning is *one*. Aeschylus even calls *"stasis"* the Greek-Persian War, using a generic term that may be applied to civil war as well.

Here Cacciari is again following Schmitt: politics begins with the separation between friend and foe. Contrary to Schmitt's personal mythology, however, he points out that there is nothing primordial about the separation. Aeschylus recognizes that friend and foe are united and remain united even when they are separated. Western philosophy, in its endless rethinking of the relationship between the One and the Many, elaborates and multiplies the same paradox, the incomprehensible difference of opposites. When dreaming of peace and harmony, we must not forget that we are "in friendship" with others not despite our differences but thanks to the incomprehensible difference that stems out of our unity. One of the most intriguing chapters of *Geo-filosofia dell'Europa* (not included in this selection) is devoted to *Venise sauvée*, Simone Weil's unfinished drama inspired by the Spanish conspiracy to destroy Venice on the last night of the 1618 Carnival.[19] The French and Spanish conspirators are determined to "make history" by crushing the resistance of the Venetian people in one night. They are about to succeed when one of them, Jaffier, unexpectedly denounces his comrades, suffers to be called a traitor and nonetheless dies as a soldier in the vain attempt to join the men he has betrayed in a last gesture of defiance. Jaffier feels no pity for the people of Venice, nor does he care about the historical destiny of Spain. He betrays his comrades because at night he is struck by the sheer beauty of the city and decides that he will not allow the destruction of that beauty. Cacciari observes that the Spanish conspiracy was a perfect power game as long as it was devoid of values. But beauty is a factor in politics, and as good as any other. In the name of beauty there will always be a traitor, someone who reintroduces values in the icy game of politics.

And yet, Venice is cynical enough to take advantage of those traitors without acknowledging them. Jaffier has saved Venice, but Venice is not thankful to him. Revolutionaries are sometimes merciful; power is not. By extolling the beauty of Venice without considering who created that beauty and how much violence and exploitation the peoples of the Mediterranean had to suffer in its name, Jaffier is unable to transcend the atrocious realpolitik on which Venice is based. Jaffier says that Venice is beautiful, but why should beauty be a value? What happens to what is beautiful? Is this beauty destined to pass or is it supposed to last forever?

As awestruck by Venice as Nietzsche and Simmel were, the Russian exiled poet Joseph Brodsky made a point when he observed that Venetian space, with its doubling of the palaces' images in the water of canals, opposes beauty to time, since beauty is the only possession that time does not have.[20] As disdainful as he was of the "herds in short pants" shuffling their sandaled feet through the city on the lagoon in every season of the year, even Brodsky might have fallen prey to the aesthetics of eternity that every visitor in Venice instantly adopts. It is impossible not to want this beauty to last forever. This is also what Jaffier wants, as soon as he leans over the edge of his balcony and takes a look of Venice at night. Venice's rulers want this too, but with a difference. They may not care about Venice's beauty the same way a visitor does, but one thing they know: their power must last as long as possible, even forever if eternity is an option. Venice does not want to die, but its natural impulse to survival has nothing to do with the justice or injustice of time. Why should a mortal creature (and Venice is nothing more than a mortal creature) be preserved from decay? Venice, Cacciari concludes, must not be "saved." It is not the city of God. It is only human. And, if it is human, it will die. The good-hearted people who want to save Venice because of its beauty are just reversed *realpolitiker*. Like Jaffier, they do not really care about the Venetians, which means that they do not care about life being subjected to decay and death. And yet, if Venice cannot and must not be saved, it still can live as everything else lives, facing its own mortality and exploring the limited but innumerable possibilities of life.

Cacciari writes his analysis of Simone Weil's *Venise sauvée* at the beginning of the 1990s, while he is running for mayor of Venice—which makes his argument even more intriguing. In another essay, "Venezia possibile"

(Possible Venice, 1989), he had already tried to connect the threads of his philosophy to Venice. What does "Save Venice!" mean, Cacciari asks? The cry is so old because the very existence of Venice has always been exceptional. For centuries, the geopolitical order of Europe has seen nothing more unnatural than Venice's government, ruling class and power. During the eighteenth century, however, Venice lost the capability of representing itself to the eyes of the world. The subsequent transformation of Venice into a tourist attraction coincided with the universal cry of "Save Venice!" addressed to no one in particular. But Venice is a living organism, and not, we may say, the European franchise of the Las Vegas version of itself (when the Venetian Hotel opened in Las Vegas, Cacciari was invited as the mayor of the "real" Venice; he obviously declined).[21]

It is entirely possible, Cacciari writes, that Venice is nothing but a living organism (just as Nono's microintervals are possible precisely because they are not perceived as real). One needs to reflect on Venice's particular *forma urbis*. Mestre and Porto Marghera failed to turn Venice into a purely industrial town, and yet they cannot be separated from Venice unless you want to reduce them to merely suburban spaces. Besides, Venice's architecture stands as an immanent criticism of modernity. Venice cannot be modernized, but it can be made the subject of great architecture (not "modern" architecture). Venice is "untimely," and it will save itself only by remaining an island. But islands, as Cacciari explains again in *L'arcipelago* (1997) are the symbolic units of Europe (one is reminded of Fernand Braudel, who spoke of sixteenth-century Europe as made of islands). Of course, if Venice can die, Europe can die too. In the world's geopolitics, Europe's destiny may be a long twilight, but it is no one else's twilight, it belongs to Europe only, and it is still rich with unexplored possibilities.

At the end of Italo Calvino's *Invisible Cities* (1972), Marco Polo is having his usual conversation with Kublai Khan. This time he is about to say something that he has never admitted before. The hundreds of strange cities that he has described to the emperor were just the masks of Venice. In his reports to the emperor, Marco Polo evoked no other city than Venice. Cacciari's theoretical, political, and literary essays have traveled a long way, but Cacciari's *writing*, in its ambitious totality, perhaps has no other desire than to be the written metamorphosis of Venice's thousand patterns.

The last chapter of our selection is a recent essay, published in 2006 as an introduction to a new Italian paperback edition of Max Weber's *Science as a Vocation* and *Politics as a Vocation*. Weber gave these well-known lectures in November 1917 and January 1919 at the University of Munich.

Facing a crowd of young students who were hoping for the renewal of humankind after World War I and were ready to embrace whatever theory promised to lift them into the realm of ideals, Weber disappointed them bitterly. He warned his audience that the scholar's career may be more the outcome of sheer luck than anything else, and he spared no words in describing how the university system seems particularly suited to the advancement of the mediocre. As for the politician's career, that one too had nothing glamorous to offer, unless for the born demagogues or whoever was ready to be at their service. Politics, to him, was a *Beruf* in the sense Martin Luther intended ("All are called [*berufen*] to their calling [*Beruf*]"), but the call in itself did not call anyone to serve the common good or other pieties. Politics is the use of power, which means the use of violence. Whoever can decide when and how to use violence has the power. Laws legitimate power, but power is enforced by violence. The final pages on the ethics of conviction and the ethics of responsibility must be read with this unsentimental premise firm in mind, while the beautiful souls are kindly requested to hurry up to the exit. And yet, Weber lives in a time when the professional politician (the bureaucrat) is still proud of his professionalism, while the vocation politician (natural leader or demagogue) is still requested to qualify himself as a politician in the full sense of the word. Today, we may say, a privileged path for vocation politicians to acquire credibility is to present themselves as champions of antipolitics.

This is why, as Cacciari argues, Weber's phenomenology only today appears in its whole tragic light. The two "types" of Weber's *agon*, the scholar and the politician, are in open conflict. The order of this conflict is the object of political science, and there is no room here for "philosophies of life" or religious values. But the very independence from any hierarchy of values that the scholar experiences in his field is in itself tragic. This is what Max Scheler or Leo Strauss did not understand when they saw in Weber's "absence of value" the ultimate metaphysical value assigned to research. Weber constantly rebels against what Carl Schmitt would later call the "tyranny of values." And yet, even though science does not decide between values, that does not put science above them. The scholar is not competing with the politician for any kind of supremacy, and the modern *civitas*, as Cacciari points out, is defined by this fraternal enmity between the citadel of science and the citadel of politics. In the latter, the absence of values as the only possible value; in the former, the "universal value" as the only interest worth pursuing. And God is absent from both cities.

Yet the politician cannot be reduced to a mere witness of the increasing bureaucratization of his vocation and the groundlessness of his values. The politician's decision may be groundless, but it is not "free." Decisions require planning and research, and only action paired with knowledge constitutes Max Weber's true "philosophy of praxis." The primacy of politics has no other ground than this. Even the politician who follows a strict ethics of responsibility must be "convinced" of the values that he champions. He cannot, however, allow himself to be "enchanted" by them, avoiding therefore responsibility for their outcome. Only his disenchantment will be the measure of his responsibility.

Cacciari observes that the politician is also responsible for the values he opposes, insofar as he is "called" to answer them. In the polytheism of politics, he who wins does not kill the enemy god, but merely answers to it. And yet this polytheism is tragic, because it will never dissolve itself in an all-embracing monotheism. Once the decision has been made, one god has been chosen against the others. The politician has therefore "sinned" in the eyes of the gods he has not worshiped, or the values he has not embraced. Contrary to Hannah Arendt in her most Aristotelian and eudemonistic moments, Cacciari knows very well that politics is not a search for happiness. Not only does the politician renounce happiness (as we see, his early essay on renunciation has run like a subterranean river, only to resurface at this point), but he also feels all the weight and guilt of his renunciation. Yet there is more: Cacciari's refusal of the implicit monotheism associated with the "right" decision liquidates the Schmittian obsession about friend and foe. Regardless of the polarization that has marked the political life of the twentieth century and threatens to shape the twenty-first century as well, Cacciari reminds the reader that the political opponent is also *hospes* (host) and not only *inimicus* (foe). Political opponents are those whose values we cannot embrace, and since they are our "limit," they contribute to the shaping of *our* values.

The ethics of responsibility says, "I want," while the ethics of conviction confesses, "I must." But the only thing that the politician "must" do is to try to compose responsibility and conviction. The ethics of conviction must not be opposed, as long as it does not invade the field of politics. Weber is not extremely clear on this point (and the huge literature on the two ethics confirms it), but it seems safe to say that the saint is not an enemy to the politician, as long as he restrains from imposing his faith as the resolution of political conflict. True sanctity, on the other hand, cannot be dismissed precisely because it knows that its kingdom is not of this world. Weber's politician turns into a truly tragic hero when he realizes that his power, which is entirely based on the game of possibility, does not count for much against the power of the impossible, and that his proud decisionism dwarfs when compared with the saint's obedience, which alone harbors the *pax profunda* denied to the politician.

In the end, the politician's ultimate goal lies beyond the "common good." Grand politics happens when the politician raises himself over the utilitarian level, only to understand that politics will never be able to "comprehend" the flame of pure conviction. The Sermon on the Mount is forbidden to the politician. And yet its impossibility must be taken into account in every possibility that politics handles. Grand politics and grand mysticism are compatible, if only as stellar friends, whose orbits will coincide in the infinite, or in God.

Weber conceives the state as a great rational artifact, where law and legitimacy provide the only possible foundation for the use of force. Yet Weber also contemplates the failure of his ideal, which is, tragically, the failure of politics. Many years after the turmoil following the end of World War I, the technical-economical organization of today's world does not suffer to be held in check, neither by the state nor by national or international law. Its goal is the complete removal of politics as a useless remnant of the past. At the same time, antipolitics grows from the grassroots level as well. As Negri and Hardt would have it, both the multitude and the multinational corporations are now calling the Empire into being. Cacciari is much less happy about this development than they are, since he does not see in the advent of Empire any implicit potentiality for liberation. He is more inclined to thinking that, no less than Nietzsche, Weber too would have recognized in the coming Empire a new "icy monster," whose absolute power will allow freedom only as the supreme right of liberators and submission of the liberated, where individual conscience will be made obsolete in a world ruled by perpetual destruction and replacement, and where everything that is solid will melt into the air at a faster pace than it has ever happened in the past.

Indeed, in this world the true politician may be as stranger as the saint is. Maybe the City of Man and the City of God are both out of this world, and the politician and the saint are both unpolitical. I do not think, however, that the total disenchantment of this conclusion casts a negative light on Massimo Cacciari's political philosophy. As Mark Lilla has recently argued in discussing the conflict between liberalism and "the politics of God," which is another name for the contrast between ethics of responsibility and ethic of (absolute) conviction, the pure and simple defense of high liberal principles will not help securing the independence of politics from claims based on divine revelation. And he observes, "But we need to recognize that coping is the order of the day, not defending high principle, and that our expectations should remain low."[22]

In his own way, Cacciari has always advocated "coping" under many names. What are Grand Opportunism and Grand Politics, when they are stripped bare, other than Grand Coping? The decline of politics does not stem only from the external fundamentalist threat and the rigid answers such threat provokes. As the West progresses from liberal democracy to empire, its political crisis grows from the inside of liberal democracies as well. Twilight is their destiny. But twilights can be very long and not every coping is coping out. It is in fact the last resort to keep political theology at bay, precisely by refusing to discuss political decisions only in terms of absolute choices. As Cacciari has often repeated after Musil, now one thing, now another . . .

CHAPTER I

Impracticable Utopias

Hofmannsthal, Lukács, Benjamin

"Romània" and Calderón

Hugo von Hofmannsthal's work seems to amount to a research project on the languages and forms of "Romània." But this "Romània" is not at all the stable dwelling that many interpreters have claimed, in the shadow of whose authority Hofmannsthal would overcome the aestheticism of his youthful dramas, of his Loris.[1] Loris's "great art," as Hermann Bahr would say, "has no feeling."[2] Loris belongs to the Jugendstil that reflects upon the formal elements, the style of composition, rather than evoking feelings and moods. It is, after all, Jugendstil that is perfectly suited to its "problem:" transience.[3] How can transience be stated and saved at the same time from the pure line of words? What power do words possess, and, therefore, what are their limitations with respect to transience? But transience is also the past. Its problem is also the problem of saving the past. The limitations of language in "comprehending" transience are its limitations in preserving and reliving the past. Hofmannsthal's uncanny (*Unheimliches*), which fascinates and scares, is this "second being," namely language, where present, every day life relives the past—the transience of words and forms.[4] Life itself, here, perceives a substantial continuity, an elective affinity, not beyond but in every contradiction and dissension.

Transience returns as present. For the poet "the dead resuscitate, not when he likes, but when they want—and they resuscitate without respite."[5] The poet saves the past, as the idea saves the phenomenon. But the present of poetry is not an abstract unity, a meeting as one of primordial, mythical elements so alike as to be bound to meet beyond any separation—destined to meet. This is the literary and conservative image that we often have of Hofmannsthal. His dead, on the contrary, revive with the multiplicity of their voices and, above all, their forms, their questions, their interrupted paths. If "the invented word" is spiritually and morally impossible, if originality betrays the necessary presence of transience in every voice, it is equally impossible—an equally indecent pretension—to believe in the "word," which eliminates every difference, dissolves every contradiction, gives peace and unity to traditions and reconciles them with the present. The poet "comprehends" the problems, listens to the questions of those traditions, talks about them, since they necessarily speak his language (the dead revive whenever they want), but he does not have at his disposal synthetic Esperantos. The poet is suspicious of profound, substantive truths, according to which we should "go around naked, as if [we were] wandering abysses and vortices."[6]

"Romània" is the place where Hofmannsthal's problems and contradictions are located. It is the space of his language. But this space does not represent an abstract totality; it already stems from a choice. It cannot be identified at all with the idea or destiny of Europe or with the intellectual cosmopolitanism of the Enlightenment. Hofmannsthal's Romanity encompasses the multiplicity of languages that revolve around the great Habsburg Empire. In Hofmannsthal, European history is reshaped around the events of the last universal monarchy instead of the traditional axis: from the Renaissance to the Counterreformation to the French Enlightenment.[7] Austria is at the center of this Reich, but not in the sense of supremacy or spiritual synthesis. In Hofmannsthal's *Austria in the Mirror of Its Poetry*, only the roots of Austrian culture are discussed. With slight irony, the *Magic Flute* becomes a child's fairytale, and Schubert's *Lieder* acquire a "somewhat popular superiority."[8] The essay, in subdued tonalities difficult to detect, is a critique of the myths of German culture, a search for "delicate divisions." To distinguish and separate does not amount to provincialism. On the contrary, it means "letting-through" the different. The idea of Austria at the center of the Habsburg universal monarchy turn for Hofmannsthal into a "letting-through," acceptance, a way of giving-itself to the multiplicity of forms and traditions that make up the Empire. Austrian universalism consists in making room and words for the different, in accepting its problems, in giving itself to it.

Hofmannsthal's "Romània," completely alien from Stefan George's "magnificent intolerance," not only represents a choice, which defines and delimits *a* linguistic-cultural space, but it is also a concrete, internal multiplicity, where the art of uniting, of *Verbinden*, is indissolubly linked to the art of distinguishing, of *Scheiden*.[9] The arch of this "Romània" is stretched between Spain and Venice. Venice is Hofmannsthal's Italian home as Florence was George's (*Essays*, 147). And with Venice, Hofmannsthal could conceive the union of East and West. Venice was his Byzantium, the memory of a primordial and disappeared Romanity. And yet Spanish poetry is very different from Venice. Venice is the city of masks, of the self that splits and travels in quest of itself through the adventures of chance, the place of encounters and enchantments without name. In the *Adventurer and the Singer* or in *Christina's Journey Home*, Casanova the master of initiations, "who must always journey," represents the exterior of the Venetian mask, which *Andreas* in the end will turn into the tragedy of the impossible bildungsroman.[10] Spain, instead, is the poetry of solidity, fidelity, permanence. It is the mystical soul of the Empire where the great problems are assumed *sub specie aeternitatis*, *Theatrum Mundi*, expression of a symbolism that illuminates and transfigures the characters of the period as eternal figures of the conflicts of the spirit (*Essays*, 161). This symbolic construction dominates from *The Smallest World Theatre* to *The Salzburg Great Theatre of the World*, which, as Goldschmit correctly remembered, premiered "six weeks after Rathenau's murder and while in Munich Falckenberg was completing rehearsal for *Drums in the Night*."[11] And yet the idea of *Theatrum Mundi* would seem opposed to that of masks. The world of chance, adventure, of the discordant multiplicity of characters, is a theater of the transitoriness and vanity of worldly interests, of their eternal return and collapse. It is in this theater that the fundamental conflicts of the era take place. The great ceremony that the theater represents does not crystallize these conflicts, does not arrest their becoming.[12] Only their "play" acquires the form of ceremony—is rescued from chance. Here, too, there are masks—ceremony is also mask. In this case it is the mask of cult, of the eternal symbolism that prevails over the individual multiplicity of life. There, it is the mask of the individual and the wanderer that renounces the plasticity of forms. One pole could not exist without the other, which does not mean that one is any less remote and different than the other. This substantial diversity—which once recognized appears to be necessary and insurmountable—is contained in Hofmannsthal's "Romània," in the multiplicity of its languages and in its dramatics, since the Spanish ceremony cannot "comprehend" the Venetian travels, nor can the Venetian mask reach the solidity and permanence of ceremony. Hofmannsthal will analyze both of these languages in their inseparable difference until his last days and in his two greatest works: the Spanish *Schauspiel* in *The Tower* on one hand, and on the other in *Andreas*, the novel of Venice.[13]

Now we should examine the Spanish side of the antithesis (without, however, forgetting that it remains incomprehensible without its opposite). The great figures of this side of "Romània" are a decisive part of this same Austrian tradition. Grillparzer had translated *Life Is a Dream* in 1816 and had remained under the sign of Lope de Vega and Calderón throughout his entire work. Lenau tackled another decisive symbol of Spanish poetry in *Don Juan* (the link between Spain and Venice? between metaphysical ceremony and mask?). The encounter with this tradition on the part of Hofmannsthal is immediate. The fairytale *The Emperor and the Sorceress* (*Der Kaiser und die Hexe*, 1897) derives from Lope and Grillparzer. The idea of *The Salzburg Great Theatre of the World* is entirely in the spirit of Calderón. The world is a stage where man lives the part that God assigned to him. From 1905 on, Hofmannsthal works on Calderón's *La hija del aire* and the idea reemerges in 1907–1908 in the correspondence with Strauss, this time as the project for an opera, *Semiramis*.[14] In 1918 Hofmannsthal confides to Hermann Bahr the intention of preparing every year an adaptation of Calderón for the Burgtheater.[15] From this idea originates the translation of *Dame Goblin* (*La dama duende*) (*Hofmannsthal*, Chapter 3). But the link with Calderón is centered on the symbol of Sigismund in *Life Is a Dream*. From this symbol Hofmannsthal will not be able to detach himself. Between 1901 and 1902 he works at a trochaic version, but as the *Notes and Diaries* (*Aufzeichnungen und Entwurfe*) of spring 1902, revised in August 1904, show, he is already thinking at a complete adaptation of the play.[16] In a letter to his father, he remarks on the incompleteness of Calderón's work and the need for a bold transformation. And, shortly after, in another letter to Theodor Comperz, he writes that he is working on "an adaptation of Calderón's *Life Is a Dream*, a play profound at times, but at times unsuccessful—a completely free adaptation . . . that relates to the original not like Kleist's *Amphitryon* to Molière's but, comparison not intended—as a Shakespeare play to the Italian novella."[17] In 1904 he writes to Hermann Bahr, "It is a question of descending in the heart of the matter of *Life Is a Dream*, which now fascinates me more than ever, into the most remote depths of the ambiguous, deep realm of the self, and of finding the no-longer-I, or the world" (*Briefe 1900–1909*, 73, 155). But the adaptation runs into a major difficulty, not of a technical but of a spiritual nature as Hofmannsthal himself remarks in his preliminary remarks (*Vorbemerkung*) to the incomplete edition of 1910—a difficulty that makes the conclusion of the play impossible. After the war, Hofmannsthal's work starts from this point. From October 23, 1920, on, he labors every day on the "major work."[18] In October 1921, having reached Act V, of which he sketches the basic structure, he interrupts it for *The Salzburg Great Theatre of the World*. In 1923 he writes to Burckhardt, "By now this work has become almost mysterious to me and this last act is like a castle built over an abyss."[19] He interrupts the work once again and writes *The Egyptian Helen*. Finally, the first version is completed, and Schnitzler, who gets a copy at the beginning of 1925, stresses its novelty with respect to Calderón not only as far as the characters go, but also for "the problem."[20] This version appeared in two issues of the *Neue Deutsche Beiträge* that Hofmannsthal published with the Bremer Press from 1922 to 1927. The Bremer Press published a second version, but as a separate volume, that was essentially identical to the first with the exception of numerous abbreviations and the scene with the Gypsy woman in Act V (the Gypsy woman appears in only one part).

But *Life Is a Dream* is not finished yet. In his reply to Leopold von Adrian, who admired the unity of the work, Hofmannsthal speaks of his decision to change the final two acts.[21] The motive of dramatic surrender conceals a deeper, substantial change in the conception of the entire work. The new version appeared in 1927. The harsh disenchantment of the last scene must have haunted Hofmannsthal. Burckhardt rightly sees how "the glassy look of this tragedy" weighs also on *Andreas* (*Ricordi*, 47). How is it possible, through suffering and with recourse to the spiritual energy one gains from it not to reach the "flash of reconciliation," the presence of a "superior morality"? Precisely this ending seemed impossible to Hofmannsthal after the first version. The subject matter had changed to the point of negating such an ending. But this negation escapes Hofmannsthal as a foreign power. The irruption of the *Trauerspiel* through *The Tower* "in these destitute times" was destined to remain a crucial presence of the contemporary uncanny.[22]

This brief account already shows how the relationship between Hofmannsthal and *Life Is a Dream* is not at all sympathetic. It is neither a model nor an answer to Hofmannsthal's questions, but a continuous questioning of the reasons of his entire work and its forms. Hofmannsthal's work is a tireless reworking and transformation of the incomplete *Life Is a Dream*—the essential incompleteness of its symbolism. With the 1925 and 1927 versions, this reworking and transformation gets to the core of the drama's sense without providing any cure for it. This sense relates to Hofmannsthal's overall idea of "Romània." *Life Is a Dream*—incomplete, and whose analysis appears endless [23]—is an open wound in this idea—the contradictory being of this idea—its specific uncanny. Removed with effort from the first version, the wound reappears uncontrollably in the second.

But this outcome develops ever since the first trochaic version in 1901–1902 and from the *Notes* of 1902–1904.[24] The stylistic differences are decisive. Calderón's universe of metrical forms, rhythms, arrangements, symbols, and similes is replaced by a functional language, attentive to the collocation and role of the characters (*Hofmannsthal*, 24). The long monologues disappear, and the dialogues are interrupted whenever the functional tension of the discourse seems to fall. Plays on words, maxims, and witticisms (the figure of Clarín) no longer adorn the verses (*Hofmannsthal*, 109). This reduction of Calderón's language conforms to the nucleus of the work's idea. Far from having a mere decorative function, the polyvalence of the linguistic character in Calderón is symbolic of the harmony of "the great theater of the world." The language stands as symbol for the system of relations, weights and counterweights, thrusts and counterthrusts, which rule in the order of the universe (*Hofmannsthal*, 100, 105). The wealth and breadth of the empire of language is symbolic of the "great theater" as *kosmos*, order willed and kept inscrutably by God. There is no silence in this empire. The word is never missing. The empty spaces, the pauses that populate the subject of *The Tower* could not be found in Calderón—for important reasons, which conform to the age and spirit of the two authors, their questioning, not their style. The word in Calderón develops its power to the point of covering the most sublime ideas, while this same power is precisely Hofmannsthal's problem when approaching *Life Is a Dream*. Hofmannsthal's *The Letter of Lord Chandos* is published in 1902, and *The Tower*'s Sigismund is the brother (sharing even the memories, as we shall see) of the despairing Lord.[25]

A Divine World-Play

In Hofmannsthal's reworking and transformation the linguistic concentration reduces the events to the essential—to the *new* essential. The role of many characters in Calderón is compressed to the minimum, and some secondary relationships are suppressed, namely, that of Astolfo and Estrella. This new essential is Sigismund, the destiny of the imprisoned

prince whose "moving star threatens endless tragedy and grief" (Calderón, Act II, Scene I), whom we meet in chains and covered with rags
("man's worst crime is to be born") and to whom "history" teaches to
repress his wild nature by showing precisely that "to live is already to
dream": "My master in this was a dream, and I still tremble at the thought
that I may waken and find myself again locked in a cell. Even if this should
happen, it would be enough to dream it, since that's the way I've come to
know that all of human happiness must like a dream come to an end" (Act
III, scene XIV).[26] "Essential" is only what rotates around this figure, the
forces that correspond to his problem and his secrets. Thus minor figures
acquire an importance that is completely absent in Calderón. Soldiers get
to speak, while the rebellion acquires characters and faces, as it was the
case in *The Salzburg Great Theatre of the World*. But above all the figure of
Basilius the King changes aspect. Hofmannsthal believed that the king in
Calderón appeared deeply contradictory. He is the prisoner of destiny for
having banished the prince to the Tower "in the crags and rocks of those
mountains" (Act I, scene I), and he wants him back. For this reason the
king wants to "try the Heavens," "because man prevails over the stars."
But Sigismund is not mature for the trial, he fails because he ignores that
life is a dream. To exile him again seems still his fate, "How little does fate
lie when he foresees misfortune!" The king defends order and stability "in
the theater of the world" by defending himself against Sigismund's wild
nature, and yet this necessity is also his guilt. Calderón already voices this
essential contradiction through Basilius, which undermines the very idea
of kingdom: "Wishing to restrain another from tyranny and cruelty, I
become one myself; or . . . by preventing his committing crimes, I may
commit those crimes myself" (Act I, scene II). Or as Sigismund says: "My
father . . . using as his excuse the auguries of my foul nature, made a brute
of me, a half-human creature . . . no vengeance or injustice can alter the
course of fate" (Act III, scene III). The reconciliation of this contradiction
occurs in Calderón through a double deceit. Both Sigismund and Basilius
recognize that the decrees of Heaven never lie and that life is "illusion,"
"shadow," "fiction," a great "play," a cross between human destiny and
stars, magic formulas and rituals, where nonetheless, in the end, divine
grace and wisdom win out (*Viaggi*, 159). The recognition of the divine
world-play (*Weltspiel*) occurs through the passion that is necessary in order
to detach oneself from the false appearances of the world. This recognition restores the wavering principle of the kingdom: the king is he who,
through passion, is now free from the prison of worldly illusions, is disenchanted and awakened to the awareness that all life is a dream—not in the

sense of chance but of Christian wisdom. "Man always acts according to cosmic and religious ties," (*Viaggi*, 160) before which the weight of single words and of individual characters is annihilated.

Therefore, the king reestablishes order or creates order because he recognizes divine order and decrees. The order of the kingdom is justified and is based on divine order. Royal passion brings order back on earth and punishes those who want to impose the dream as reality, illusion, and worldly vanity as law. Sentencing his accomplices in the revolt, Sigismund, the new king, proclaims, "Once the cause of treason's past, there's no need to keep the traitor" (Act III, scene III). This central idea of the great Baroque Spanish play is intolerable to Hofmannsthal. We need to find the basic reasons for this rejection, from which derive Hofmannsthal's differences in style and form. Hofmannsthal finds it impossible to conceive complete immanence of grace in the political and religious order. Walter Benjamin has made clear this fundamental trait: "Spanish drama . . . resolves the conflicts of a creatural state deprived of grace by somehow reducing them playfully within the sphere of the court, whose king proves to be a secularized redemptive power."[27] In fact, within the *stretto* of the third act, the great symbol of the relation between transcendental and immanent political order comes to light. To awaken this symbol and looking after it: such is the mission and destiny of the Christian king.

But how can such a symbol be established? How can grace become immanent when at the origin a crime has been committed? The Doctor expresses this central idea in the 1925 and 1927 versions. Where this life has been torn by the roots, a vortex has been opened that carries away everything with it. Life is a dream, but the immanent political decision has condemned Sigismund to his Tower. What power can show that this decision is the result of a divine plan? For Hofmannsthal, this synthesis of decision and grace seems vain even in Calderón. Sigismund's martyrdom cannot be resolved in continuity with the previous reign and its order. It cannot consecrate the kingship that has committed the crime and in so doing has separated itself from grace. Political power alone removes Sigismund from the tower, is able to free him—power that fights Basilius on his same ground. How can a new kingdom be established from this conflict? How can the immanence of this conflict be overcome, which no longer has anything to do with the immanence of divine grace? These questions lead Hofmannsthal away from the specific form of the Spanish drama. It becomes difficult, contradictory, and a struggle to affirm the teleology of the martyr's passion. According to Benjamin, it is by reflection to the Spanish making grace immanent that emerges "the comprehensive secularisation of the historical in the creatural state" (*Origin*, 92).

Sigismund is transformed in a creature of the *Trauerspiel*, thrown in a play that no force will be able to reconcile to the religious idea of a cosmic order—a play that knows only the nihilistic element of Spanish drama (the appearance of Being, the collapse of every Being in the dream), not the assertion of the superior reality of divine order.[28]

But what content should Sigismund's presence, his witnessing assume? A new order, a new empire? And what forces could realize this witnessing, once the impossibility of a theoteleology of historical events has been recognized? In history, only the political is, only the will to power—not the establishment of order. Or is Sigismund's witnessing utopia, *the* utopia— witnessing the absence of its very idea? The vortex created by the Spanish drama (with no healing in sight) constitutes, according to Hofmannsthal, the theme of *The Tower*—a question that, like Andreas's voyage, remains without answer.

This decisive turning point in the meaning of the *Trauerspiel*, inherent in the new centrality of Sigismund's character, is subsequently strengthened in the drafts of 1902–1904. The figure of the king is now subjected to a veritable devaluation (*Hofmannsthal*, 110) that reveals the fundamental contradiction intuited by Hofmannsthal in Calderón.[29] As for Clotaldo, he too undergoes the transformation from faithful servant and wise Christian, to pure politician. Here great importance is given to the injustice suffered by Sigismund, which is indissolubly linked to the disorder that dominates the country. The devaluation of the king is complete: his baseness, his "animality" is emphasized by the impotence that afflicts him after condemning the newly born Sigismund to the Tower. The king's impotence too becomes rebellion, destruction of the order. Insofar as it is caused by the king's guilt, the rebellion is now an inevitable turning point, and a necessity. Sigismund's martyrdom is symbolic of the king's sins. They have created the vortex that plunges the order of the kingdom to the bottom. They determine the turning to necessity, to misery: "This son is not there in the Tower, but here in my conscience as a worm which devours me."[30] The son is freed to restore the fallen order, to heal the impotence of the king. But how can one restore what by now lacks foundation, what by now is in the vortex of his guilt? The test fails because Sigismund can only be manifest in the political as political, can only assert his will to power against that of his father. The father had summoned him to restore the kingdom that he had founded on that crime—not to reconcile, not to erase the guilt of the political and of the crime that he had committed in his name. The same goes for Calderón. It is fundamentally a reason of state that puts Sigismund to the test. But, then, for Hofmannsthal the test *must* fail and Sigismund must be thrown again in the Tower, in what he perceives as reality. Here the fundamental transformation of his character occurs; Sigismund recognizes all the real as "play of shadows," "dreamt things" and succeeds in conquering from the world a "liberating distance." This makes him politically expendable. The rebels take Sigismund to be mad, just as he was for his father wild and violent, and they kill him. They introduce to the joyful people the new Sigismund as the king, yet not Sigismund, but the mask of Sigismund. His spirit cannot rule. An incurable wound is established within Sigismund's conscience conquered through martyrdom, between the fact that life is a dream and the reasons of the political. With every effort, Hofmannsthal will try to overcome the hopeless conclusion of the 1902–1904 drafts, but he will have to turn to it again in the last version.

It is very understandable why it was decisive for Hofmannsthal to reconcile somehow with the teleology of Calderón's drama. The crisis of that teleology would signify the pure impossibility to entertain the very idea of "Romània." As we have seen already, not only do the forms of that idea appear contradictory—not only does the idea derive from a choice and therefore a renunciation—but now it seems that the internal dialectic of those forms leads to something other than itself, reaches its own crisis. Around the kingdom the great ceremony took place where East and West played their destined roles, the conflicting voices of the harmony of the last world monarchy. The passion play of the martyr leads to this order. Here the richness of the word has the power to denote and comprehend. Now, instead, that kingdom appears without foundation, the ceremony is transformed in politics for the preservation of power, and the conflicting voices are transformed in rebellion. The passion play does not conquer new earthly orders, but only bears witness to an indelible difference between spirit and power.[31] The Spanish drama collapses in the creatural space of the *Trauerspiel*, and this occurs by "working through" the very subject matter of the Spanish drama, by almost analyzing whatever is removed, by laying bare the questions, by exposing the transience of the stability of the social order that it meant to represent.

And yet, beyond all doubt, this stability was Hofmannsthal's idea, its reaffirmation in the present, its continuity. This is precisely Hofmannsthal's idea: to recapture once again in the word *Stimmung* the concept of universal harmony. In Calderón's baroque language he heard "Ambrosian choirs and synesthetics,"[32] the full immanence of grace, the full realization of universal harmony in time transforming "pantheistic fullness into Catholic polyphony" (*Harmony*, 32). "The harmony of the skies is no longer an object of nostalgia" (*Harmony*, 112). It has become reality in the word or in the music of the artist—just as in the order that the kingship through the Passion play affirms in the political, in the mundane. The harmony of the spheres comes across clear in these languages. They are its fullest symbol. But this "Romània" is not given neither to Spitzer, who published his study during World War II, nor to Hofmannsthal (quoted by Spitzer together with Calderón). The present is not the *Stimmung* but its crisis: "That process of 'demusicalization' and secularization" that Novalis, according to Spitzer, described in *Christendom or Europe*, and that led to the present "anarchy," to "this era of disintegration" (*Harmony*, 138). Hofmannsthal's nostalgia, however, appears to be deeper and more disenchanted. This era of disintegration is the decline of an order deeply torn apart. This order generates the forces of its own end. And the same process of disintegration entails the affirmation of new historical powers that have to be desperately comprehended, without consolation. *The Tower*, in its two basic versions, probes this entire process. The possibility of a reaffirmation of the Baroque concert in this era of misery, in the misery of this epoch; at the same time, the failure of this possibility and the necessity, then, of understanding those powers in their human solitude, in their being-divided for always from the Order of the *Stimmung*, in their essential anarchy.

Hofmannsthal is not even original in this (*Essays*, 186).[33] This relation with the Baroque *Stimmung*, as conclusive element of the idea of "Romània"—a relation as profound as widely known and hopeless—was steeped in the more universal tradition of Austrian poetry. It constitutes the theme of the most extraordinary work by Franz Grillparzer, *Family Strife in Habsburg*.[34] Here the idea of the Habsburg universal monarchy emerges *together* with the forces that from the inside lead inexorably to the end. Hofmannsthal places the figure of Rudolph II with that of the *Poor Fiddler*, among the strongest in Grillparzer. In my opinion, *Family Strife in Habsburg* constitutes the true spiritual precedent of *The Tower*. There is the same affirmation of the idea that obsessed Hofmannsthal and the same tragic solution. This idea finds its expression in Rudolph's being almost condemned to rule—hopeless in his attempt to keep the world in the *Stimmung*. He rules like Sigismund of the first version could rule, exhausted, having reached his final years. Around him, new powers are unbridled that he knows he cannot comprehend. Order has now withdrawn completely "there": "Then learn that *order* is the cause, young man. / There order dwells, there order has its home / While here confusion lives and vain caprice." The great Baroque symbol is broken. Rudolph's attempt to preserve it is a desperate one: "But what was my own duty, that this world, / A mirrored image, should reflect Thy order . . . / That shall I do, if Thou wilt grant me aid!" The state is a foundation placed by God, an element of cosmic harmony, instrument of divine concert. There cannot be state if this foundation is abolished, or is demusicalized, secularized, because then the end of the political is not the realization of the great symbol, but the interest and the will to power of the particular: "For power? More power is what they wish. / May be, this schism at its start concerned / Religious questions, statutes of the faith. / But now its greed has drawn within its sphere / Much else of evil active in the world." Rudolph would like at least to preserve "the idea of kingdom" (precisely the Hofmannsthalian *Königtum*) to the world ("the world needs it"), but the tragedy closes on the image of the total powerlessness of the Habsburgs to avoid "slaughters and civil war." The figure of Wallenstein, in the last scene, overpoweringly recalls Olivier in *The Tower*, and this figure asserts itself, while Matthias, the force that undermined the divine foundation from within the *Königtum*, also moves to the tomb "without power." Ferdinand too appears to be prisoner of the "Wallenstein principle" (Hofmannsthal's "Olivierian principle").

On the other hand, how can Rudolph oppose the new powers if he is forced to speak their language? He says, alluding to his brother Matthias, "Then let Matthias rule. And let him learn / That blame is easy, better ways deceptive, / When toying with a realm of distant dreams, / But action very hard since it is real / And in a real world faces hardest fact." The art of ruling cannot reconcile, it can only be affirmed in the "stable revolt" imposed by opposing interests. Of a different kind, and by now completely impotent, is the idea of the political that Rudolph would like to bear witness to. Namely, to let man and his state partake of the whole, to comprehend it in the continuity of its history and traditions, allowing them to develop naturally, organically—and "to hesitate" before the new, assimilating it slowly without anticipating it or preceding it, following "the way of eternal Nature" and waiting "in the center of its forces" "that the wandering minds return." With painful and profound resignation, Rudolph bears witness to the end of this idea. He renounces to affirming it politically. That idea has withdrawn in the "constant orbits" of the stars, in the "eternal laws" of heaven.[35] The only kingdom of God now resides in those orbits. The divine order, its peace, its music have become completely transcendental. "The new is pressing," extinguishing ancestries, dissolving bonds, ruining individuals, destroying "Romània." Rudolph remembers, "When I came out of Spain where I was reared, / And word was passed that now the German coast / Was sighted. . . . / I hurried up on deck, with open arms" and cried: "My fatherland! My precious fatherland!" The fatherland is the country, the dwelling, the Habsburgian universal monarchy as symbol of a foundering heavenly country, of being at home everywhere. The spirit of this symbol has withdrawn in the pure word of Lope de Vega, in whose reading Rudolph is immersed as he appears on stage, or in the Paracelsian image of the Scotsman Dee, "a prophet, seer, / Who peers into the night of all creation / And brightens it with light that comes from God."[36] Not only is this symbol other than the new, but it can also be imagined solely as the no longer attainable, the no longer reachable. Rudolph rejects consolations, just as Sigismund does in the concluding pages of Act V of the last version. Their witnessing is not practicable; it moves into the impracticable. This witnessing is the *idea* of Order as Baroque-Catholic symbol but caught in its tragic and necessary fall.

It is truly meaningful that speaking of Grillparzer on the fiftieth anniversary of his death, Hofmannsthal praised *Family Strife in Habsburg* for the plastic force with which it expressed the historical content of an era but did not even mention the central problem posed by the work and that was posed by Hofmannsthal himself, namely, the irruption of the *Trauerspiel* in the Baroque symbol.[37] Grillparzer is understood solely within the idea of continuity and tradition. He almost seems the realization of the *idea* of his desperate Rudolph. Grillparzer, too, hesitates before the new; he waits for nature to discern "visual errors" and "hysterics" from the real force of concepts. His ideas develop like a language, untouched by anxieties, constantly embodied, rooted in the history of the nation and in the plasticity of figures. That is why they carry "in the shaky and confused nature of the world the magnificent order reflected in his poetic works." Magnificent order! Precisely what *Family Strife in Habsburg* does not reflect! This is how Hofmannsthal deceived himself in 1922 at the onset of his last attack on *The Tower*. Nothing could express better the weight of utopia of the Baroque-Catholic symbol in Hofmannsthal than this reduction of Grillparzer to an Austrian provincial, *völkisch*, Stifterian dimension.[38] No doubt Hofmannsthal was searching for this symbol, but the outcome of the search is already sealed in *Family Strife in Habsburg*. It could not even be reversed in the first version, and with the 1927 version it will be asserted fully. An outcome not wished for, not hoped for, a disturbing and haunting outcome, an outcome against which Hofmannsthal had battled all his life. For this reason, as Benjamin immediately recognized, it was even more decisive.[39]

Drama, Tragedy, Trauerspiel

The endless irreconcilability of conflict concludes *Family Strife in Habs-burg*: the prophecy of an era of wars. Even the second version of *The Tower* concludes with the affirmation of the spirit of conflict, not of order. Oliv-ier cannot be order, peace, because his "political" is in the complete im-manence where instincts and favoritisms rule. Olivier's order could never be form. But Rudolph's forms could never be life. This dualism is analyzed by Georg Simmel in his work as a whole as the tragedy of culture, and especially in two essays that I believe to be essential to Hofmannsthal's problematic: "On the Concept and Tragedy of Culture" and "The Con-flict in Modern Culture."[40]

In the former work, contemporaneous with Lukács's *Soul and Form*, the tragedy of culture is viewed in its necessary self-fulfillment in forms that exhibit an autonomous logic that leads always further away from their original goal to realize the subject, to give a home to its strife. The forms of culture emancipate themselves from the subjective spirit and we end up by feeling them as external natural powers. They take on an immanent and impersonal logic that develops in a bitter and growing contrast to the impulses and norms of subjectivity (*Culture*, 27–46). In "The Conflict in Modern Culture," Simmel analyzes this tragedy in the different manifesta-tions of the spirit. Life can be realized only by creating itself as form, as essential content. But this form becomes its opposite. This is essentially the situation of our own epoch since it extols the dominion of objective form and its autonomous capacity of development. As civilization proceeds "the forms themselves . . . in their rigidly individual shapes, in the de-mands of their inalienable rights, they boldly present themselves as the true meaning and value of our existence" (*Culture*, 25). This conflict can-not be overcome (as "philistine prejudice" believes for whom problems are "dreamt up merely for the sake of their solution") but can only be transformed, continuously transformed. The transformation of forms (forms are only transformations) changes continually the relation of the subject with their autonomous power, but the subject will never be able to "be at home" with them, as the classical idea of culture used to promise. Culture, in fact, is equivalent to unity of subjective and objective spirit. The subject creates itself as object, finds itself in it and transforms it ac-cording to its needs, its understanding (*intendere*). The concept of culture is entirely on this side of the autonomization of forms and contents, of the subject's silence in them.

The idea of this culture is Hofmannsthal's unattainable end. Plastically, it is imagined as Habsburgian "Romània." But Simmel's tragedy ends up by imposing itself objectively. Politics as the element of that culture is Rudolph's desperate memory. Politics as form in which the subject finds a dwelling. A law that is not foreign to the movements of individuals. A law ingrained in them, as the heavenly one is to the stars. And yet politics, where this idea has become objectified, by now moves autonomously, by now has at its disposal languages that are incomprehensible or uncontrollable by that idea. Politics has become totally immanent. The reassertion of politics as culture is the utopia that still animates Sigismund in the first version when, mortally wounded, he speaks to the lords of the realm. He acknowledges the end of the old order, but the old order becomes that of division and conflict. In order to sustain his utopia, Hofmannsthal reverses the terms of the contradiction. The new promised by Sigismund is politics as dwelling ("and so we want to be all together citizens of the new"), that is, of the old order, the discordant multiplicity of individuals. In actual fact, the old order is both feudal multiplicity ("your tiny kingdoms . . . your houses . . . your faiths . . . your people") and idea of politics as culture, Europe or Christendom. The new is the conflict between the idea of culture and the autonomous language of the political, objectification with no return of the forms of the spirit. This is precisely the conclusion reached by Hofmannsthal in his 1927 version. The disappearance of the political Sigismund makes tragically obvious that the idea of politics as culture is now confined to mythic memory.

The irreconcilable conflict ("the struggle in the absolute sense," as Simmel puts it) is the new of which Rudolph was afraid and was powerless to avoid (he could only delay it), and against which, once it explodes in *The Tower*, the Sigismund of the first version fights to the death. The languages of this conflict take the place of this culture, the unceasing objectification of forms in contrast with the norms and impulses of the different subjects, and this contrast reproduces the conflict on new grounds through new contents.

But how is this conflict articulated? Simmel speaks of tragedy. The unceasing assertion of form on life, of the reification of form against life, is tragic in its essence. Tragedy is conceived as form in which conflict exists, comes to expression. Simmel does not subject the concept of tragedy to a critical examination even though it plays a fundamental role in its conception of the relation between life and forms. The form of tragedy is almost antithetical to that of culture. Where culture is reconciliation, continuity, tradition, dwelling, tragedy is the irreversible event of the autonomization of the logic of forms from the impulses and the necessities of life. That is why tragedy deals with situations and not with characters (*Essays*, 191).[41]

Tragedy concerns the logic of objectified spirit, its relentlessness, and not the spirit, that is, the aspirations, the duties, the sentiments of the characters, or only to the extent to which it founders against that logic. Historically, it could be said that the destiny of culture is tragedy. For Simmel, tragedy does not forget any aspect of the necessity marked by the times. It does not give itself up in the face of the reification of forms, to the mere impressionism of life, and not even to the impotence of life in dominating the logic of forms, to a mystical sublimation of them, almost as if they came from other worlds (from the "heavenly order" that for Rudolph reigns "above") and not from the constitutive misery for which man produces. Tragedy does not forget; it takes on the entire weight of its content. But here opens up a lacerating aporia. Essentially, the conflict signifies the unrepresentability of forms on the part of life. It is precisely this relation that tragedy expresses and represents. But tragedy thus becomes the representation of the unrepresentable. Tragedy imagines (places in images) the autonomy of forms that are no longer comprehensible from life and, at the same time, this life current that is no longer "at home" in these forms. But in this fashion, tragedy dominates the entire contradiction. It represents the entire conflict. In its word one finds form and life. Their conflict attains to the word, the tragic word.

Here comes to the fore a decisive utopia to comprehend the development of contemporary culture. The *content* of this culture is recognized as conflict, and as inconsolable conflict, but to this conflict it is possible to confer a form, a unitary form. The difference between form and life is insurmountable, and yet it appears dominated in the form of tragedy. Tragedy subsumes its elements. It does not take away, does not negate the contradiction, the content of the contradiction that, in fact, it reasserts with absolute disenchantment and total refusal of any utopian consolation. Tragedy subsumes contradiction formally. It is a formal domination of conflict. There is no real dialectic that can reestablish the order of the Baroque symbol or form new communities where the idea of culture dominates. But tragic form can express this content in its totality, that is, represent form and its logic, together with life and its currents, even in the incessant repetition of their conflict. Tragedy is the key form of contemporary utopia. This is how it develops in the crisis of Enlightenment in Germany, but only Hölderlin understands it in its irresolvable aporia.[42] How can there be full formal "comprehension" there where languages are untranslatable? How can there be a form that represents the totality of conflict, if conflict means precisely separation, difference, distance? Utopia

stops looking at the actuality of culture to latch on with greater persever-
ance to the form of representation.

This utopia of tragedy, as form of the same conflict, while it no longer
appears either compatible with tradition or dialectically surmountable, is
implicit in Simmel and explicit in the Lukács of those years. Lukács, consciously, sees tragedy as the very duty (*Sollen*) of contemporary artistic
form, but does not analyze at all its debacle—or its many debacles—and
reproposes it as the only possible and real domination of Simmelian conflict. Tragedy originates from the radical assertion: life = dream, and describes the awakening "from obscure dreams," from the anarchic
chiaroscuro of existence. Its form is the "deprivation" of temporality.[43]
"[Its] judgment is a cruelly harsh one, without mercy or reprieve: sentence
is passed ruthlessly upon even the smallest fault, the faintest suggestion of
a betrayal of the essence" (*Soul and Form*, 157–158). Existence silences the
voice of the god and tragedy tries once again to detect it, to listen to it, to
establish this fatal relation. In Lukács, therefore, the Simmelian conflict is
strained to the end. Any hope of a bridge between form and life seems to
fall apart. Tragedy is the voice of this absence of bridge, of passage. But
here tragedy forgets his holding on firmly to life. The simple annihilation
(*Vernichtung*) of life is not tragedy, is a paradoxical ethics. In fact Lukács
speaks of ethics not of tragedy. By exacerbating the conflict, he can no
longer give voice to life. On the other hand, there is no language that can
speak at the same time the logic of forms and the chiaroscuro of life. Lukács refuses as utopian the possibility of tragic form as formal synthesis of
the conflict. But this refusal, this renunciation on which he decides, leads
to tragedy as pure expression of divine ethics, to tragedy as death drive of
every determined existence. A paradoxical ethics of neo-Kantian origins
and the problem of tragic form are confused indissolubly. Tragic form
becomes an ethical fact and tragedy appears as "a form which has been
purified until it has become ethical" (*Soul and Form*, 174).[44] But this form
becomes the unrepresentable; it withdraws totally in the "harsh mountain
air" where "naked souls conduct a dialogue here with naked destinies"
(*Soul and Form*, 155). "Naked" here means without words, in silence.

A different concept of tragedy could be derived from the Simmelian
conflict, namely, tragedy as togetherness (*forma-insieme*) of existence and
of forms that grow autonomously out of it. This form of tragic utopia is
revealed by Lukács in its groundlessness. If there were a language that
comprehended life and forms there would be no tragedy, but culture once
again. The tragic Lukácsian utopia consists, instead, of wanting to represent the annihilation of existence in the affirmation of the absolute autonomy of ethics. But this annihilation is a process that concerns existence. If

tragedy must represent it, we are dealing once again with Simmel's concept of aporia. If tragedy originates from its fulfillment, it has nothing to represent, its content is the unrepresentable (*Unvorstellbares*), the inner ethical, inflexible decision. The destiny of tragedy becomes the paradoxical ethics, as in Simmel tragedy was the paradox of culture.

But why do Lukács and Simmel speak of tragedy? In both of them but more clearly in Lukács, tragedy is opposed to poetry and to contemporary dramatic forms. "Life is the most unreal and unliving of all conceivable existences," says Lukács (*Soul and Form*, 153), but the content of contemporary drama (Lukács calls it "modern lyric tragedy") is precisely a mere "becoming-poetic of ordinary life, that is to say, only the intensification of ordinary life" (*Soul and Form*, 162). The ethics of this poetry "is one of understanding all and forgiving all."[45] In Simmel, too, as we have already seen, tragedy is the refusal of culture as reconciliation of conflict. But the term *tragedy* cannot have value in opposition to contemporary lyric drama alone. Lukács's concept of tragedy is consciously opposed to that of Baroque drama and to that of *Trauerspiel* and as such it represents a decisive element in our study of Hofmannsthal. In Baroque drama, in Calderón, the creature caught in its radical immanence and "natural state" is reeducated to the recognition of divine grace that dominates all the events. The plot is always rescued by the full immanentization of grace. The Baroque symbol actually synthesizes through the passion of the main characters the political-worldly word and the form of the transcendental order. The modernity of this drama's "grand symbolism" is precisely what Simmel rejects on historical and theoretical considerations. From these Lukács develops his own conception. In the mourning play (*Trauerspiel*), instead, play and mourning are entirely secularized. The Baroque onto-theo-teleology has no longer a place where it can be manifested. The scene is completely dominated by the ephemeral writings of history. But here, then, form, which constitutes for Simmel and Lukács the specific content of tragedy, cannot find expression. The *Trauerspiel* is only vanity (*Eitelkeiten*), where the paradoxical ethical imperative (which contains in its meaning every form) can only be as absolute silence, *Unvorstellbares*. The utopia of tragedy is, thus, a refusal of both drama and *Trauerspiel*.

This refusal is a renunciation of "outward richness," a renouncing of Shakespeare. It goes in the direction of a reborn *tragédie classique*, but this time conceived only as a return to the "eternally great model," to "the *Oedipus* of Sophocles" (*Soul and Form*, 164). This conclusion defines Lukács's tragic utopia. It consists in the recovery of tragedy as classical tragedy in opposition not so much to contemporary drama but to the different forms of the Baroque drama and *Trauerspiel*. In this Lukács is associated directly with the utopia of Hölderlin's tragedy while marking its profound distance from Schiller.

The utopian character of Lukács's tragic consists in the determination—in a paradoxically ethical sense—of *tragédie classique* and the self-evident manner with which its relation with the classical is posited. It is true that in the *tragédie classique* the only true reality, the only essence is the divine, but this reality is an absolute transcendence.[46] The present is the essence in its insurmountable distance from the subject that seeks it, that demands it. The present is therefore the *absence* of this essence. The problem becomes: how can one live with the feeling that God is looking at him? Solely by annihilating existence. But then tragedy has this basic content: an insurmountable relation with existence, that is, a continuous repetition of the annihilation of beings. This is the content of tragedy: neither God's glance nor the annihilation to come. Although this tragedy originates in the anguish before the silence of the absolute as experienced by man immersed in the universe of Cartesian rationality, it deeply partakes of the decisive forces that form this same universe. The annihilation of beings is also symbolic of its reduction to *noeta* and *mathemata*. The *tragédie classique*, therefore, differently from the way Lukács idealized it, is indissolubly presence and absence of the divine, but this is also the reason why tragedy is rooted in the fundamental current of contemporary rationalism.

There is in Lukács a leap that the *tragédie classique* always refuses to make. Reading "Metaphysics of Tragedy" in *Soul and Form* makes it seem as if not-seeing appearances—the annihilation of beings—corresponds naturally to seeing essence. The vanity of the real and of the visible symbolized by tragic man is instead a continuous repetition. The inessential existence in which "we travel" is the only real presence. The absolute refusal of this presence would not be tragic but mystical. The tragic man of *tragédie classique* does not live in the "harsh mountain air" but in the world, he knows the vanity of this existence, but also knows that to know the vanity of beings is the not the same as seeing essence. He repeats the annihilation of beings, which is knowing beings and knowing the limits, the misery of this same knowledge.[47] In fact, Goldmann calls this relation an "interworldly rejection" of the world. Lukács ignores this dialectic.

It is true that this dialectic can be expressed ethically. But its morality has nothing to do with Kantian ethics, and even less with the paradoxical ethical rigor that Lukács seems to derive from it. On one hand, this ethic is founded on the concept of presence-absence of the divine (from which stems the behavior of the hero in the world: "living in it without taking part in it," says Goldmann), that is, on a religious-cosmic concept that cannot be absolutely deduced from the structures of reason, of his "solitude." On the other hand, this ethic is effective and reflects a precise social order. To be sure, it is an ethical *form*—but form powerful over life, not a simple imperative of that solitude—but actuality of recognized human and social relations. Here there is contact between *tragédie classique* and Baroque drama. Already Hölderlin, when he confronts the problem of the tragic, starting from an analysis of Kantian forms, clashes with the insurmountable aporia of the ineffectiveness (and unrepresentability) of these forms. Lukács exasperates the aporia and looks for a solution precisely in this exasperation, namely, in the tragedy of the absolute solitude of ethical form, of the absolute condemnation of any existentiality. But this is what makes his discourse an absolute ethical discourse that has nothing to do with tragedy because it annuls the process of annihilation, which is the authentic representable of tragedy, and identifies immediately this absolute annihilation with the possession of the divine. Therefore, despite the apparent absoluteness, the tragic Lukácsian utopia is deeply consolatory, and especially when he tries to establish a direct relation with classical tragedy. If ethical form can still serve to interpret the *tragédie classique* (but an ethical form entirely opposed to the neo-Kantian one within which Lukács is forced to think), ethics as such, the ethical consideration in itself and for itself is entirely impotent to interpret classical tragedy. Hegel had already pitilessly shed light, against any possible tragic utopia, on the insurmountable difference with the classical.[48] Tragedy is interested in the "what" through whose vicissitudes the multiplicity of the justices (*dikai*) is brought to reconciliation.

The individual is the bearer: *what* he does and lives, shows this vicissitude. What matters to tragedy is not intention but the substantial clash provoked by the act. Thus, the whole of the event is present from the beginning. The movement unfolds in the "embrace of the divine" fulfilled in and for itself. The end is constantly in relation with the beginning. Tragedy's unity of place is in fact the resting of tragedy in the "clearing" of truth (*aletheia*). The tragic truth is this unhidden space, not created and not formed by the questioning but that gives itself to the questioning. That is why ethics does not decide anything. When the decisive experience becomes the absence of God and the truth withdraws in the inner being of man who lives in the search for essence and in the annihilation of beings (an aspect absolutely foreign to the classical), the ethical dimension takes over while the tragic one, in the sense of classical tragedy, disappears.

Vicissitudes unfold in an adventurous line: the character emerges, the plot becomes more complex, and the fortuitousness of the encounter develops. This is the creatural man of the *Trauerspiel*. Ethics is a form of this adventure. Ethics is only worldly effective. Ethics as absolute form destroys representation and therefore the very possibility of saving phenomena. By becoming absolutely paradoxical, it goes beyond the possibility of dialogue. It becomes silence, which is betrayed and falls in the inauthentic as soon as it states itself as silence.

The inauthenticity of Lukács's utopia can be better understood if we closely analyze the example of the recovery of tragedy that it purports to point to.[49] Critics of the young Lukács have never looked at Paul Ernst, and yet this figure played an important role in German culture straddling World War I.[50] The reference to Ernst in "Metaphysics of Tragedy" can in no way be considered secondary or casual. In *Brunhild*, a tragedy that even Ernst, as we shall see, considers central to his evolution, Lukács sees characters who are "by their deepest nature, Greek . . . perhaps more Greek than those in many ancient tragedies" (*Soul and Form*, 164) because they are conscious of their fate and call this consciousness guilt (*Soul and Form*, 175). And yet this consciousness now entails a harsh renunciation. The form of this awareness is felt as renunciation (*Entsagung*) with respect to the concrete historicity of life. This feeling is completely anticlassical and brings us back to the problematic of the *Trauerspiel*. In fact, Lukács speaks of the *Trauerspiel* when he analyzes Ernst's historical drama as dominated by the problem of ethics. Ernst had already recognized the absolute utopian character of tragedy in an essay of 1909.[51] Tragedy is possible only where a community (*Gemeinheit*) welcomes it, knows its myth, where the subject emanates an absolute objectivity. The absence of God in the modern world cannot be a condition of a tragic experience but of its exact opposite, the negation of tragedy. Tragedy as absence of the divine is a contradiction in terms. For Ernst his own *Brunhild* is founded on this contradiction. How is it possible, then, to keep Lukács's rejection of the *Trauerspiel* (understood as play of Beings: godless, *gottlos* in its deepest sense) without at the same time seeking refuge in the absolute utopia of tragedy?

By now for us tragedy is only the process of annihilation of beings. For Ernst this is the only form of *Brunhild*. But, we must repeat, annihilation of beings does not coincide with a vision of essence. We must overcome this form, which Ernst confuses with form of tragedy in general, toward the redemption play (*Erlösungdrama*), toward drama as religious fact, as return to the divine, to the centrality of the divine.[52] The problem of modern drama is to liberate the nonsense of the worldly and of the historical toward the religious, the essential understood as religious. A key character of this drama is the martyr who is not limited to the ethical negation of beings, but arrives at the affirmation of the solitary, sole relation with the divine. Religious experience is understood in an absolute Kierkegaardian sense:[53] the individual (*der Einzelne*) risks the religious relation leaping beyond any ethical-worldly relation. Drama is the *Passionspiel* of the individual.

The redemption play (*Erlösungsdrama*) strips naked the groundlessness of tragedy as absolute morality and seems to be closer to specific forms of Baroque drama, of its symbol. But this symbol was already broken in Schiller and Goethe (and Lukács recognizes this failure when he speaks of Ernst as the first and decisive abandonment of the utopian synthesis between Sophocles and Shakespeare). As we have already seen, it lived only as memory in Grillparzer, and its content is not the Ernstian problematic at all. The religious experience that it represents is not that of the individual, but of a well-determined order. The relation of man with the religious is lived as a cosmic process. The *Passionspiel* of the hero-martyr in the Baroque drama, such as *Life Is a Dream*, is fulfilled with the actual reaffirmation of order, of the symbol between politics/ethics and the divine. How can there be drama of the Kierkegaardian experience? The redemption (*Erlösung*) to which it gives rise is neither ethically nor aesthetically communicable. Grace becomes immanent in the individual—in the absolute individual, not in the great play of the world. The individual not only continues to repeat the doubt on the voice that has struck him, but he will also never be able to represent this announcement, turn it into images. Ernst does not even scratch the complex problematic of the redemption play. He deals with this form in terms that are almost vulgarly consolatory, as conquest of the center, overcoming of tragedy, but of tragedy understood, generically, as experience of the Simmelian conflict.

The problem of tragic form was posited as the fundamental utopia of contemporary culture inasmuch as its purpose consisted in holding firmly onto the essentiality of conflict while at the same time being able to represent it in its totality. In Simmel this representation appears rather as formal "comprehension." In Lukács it appears as ethical annihilation of beings and as representation, as a result, of the absolute. In both cases, the conflict from essential is transformed to apparent. This is reflected in the nostalgia toward the classical forms of tragedy. In fact, there cannot be tragedy of the Simmelian conflict taken in its most radical sense. From this ensemble of relations emerges a hard necessity from which branch off the lines of Benjamin's critique and of the last Hofmannsthalian *Trauerspiel.* Not only are we not given a dwelling, but the sense of the conflict also does not promise homecomings. Not only do we not have natures to return to, utopias that ground our nostalgia, but there is also not even tragedy—communicable, ethical annihilation of beings, or Baroque symbol, or religious redemption—and not even the tragic *aletheia* of classical tragedy. Nor should we console ourselves calling our silence or the exhausted repetition of forms without life tragedy. This disenchantment brings back to the *Trauerspiel* and to its absence as form. It is the space of the absence of tragedy and of dwelling together. It denies primeval dwellings just as it denies possible theories of our conflict, since theory belongs to tragedy alone, as a vision of God.

Benjamin's Critique

The form of *The Tower* consists in renouncing the illusion of a new tragedy.[54] The *Origin of German Tragic Drama*, which in part, as is well known, was published by Hofmannsthal in his *Neue Deutsche Beiträge*, was devoted in large part to illustrating the radical difference between tragedy and *Trauerspiel.*[55] Failing to question the "competence" of the "unguided feelings of 'modern man' " with respect to tragedy, there is still "the presumption that it must still be possible to write tragedies" (*Origin*, 101). Nietzsche was the first to criticize this feeling by affirming the complete autonomy of the tragic from ethos, but he confused in a vague aestheticism the historical-philosophical search for myth (*Origin*, 102). Benjamin does not analyze the further development of Nietzsche's thought, and strangely enough, does not criticize Lukács's position, which constitutes, in fact, an overturning of the renunciation of tragedy. This lack of development in Benjamin's discourse is even more surprising when in the pages that immediately follow the analysis of the Socratic genius as crisis of reason sounds absolutely Nietzschean (*Origin*, 113). This is also the position of *Soul and Form*, but with the basic difference that here Socrates becomes the hero of longing (*Sehnsucht*), and it is on the basis of the "great ascetic love" that Lukács creates the utopia of a new tragedy (*Soul and Form*, 94). For Benjamin this utopia is not a *Holzweg*, a path that leads to the woods, but a path that leads nowhere.

"According to the Greeks the scene is a cosmic *topos*," and "what takes place in it is . . . a decisive event of the cosmos" (*Origin*, 118–119). Every character is this atemporal event that no adventure can alter and whose movement is *peripateia*, turn of fortune. Mourning is absolutely foreign to tragedy. Its aim is theory not mourning, not representation of mourning. Benjamin is aware of the substantial affinity of tragedy with prophecy (*Origin*, 117). Even prophecy is based on theory, on the mythic recognition of the cosmic order. Ethical and psychological considerations are completely foreign to tragic prophecy. Instead, they become central there where it is a question of stirring up mourning by means of the *Passionspiel*, of worldly determined characters, and no longer by mythical or cosmic events. The intrinsic problematic of tragedy, totally foreign to the characters of the *Trauerspiel*, consists of an "anti-Olympic prophecy" that permeates it. Tragedy is "a debate on the Olympians to which the hero is a witness" (*Origin*, 107). But this debate is not the result of man's conscience that he is "better than the gods" (Here our interpretation differs from Benjamin's), rather of the fact that the very power of the gods is weak, that it is also a cosmic event, a destined event, which can be subject of prophecy and subject to it, but not foundation of prophecy. It is this knowledge that silences the tragic. This silence does not stem from, as Benjamin seems to think, following Rosenzweig (and in this he is very close to Lukács), the "glacial solitude of the Self."[56] It stems from the progressive disappearance of the Olympic on the scene. And this experience is common, is political. The anti-Olympic prophecy that echoes powerfully in the *Prometheus* is not represented in the silence of the hero, shut up in his glacial solitude, but in the new theory of cosmic event, of the chain of cosmic events that myth represents. When the anti-Olympic prophecy becomes word or silence of man, the hero has already exited the classical scene and walks "the earth as arena of mournful events" of the *Trauerspiel* (*Origin*, 119).

This analysis does not contradict but reinforces Benjamin's basic thesis of the irreducible otherness between tragedy and *Trauerspiel*. We could add, between tragedy and Baroque drama, play of divine grace that through games and apparent adventures manifests the intrinsic teleological character of history. Teleological judgment is absolutely foreign to tragedy. The tragic event is totality that does not refer to anything but itself to achieve its sense. We have already indicated the difference between Baroque drama and *Trauerspiel*. Since tragedy is opposed to both, its space in modern tragedy becomes that of absolute utopia (the reasons for this utopia are not analyzed by Benjamin; that is why I have discussed them in the previous pages).

Under the sign of the symbol, the "great play" of Baroque drama, of Calderón's genius unfolds. The play of Vanities (*Eitelkeiten*) describes, stirs up mourning for redemption (*Erlösung*). Drama is naturally Christian. The *Passionspiel* is always symbolic of the redemptive passion of Christ. The play of vanities is completely secularized in the *Trauerspiel*. Vanity's dance of death replaces the redemption of the *Passionspiel*. Not *Trauerspiel* but *Schauspiel*, comedy is Calderón's *Life Is a Dream*. *Trauerspiel* is Lohenstein's *Sophonisbe* (*Origin*, 173).[57] Not even death stops the play. The events precipitate toward the grave, and in the grave time continues to "play with us." Mourning has neither end nor redemption. The radical experience of time, living-in-time as fundamental alienation and radical mourning is the experience of the *Trauerspiel*, absolutely opposed to the *Schauspiel* of the Baroque Catholic drama. In the *Trauerspiel* the opposite of the annihilation of the vanities of time occurs, but the repetition of alienation-in-time continues. The annihilation of drama is conceived plastically in the conclusive symbol of event and form, event and grace. The impossibility of annihilation will have to be conceived in terms opposed to the symbol or, better, the *Trauerspiel* will have to take on as its own substance that same formlessness whence the Baroque symbol emerged victoriously. In the course of the martyr's passion, this symbol prevailed on the multiplicity of figures, events, deferments and meanings presented by worldly vanity. This troubled background of the symbol becomes form of the *Trauerspiel*. It develops under the sign of allegory.

Against the symbol as theological paradox of the unity of sensible and supersensible (*Origin*, 167), there is allegory as expression, "just as language is expression and, in fact, writing" (*Origin*, 170). Sign, writing are allegory—discourse, theology are symbol. Vanity is no longer transfigurable "in the light of redemption." Allegory presents to the spectator "the *Hippocratic face* of history as a primeval petrified landscape" (*Origin*, 174). This originality of allegory is expressed in its being background to the symbol: "The dark background against which the world of the symbol had to loom clearly" (*Origin*, 168). This background now liberates its own signs, its own writings, and its own dialects, against the language of the symbol.[58] Sign, writing, is history but secularized history without residue, exposition (*Vorstellung*) of the pain of the world, as Benjamin recognized. *Trauerspiel* is the play of this pain, which has meaning insofar as it cannot be emancipated from the world, as it is inexorably driven in time. Death itself is a figure of time, as we saw, not a deliverance (*Erlösung*) from time. And signs, scriptures, allegory are inextricably linked with time and death. If in the *Trauerspiel* "history arrives on the scene, it does so as writing. In front of nature it is written 'history' in the characters of its transience" (*Origin*, 187). The martyr is the victim of history, and its witnessing is the

witnessing of the vanity that reigns there. But its presentation as symbol of
Christ would be blasphemy in the world of allegory. Allegory is existence,
absolute existence of signs, writings, and not appearance, which refers to
essence, even if it can waste in the longing of being this appearance and in
the task (*Sollen*) of reuniting with its utopian essence. Either there is symbol, not reference but unity of sensible and supersensible, or there is allegory, sign writing, absolute in itself.

But can we still define this *Trauerspiel* as Christian? This is the decisive
question that results from Benjamin's critique. As a matter of fact, Benjamin tends to coordinate drama and *Trauerspiel* in the light of a fairly wide
conception of the Baroque. But the concrete analysis that he develops differentiates then radically between drama and *Trauerspiel*, and the difference points precisely at this question: the symbol belongs solidly to the
world of Christian theological discourse, while allegory can be understood
as the background of the symbol. But the background of the "paradox of
the theological symbol," once freed, having reached the existence in itself
and for itself, which relationship does it entertain with that paradox? This
is the real rending question (*Fragwürdiges*) of Hofmannsthal's quest. Is not
the *Trauerspiel* already a radical alienation from the theological? Is not the
Trauerspiel already the end of Christian discourse, of the Christian sense
and dominion of the world? Since the Christian dimension is not at all
reducible to the exposure of vanity, this exposure must become interworldly refusal and salvation of vanity in the symbol of heavenly order
and social order. The existence of vanity, the mourning provoked by its
representation is the simple absence of God and, once again, no representation of absence is in itself reflection of essence.

Immediate absence of God—this is how the form of the *Trauerspiel* ends
up by appearing. This is the type of conclusion that Hofmannsthal will
try to forbid himself in *The Tower*, which, instead, appears self-evident to
Benjamin, both in the close link that he establishes between the theological and the symbolical and in the efficacy that he attributes to the allegorical, which becomes truly a key concept of contemporary art. How much
does this death of the symbol (which is essentially what *Origin of German
Tragic Drama* is all about) weigh on Benjamin's relation with some currents of Hebrew mysticism? Decisive in illustrating this relation would
seem to be the impossibility of viewing the martyr as redemption, as historical fact, as idea-force of the symbol.[59] In the definition of the Baroque
scene as nomadic stage, in the radical conception of vanity put forward by
Benjamin, in the emphasis with which allegory is interpreted as sign and

writing—this relation seems to me to be a true leading thread of Benjamin's work. And the problem of Jewish history is also an important aspect of *The Tower*.[60]

The critique of the symbol, that is, the exposition of the historical crisis of the Baroque symbol in the *Trauerspiel*, constitutes anyhow an essential caesura of theological discourse. This discourse is symbolic in its origins and in the entire course of its development. Scripture, as the Son, is the incarnation of the Logos.[61] The Logos becomes flesh "through each of the words in Scripture." No autonomy of the sign, no independence from Scripture. The multiplicity of words and signs comes from the Logos, is flesh of the Logos. Saint Iraeneus says: "Inseminatus est ubique in Scripturis Filius Dei." And the body of the Logos is not only Scripture but also the Church: "Not dispersed words" (*non verba disiecta*) but writing of the Logos; not signs, but symbolic existence. The whole of the Christian is a symbolic existence ruled by the primacy of the word, of the Logos: "Words of which much is spoken are of one word" (*verba, quae multa locutus est, unum verbum sunt*). This is the fundamental scheme of symbolic existence.

Where the Christian speaks of allegory, he understands the opposite of the *Trauerspiel*'s allegory (*Histoire*, 124). Allegory concerns not just the historicity of Christianity, but also the historicity saved in its essential. Allegory understands Scripture as the coming of Christ, of Christ's turning point, that is, the beginning of an era dominated by the Logos become flesh, finalized by the Logos. Christian allegory is fundamentally onto-theo-teleology. It is interpretation of history insofar as it is writing of the Logos, in which nothing happens "in case, in the event, at leisure, accidentally, uselessly, in error" (*casu, eventu, otiose, fortuiter, inaniter, frustra*). Allegory is not prisoner of the letter because it recognizes in the sign the incarnation of the Logos and therefore it frees itself from the sign at its origin, at the theory. The *allegoresis* establishes in this fashion symbolic relations. Where there is multiplicity of figures, types, events, allegoresis sees the *Unum Verbum*, unity in the Logos.

Goethe's utopia of the symbol aims at this same *allegoresis*. For Benjamin it has become equally illusory as tragic form. The allegory of which Benjamin speaks is the shipwrecked Christian allegory that is no longer able to rise from signs to the Logos, that sees in Scripture the absence of the Logos, allegory as exposition of signs, as conscience of their vanity, or solely referring from one sign to another. The historicity of these signs has nothing Christian any longer. The only thing announced by this allegory is a ghostly Messiah to come, an unspeakable turning point because it has not yet come. Benjamin's allegorical world ignores the turning point on whose bases Christian allegory alone works (it is the conversion of the times that determines the subsequent development and makes history essential, even the previous one in as much as it is finalized to conversion), or considers it as exhausted by now. The constant hearing of his Word has been transformed in the constant listening to its silence.

The *Trauerspiel* insofar as it is opposed to the *Schauspiel* opposes therefore its own allegory to Christian allegory. This inevitable conclusion of Benjamin's critique goes directly to the heart of Hofmannsthal's elaboration of *The Tower*. Just when he is about to conclude the first version of *The Tower* and among many doubts, he imagines, as we will see, a possible reconciliation between the historicity of the *Trauerspiel* and Christian allegory. Hofmannsthal reads Benjamin's "Goethe's *Elective Affinities*," where it is precisely a question of the dissolution of the symbol and of the assertion of the allegorical "dark wood" through the real dialectic of the contents of Goethe's novel.[62] Hofmannsthal called Benjamin's essay "beyond compare." In conversation with F. C. Rang, who had criticized Benjamin's essay because of its eclectic character, Hofmannsthal replied: "Too many-sided in its aspects (*vielseitig*)! I am well aware of the weight of this reproach. May it not be applicable to everything that I undertake from now on, because if it is appropriate for this essay, then it is by now entirely worn out." Benjamin's essay on Goethe "has been a landmark in my life," and this judgment can only be understood with reference to the destiny of the *Tower*.[63] Only in the mirror Benjamin offers him, Hofmannsthal can see with clarity the necessity of the *Trauerspiel* and develop his work in this direction with absolute radicalism. The end of the second version of the *Tower* is truly in the spirit of Benjamin's *Origin of German Tragic Drama* and "Goethe's *Elective Affinities*." Hofmannsthal's greatness consists in having let this spirit in so that it could destroy any of its residual utopias and in having recognized this outcome as the logic of his own work.

Goethe's *Elective Affinities*, what do they *see*? At the height of culture, at the height of the apparent transformation and devaluation of the natural, forces of an "incomprehensible ambiguity" are being liberated. The many-sidedness, far from being a characteristic or a limitation of Benjamin's essay, constitutes the problem that dominates the *Affinities*. Where everything seemed reducible to the *Unum Verbum* of culture, the "dark wood" of allusions, echoes, references bursts in, an infinity of allegories without a country. The symbol of culture is revealed to be illusory, just as illusory is the possibility of shaping this "dark wood" of allegories into a tragedy, since in tragedy it is not a question of relating the word to the Logos, writing to essence, but content of reality and content of truth are one and the same. The allegory we described earlier is Christian not tragic. Christian allegory is already the end of tragic theory. Beauty is the sign that more distinctly reflects this world of allegory without a country. It is sign, absolute writing, has no memory. It is exactly the opposite of Beauty in the *Phaedrus*, and that is why it leads to ruin, it represents and creates mourning. Ottilie's beauty is a character of the *Trauerspiel*. On one hand, it refers to the creature and to the naturalness of her passions; on the other, it refers to the infinite and interminable search for reconciliation. Since this is not possible, because allegory is essentially other from the symbol, there is only the exteriority of the legal norm and the renunciation that it imposes. The characters of the *Trauerspiel* cannot relate to any truth content outside the will of the institution. Their creatural condition, without residues, is not reconcilable, it can only be ruled. Time after time this synthesis will show its own transience and vanity, because it is not symbol and is not reconciliation. And time after time, the allegorical many-sidedness will assert itself against the institution and time after time the legal norm will repress this "dark wood" of allegories. The essence of the *Trauerspiel* consists in this play.

Utopia of tragedy, irredeemability of the allegorical together with the question of the norm, of the institution, of the law that, however transient, tries to prevail over the allegorical, which though ephemeral as the signs and the dialects of allegory still has to dominate them. This is the complexity, the "dark wood" that asks to be heard in *The Tower*.

The Tower

The historicity of the creature is expressed essentially in its being rooted in the universe of the political. When culture reveals to be impotent, when the harmony of the symbol ceases to take hold, what is asserted is not allegory as simple natural transience but allegory as political game. Norm asserts itself on the shaky allegory.[64] But the political does not depend on the theological symbol and is not even its reflection. The political can try to represent itself as an analogue to the theological symbol, but in reality it is a form of organization of the allegorical that originates and develops on this ground. The political does not recover any theological dimension, any transcendental level of justification. In fact, it would be guilty if it presumed to. Thus, the *Trauerspiel* is political in its essence.

It is incapable of the symbol's real peace.[65] There is real peace only in theological unity, in the overcoming of conflict. Since this is impossible, to keep pursuing it means continuing the war. "Why don't you try to reconcile?" asks Julius of Brunswick to Rudolph in *Family Strife in Habsburg*. Because this would entail continuing the war forever. Whereas the conflict cannot be overcome, peace is possible only by "abandoning" conflict. This means in fact the radical secularization of the political, which recognizes that the political is impotent to reach real peace, that it is a mere instrument of apparent peace (*pax apparens*). Between the theological and the political an abyss opens up that is form and content of the *Trauerspiel*. The political animal is not man in general but the creature of the *Trauerspiel*. It lives in the apparent peace of the political. It deceives itself at times that this peace is real, it longs powerlessly for this peace but it can only give shape, give an order but never the Order, to the historicity without residue of its becoming.

The real peace is the profound peace that announces the "god in us." Profound peace, great peace is conceivable only in the light of the symbol that connects the glory of God *in excelsis* to the dwelling of man on earth (*Re*, 19). "And then indeed the Kingdom of God is amongst us" (*Et tunc enim regnum Dei intra nos est*) (*Exégèse*, 2:498). In this light, the political can only be the pontifical. The king is conceivable only as pontiff, builder of bridges (*pontifex*), mediator, rainbow, "pledge of God's alliance with his people" (*Re*, 19). The political is here existence of the symbol, of which Rudolph only retains the memory and Sigismund, in the second version, shows its radical distancing. The tradition of this symbol has been definitively broken. The collapse of tradition is the same as the symbol, since the symbol can give itself there where a tradition can preserve the idea of the world as harmony, "the very reflection of divine Unity," of the divine Logos as "site of possibilities."[66]

At the back of the symbol's cave we find the light. In fact, even in the symbol there is labyrinth, journey—but as initiation. The symbol ignores the journeying and its nostalgia. It only knows the pilgrimage.[67] The cave of the symbol leads to the center. In the *Trauerspiel*, instead, the cave is transformed in a mere "shadow of darkness" (*umbra tenebrarum*), an allegory of erring and loss of light. Shadow of darkness and shadow of light are not arranged any longer according to a well-arranged ladder, as in symbolic metaphysics from Ficino to Bruno.[68] The long struggle between shadow and light, imagination and reason has become, so to speak, self-contained and no longer brings to the contemplation that leads to God. Our faculties, such as the political, waver freely in its absence.

Where there is no real peace, where the nomadic journeying of the subject takes the place of the labyrinth of initiation over which the pontiff rules, there also cannot be true justice. The love that holds the city of man is evil, "exclusive or predominant love for earthly things," and divides because it is without the center of the city of God.[69] The citizens of the city of man cannot be reconciled, have no dwelling, because according to its essence the city of man has no transcendental foundation, does not know the truth. This city of evil could be defined as Babel, since it is not interested in reordering the multiplicity of languages and tolerates controversy and dissent in its bosom: "not over fields, the home and money questions, but what constitutes life's happiness or unhappiness."[70]

Pagan wisdom (*Weltweisheit*) is intrinsically diabolic. It is forced to tolerate division since it does not know the center, does not possess truth.[71] The city of God, instead, reconciles, harmonizes, redresses dissent. It possesses truth, a revealed truth. But it is here precisely that we encounter the aporia that is a condition of the *Trauerspiel*. The city of God is in endless war to impose on the conflicting "loves" of man the spiritual intelligence of history, the uniqueness of truth. Precisely because it is intrinsically intolerant, the profound peace of the city of God has to impose its own justice, as it cannot allow different "loves." It is the dwelling. But its peace lives historically only as war, division, dissension with respect to the forces of the city of evil. Therefore only apparent peace is possible on earth. The pretense of real peace condemns to endless war. Also, apparent peace must be atheistic, since it would be impossible, knowing what constitutes happiness, not to want to make it the foundation of the dwelling of man.

In a world abandoned by the idea of profound peace, it is supreme vanity to want to mask the subjectivity and partiality of conflict with the light of the symbol, with promises of dwelling. Here Augustine's idea of real peace and real justice can be of value only as "instruments of the kingdom" (*instrumenta regni*). The intrinsic intolerance of the city of man that believes it possesses the truth becomes tyranny, which, so understood, is a central figure of the *Trauerspiel*, the image of the vanity of earthly power disguised as eternal. The fool, the *Narr* of the *Trauerspiel*, must dissolve precisely this vanity, this transience, which is supposed real and grounded, which pretends that its authority is legitimate on a transcendental basis. In *The Tower* this dissolution is accomplished not by the Fool but by another figure of the fool-for-the-world, Brother Ignatius, the former Grand Almoner of the king. He calls Basilius's war useless and sacrilegious. Useless because abandoned by the symbol, because it is conducted on the bases of signs that no Christian allegory can interpret. It is sacrilegious because its leading power curses the name of the center, of truth,

disguises itself as real peace and real justice. Ignatius reveals the groundlessness of this power, revealing the absence of God from the city of evil,
which remains the only dimension of the political. God has withdrawn
from its nomadic scene. To the tyranny that pretends to be still carrying
on the signs, to be still capturing the voices of the divine, Ignatius retorts
by reminding the king that the divine is not a mirror in which he can
justify the existence of his power. The divine is "an ear behind your ear, a
nose behind your nose." It compels the tyrant to listen to his own cry,
what despairs behind his despair, what horrifies him behind his horror,
and yet will not leave him to himself and will not allow him to forget
himself. This is what the divine is, the endless tearing of the tyrant's
masks.

In the essence of the *Trauerspiel*, therefore, there is not only the hidden
being of the divine. In the political of the *Trauerspiel* the divine is not
simply at rest (*otiousus*). The divine is what prevents the figures of the
Trauerspiel from freeing themselves from their own allegorical groundlessness; it is the wall that forces any cry to echo. The intertwining of these
echoes is the true scene of the *Trauerspiel*. Not mere transience, mere apparent peace forever shipwrecked, but transience felt as such, apparent
peace compelled to tear its own masks, its own pretense to eternity, its
own illusions of stability and duration. Not mere absence of dwelling but
necessity of roaming and of conflict.

This worldly order realized by the political, therefore, is deprived of
transcendental foundation. Its ceremony cannot be preserved on the basis
of the *value* of the symbol. The legitimacy of this law is preserved if it has
more real *force* than that of the other subjects that are in pursuit—the other
figures of the *Trauerspiel*. This order must be preserved in compliance with
the law, because otherwise it would be an inextricable "dark wood," but it
could never be preserved in the name of the theological symbol, in the
name of the theologically grounded and finalized order. Therefore this
order is transient, just as is any figure, any situation in the *Trauerspiel*, and
it is powerful the more it recognizes this condition. The political is also
vanity before the symbol; this is its necessity (*Notwendigkeit*). And on this
necessity the political grounds its *ratio*: calculation, measure, and constant
search to reduce history to natural becoming in order to realize an actual
comprehension—to ground an actual dominion. This search is the destiny
of the political, of its essential rationality (in the sense of modern metaphysics), and "grand politics" (*grosse Politik*) will never come short of this
destiny. It has to try to reduce social movements and relations to the order
that reigns up "there," but this order is now understood in an absolute

physical deterministic sense. This reduction persists as idea of the political precisely because there cannot be symbol between natural order, conceived as *more mathematico* and historical, social order. There was symbol between the political order and the theoteleological ordering of the universe, but mere physical regularities are nothing but a spectral *analogon* of the latter.

Not living in the light of the symbol, not being able neither to form nor to simply promise a real peace (on the contrary, having to be opposed to its pursuit), the political is not dwelling. The *Trauerspiel* is, in fact, the absence of dwelling. Its stage shifts from city to city, and from court to court.[72] The court is the place of the political, of political decisions. At court the political is represented as *Trauerspiel*, because the court, as site of political decision is precisely the negation of dwelling.

The problem of the court is the problem of kingship, of sovereignty. As we know, it constitutes the center of the entire Hofmannsthal's *Weltanschauung*. But only now we can understand the reasons. The problem of kingship is that of the sovereignty abandoned by the light of the symbol. Where is the kingship being legitimized? It is no longer at home in an ontotheologically grounded universe. It is no longer the realization of a real peace. The sovereign, Benjamin writes, is only a "representative of history" (*Origin*, 48), the incarnation of history. Government is art, is technique, an artifice of apparent peace pursued and, transitorily, even realized by the norm (the apparent peace that concludes Goethe's *Elective Affinities*). The kingship, therefore, is being legitimized in two directions: as decision not a priori grounded on the symbol, not inscribed in the order that reigns "up there" (as subjective, historical, immanent decision); and as foundation of an apparent peace preserved by means of norms and laws that can be applied. In the concept of apparent peace is inherent that of law. Peace, not being real, is only organization of conflict, discipline of multiple interests and points of escape. The very same term *peace* becomes allegorical.

The sovereign decides. This decision grounds the law, the norm. There are no symbols from which the decision can be deduced. In fact, the decision as such is the power that breaks the old theological symbol once and for all. To decide politically is to divide the political from real peace, but at the same time is to divide the political from the order of natural sciences. The decision allows the dimension of the political to burst in the dimension of the irreducible conflicts and of the play of the *Trauerspiel*. This decision is exceptional. "Sovereign is the one who decides in exceptional conditions."[73] This ulterior specification goes deeper into the nature

of the *Trauerspiel*. In it the becoming of the creature cannot be theologically preordained. The observation of the regularity of history is a farcical
analogue of the regularity of nature. In the reign of allegory different no-
mads always appear. The new, which causes anxiety for Rudolph (that
which does not recognize either tradition or continuity), is the permanent
character of allegory. The exceptional state is its form. Faced with this
situation, the political is constantly called on to decide, to preserve the
law, to form the new into law, to force the new to linger. Here the form
is not as important as the effectiveness of the decision. According to the
disposition of the play, either one or the other will be the decision that
leads an action to a result. The outcome alone legitimizes the decision.

But are we not faced with a kind of sublimation of the decision? No
doubt, if from the analysis of the decision we pass immediately to the
concept of tyranny.[74] Tyranny sees in the decision and in sovereignty (necessary sovereignty) the premise of the order, of the overcoming of conflict.
But the decision plunged in the continuous transformation of the political
relations is the negation a priori of the effectiveness of tyranny. Sovereignty, kingship, far from overcoming the essential historicity of the creature, *are* the creature. Their decision will never sublimate the vanity of the
multiple, the scattered orders in which and with which the creature plays.
This is the meaning of the "animal" traits with which the king is often
characterized in the *Trauerspiel* (*Origin*, 76–78), and that Hofmannsthal
takes up in the powerful character of Basilius. Even the king is determined
by the creatural state. His very tyranny is thus creatural, and not at all
sublime with respect to the mourning of the world.

But this is not all. The kingship of the *Trauerspiel* lives in the substantial
contradiction of not being able to obtain consent to his law, to his norms.
There cannot be universal consent to an apparent peace. There cannot be
universal consent to a subjective decision on the part of a subject who is
also creature, who gets recognized and is manifested as such and not as
intrinsic part of the theological symbol. The transgression of the law is
here by now inherent in the law itself, since the law cannot a priori obtain
consent. The sovereign's decision can even try to assert itself with high-
handedness, but this will only make clearer its constitutive impotence.
Masking the decision of form can only bring about a more precise measure
of the distance between decision and form. The decision and its order are
always weak and transitory like the creature to which it applies.

Benjamin understood very well this dark side of the decision (completely masked by Schmitt) when he writes "of the decisiveness of the
tyrant" (*Origin*, 71). His words could be applied to an interpretation of

The Tower where the question of legitimacy and effectiveness of the political clashes directly with that of consent. In Lohenstein's sovereigns, for instance, "what is conspicuous about them is not so much the sovereignty evident in the stoic turn of phrase, as the sheer arbitrariness of a constantly shifting emotional storm in which [they] sway about like torn and flapping banners" (*Origin*, 71). They are creatures called on by exception to restore an order. It seems that this task can be accomplished only in tyranny. But its form is perfect utopia, because a historical decision taken by a creature will never be able "to replace the unpredictability of historical accident with the iron constitution of the laws of nature" (*Origin*, 74). The utopian content of tyranny consists in the idea of substituting to the theological symbol of the past one between the secularized political and physical and natural determinism. This is indeed theology of antitheology (*Theologie*, 86).

The idea of tyranny is outside the political, just as the empty repetition of nostalgia for the symbol and its drama, or for myth and its tragedy (history is the object of drama, myth of tragedy) (*Origin*, 48). In the space of the political, here it resists the conscious decision of the political's radical immanence, of its being part and not whole, subject and not totality, and therefore, conscious of the intrinsic problematic character of its relation with *consent*. The absence of dwelling (*Heimatlosigkeit*) of the political is the entire "sayable"—which does not mean: everything. It does not even mean the essential. It means simply that the space of its could-say [*poter-dire*] is solely that of the *Trauerspiel*. Therefore the political decision can also appear as that of a martyr. A strange martyr turned upside down, that is, one who refuses *askesis*, one who refuses images of redemption and of order, both worldly and superworldly.

There is and there can be utopia but without any passage, any bridge to the sayable of the political, which is absolutely extraneous to the scene of the *Trauerspiel*. In the *Trauerspiel*, utopia appears as silent background. Utopian is the decision applied to the reform of the theological symbol, founded on universal consent. Utopian is true peace. But utopian is also the apparently disenchanted arrogance of tyranny. The legitimacy of kingship cannot stand its weight. Hofmannsthal's road to the *Trauerspiel* crosses all these questions. This same road describes a history of the possible forms of the *Trauerspiel*. In the first version Hofmannsthal tests the possible mediations with drama, its power to sustain the utopian word. In the second version this power disappears, but also because it had already appeared masked in the first one. Therefore, in the last version of *The Tower* the basic problematic character of the political, which is the specific object of the *Trauerspiel*, namely, its having to be order, its not being able to be consent, is placed in even greater emphasis.

"The dream as cornerstone of historical events."[75] This fascinating and strange (uncanny) formula is at the basis of both versions of *The Tower*. But its relation to the formal richness of the Baroque serves rather to emphasize its distance. The function of the dream is completely changed. In Calderón, the dream is "like a concave mirror" tearing the veil that separates from the "incommensurable backdrop" of inwardness—which dream contains in the light of the transcendental. In Hofmannsthal, instead, the dream is "a world more real" constantly crossed by the waking world. This confers completely new life to Calderón's subject matter. Calderón's play is spectacle (*Schauspiel*), is the great theater of the world in which the dream "at the center of every drama" (*Schriften*, 30) still lives in the light of the symbol. Hofmannsthal's play, instead, is mourning play (*Trauerspiel*), because the dream shows, on the contrary, the irreconcilability of worldly events with the transcendental. *Trauerspiel* is division and tension (*Spannung*), and insofar as it is tension it has an affinity to decision, *Entscheidung*. Tension between speech and performance, between *Rede* and *Tun*. That is why Baroque rhetoric loses its richness in *The Tower* and almost disappears in the second version, because in Calderón's drama such rhetoric represented symbolically the power of speech. The tension between word and action makes the possibility of the power of speech absolutely remote. Calderón's Christian optimism is replaced with Sigismund's silence, the ritual as pale substitute of the symbol or, better, a ritual where by now the symbol appears topsy-turvy and destroyed. On the symbol "the evil powers of the earth" march; "from the earth dreams rise and from them, for a long time now, the Christian heaven has withdrawn" (*Schriften*, 33). The span of Calderón's drama went from the creature to Christ. The conquered Christian wisdom of Christ's symbol founded kingship. In Hofmannsthal this span is broken. The kingship is *decision*, which has nothing to do with the formula that life is a dream. This formula can be maintained only as *instrumentum regni*, instrument of kingship, as ritual, ceremony reduced to ideology. But the *kosmos* is no more, it is no longer the original order or return to it, to the power (*Gewalt*). Here Hofmannsthal overturns Calderón's subject matter. As we have already pointed out, he applies pressure to overturn the Baroque utopia. Power cannot be order, symbol of divine law, if it is founded on unnaturalness, if it depends on decision and on the decision of a part, of a subject in conflict with other parts and other subjects, a decision devoid of consent and founding a mere apparent peace. Basilius's power is founded on unnatural-ness. The power of those who will unseat Sigismund is unnaturalness. But unnaturalness is also Sigismund's power in the first version: break with the father, war. How can the reconciliation derive from the vortex of unnatu-ralness? The nature of the political is unnaturalness. It makes manifest the impossibility of the cosmos, of order, of musical harmony in whose utopia (Romània's) Hofmannsthal had desperately lived. Hofmannsthal gets to the bottom of this life in *The Tower*.

Benjamin reads the first version of the *Tower* in the spirit of the second, namely, of the break with drama and the end of illusion of a new tragic drama. In May 1925 he announces in a letter to Scholem that he sent to Hofmannsthal the "manuscript of my book on the *Trauerspiel*" (*Briefe I*, 383). Even earlier in his letter to Hofmannsthal of January 13, 1924, he had outlined his "working program" on "the ancient words: destiny (*Schicksal*) and character (*Charakter*)" (*Briefe I*, 328), an analysis that will be central to his essay on Goethe's *Elective Affinities*, as was already men-tioned. Between 1925 and 1928 the correspondence becomes more in-tense. In a letter of October 30, 1926, Benjamin writes that he is waiting anxiously for the new conclusion of *The Tower*. He will read it for the first time in February 1928 and immediately reviews it for *Die Literarische Welt*. In the first version, Sigismund appears as a prince still able to exorcise conflict and its dark power. While it is true that he dies upholding this reconciliatory will, this is taken up by the Children's King (*Kinderkönig*), who appears at the end of the play singing. His own language seems to embody this new harmony. But this harmony remains absolutely utopian. Sigismund's witnessing is utopian. The real prince, who actually pursues true peace, goes to the bottom of it, and true peace withdraws to the abso-lute utopia of the Children's King. We do not even find this much in the second version. Here Sigismund does not even bear witness to the utopian kingdom of the Children's King, but to its absence. He bears witness to his complete impotence with respect to the political together with his dis-enchantment with utopia. The Sigismund of the second and last version is more silent and more determined.[76] The attitude of the martyr's worldly rejection still guides the prince in the first version. However desperately, he complies with the people's need for peace. In the second version, in-stead, the separation of word and action, utterance and speech, is com-plete. Sigismund has no words for that necessity and knows that that necessity will not find satisfaction in the political. But he coldly and harsh-ly rejects the utopia of the Children's King. Thus, in his own silence he can call "as a lark's call" (*Schriften*, 39).[77] His own silence calls not the political, not utopia, and not even the symbol or the tragic, but an unmodifiable condition that is naturally Christian, absolute, and separate from any allegory. However, this is the condition of the One (*Unico*), of the unrepresentable Christianity of the One. That is why Sigismund is no longer a martyr. His witnessing, in fact, is inaudible a priori. There can be martyrdom only as rejection of the worldly, as utopia of redemption (*Erlösung*) or word of a common faith that can be represented or communicated. But in the last version, Sigismund lives in the absolute solitude of the One. "Bear witness: I was here," he says at the end, "Even though no one knew me." But no one can recognize the martyrdom, because here there is no martyrdom. The only possible witnessing of this death concerns solely its paradoxical oneness—its incommunicability. Sigismund bears witness to the already realized silence of the Christian symbol.[78]

About this second version, Benjamin speaks of the elevation of the figure of the Children's King in Sigismund (*Schriften*, 100). The relation is more complex. In the first version, Sigismund has a brother who comes forward singing in the harmony of utopia. And yet, one says that the people of children "have issued new laws because the laws must always come from the young." Utopia is always in the world-in-between (*Zwischenwelt*) of the possible, which is intrinsically ambiguous, as ambiguous remains even the genre of the first version.[79] Sigismund states at the end, in the second version, "no one knew me," and yet he is designated as the star (*Sternbild*) for the people of the Children's King. His grave sanctifies the place where those who have recognized him live. His grave, therefore, establishes a new dwelling. There is none of this in the second version. The Children's King disappears, whereas Olivier lives, the negation, the absence of dwelling. Sigismund no longer expresses utopias, rather the disenchanted consciousness of his absolute separation from the political. He is also removed from the figure of the Children's King, namely, he radicalizes the utopian aspect to the point of rendering it unmentionable and unrepresentable, to the point of confusing it completely in his silence.

Transience and Silence

This getting to the core of utopia, however, is not at all an indirect sanctioning of the political. This would be a vulgar interpretation of the *Trauerspiel*. In fact, the absolute separateness of the figure of Sigismund from the political desecrates the very idea of the political. The problematic of its principle is resolved in complete immanence, in its substantial groundlessness. It can no longer make claims of stability (*Festigkeit*) and durability (*Dauer*). Precisely the bursting in of Sigismund's solitude in the space of the political demonstrates the vanity of the political. Its assertion does not take away from its character, but in fact affirms it irreversibly because in the world of allegory, of allusion, of vacillating interests and of the relations founded solely on it, nothing but the political could be of value. For the silent presence of Sigismund alone, the political can be caught in its intrinsic problematic character and its claim to foundation denied.

This outcome is impossible in the first version, since Sigismund is still speaking politically, since at the end of the play the "sung" laws of the children, which are still symbols of harmony, still seem to assert themselves. Instead, the formula of the second version is that the young will never dictate laws. But that is why the laws (the only possible norms), are inscribed in the *Trauerspiel*, and nomadic as the scenes of the *Trauerspiel*. They are apparent peaces, subjective solutions to the conflict, not grounded on consent, made legitimate only by their outcome, and therefore as weak as the links holding the allegorical chains of a *Trauerspiel* monologue—mere creatural voices. In this wider context, one should understand the interpretation of *The Tower* given by Curtius as a "tragedy of social revolution" (*Essays*, 187–188). As we will see, the material that Hofmannsthal employs to represent this revolution is historically well determined, but his war is seen *sub specie aeterni* in this sense: revolution is an insurmountable conflict. It points, on one hand, to the state of exception, the turning point, required by the exceptionality of the decision, and on the other hand to the powerlessness of the decision to put an end to conflict, to realize a real peace.

The tragedy (a term that Curtius uses in an ambiguous sense) of social revolution, therefore, is the *Trauerspiel* of the constant interplay between exception-decision-apparent peace and *again division*. The play of an insurmountable revolution, which, therefore, can be seen *sub specie aeterni*. But, let it be clear, revolution in Hofmannsthal is not cosmic revolution, which would inscribe it in the laws written "up there." It is not an eternal return of the same. This would allow once again a kind of metaphysics of history, a symbolic interpretation. Instead, the contents of the revolution change, just as the objects and the contexts of the decision. Each time it is part: absolute partiality and subjectivity. The decision is never reform, never leads back to nature or to dwelling. Therefore it is symbolically incomprehensible. Therefore it is *Trauerspiel*. There is here a certain continuity between first and second version because even in the first one Sigismund does not want to be "lord of forms that are customary and pleasurable, but in those that surprise you." The Messiah is armed with a sword and his decision is division from the old order: "I take responsibility to unite in this life both things: establish order and leave the old order." But the order that the first Sigismund wants to establish is still strictly connected with the idea of reform. The new order is founded—in fact it must be founded—on universal consent that is more a submission based on abnegation (*Bescheidung*), on renunciation. The old kings are dead but in their place a harmony seems to advance even more ancient than the symbol, whose banner flutters on Sigismund's tent. "You may look upon all three flags," Sigismund tells the lords of the kingdom that come to pay him homage at the end of the play. "There is that of Asia, that of the people that broke chains, that of the authority of the father. United they flap and clatter in the wind wherever we ride." And to the apparent peace of the lords, Sigismund opposes the utopia of Christian universal peace. ("What you call peace, is your power. . . . What I bear within me is the spirit of foundation, not the spirit of possession.") The new Sigismund, therefore, in the first version, is ancient harmony. His discourse is only apparently political. There is no armed Messiah.

Not only that, but since, as we know, there is no real peace, wanting to pursue it means remaining eternally in war. Since there is no redemption, to continue to want to realize it means to continue the martyrdom. To Sigismund's words the Senior Banneret replies, "Our lives and lands are yours, our Lord and King. . . . Do not let the horse's tail of the heathen wave beside your holy banner! And have the banner of the broken chains buried in the earth: for why the emblem of rebellion, since you are supreme? . . . Make a covenant with us, who are your vassals, and permit us to crown you with the crown of your fathers!" The word of reconciliation, therefore, is the politics of the old, ancient authority. And the Banneret is right to mention it. There is peace, his peace, only by burying all other banners. Sigismund rejects this alliance, but he is already condemned to death by the poison of the Gypsy. Nor can the Children's King face the conflict that Sigismund's meeting with the lords of the kingdom has represented intact, despite the victory over Olivier, despite the prince's apparent political affirmation educated in the formula: *la vida es sueño*. It is not up to the Children's King "to see evil." To the lords' swords he opposes the song: "Most mighty! The lark is most mighty! And the sun displays his glorious house, and all points to one place," the one place on earth where the source of milk and honey flows. The Children's King asks Sigismund for swords and scales to be able to proclaim new laws, whose meaning becomes that of having announced the new kingdom, of having been the Baptist. They will have to forge swords into ploughshares and set lighted candles beside the dead, to shape the world for which Sigismund was still untimely ("there is no place for me in time"). But with what words does the Children's King address the lords, the people, Asia? He shows them the perfect and absolute power of utopia, but the more his voice is pure the more it opens up the rift between it and the forces of the *Trauerspiel* that it addresses. It does not resolve the *Trauerspiel* but is one of its figures—in fact, one of its fundamental figures, because its very impotence reveals fully its insurmountable allegorical character.

Many-sidedness! Now we understand how well founded were Hofmannsthal's fears to be the target of such reproach. Many-sided is precisely the conclusion of the first *Tower*, but this many-sidedness is a cover, a defense. To the complete devaluation of the political he opposes a desperate resistance. Sigismund dies, but his grave sanctifies a new dwelling. In the real world not a single banner flaps, but Olivier is dead (though, even here, ambiguously, by means of dark and mysterious scene, and not through the play, the force of the political). And yet, in what sense will the Children's King reign over "those who live"? In what sense does he interpret Sigismund's death? Must Sigismund die because he is still destined to the political, timely only to the conflict? Has he taken on this guilt to announce and prepare the coming of the Children's King, who will finally be able to forge swords into plowshares? This is not stated in any way; on the contrary, as we have seen, Sigismund's encounter with the lords (a memorable scene where on one hand all the forces of misinterpretation and ambiguity are at work and, on the other, there is a desperate will to be understood and loved)[80] reiterates the fact that the reconciliation is apparent, that *three* are the banners after all. The Children's King ushers only the silence of the second Sigismund (and perhaps this is how Benjamin understood it) as the pure utopia that precedes absolute disenchantment and silence? To be sure, he is utopia, but utopia that asks for sword and scale. For this world? For the world of unreconciled conflict? No, but he retains this utopia, preserving it in the light of his hidden realm so that it may be asserted "in another time." How should we interpret the Children's King? Solely in the way in which Heidegger has interpreted Trakl's "Stranger on Earth."[81] There is no doubting Trakl's influence on Hofmannsthal. The Children's King is the stranger, the unborn that calls toward the earth, an earth not yet unveiled. The Children's King, as Trakl's Elis, looks after the earth for the unborn, "those who will live." Sigismund's corpse is finally brought to this land; this is the land that he sanctifies. Sigismund withdraws in the *parsi-fal*, in the "pure folly" of the

unborn. But this unborn, differently in my view from Trakl but as it occurs, instead, in Heidegger's discussion, appears, sings, calls, suddenly and
mysteriously no longer passes near "dark villages, solitary estates" (Trakl)
but crosses them. In Trakl is not the soul, the stranger who sings but only
his friend, the one who takes leave, and must take leave, without first having listened to the song of the unborn, to the promise of the West. That
is why the many-sidedness of the first Sigismund was untenable. Sigismund had to go without the Children's King, without being able to wait
for the call of the unborn and without hoping to have announced it in any
way. That is why to say that the position of the second Sigismund toward
the political is more abstract is misleading (*Dramen*, 264). The opposite
is true. Sigismund recognizes the harshness, the rough terrain and the
chiaroscuro of the political. His position with respect to it is not abstract.
It is absolute. Precisely because he recognizes the real power of the political, he knows that he cannot intervene, that he can find neither reconciliation nor Children's King. That is why the historical event is treated much
more politically in the second version. In fact, only here does history, as it
is in the essence of the *Trauerspiel*, become politics, absolutely independent
of physical and natural determinism. It is true that Sigismund is no longer
a martyr in the second version. His witnessing is by now exiled to pure
inwardness (*Dramen*, 267),[82] and it has no voice to exist, not because Sigismund's purity may become "aesthetic" (an aesthetic escape from the
world) but for precisely the opposite reason—namely, that Sigismund exists only in this world. He knows that only this world is sayable and that
the soul, therefore, a stranger on earth, does not belong to what can be
said. Not an escape in the unsayable but the silent presence here till death.

The relation between speech and silence is decisive for an understanding of *The Tower*. In the design of the *Trauerspiel* speech marks the beginning of becoming-man: the separation from the animal (*Tier*), the
transformation of the animal motif (*Tiermotiv*)—as we know, the motif of
animality is also fundamental in Benjamin—in incarnation (*Menschenwer-
dung*) (*Sprachtematik*, 96). Where speech is missing, the animal corpse
(*Tierkadaver*) is there once again: "the limits between silence and speech
are those between 'wolf' and 'man'" (*Sprachtematik*, 96). Man is on his
way to language. His sign is the endless "metamorphosis of the world in
speech," the endless dematerialization (*Entstofflichung*) of the world
through speech (*Sprachtematik*, 97). In *The Tower* speech is positioned at
different levels. In Olivier it is purely functional: names, simple imperatives, scattered words. It exists solely to command, it neither questions nor

answers.[83] On the contrary, in Sigismund it reaches the full dematerialization of things (*Entsachlichung der Dingen*) the full spiritualization of the physical (*Sprachtematik*, 100).

But this is not at all essential. This kind of interpretation reduces Hofmannsthal's *Trauerspiel* to empty formulas (contrast between speech and action, etc., the whole conducted by means of external, sympathetic, sentimental lines and not according to the logic of the *Trauerspiel*, of its form, of its materials and their relation to drama and tragedy). The spiritualization of the physical is not what is essential to the angelic language of Sigismund. What is essential is that this speech does not constitute in any way the passage to the transcendental, and that it is inextricably linked to silence. If in the first Sigismund angelic language still seems powerful, in the second it withdraws completely in the inaudible. Hofmannsthal points to this characteristic more than once. When he meets his father, Sigismund "speaks, but from his lips comes no sound." In his encounter with the Voivode of Lublin in the throne room after the coup against Basilius "he barely says a word." He is once again silent, insistently, before Olivier. Even before the people who call for him he must be silent: "My teacher, why do you speak to him? To say those things that would be worth saying our tongues are too thick."[84] The angelic language is silence. It is a devaluation of language as such insofar as it is utopia of spiritualization or, which is the same, of the full comprehension of the world. Sigismund, therefore, is not the overcoming of Lord Chandos but the true brother of the desperate Lord. Even their memories are the same: "Wood lice, worms, toads, grasshoppers, vipers! They all want to attack me. I beat them to death, they are released, the hard black beetles come and bury them." Sigismund is Chandos left prisoner in the cellars where "those rat people" fight against the poison.[85] Sigismund carries within himself Chandos's same capacity to feel every inanimate thing and the drama of creatures: "Do you remember the pig that father slaughtered, and it cried so loud and I cried with it. . . . When it hung on a rafter in the passage, by my bedroom door, its inside so dark, I lost myself in it.—Was that its soul which had fled from it in the last terrible scream? And did my soul enter into the dead animal in its place?"

It is not a question of a simple reformulation of the Baroque theme animal-man-God. Whoever is more detached from the instrumentalization (*Verdinglichung*) of language is the one who, on one hand, is in tune with the naturalness of the creatural state and, on the other, the impotence of language to express this cosmic relation. The angelic language thus is transformed in a critique of language. Life is a dream means that it is a dream to think that language can dematerialize, or that language is a dream before essence, before the symbol. Speech reveals itself to be intrinsically allegorical. Whoever has to bear witness to speech as opposed to the instrumentality of technique can only bear witness to its silence. Sigismund's extreme remark, "Bear witness," of the second version has no relation to a similar remark in the first where the full spiritualization of speech seemed utopian in the Children's King, of whom Sigismund was brother. The first Sigismund was not a Messiah, but speech on the Messiah, announcement of the Messiah. The second Sigismund, Chandos's true brother, knows the impossibility of language to announce a Messiah. His *Passionspiel* comes out empty.

But the desperate conscience of the limits of his own language gained by the second Sigismund also transforms the sense of the other languages. Around Sigismund the central figures of the *Trauerspiel* are being modified. Precisely because Sigismund conquers the conscience of the insurmountable limits of spiritualization, he can lay bare by his own presence the limitations of other languages that purport to be realized and effective. From his own language, precisely because it is ruthlessly criticized, Sigismund can lay bare the groundlessness of the others, their essential vanity. In *The Tower*, therefore, we do not have at all the simple shipwreck of angelic language before the dark powers of the political-allegorical. That shipwreck is also and intrinsically critique of the language of these powers. This is immediately true of Basilius, whose lawlessness, still profoundly rooted in the animal world, in instinct to life, undermines any possibility to found an order, even just an apparent peace, to preserve the kingdom. But this is also true of Julian, even though he is Sigismund's teacher in acknowledging that life is a dream. He loves the beautiful dream, he wants the beautiful dream, he wants to realize that power that his spirit has told him to be a dream. And it is also true of Olivier who, in my view, is the character who has undergone a greater transformation in the second version. In the first, the presence alone of Sigismund on the political field had confused Olivier's behavior. In Act IV he appeared as a storm-and-stress bandit, not as someone aware of the language of command, of functionality and technique. His relationship with the Gypsy, the very manner in which Hofmannsthal announced his death, further romanticized the traits of this central character.

In the second version, Olivier is absolutely purified of any romantic trace. The final encounter with Sigismund occurs between two languages reciprocally and ruthlessly laying bare their own limitations and their powerlessness. The central question of Sigismund is, "Who gave you the power so that you could pass it on to others?" This is the decision that the exceptional state requires. No God, as the kings of old pretended, as Basilius had still fancifully told Sigismund during their first encounter. And Sigismund had asked the same question of Basilius. Olivier is aware of his own exceptionality. "Who is before you, you have not known him yet. What you have known till now were Jesuit practices and nonsense. But what is here now is *reality*." Olivier knows that he represents the devaluation of power, of the political as instrument of the conquest and preservation of power. Sigismund answers him: "I understand you well. I know, *the here and now*, puts many into chains. . . . You did not get hold of me. For I belong to myself. You cannot even see me, for you do not know how to see." What is it that Olivier does not have? It cannot be a question of Sigismund's speech, of his speech between spirit and spirit, in the absolute interiority of silence. Olivier is other than that. He does not have something he should have. One does not have what one feels the absence of. What absence does Sigismund reveal to Olivier? The absence of consent. In his political apparatus, Olivier lacks this fundamental instrument of power. In fact, why does he have to turn to Sigismund? Because Sigismund has consent, because he is seen as announcing peace. His image is in every house where "candles are lit as before the image of a saint." Olivier cannot do without it, and because Sigismund refuses to instruct the people mute before his image touring the town on a cart pulled by twelve pairs of oxen, as if it were a church on wheels, Olivier needs "an individual similar enough to confuse them and that would obey me like a glove the hand." But why does Sigismund refuse and go to his death? Simply because in the age of Olivier the spirit cannot be reality? Simply because the political is, as we have seen, other than the symbol of the spirit? He goes to his death for a more profound and decisive reason, namely, that Sigismund knows by now the intrinsic limitations of his own language and has recognized its political impotence. This language has nothing to do with orders, peace, and the revolutions of the political. Olivier cannot have him, not because Sigismund chooses to refuse himself but because by now he cannot will anything else but his own separation from the political.

Only the mask of Sigismund is possible in reality, not Sigismund himself.[86] But this also reveals the insurmountable groundlessness of the power of this reality. Sigismund cannot but refuse. Olivier cannot but feign him on the oxcart that represents false peace, apparent peace: a frail attempt at power and government. All is vain, Sigismund tells Julian (whose prayer "is not without power, though you clench your fists instead of folding your hands") except for the dialogue between spirit and spirit.

But this dialogue is powerless where the "no names" rule. The spirit has name, dwellings have a name; a name establishes and defines. Masks and allegories have no names. But the impotence of the dialogue of the spirit and of its names in Olivier's reality is at the same time transience and groundlessness of the political. It cannot transform disorder into order. This still constitutes the utopia proper to Julian. He fights for power but still aims at power as sovereignty legitimized by the establishment of order. For Olivier, this is Jesuitical nonsense. He knows he is chained in the here and now ("I am too in the hands of Fate"), but he will have to fight with greater toughness the more he recognizes the weakness of his principle. The true center of *The Tower* is not the dialogue of the spirit with the spirit but this final dialogue of two impenetrable voices whose reasons are condemned reciprocally to vanity and to impotence, to transience and to silence. Two mirrors that reflecting each other understand their own principle through the impossibility of understanding the other. The political is visible only in Sigismund's mirror, but Sigismund is visible, comprehensible only in Olivier's mirror. Not symbol, but absolute difference: and yet only difference makes it possible to understand the different. This is the paradoxical presence of the symbol in the desert of allegorical life: having to be together in absolute difference, in absolute misery and solitude. In fact, Sigismund is not the only one who is alone; so are Julian ("My years were hauntingly lonely"), Basilius ("I too have not had a friend around me"), and Olivier. Loneliness is the incommunicability and the impossibility of translating their languages—it is the full awareness of their limitations. One's limits call for the other's, imposing on the other one's own limits, one's own loneliness. Each has in the other an unbreakable mirror of his misery.

Not Olivier but the overall structure of this *Trauerspiel* abolishes "the language of priests and players" and makes it possible for a disenchanted day to fall on the world. In fact, even Sigismund rejects the language of comedy; even Julian has nostalgia for a power grounded in actuality not on the symbol, on immanent order and not on divine kingship. But Olivier himself can be a disenchanted thinker solely because one reflects on the absolute otherness of Sigismund and not, as in the first version, on a Sigismund ruled by utopia. In fact, in the first version, Olivier's language, far from being sober and simple, was intoxicated and magical. Where in the first version Olivier was ruled by the "I," in the second he is thoroughly a "no name." Not even after his victory does he want a name. He knows that he can preserve himself only as the principle opposed to the name. The impossibility of the symbol asserts itself therefore as the impossibility of the "I," as it is split (*Spaltung*) in itself.[87] The impossibility of the name is the impossibility of naming oneself. The allegorical is above all the allegorical of one's own "I" and *inside* one's own "I." This is how Chandos-Sigismund and Olivier are represented.

In Simon's words, the world that no longer possesses a name or a dwelling is reflected, where the old king is animal, the messiah is silence, the political Julian and Olivier are in Sigismund's *mirror*. It is the world of precariousness lived by Hofmannsthal.[88] It is Benjamin's world of expressionism and allegory. The wonderful image of inflation outlined by Simon is truly the image of the definitive fall of the allegorical.[89] Loss of center, loss of trust, deception over "true weight."[90] The collapse of every certainty on the *value* of money is the precariousness of the allegorical.

Here Hofmannsthal's apocalypse ends. In *The Tower*, the Spanish side of his "Romània" arrives at the radical *Trauerspiel*, just as his Venetian side does in *Andreas*.

CHAPTER 2

Nietzsche and the Unpolitical

Wagner's music is anti-Goethe. In fact, Goethe is missing in
German music as he is in German politics.

FRIEDRICH NIETZSCHE, *Posthumous Fragments*, Spring 1888

The most authentic reactionary thinking of the German crisis remarked
with sound intuition its own distance from the "political" Nietzsche. In
August 1918, in reply to the accusations of "allied *Zivilisation*" against the
Kultur of *Deutschtum* and its "presumed advocacy of violence," Ulrich von
Wilamowitz-Möllendorf wrote, "And finally, Nietzsche. It just makes us
smile to see pitted against the advocates of the power of our State one of
those individual anarchists who can afford to negate the social order precisely because he is protected by this society squarely set within the order
of the State. After all, if one looks at Nietzsche's precursors one will not
find Germans, but French moralists and Greek cynics. Treitschke's conception of the world and Nietzsche's are worlds apart."[1] Between the
"spirit of 1914"—in all its academic variations, from Wilamowitz on one
hand to Troeltsch or Meinecke on the other—and Nietzsche, the critic of
Wilhelmine *Sekurität* (that is, the outcome of that Prussian militarism and
nationalism that believed to have been called "to lead the history of Humanity"), the clash is head-on.[2] The "great reaction" understands Nietzsche's uselessness within its cultural-political project. Its philology is too
good to translate *Will to Power* (*Wille zur Macht*) into *Waiting for the Leader*
(*Führererwartung*), and to aestheticize Nietzsche's political as *völkisch*. To
this aestheticization—the virile power of *Deutschtum* opposed to European

decadence, to the "decline of the West" the definitive answer came from Thomas Mann in 1918, in his *Reflections of a Nonpolitical Man*.[3]

In Mann, Nietzsche becomes the center of German *Kultur* precisely because he is unpolitical. "The spiritual conversion of Germany to politics" (*Reflections*, 18) constitutes the process *against* which Nietzsche testifies to the authentic German destiny. Thomas Mann's hatred for any aestheticization and politicization of Nietzsche finds here, therefore, its essential motives: Nietzsche is the unpolitical, but this unpolitical is the spiritual power of Germany itself. Therefore, Nietzsche belongs to the heart of Germany. The whole book is but the development of this one theme: Nietzsche read according to Theodor Storm's "renunciation" (*Entsagung*) (*Reflections*, 74), educated to the pessimistic German and bürgerlich ethics of Schopenhauer and Wagner, belonging to the *Humanität* of the classical-romantic period, of the German *Bildung* (*Reflections*, 85, 90).[4] The entire German nineteenth century is interpreted according to the schemes of the myth of Weimar: a relation of sacred continuity links the Goethe of that myth to the heroic Nietzsche for his being unpolitical, for being absolute and paradoxical in his ethical pathos (*Reflections*, 104). His figure undermines the utopias of Troeltsch and Meinecke. The era of Goethe (the *Goethezeit*) no longer expresses the alliance of spirit and power, "German spirituality widespread as the world, and solid Prussian state," rather the absolute superpoliticality and nonpoliticality of that spirit.[5] The spirit, insofar as it is bürgerlich and German, is essentially *Kultur*. *Kultur* is *Weltbürgertum*, cosmopolitanism; it is the expression, that is, of the substance of *Bürgertum*, universal substance opposed to the Latin concept of the bourgeoisie. The essential meaning of *Weltbürgertum* rests therefore on the concept of the unpolitical. Mann sees war itself, differently from those other greats of the liberal-conservative tradition, as a clash between the affirmation of this idea of *Weltbürgertum* (*not* of the synthesis of spirit and power!) and the affirmation of political civilization controlled by the bourgeoisie. The German mission consists in affirming the power of the unpolitical, and in this consists its supra-Germanity.

This Mannian interpretation of Nietzsche, however, so contrary to the myths of the "spirit of 1914," to the vision of German *Bildung* typical of the latter, so fiercely opposed to the Nietzschean popularization of reactionary *Deutschtum*, follows the same historicist method that it questions in many of its single assertions. A deep, strong continuity sustains German history from its classical era—but even before: from the age of the German cities, of the German Hanseatic League, of a Wagnerian Nuremberg more

than merely medieval (*Reflections*, 80)—until the test of 1914. And Nietzsche is supposedly the symbol of this continuity, which is hatred for the
political. However, Nietzsche, instead, is precisely the critic of this symbol
and this continuity. As Löwith has masterfully pointed out, the Nietzschean position with respect to the "age of Goethe" is completely different from the interpretation given by Mann. Goethe is for Nietzsche an
accident without consequences in German history. Far from perfecting a
tradition from which Nietzsche himself could draw, his conservative and
conciliatory attitude appears in actuality to be the mask with which he
detaches himself from the German *Weltbürgertum*. The latter is Hegelian
and dialectic, not Goethean—it is dominated by the philosophy of history
and by the idol of success sacralized as rational necessity. Goethe's realism
seems to Nietzsche to be, in actual fact, a heroic antinihilistic attempt at
overcoming nihilism, at Dionysian affirmation, absolutely eccentric with
respect to the forces of German *Kultur*.[6] This radical misunderstanding of
Nietzsche's Goethe on Thomas Mann's part conceals, obviously, an even
more substantial misunderstanding of the antihistoricist direction of
Nietzsche's thought, absolutely opposed to any continuist reconstruction
of the cultural event, to overcoming it in synthetic forms.

Many other reductions should be performed so that Mann's interpretation can stand up. Nietzsche's genealogy of morals should be reduced to a
simple critique of political morals, or a critique of morals mixed with interest, or maybe a mere critique of ideology, without independent theoretical
relevance.[7] The illuministic side of Nietzsche should be flattened to a dimension of pure appearance or simply comprehended in the concept of
cosmopolitanism—but this analysis would stray far from the topic of this
essay. The real central question posed by Mann's *Reflections of a Nonpolitical
Man* is another: Should the political in Nietzsche be understood as an
issue of the unpolitical? Is it a question of a reversal of values? And what
should we understand by the unpolitical? What is the "thing in itself" that
Nietzsche thinks in the question of the unpolitical? It is very clear that
Mann understands it as the refusal of the political dimension, as the idea
of the will to power as heroic process of *askesis*, of renunciation in the
Protestant sense. The political is for Mann a nonvalue. Its dimension
makes impossible the unfolding of that process which is the affirmation of
the values of *Humanität* and *Bildung* of the German cosmopolitanism. The
unpolitical, therefore, for Mann is an affirmation of value, not its reversal.
The political, rather, is the reversal of values. The politicization expresses
the disruption between *Seele* and *Geist*, Soul and Spirit, whereby the *Verge-
istigung*, or spiritualization (the process of spiritualization or rationalization of social relations) appears and dominates as *Entseelung* or

despiritualization (the extirpation of romantic individuality, of the cultural individualism of the classic bourgeoisie).

Is this Nietzsche's unpolitical? To be sure, it is radically different from Weber's vision. Mann can prove the utopian character of the conservative reconciliation between *Kultur* and the Prussian state, between spirit and power politics, but his nostalgia for the Weimar myth is entirely powerless with respect to the Weberian analysis of the process of politicization as necessary despiritualization. The unpolitical as affirmation of values preceding the era of politicization, or struggling with its destiny, constitutes the spiritual attitude that more explicitly is opposed to the Weberian disenchantment. To which horn of the dilemma does Nietzsche belong? And can his position throw new light on this contradiction?

Nietzsche's critique is the opposite of the critique of the political as nonvalue. This critique moves already within Weber's necessity (*necessitas*, not *dira*, not adjectivized) of politicization. But, beyond Weber, it questions the meaning of the political as such. It is not enough to record its success, it is not enough to oppose to the praying devout in the old churches the new fetishism of the fact. Nietzsche's unpolitical is the critique of the political as affirmation of value. The unpolitical is not the nostalgic refusal of the political, but the radical critique of the political. It goes beyond the mask of the political (its disenchantment, its necessity, its being destiny) to discover the foundation of values, the discourse of value that still founds it. Its power analyses, and dissolves, that which even in Weber tends to present itself as the totalizing method of Western spiritualization. The unpolitical does not represent the value that frees itself from the nonvalue of the political, but the radical critique of the political as invested with value. The unpolitical is the reversal of value. And only this reversal can liberate the will to power in the direction of politics on a grand scale. Grand politics are not possible there where the critique of the unpolitical is limited to affirming the necessity of politicization. This affirmation is still historicism, tradition. Grand politics is a critique of the values that still form the basis of this politicization. The unpolitical, in Mann's sense, is but an expression of these values. And here its dialectics ends. Having left home to fight against politicization, such dialectics finds that it has to defend the same values that lie at the foundation of the still "enchanted," still uncriticized dimension of the political. Such dialectics finds itself in the dimension of the political, in a nutshell. Nietzsche's unpolitical instead develops separately from this political, and from this polar unpolitical, as an analysis of the authentic genealogy of the process of politicization and of the premises contained within it of grand politics.

The unpolitical in Nietzsche shapes up, we could say, as the critical stage of grand politics.

As we have already mentioned, a first test of this thesis could be easily made by reading Nietzsche's critique of the Wilhelmine era. But this would entail an extreme trivialization of the meaning of the unpolitical. The general theoretical significance of the unpolitical consists in the assertion of the necessity of politicization insofar as despiritualization (*Entseelung*) and devaluation (*Entwertung*). Far from coinciding with Mann's refusal of the political, the unpolitical constitutes its greatest assertion within Western nihilism. The unpolitical brings the political back to the acknowledgment of its intrinsic nihilism. This key direction opens up, above all, by attacking the concepts, the forms, and the conducts that are the substance of the political as value. But this very same *pars destruens* is already a construction of grand politics insofar as it is a nihilistic devaluation.

In the process of politicization, the political tends to represent itself as total concept. The forms assumed by the politicization, even in Weber, appear as articulation of the political as totality. The political intervenes everywhere—its logic constitutes the method of any social relation. And any form of social organization tends relentlessly to take on the form of a totality, to lock into and to subsume within itself the totality of social interests. The dialectical state expresses organically these forces; it is indeed its outcome. Far from opposing sectarianisms that are represented as such, the dialectical state comprehends the totalizing instance that emerges from the combination of forms of the politicization.[8] As totality, this state tends immediately to conceive its own form as the natural form of political organization.[9] The dialectical state absolutizes the concept of state: the historically determined work, which has led to its configuration within the sphere of Western rationalism (nihilism), appears surpassed— now the state counts as pure norm, law. Norm and law point to the universal method on whose basis every subject becomes totality.[10]

The unpolitical is the work of deconstruction of this totality. Not in the superficial sense of the term "critique of ideology," whereby this totality is said to be "false"—but in the sense that this totality is historically marked and produces the forces of its own crisis, forces whose possibility is definitely accountable. In the absolutization of its being, its totality, the state—the greatest expression of political organization, the result of the political—defines itself as value: its functions become values. Naming the multiplicity of forces that make up the crisis of that totality, the unpolitical

represents the critique of values on whose bases alone such totality is conceivable. Unpolitical does not mean, therefore, suprapolitical: its concept
moves across the entire space of the political. It is, in the political, the
critique of its ideology and of its determination.

The emphasis is placed on the second term, not on the first. The first
unfolds, substantially, by demonstrating the ethical foundation of the absolutization of the political proclaimed by the modern state. On this side,
the political falls once again under Nietzsche's overall critique of ethics.
Democratization and socialism are rather subsumed under the misery of
Christian eschatology (*Nietzsche*, 455).[11] This eschatology presupposes a
human nature that is to be liberated from the alienation to which the institutions of civilization have presumably condemned it. This eschatology,
however, is not only at the basis of socialism but also at the basis of the
idea of democratization—and, even more generally, of the modern absolutization of the political. This absolutization claims to be the redemption
of the totality of man, the overcoming of the empirical, contingent immediacy of his figure. If man could resist as an unpolitical partiality, the political could not conclude dialectically in the total state. And, therefore, the
strong eschatological tone of the ideas of democracy and socialism is the
lawful son of the political—it constitutes its necessary unfolding. For
Nietzsche, this nature, whose alienation would be revocable, is supersti-
tion—better, it is a theological assumption.[12] The absolutization of the
political belongs to the theological dimension of Western thought. But
the analysis of its condition is not sufficient: it too represents a determinate
and problematic asset of social organization. In this sense, the critique of
the ideas of democracy and socialism is essential since, according to Nietzsche, they unfold the political until baring its own constitutive determi-
nacy and problematic nature.

Democracy makes explicit the origin presupposed by the discourse on
the political (the political gives norms and laws that concern the origin
and aim at the end of man as totality), but at the same time it makes
possible for any subject as such to express and organize its own force.
Precisely insofar as it wants to make explicit the dignity of the common
origin, it multiplies the organizing of heterogeneous centers of force. This
is the process of politicization itself. It is the generalization of the political.
Any subject, in the dialectics of democracy, can be organized politically—in fact, this is what it is directly called upon to do. But this very
same process that appears as absolutization of the political, defines it in
actuality as a field of heterogeneous forces, of contradictions—as a space
where endless differences occur. The absolutization occurs through a loss

of centrality and a constant weakening of the system. Far from leading to
unity, to common origins, the total politicization increases the entropy of
the system. It undermines the relations of subordination that regulated
the course of the different subjects or selected their information. "[Total
politicization] is destined to disappear, because its foundation disappears,
namely, trust in absolute authority and in definitive truth . . . In *freer*
conditions, one will become subordinate only on condition, as a result of
reciprocal contract, that is, with all the reservations of one's own interest"
(*Human, All Too Human*, 1:245). But free subordination is the opposite of
subordination, which is based on a true social hierarchy and justified by an
overall vision of philosophy of history. It becomes an interest, revocable
at any moment on the basis of a right that derives from the relation of
force, of an "arbitrary right" (*Human, All Too Human*, 1:252–253, 2:151).
This undermines from the foundations the ancient "relation of reverence
and piety toward the state." The idea of the state is transformed into an
instrument of being able, to avail of one's own right. None will see in the
law anything else than the determined political organization that produced
it, than the contingent power that issued from it. The mission of the democratic idea consists in the perfecting of this decay of the state, of the
political as totality, in the concourse of the different subjects that by now
autonomously make it up. But this decay is at the same time the greatest
extension of the political, the perfection of the *Politisierung*: everybody
makes politics and organizes himself politically—but only because the political has lost any aura, because it revealed itself as devaluation and despiritualization. "The belief in a divine order of things political, in a mystery
in the existence of the state, is of religious origin." This belief is upheld as
long as the perception of this origin exists. None can revere the state, if it
ceases to represent the destiny that brings man back home, to the revoca-
tion of his alienation, to the conquest (or reformation) of his true nature.
If the state appears ultimately as a sectarian organization of arbitrary
laws—if in the state different competing laws surface—even the last spell
is driven away from the idea of the political. The task of the democratic
idea consists in the desacralization of the political. When it fulfils its task
and "when every relapse into the old sickness has been overcome, a new
page will be turned in the storybook of humanity"—which does not mean
that it will be necessarily chaos. If the state is not able to cope with the
autonomous multiplication of subjects, if the state is not able to stand up
on the rock of its dialectics, "an invention more suited to their purpose
than the state will gain victory over the state." No anarchic nostalgia can

be substituted here for the ethical-eschatological ought-to-be of the political—rather, the consequent refusal to speak of ends, to reintroduce a perspective of value, there where this appears by now, today, perfect in the democratization of the political. It is essential to understand the finiteness of the state: "How many an organizing power has mankind not seen die out," how many ideas of rights have we ourselves seen grow "ever paler and more impotent." The state is one of these powers whose process of absolutization coincides with that of its devaluation. The unpolitical is the recognition of the occurred perfection of the political.

The idea of socialism also belongs to this destiny. Socialism, despite its desires for "an abundance of state power such as only despotism has ever had," educates new subjects to the political, becomes incarnate in its own process of detheologization.[13] It is true that socialism accomplishes this task in contradictory forms—but the moral ideology that it preserves, more than the substance of its work, represents its mask. Socialism derives from the dissolution of the sacred centrality of the idea of the political and of the state—from the affirmation of subjects dialectically irreducible within it, bearers of arbitrary rights. The fact that everyone of these still proposes his rights as the true one, his ends as reform of the total state founded on the norm, on the law, does not change their sign—the sign in which they are inexorably entrenched: that of the dissolution of the idea and of the form of the dialectical state.

In the fever that seizes the concept of work, Nietzsche catches the most evident symptom of this process. Even Löwith, who was the first to call attention to the importance of this theme in Nietzsche (*From Hegel*, 283), has shown its roots in the ancient ethos of *otium* rather than analyzing its function within the critique of the political and of the dialectical state. Neither nostalgia for a return, as in Carlyle, to blessed precapitalistic work, nor even nostalgia to move forward toward a perfect militarization of work, understood as realization of its value, constitutes the power of Nietzsche's critique; rather, it is the attack on the very idea of work as value, an attack led on the basis of the concrete, historically determined dissolution of this idea that constitutes, in fact, the motor of dialectical construction. Only by acknowledging this idea is it possible to realize the mediation among the different operations of the different subjects. In such mediation this diversity is reduced so that the process of mediation can lead to synthesis. The value of work is constituted by its necessary dialectical function—without this philosophical premise nothing can be comprehended of its subsequent disciplinary analyses (in economics above all).

The value of work is founded on the teleological premise of the reconcilability of different operations—and of the necessity of this harmony for the development of the system.[14] This teleology is the object of Nietzsche's critique, but not just because of its general moral character. Nietzsche stresses rather the impracticability, the current powerlessness of the synthesis that it projects. The unpolitical criticizes politically the idea of the value of work as law and end of the multiplicity of subjects, as foundation of the progressive-synthetic idea of development. But let it be clear, "a *reversal*, a turning back in any sense and to any degree, is quite impossible. We philologists at least know that. But all priests and moralists have believed it was possible—they have *wanted* to take mankind back, *force* it back, to an *earlier* standard of virtue . . . Even politicians have in this matter imitated the preachers of virtue: even today there are parties whose goal is to dream the crabwise *retrogression* of all things."[15] Nietzsche's "passing by" is the very same process of the critical analysis of existing value.[16] Here it is constituted by the critical analysis of work. This analysis captures the realization of the subject in work as a process of alienation. But to stop here, as it is done usually, makes it possible to reduce Nietzsche's text to anticapitalist nostalgia. Nietzsche conceives alienation radically. The different operations are alienated by the possibility of their synthesis—they emerge as irreducible and contradictory interests. The process of alienation constitutes the subject from within, does not capture it, in the course of its dialectical realization, as an exogenous destiny. This operation, typical of these subjects historically determined, and which is impossible to reverse, this is irrevocable alienation. It generates contradiction and conflict. Its syntheses are moments of precarious balance in the relations of force between arbitrary rights.

Work, therefore, is a multiplicity of practices—and the character of these operations consists in being alienated from the possibility of dialectical synthesis. The unpolitical denounces in small politics the desperate conservation of the regressive idea of a mutual universal recognition of subjects in work as value. But why is this reduction impracticable? Because it appears by now that it is almost impossible to reduce the practices to their mere technical foundation. The doing (doing of *techné* irrevocably severed from *poieín*) is embodied in subjects that enact their own absence of home as a conflictual relation. This doing is political. The value of work is alienated in subjects politically determined. And they see their own operations as alienation—not in the banal and servile sense, that this alienation is simply imposed on them, that they are subject to it in messianic expectation of the dialectical synthesis, but in the sense that, within the irrevocable dimension of alienation, they can build their own political interest, can determine their own separateness and division as grand politics. The doing is embodied in the political power of the different class interests. Their contraposition eliminates the teleology of the value of work, whose form is the dialectical state.

Even more impossible, with respect to this form, is work itself, work producing value. The class that supplies it is impossible against the dialectical state. Its alienation—far from getting lost in lamentations—posits the alienation of the state from its pretension of totality. There is no synthesis for workers' alienation. The impossibility of the working class as class lies in its positing the synthesis as impossible, with respect to both the political of the *Reich* and to socialist pied pipers "which bid you *to be prepared* and nothing further."[17] The glorification of the value of work is the best policeman. Its purpose is to hinder the production of class and its dialectical impossibility from this work. Or better: the value of work takes the form of a point of view contrary to that of the impossible class—therefore, it is itself in the impossibility to claim to be total, comprehensive, synthetic.

The apologists of work pursue the aim of wearing down an "extraordinary amount of nervous energy," subtracting it to "reflection, brooding, dreaming, worrying, loving, hating." They fear "an empowerment of reason." The security (*Sicherheit*) is their god: a society "in which there is continual hard work will have more security: and security is now worshipped as the supreme divinity." But Nietzsche's critique does not stop at a criticism of the ideology of work. It also realizes how the transformations of the political and the state—the transformation of the subjects that constitute them—undo this divinity. What really matters is not the ideological character of that *apologia*, but the fact that the worker is now posited as impossible against his claims to synthesis, is posited as individual against them. "And now! Horror! Precisely the 'worker' has become *dangerous*! The place is swarming with 'dangerous individuals'! And behind them the danger of dangers—*the* individual!" (*Daybreak*, book III, no. 176). The opposite of an aristocratic-regressive idea of individuality: the individual is the process of separation of the worker from his work—the individual is the final product of the demythologization of the political, of his becoming democratic. This individual is impossible for the value of work.

But if the dialectical state is conceivable only in the light of this value, the emergence of the individual makes it unconceivable. The impossibility of the relation between workers and value of work posits the impossibility of the state that was founded precisely on the power of this relation. This problem should be pondered by the "state-worshippers" (*Human, All Too Human* 2:232), the "devotees" of the state, since they demand that everything should become politics, "that *everyone* should live and work according to such a standard" (*Human, All Too Human* 1:438). They should understand how this very same process of universal politicization liberates the worker from the immediacy of his technical subordination, liquidates the subordination as pivot of hierarchical construction, overturns in the political separation of individuals the alienation of everyone in the value of work. The "state-worshippers" should understand that the same process that they extol is the irreversible decay of the state. The dangerous individual is the worker as impossible class, as a class that is aware of its own condition as impossible. But impossible in both senses: both because the conditions of its exploitation are a disgrace—and because its own individuality makes impossible the dialectical process of reduction and mediation, which is a condition of the power of the state form. This form decays. Any attempt at stopping or overturning this decay is tantamount to dreaming that things proceed crabwise. Any political nostalgia for the universal foundation of value and the state form is precritical. The very same political operation is the dissolution of this form. It is transformation without foundation, that is, not inscribable in a teleological framework, in a philosophy of history. Grand politics entails resisting in the destiny of the devaluation of the political: transforming according to a point of view, to a right, organizing individuality. Grand politics has, as its condition, the unpolitical acknowledgment of the nontotality of the political: a radical critique to the state-worshippers.

Disgraceful is not the priest, but the priest who states that his kingdom is of this world. If our announcement proclaims values, let our kingdom not be of this world. If our kingdom is nothing but this world, then let our language be that of politics without foundation. And let this language know how little does one say when one says it politically. Let it recognize its own limitations—and how much silence embraces its every word. Perhaps the last page of *Human, All Too Human* is devoted to this political: "He who has attained to only some degree of freedom of mind cannot feel other than a wanderer on the earth—though not as a traveller *to* a final destination: for this destination does not exist. But he will watch and observe and keep his eyes open to see what is really going on in the world . . . Within him too there must be something wandering that takes pleasure in change and transience. Such a man will, to be sure, experience bad nights . . . But then, as recompense, there will come the joyful mornings of other days and climes" when "in the equanimity of his soul at morning" he will gather the gifts "of all those free spirits who are at home in mountain, wood and solitude and who, like him, are, in their now joyful, now thoughtful way, wanderers and philosophers." Therefore, the only glimmer, the only narrow door left to us in the era of the demythologization of the political, is to keep one's eyes open and to watch and observe well what is going on in the world, in order to work out that dissolution of values of the state that is the intuition of the "philosophy of the morning."

"Born out of the mysteries of the dawn, they ponder on how, between the tenth and the twelfth stroke of the clock, the day could present a face so pure, so light-filled, so cheerful and transfigured" (*Human, All Too Human* 1:638). "Only ghosts such as this will our descendants sometimes see in the light of day, while the sun shines through the windows—and from the spire resound not gloomy and dismal bells but the flushed, jubilant trumpets, announcing the joyous hour of noon!"[18]

CHAPTER 3

Weber and the Critique of Socialist Reason

The Possibility of Socialism

Eduard Bernstein's analysis of Weber's critique of socialism—of Second International Austrian-German social democratic orthodoxy—is only a basic prologue to the really decisive question (for Weber, as for Sombart, for Schumpeter, as for Kelsen): how is socialism possible? What is its transcendental condition?[1] The issue goes well beyond the purely historical-phenomenological sphere. The question of the origins of socialism differs from the reasons why it can actually exist as a theoretical and practical direction—or as *the* direction—of the European worker's movement. To bare without pity the errors contained in the Marxist prophecy is not only not enough with respect to this problem, but it is also self-contradictory, since the prophecy cannot be evaluated on the bases of its prophetic capacities, the way one would test any scientific statement. In case, the prophecy should be questioned to discover at least some of the reasons that condition socialism. The same can be said in regard to the simple historical analysis: it can show clearly the forms of production of socialism originating from the factory's capitalist discipline, and even earlier, from the processes of expropriation and alienation that are at the bases of capitalist production. One could attempt an immediate explanation, by relating socialism to this characteristic of actual social relations, which eternally repeats itself. But Weber appears, and rightly so, to avoid this shortcut. A similar, static fidelity of socialism to the substance of capitalistic forms of production would hinder its development and growth—it would be functional to describing its decline but not its actual existence. Weber, as we shall see, goes out of his way to demonstrate that the simple rejection of capitalistic alienation leads to insoluble logical contradictions, even before economical or political ones. And yet, one has the clear sense that this critique cannot constitute the cornerstone of his argument, since this critique should conclude by defining socialism as a passing ghost, whose consistency is destined to melt at the light of rationalization (*Rationalisierung*). The overall context of Weber's discourse (and Schumpeter's on this point) appears instead to exclude similar conclusions.

First of all, let us check the key passages—which do not coincide, perhaps, with the most explicit ones—of Weber's critique. The process of bureaucratization, which also comprises democratic form, requires the separation of the executor (at any level and of whatever quality) from owning the means of production. If the owner is replaced with state apparatus, or with one of its organizations, nothing basically changes in the form of these relations. On the contrary, one can suppose that a process of nationalization of the economy would not lead to the subjection of the bureaucratic to the political, but exactly to the opposite. Union and political representatives called on to lead the economy would find themselves in the necessity of obeying to the directives of the techno-bureaucrats to increase production, and these, in the end, thanks to this very relation, would succeed in penetrating into the political, in the area of political decisions, much easier and more effectively than it could happen in the liberal paradigm. Industrial bureaucracy and state bureaucracy would become one, a fact that Weber, differently from many of his contemporary intellectuals, defines painful.[2] A hegemonic bureaucracy would be formed that would exclude the asserting of a political managerial spirit (*leitender Geist*).

It is true that Weber's political is still close to the idea of the national state power (*Machtstaat*).[3] It is also true that in this period, and despite his relentless critique of Wilhelmine liberalism, Weber still conceives the necessity of orienting the political in this sense—but there is no doubt that from his conception emerges with always renewed vigor the invocation to the formation of a new political ruling class, whose boundaries go well beyond Naumann's liberal national party. Weber's political takes on the trait of an organizational will (*Gestaltungwillen*) directed toward the inside, toward new social and class conflicts—and therefore toward (and *versus*) socialism itself.[4] In the theory and practice of socialism, Weber finds an objective tendency to abolish the political as autonomous project, innovative-transforming capacity, decision-making power, and to the domination of a total bureaucracy.

Socialism, therefore, is dominated by this radical contradiction. On one hand, it originates historically out of the separation of labor from the means of production, and it is justified ideologically by the will to overcome this alienation. On the other hand, it pushes necessarily forward toward the control of a total bureaucracy, which not only would reinforce that separation but also would expropriate the political itself. Socialism's aversion to alienation, which holds sway over capitalistic social relations, appears even more intrinsically contradictory. Socialism, in fact, is opposed to capitalism because the latter's political form prevents, at a certain moment, the further development of the forces of production. But this development is only rationally conceivable through the strengthening of the bureaucratic structure. The end of the development of the productive forces turns the antibureaucratic aspirations into a "worthless phraseology" (*wertlose Phraseologie*).[5] What seems to justify, or establish rationally, these tendencies of socialism, which open themselves up to a number of contradictions, consists for Weber in the denunciation of the anarchic character of capitalist production. This denunciation seems to have a moral, nonrational character. Here Weber's critique coincides with Schumpeter's.[6]

If by the term *anarchy* we mean the lack of connection or interweaving between the levels of economic activity and of political finalities—in other words, if by anarchy we mean the autonomy of economics—this is historically disavowed by the processes of socialization of economic life, which constitutes not so much a phase, but the very cornerstone of capitalistic development. However, if by anarchy is meant the impossibility of rational reckoning, reduction of economic relations to the immediate level of subjective-individual profit, this critique is logically false. In fact, it is overturned by Weber for whom the socialist prophecy is logically groundless, and, in this sense, anarchic, while capitalist reason can be formulated in formally complete terms and entirely value-free. On the contrary, the judgments of socialism on capitalism are always value judgments.

Socialism and Market Anarchy

Of extreme importance, in this context, seems to be Weber's previous essay, "On the Theory of Marginal Utility and the 'Fundamental Law of

Psychophysics,'" which appeared in *Archiv* in 1908.[7] This very complex work, which attempts to counter in universal logical terms the thesis of capitalism's anarchy, seems to us to constitute the basis of his eventual critique of socialism. In this essay, he asserts the full emancipation of economic calculation from psychologism. The relation between the form that economic calculation acquires thanks to the theory of marginal utility and any subjective idea of utility (whereby the stimulus determined by an external event should always turn out quantitatively measurable) mystifies the logico-formal character of theory—its complete independence from any psychology. The premises of this theory are: (1) that a man acts, among other things, also in order to satisfy needs that can be satisfied through the consumption of goods; (2) that as the gratification of determined needs grows, the need of nonconsumed goods also develops; and (3) that men are able to act rationally in the light of past experience and anticipation (*Vorausberechnung*). This calculation does not question at all the meaning of terms such as need or purpose. Psychology is entirely indifferent to it. Economic calculation wishes to be only a rational theory of the formation of price—a theory pragmatically and not psychologically founded. It presupposes certain data of human behavior (and only some—it does not pretend any universality), and on these it builds its calculation.

It is clear within which philosophical family Weber develops his thesis. It is a critique of psychologism as it is developed by the neo-Kantian school rather than by Husserl. The neo-Kantian origins of Weber's analysis are particularly clear where there is more explicit use of the category of "as if" (*als ob*)[8] in defining human behavior (men must be considered *as if* constantly involved in an economical enterprise, *as if* "under the control of commercial calculation"). Here one does not "feign hypotheses" with respect to human nature or human psychology. On the bases of extremely banal factual data at hand, marginal economy defines some presuppositions from which results a perfectly resolved calculation, without contradictions. This calculation does not pretend at all to appeal to man's general nature—let alone knowing it or being able to express it. It is totally specialistic and therefore completely indifferent to psychology itself. This analysis is important because it shows that the socialist critiques of neo-classical schools (especially Austrian ones) are untenable, psychological and subjective, or that they mystify the determined historical characters of capitalist means of production by assuming universal psychological presuppositions. But above all, Weber's analysis vindicates the normative-conscious character of capitalist economic calculation. The normativeness of economic action excludes any naturalistic presupposition. No nature grounds the ratio of such action and legitimizes it. Economic action proceeds on the basis of definite conventions to the solutions of definite problems. These conventions hold a binding power, which is social and political in character. They dictate the frame of reference that must necessarily be maintained in order to act rationally within the sphere of capitalist economical calculation, that is, of an economical calculation based on expectations of growth and development. This calculation and these expectations are not at all determined; they do not pretend any metaphysical status. The accusation of naturalism is reversed in socialist criticism. When this critique speaks of anarchy in the marketplace, is it not forced, perhaps, to refer to a rational-natural order in which conflicts of interest would be dialectically overcome by the consideration and imposition of the general good, of the *res publica*? The discourse of socialism on general interest, on community (*Gemeinwesen*), versus capitalist irrationality: is it not forced to assume as its own foundation the metaphysical presupposition of a substantially common nature? Böhm-Bawerk traced these presuppositions, which also constitute the cornerstone of socialist prophecy, back to the more properly analytical and economic body of Marxism, to the reduction of the Marxist theory of value (of its complex problematic) to left-wing Ricardism.[9]

Against this socialist pauperism Weber opposes the rational disenchantment of economic calculation and the specific, concrete, political normativeness that derives from it. Mobile normativeness is capable of transformations coherent with the development of the economic system and its social composition, because it is extraneous to any metaphysical or naturalistic foundation. Schumpeter's critique of the socialist myth of socialization as the overcoming of hypothetical market anarchy follows a similar method, as does Kelsen's critique of Marxism as a "nineteenth century system" preceding the "epistemological revolution" of the end of the century.[10] Weber's rationalization, worked out by the professional intellectual and politician at the height, so to speak, of its immanence, appears as a critique of things opposed to socialism as ideology-prophecy, or as metaphysics reduced to ideology.

Socialism and the American Worker

But how can we be satisfied with this critique? Not only does it remain a critique of ideology, but it also presupposes, more or less consciously, that its object is constituted in the last instance by ideology. Socialism's image as an epochal political and organizational force, whose structure is grounded, however, on the effectiveness of ideological appeal, of the invocation of ends; it is such a reduction to make the subsequent critical operation politically sensible. In fact, it is for this reason, that the critique of ideology becomes politics, an effective moment of political struggle. But it is precisely this shift that is problematic. Is the substance of socialism an ideology? Is it ideological pauperism? And after having analyzed and criticized it, can one believe that it dealt a decisive blow to the socialist political organization? Or is there a specific autonomy of this organization with respect to its ideological expressions, an autonomy that makes possible its capacity and explains its effectiveness? The question of socialism is not resolved at all within the sphere of a critique of socialist ideology. This critique does not explain the foundations of the real movement expressed and represented by socialism, and therefore does not seem capable of contrasting it politically. The vulgar technocratic utopia that applies to the crisis of ideology, the proverbial *urbis et orbis*, does not even touch the authors considered here. Socialism's ideology has to be accounted for in terms of economical and institutional transformations, and in its relation to them. The lines of strength and frailty emerging from this analysis make possible to situate and define that decisive political process that, conventionally, we call socialism.

In this sense, it is useful to compare Weber's program, so far outlined, and Sombart's essay of 1906 on socialism in the United States.[11] Weber's question concerning essentially the very possibility of socialism is here already explicitly formulated, and it is significant that the answer given does not deal at all with traditional ideological reasons. In Sombart, the political ineffectiveness of a socialist critique of ideology is taken for granted. What is examined and what is fascinating in the American experience is the critique of things that appear to have been realized there versus socialism. If we study such an experience, the lines of a political program can be seen to emerge—not only, and at last, theoretical and scientific. In other words, if that critique of ideology, which in Europe has already given important results, can be redefined within the sphere of a concrete political program, which disposes of its own credible models, it is possible to posit sensibly the question of the overcoming of socialism. Therefore, the study of the United States is seminal in this twofold and complementary direction. On one hand, it makes possible the definition of a model of social-political organization *without* socialism, a model of the nonexistence

of socialism. On the other hand, this same model renders apparent, indirectly, the overall economic-institutional reasons at the bases of socialist
organization, its effectiveness and its development, despite any "critical-
critical" effort on the side of ideologies.

How is it possible that in a country with the greatest capitalistic development there is no socialism? That in this "country of our future" there
is a great labor force "that is basically not socialist"? Will the social future
of the United States move in the same direction as the European one, or
vice versa? "For the social politicians there is nothing more important"
than trying to answer these questions. Sombart's answer takes its starting
point from an analysis of the behavior and the ideology of the American
worker. This part is the least successful and thought out of the essay. We
find all the commonplaces on the worker's patriotic identification with the
system and on union integration. More interesting, but equally dated, the
pages on the political system and on parties where the diversity with respect to the European situation is derived from the "total absence of principles" that characterizes the American political party system, and from
the almost insurmountable obstacles that the spoil system opposes to the
birth of competing political forces and, also, therefore, to the establishment of a social democracy. The clue to Sombart's answer is to be found
elsewhere and, precisely, in the happy combination between "the fact that
American capitalism developed in a country with enormous free land
space" and the emphasis on the radically democratic character of the Constitution and of American political life. On one hand, the American industrial takeoff occurred in the presence of humanly and economically valid
alternatives to the factory system, in situations that made actual freedom
of choice possible for the labor force; on the other hand, and thanks to
this phenomenon, the process of democratization of political and social
life has taken on such wide and profound proportions to involve the very
same common sense of the people (this process, according to Sombart,
also involves industrial relations). In short, the decisive factor that explains
the nonexistence of socialism in the country that by now is the leader of
capitalism is the democratic form of American public life.

The political program that emerges from Sombart's paper, therefore,
and that reorganizes and consolidates the socialist critique of ideology, is
based on setting up wide processes of democratization, not only of institutional apparatuses but of economic life as well.

This is the pivot for a political confrontation with socialism. Here, the
virtue of a new national liberal ruling force, opposed to Wilhelmine conservative liberalism, should be measured. In more general terms, but that

at the same time indicate the direction the discourse is taking, this political program is based on two complementary propositions: that socialism can be developed out of the contradiction between capitalist development and democratization, and that this contradiction can not only be resolved but there also can be complete convergence between unfolding capitalist spirit and radical democratization, as the American example shows us. This is the conclusion that seems to emerge forcefully from Sombart's study. And yet, it contrasts with Sombart's conclusion that the reasons that have made impossible the development of socialism in the United States are slowly disappearing, and that one expects its full blossoming in the next generation. The proof of this statement is postponed to further studies, which have never been done.[12] How can we explain this apparent, abrupt twist in Sombart's thinking?

The problem of socialism has shifted inadvertently to that of democratization. The times and forms of democratization will explain socialism. It is possible to maintain that the material conditions of the American take off will deplete, or are already in the process of depletion, but this has nothing to do with the political constitution, the radical democracy of the United States. Is this, then, the democracy that Sombart believes to be in danger? Is this why he expects a full blossoming of socialism even in the model country of its nonexistence? I believe that an answer lies deeper, and within the context of Weber's research (from Weber to Schumpeter) on democratization. These are the problems and contradictions of the democratic state, which, emerging historically and theoretically, seem to render it powerless again with respect to socialism as real movement and organization. The critique of socialist ideology can become the political critique of socialism only through an adventurous critique of the democratic state form itself.

The Specter of Bureaucracy

Can this form support Sombart's program? For Sombart, his own intellectual and political experiences suffice to reply.[13] But that program was in sympathy with the one "desperately" pursued by Weber. Is there in Weber a critique of democratic form capable of demonstrating its political effectiveness versus socialism? Is there in Weber a form of democratization capable of neutralizing and integrating socialism, by putting into question its historical and material conditions?[14] This critique is not satisfactory. Even more lucid than in Sombart is Weber's representation of democracy as bureaucratized democracy. The best guarantee of the democratic system's tenure is in the professional effectiveness of its bureaucratic structures. These structures are dominant in political life as in the economic one. The new industrial organizations—and the overcoming of the nineteenth-century idea of market that they carry out—are but the most accomplished manifestation of this process and of this destiny. But the complementariness of democratization and bureaucratization makes even more evanescent the political effectiveness of democracy versus socialism, and the comparison with it seems still destined to be reduced to an enlightenment sermonizing. Here, however, the argument has made a jump forward. We have singled out a precise line of weakness in democratic form. As mere bureaucratization (this is also what emerges from Sombart's analysis of American political parties) democracy "intends" socialism. Conversely, if democracy does not develop in a bureaucratic sense, it will end up by contradicting the essential productive forces of contemporary life, by appearing to them as an idle superstructure, without any actual authority. This process, too, produces socialism. If bureaucratization cannot reduce democracy to mere formalism, then the democratization of social life, the forms of political participation that it requires, cannot spectralize the effectiveness and authority of the bureaucratic structure, without which democracy does not seem legitimate today. On one hand, socialism is produced by the tendency to bureaucratic incorporation of democracy and, on the other, by the tendency to the disintegration of bureaucratic structure on the part of disclosed democracy. In the first case, socialism is request for representativity and participation, in the latter for stability and harmony. This duplicity of socialism is, however, politically grounded. It does not derive from ideological-prophetic enchantments but from the particular aporias of democratization. To confront them is equivalent to confronting the problem of socialism.

The weakness of Kelsen's *apologia* (*Socialismo*, lvii–lxv) seems clear. It is developed at an almost exclusively methodological level. Democracy is a problem, insofar as it must remain a *quaestio facti*, dissolution of every absolute value, an endless search for compromise. Democracy is expression of political relativism and, therefore, it not only presupposes a minority, but coherently pursues its defense. This antitheological definition of democracy is not capable in any way to confront the particular aporias that tend to disintegrate its structure. The question, in fact, does not concern the relativism of democracy (coherent with the epistemological turning-point of century's end—and Machian—for Kelsen, in particular), but the

political effectiveness of this relativism, specifically, its power versus socialist ideas and organizations. In the end, even in *Socialism and State*, socialism is not criticized through a political critique of democracy but as
ideology and/or metaphysics. The simple methodological-formal construction of democracy still compels to a critique of socialist ideology.
This insuperable limitation of Kelsen's analysis seems to me to be at the
heart of Schmitt's critique (*Socialismo*, cxi, clii), and of Scheler's and
Schumpeter's.[15] Such a critique involves the very real functioning, the very
constitution of the Weimar Republic. In this critique, and in the social
democratic political and parliamentarian praxis, Kelsen's neo-Kantianism,
which makes possible the inference of the community (*Gemeinwesen*) from
the identification of state and norm, remains intrinsically unable of capturing dynamically and conflictually the process of democratization. And yet,
such critique is more valuable than Weber's political, whose problematic
involves exactly that aporetic interlacement of democracy and bureaucratization, from whose development depend, in one, the destinies of democracy and those of socialism.

Weber's answer to this question is extremely complex. For democracy,
the necessary condition of success is that political competitiveness can
guarantee the self-assertion of "guiding spirits," capable of employing bureaucratic structures or preventing their institutionalizing tendencies. A
situation of tense competitiveness is the sole ground on which an effective
autonomy of the political can be produced. Weber studies the process of
parliamentarization (Mommsen, *Max Weber*, 188) entirely in this direction, for this purpose. If democratization succeeds in giving life to a parliament where the competitive mechanisms, far from provoking neutralizing
compromises, lead to the affirmation of leadership capable of deciding on
actual questions, beyond all theological pretense, this outcome can, on one
hand, confront effectively the inevitable knot of the relation with bureaucracy, and, on the other, liquidate the essential reason of socialist struggle:
the demand for general representation (which can also be reduced tacti-
cally to a demand for participation in government). If parliamentarization
guarantees such competitiveness, socialism will have to measure up concretely on its ground, on the ground of its actual political immanence.
From this confrontation, the evolutionary perspective that Weber points
out in *Socialism* will be either radically defeated or entirely transformed.

But this reasoning is kept entirely formal. The competitiveness of parliament, which ought to produce that guiding spirit (*leitender Geist*) capable
of dominating bureaucracy, even though recognizing its necessity—
capable, that is, of embodying Kelsen's methodological relativism—is

based, in its turn, on a productive-neutralizing process. Parliamentary competitiveness can function solely through the formalization of conflicts produced by democratic life. The range of political decision has definite limits—if a subject gives signs of wanting to go beyond them, the democratic game comes to an end immediately. The game can never involve the rules of the game. In other words: none of the subjects in play turns out to be politically voidable. The decision concerns a conflict neutralized a priori. This makes possible that, intrinsically to the democratic organisms, conservative-neutralizing tendencies can develop, and that the moment of reflection on the compatibility and the rules of the game be asserted on the production of transforming leadership. Not only that, but this tendency also reintroduces in democratic relativism traditional theological aspects. In order to uphold their own autoconservative efforts, the political subjects of parliamentarization will tend to develop, in fact, their own common system of values, a substance in which they can recognize themselves together. The conservative tendency of democracy is sublimated thus in faithfulness to principles—and the democratic relativism, far from developing its revolutionary potentiality, is sublimated in a metaphysics of community, rich perhaps with nationalist inflexions.[16]

If democracy does not know how to react to this tendency, the process of parliamentarization not only does not contrast with the affirmation of the bureaucratic principle but also nourishes it, and for two complementary reasons. One is that a neutralizing practice bureaucratizes the same political subjects, and that, together, these subjects will always be amateurs of bureaucracy compared to expert, prestigious officials who are educated as specialists. True bureaucracy, therefore, will form the actual government, from which the same political men will be guided, in the end. Or the political, this bureaucratized political, will try to get rid of true bureaucracy—even appealing to democratic values—substituting it, in the key places, with men from the machinery. The political can also come out a winner in this struggle, if all the subjects that constitute it essentially agree to lead it. But this will lead to a terrible, techno-intellectual impoverishment, to a condition of blockage of the productive forces, to results that delegitimate the entire democratic force. The absence, together, of an effective autonomy of the political and of an authentic bureaucratic structure, will condemn democracy to the loss of any authority. Then, an always more cogent political demand for capable techno-specialistic structures of power will arise, which will end by liquidating the powerless resistance of the political democratic. Parliamentarization may assert itself as ground of real struggle, from which political decisions can emerge, whose subjects detain actual autonomy with respect to bureaucratic structures and given civil interests—as ground of struggle in continuous transformation, capable of guaranteeing the renewal of leadership and an effective relativism. Or democratic form will end by contradicting, by means of short cuts and detours more or less complex, the form of the contemporary social brain, specialized and bureaucratically organized.

Different Crises

But this initial conclusion raises more problems than it answers. And I am not referring particularly to the techno-institutional solution that Weber seems to offer to the problem of mobility of the managerial class, blocked by the pure parliamentarian game, namely, the presidential perspective, where the moment of custody of the Constitution and the decisional-innovative moment are contradictorily confused. I am referring to the more complex model that we can derive from Weber. The effectiveness of the parliamentary game seems to consist in keeping open the conditions of growth of particular branches of knowledge, of specializations that make up the social brain. In order to follow this growth, parliamentarization must be able to assert itself as an innovative process. But the form of these specializations is interpreted bureaucratically.[17] They do not reveal contradiction either among themselves or within themselves. The particular branches of knowledge pretend that the conditions for their growth are guaranteed. They pretend a state form relative to this end ("development of productive forces")—but they never act as political intention, they are never organized as political power. In Weber's model there is a functional division between the political and specialism, but in order to reach such an equilibrium one must reduce or formalize specialism to bureaucracy, however active, responsible, or educational it presents itself. If the linearity of the relation between specialism and bureaucracy is broken, and the particular types of knowledge are understood also in internal and reciprocal contradiction, as political intention, expectation of power, the decision that the political is called on to assume ceases from being able to be interpreted formalistically, within the framework of a constitutional *Grundnorm*, of an ideal community—and the democratic form itself comes into question. The actually diriment decision threatens democratic relativism, represses the aspirations of representation and participation, reproposes the caesaristic theme contained in the presidential model.

Therefore, the possibility of socialism—its a priori conditions—does not seem to be overcome by these deductions of democratic form. The democratization seems to be a tactical response to the real forces that from within reproduce socialism as real movement founded on real processes and contradictions. The same substantial ambiguity of socialism is coherent with the form of these processes and contradictions. *Capitalism, Socialism, Democracy* concludes this problematic arch, which begins with Weber's critique of liberalism and of nineteenth-century *Kathedersozialismus*. But between this conclusion and that beginning there are not just the events of Weimar, on which Schumpeter himself writes with a cold, Weber-like tone.[18] There is the Great Crash, first the formulation and later the assertion, after the war, of Keynes's economic policies. These epochal experiences find their more appropriate meaning within the framework of the confrontation between socialism and democracy. Even though critical at the analytical-scientific level and reductive in pointing to the importance in the history of economic thought, Schumpeter views Keynesianism as an authentic cultural revolution, through which theoretico-practical principles that undermine the capitalist social system are asserted as general objectives or common sense. Keynesianism materializes as labor capitalism, but this capitalism destroys the parameters, the centrality, the mindset that made it a system and that guaranteed its authority. The setting of capitalist competitiveness (in Schumpeter's discourse a factor absolutely irreducible to the legend of laissez-faire) goes hand in hand with parliamentary competitiveness, determining the affirmation of the techno-bureaucratic activity over the entrepreneurial-innovative one. The disappearance of the responsible entrepreneur, of the entrepreneurial call (*Beruf*), is at one with that of Weber's political, of every guiding spirit. But it becomes highly problematic to ask obedience to authorities by now absent. Socialism therefore does not appear any longer as an exogenous force that attacks, destroys, and substitutes the democratic mechanism and market economy. It is nothing but the development of this mechanism, the probable end (in no way predictable) of a process of continuous social transformation, even if slow and contradictory, of which the Great Crash is the formidable accelerator.[19]

Sombart concluded his already quoted study of 1906 in similar ways. Weber, too, does so when at the end of *Socialism* he states, "Workers will always be socialists in one way or another." In a certain way, the idea behind Schumpeter's greatest work is that democratization cannot overcome socialism, except that now Schumpeter is able to see organically the connection between capitalistic economic development, democratic fragility, and socialism. He can now disenchant Weber with respect to the antisocialist potentiality of democracy. And yet, especially here, between Keynes and Schumpeter, the theory and practice that socialism had developed suffers the most effective attack. Let us begin first, so to speak, with some methodological reasons. In Schumpeter, the recognition of socialism equals its radical reduction to *quaestio facti*. Socialism is entirely subsumed within the relativistic circle proper to democratization. The inquiry on the possibility of socialism is reduced to its capacity to function. Socialism seems possible as mechanism of economical and political management and administration. The devalued (*wertfrei*) viewpoint of the analysis is anything but painless with respect to its object: it formalizes it, tends to make it indifferent with respect to the social tendencies taking place, no longer content of a radical choice. This viewpoint is made plausible and, therefore, can actually appear neutral, insofar as it is certainly applicable to the capitalist system. But the representation of the capitalistic system as immanent crisis of value and therefore of the system itself, as mere machinery for development, makes socialism's pretense to establish itself as an alternative system or value—appear senseless. While that viewpoint is absolutely in agreement with what constitutes the power of contemporary capitalist reason (its functional relativism, the bureaucratic growth of special competences), the same viewpoint tends to delegitimate the socialist perspective, to the extent to which socialism relates to capitalism as system and presents an image of itself as comprehensive, alternative value. What Schumpeter means to get, therefore, is either the formal reduction of socialism to laborist capitalism or its autosublimation in pure ideology.

But these reasons follow along substantial transformations of economical functioning and of democracy itself. Democratization is anchored to the pursuit of determined objectives; it asserts and legitimates itself as a guarantee of specific solutions to determined problems, imposed by the great crisis years. On the classical themes of representation and participation follows the direct effort at defining some universally credible and desirable objectives and their satisfaction. The procedure is formally analogous to the one we have seen with respect to Weber's definition of marginal calculus. These politics do not come forward in any way as a promised land, new system, stability, or authentic representatives of human nature however defined, but rather as immanent calculus of concrete and priority problems, on the basis of vulgar experience. Democratic form finds legitimacy on the satisfaction of such problems. The instruments and economical mechanisms to reach this end are uniquely *quaestio*

facti. Because of the effectiveness of this political calculation and the economical instruments that it was able to use, an actual crisis of socialism
occurs between Keynes and Schumpeter. A formal democratization is neither opposed to it nor a simple ratio of marginal calculus is called to contradict the accusation of anarchy. Rather, decisional capacity is required,
determined from the field of action and techniques of political economy
that assume programming characteristics. The reality of this democratic
form—that ceases to oppose socialism on principle—consists of the degree
of satisfaction that it can guarantee to a definite system of needs. The
science of means, of which it disposes, and that neither Sombart nor
Weber nor Kelsen had at their disposal, is truly, in its apparent respite of
brief period or short term, the strategic lever with which socialism is all
together subsumed, formalized, and defused—with which its twofold instance of real democracy and effective state authority, of programmed intervention, is "vulgarly" realized.

One does not respond to this crisis of socialism by showing the crisis of
Keynesian's politics, of their sociopolitical paradigms, or of the equilibrium that they have made possible so far. These politics and these instruments have arisen, and have become effective, insofar as they were
temporary and partial. Their very same formal correctness stems from
precise limits, from clearly reductive hypotheses. The very meaning of the
term *crisis* therefore takes on, when compared to them, quite a different
sense from Marxism or the socialist tradition to which it refers. Actually,
to this crisis of socialism one can answer only by transforming it, by moving the entire theoretical and political structure.

Socialism and Alienation

It can no longer appear as a science of "what," or of how capitalism "is
going" on the basis of a privileged-hegemonic language (critique of political economy).[20] This science defines capitalism as system precisely for its
unprogrammability, capturing the permanent, substantial character of
capitalistic social relations precisely in their anarchy. On one hand, a similar science is more and more irrelevant. On the other, it shows a clear
imperative and normative character: the attainment of an authentic system
of total public-state programming. This imperative, in turn, is based on
the idea that the widest socialization of the productive forces coincides
with a process of real democratization, and that the end of this process, its
most deeply awaited promise, is a state of political tranquility (*Ruhe*), not

of perfect material satisfaction, rather, of perfect ethico-political satisfaction. The programming, that is, the development, the deepening of instruments and of the forms of programming intervention—is a factor in this teleological picture. Programming provides conscience and rationality to the material process of socialization, overcoming it, in the sense of *Aufhebung*, in real democratization tending to the state of dealienation, as perfect ethico-political tranquility. Alienation becomes, then, the key word, perhaps. The pivot of the socialist's critique of ideology, from which we started, concerns precisely the impossibility of overcoming alienation within the framework of the economical and political processes proposed and foreseen by socialism, and the inevitability of having to resort to naturalistic presuppositions in order to infer its notion. But the argument could also be overturned, and here we meet Weber again. One could state, in fact, that it is precisely the impossibility of overcoming alienation in the social relations of production—produced by the unfolding universe of technology—that constitutes the conditions for socialism, or the true name of socialism. Any move toward disenchantment, language hygiene, or ruthless reduction to the calculability of relations, also explains that these relations of production and their possible processes do not contain an answer to the problem of the overcoming of alienation. The critique of the theoretical groundlessness of socialism consists in the reaffirming of alienated relations, which socialism would not recognize as necessary. But their necessity is the very necessity of socialism.

This short-circuit leaves traces in Weber. The same contradictoriness of democratization in answering to socialism and the same aporetic character of the relations, which Weber would like to disentangle linearly, between socialization, bureaucratization, and specialism, are projected on the background of this question. The same scientific demonstration of the nondeductibility of a dealienating perspective, within the sphere of technology, renders inevitable the socialist attitude, the real movement we call socialism. Trying to understand the systematizing-totalizing theoretical claims that it has produced (the liquidation *more geometrico* of its teleological asset), only underlines its reasons even more. The same demonstration of the ethico-moral premises of the socialist objective—its idea of a political tranquility, so structurally contradictory with respect to the "restless heart" of technology, of which socialism too is a product, does not affect at all the question of the intrinsic relation between socialism and alienation. Weber explains it in the following terms: Socialism appears as that political-theoretical movement through which the materially irrational aspect of capitalist reason becomes apparent, resulting from

corporate control as a labor class, or from the dispossession of any decisional capacity of labor on the part of capitalistic discipline.[21] This alienation is irrational, in the sense that it has no rational foundation, that its
necessity is not deducible. But now the argument could be pursued further. This alienation refers to something even more general than the specific capitalistic form of the means of production. If in the place of the
corporate as class and of their discipline we put the governing of a state
bureaucracy that, let us suppose, may even believe to be acting according
to a goal of perfect democratization, the essential dispossession—which
concerns the decisional force, the power—persists or grows even stronger
(since the holder of power multiplies, loses physiognomy, becomes elusive). And even this form of organization of the social means of production is irrational, cannot show itself formally as necessary. It is a mere
possibility that, however, pretends to be necessary. To this, then, one
could counter with that political movement we call socialism, a political
possible we call socialism. The classical capitalistic control is not the only
one to appear irrational, but also the forms of the decisional process that
take shape in the universe of technology, because intrinsically alienating.
Socialism is the political affirmation of the nonnecessity of these forms.

Weber's *Kreis*, in order to respond to socialism, must picture it as an
image reducible to the reformism-extremism circuit between the Second
and Third International. This analysis and critique capture a very wide
phenomenological horizon but have no answer for the fundamental problem of the conditions of existence of socialism, as real political movement.
This critique does not succeed in dissolving its object because this object
was defined by means of a priori reductive operations. Only the analysis
of democratization and its contradictions allows, in the end, proposing the
problem in all its complexity. There is the possibility of socialism not as
an ideology of the end of the dealienated state, but as immanent critique
of the necessity of alienation. The sphere of this critique is political. It
defines alienation (it cannot but define it) politically, as concrete state of
the social means of production from whose contradictions concrete organizational and political movements can arise. The interest (*interesse*) of
these movements consists in preventing that the bureaucratization processes, which constitute the immanent notion of alienation, organize
themselves in separate totalities, strengthening within each single form.
What can be understood from within these movements, this interest?
What is made transparent, according to this point of view, which the mere
affirming of the necessity of alienation cannot grasp? The often subterranean breakthrough movements that are at work in every language, the

endless transformation of boundaries between one and the other, and, more generally, the impossibility for this state (thus constituted on the fundamental irrationality of the relations of alienation) to impose as totality the sum of its constituted forms. The intrinsic character of socialism and alienation is the immanent critique to the existing system, the emptying and breaking through of the existing as system.

Does this mean waiting for an end? Is it a waiting or a preserving mode? Or is it a mere pushing beyond languages in their instinct of spiritualized power?[22] Is it a way of repeating the wait, not betraying it anymore in the guise of scientific prediction or ideological prophecy? Or a productive transforming of languages? A form of their actual productivity? Perhaps one and the other, according to chance, "without quality." Perhaps, the activist "in his anxious actions is in his own way also a dreamer of God."[23] And perhaps, in order to dream the dreams of God, it is necessary to understand the ways of the world, with a lot of worldly clarity.

CHAPTER 4

Project

Ambiguity of Terminology

What do we mean by the term *project*? The question seems just as super-fluous as it is normal-sounding in our language. Its basic emphasis is simi-lar to technology. One only truly disposes of the world when there are paradigms at one's disposal that make it available. The present dominion has actual value only insofar as it is productive of future dominion. *Produc-ing* and *project* are joint terms representing, in our language, a single fam-ily. The project is understood as intrinsically productive: it elaborates models of production. Producing is included in the project whose meaning and purpose it illuminates. In the project, therefore, it is question of a strategy on whose basis something must be produced, something must be brought out, to presence. The project foresees, so to speak, this future presence; it unfolds its character in advance. But in the project, precisely, one is not limited to "project" (*ideare*) this presence; one also has to show with what means and in what ways presence is actually producible. The tone of the project, therefore, is that of anticipation, of prediction and of concrete production. Let us keep this point firmly in mind—whereby in the term *project* we mean essentially the techno-scientific project—before returning to it critically. It is also necessary to realize how the anticipating emphasis of the "pro" tends to conceal a presupposition. It is as if in the project a predictive-productive force was being expressed free from any presupposition (the German term *Gesetz*, law, is the exact translation of presupposition), a way-in-the-future without a way-from. As we will see, this connects since its inception the term *project* and its family to that of "freedom." It is easy to realize that the essential content of freedom consists for us in being able to project. And so much richer this freedom appears to us, as the projecting ability seems free from any presupposition. But this is not to be taken entirely for granted. If we analyze, for example, the German term *Entwurf*, then the root of the project reemerges with force. In the *ent-*, the anticipation, the before (*avanti*) do not resound; what resounds, rather, is the way-from, the separation-from, the departing—not so much the constructive-productive in its advance, as much as the destructive or the overcoming. In *Entwurf* one perceives the "pull" (*strappo*) of the "throw" (*lancio*), not its eventual prefiguring, predictive force. Thus, in terms such as *Entwicklung* or *Entfaltung*, the *techné* of unfolding, of unwinding, of developing is portrayed with its eyes turned backward: to the "already developed" that must be newly unfolded, to the refolded, to the "congealed" that must be disentangled, unraveled, analyzed.[1] It is in the *Fortschritt* (progress), in any case, that we find the tone of the project. The term *project* is proper to the overall aura of progress, while in *Entwurf* this tonality is extremely faded, if not absent. In it one thinks the hardness of the presupposition to be removed, the laborious flowing toward the presence beginning from an obscure, an unknown. This presupposition is precisely the compact, the immediate, to be deconstructed, mediated, analyzed. And in the *ent-* resounds exactly this *de-*: the dramatics of an analytic-deconstructive work, suspended on the "beyond" that in the term *project* instead is announced, predicted, prefigured, anticipated with so much certainty.

Because of these considerations, too, Heidegger's *Entwurf* does not seem to be translatable as "project." Heidegger asks, "Why does the understanding—whatever may be the essential dimensions of that which can be disclosed in it—always press forward into possibilities?"[2] Why in the understanding (*Verstehen*) the mode of being of *Dasein* is potentiality-for-Being? (And here potentiality-for-Being does not indicate a fluctuating *libertas indifferentiae*, but "the most original and extremely positive ontological determination of *Dasein*"). "It is because the understanding has in itself the existential structure which we call *projection* (*Entwurf*)." Understanding has projecting character. *Dasein* is "thrown in to the kind of being which we call projecting." Therefore, the project itself, so understood, belongs to that "ontologico-existential constitution of being precisely within the sphere of the actual potentiality-for-being." Heidegger's *Entwurf* has nothing to do with a techno-scientific plan, with the anticipating predictive-productive dimension of the project, with its inevitable progressive aura. Heidegger's *Entwurf* constitutes the mode of *Dasein as thrown*. In *Entwurf*, *Dasein* is caught as constitutively projecting "possibility as possibility." *Dasein is* project (*Entwurf*)—the project belongs to its ontological determination. Therefore, the emphasis cannot fall here on the not yet present—indicated by the *pro-* and in whose sight it would be positioned, but on the actual structure of *Dasein*. To think of the content of the project (*Entwurf*) as what one projects onto means degrading the projected to "a given and existing thought," to something external and extrinsic with respect to the essential dimensions of *Dasein*.

To what extent Heidegger's phenomenology is decisive for the later political-philosophical culture, lies outside our present purpose.[3] Its essential gesture almost consists in removing the term *project*, *Entwurf*, from the family of progress, *Fortschritt*, in defining the project as an original existential structure, disentangling it from the onto which it is projected, from the factual determination of the not yet present. The project, here, does not pierce at all the being-thrown, since the projecting is essential determination of our being-thrown. Radically understood, the project reveals the structure of being-thrown—is this, the *Verfallen*, the horizon within which the analysis unfolds. We should have, therefore, at least three areas of definition of our term: (1) the one most immediately evident in the project, devoted to the production of the projected, which is prefigured and anticipated in the project; (2) the one which emphasizes the "tear" (*strappo*) of the presupposed, the being-*thrown*-away-from, in a continuous deconstructive work of the already unfolded, already entangled; (3) and that which conceives the project as ontologically constitutive of *Dasein* as *thrown*, and therefore, somehow, reassimilates it fully to the presupposed. Only in the first instance, for the first area, the term *project* seems appropriate. For the second area, *Entwurf* is rather valid. For the third, *Entwurf* can only be valid as opposed to project and recalling the presupposed with respect to the content anticipated by the project, but takes on a tonality of its own only within the overall framework of being-thrown, of *Verfallen*. It is as if, in this case, the tear (*strappo*) belonged constitutively to *Dasein* and did not arise as choice or decision. In this *Entwurf* one becomes what one is; the *ent-* leads away, "seduces," in order to lead back to the root—absent *epistrophe* in the previous two areas.

It is deeply meaningful that these differences seem today almost unnoticeable and that the project as productive construction, anticipation of the projected and strategy for pursuing it, dominates unchallenged in our language. Within the sphere of numerous existential-psychological arrangements that make up contemporary babble we have arrived, in fact, at the point of conceiving in substantial terms these very same differences. Since understanding is constitutively projecting, we may tear ourselves away from every presupposed, and since we are free from every already developed thing, we can proceed further, progress, and in this projecting process, anticipate destinations, ends to be pursued concretely, to be produced actually, that is, leading them to full presence. The dominant project is not at all interested that *Entwurf*, as ontological constitution, is constantly more than any simple presence, or, better, ontologically different from itself. Or, on one hand, that the throwing itself away from the presupposed may realize dramatically its difference from Heidegger's *Entwurf*. On the other, the dominant project knows nothing of determined contents of its potentiality-for-being. And yet we must recognize the dominance of the current notion of the project in order to define its limits, problems, aporias. Let us take heed of a note from Derrida that it is not a question of rejecting this notion of project; it is a question of not thinking of it anymore naively, as a kind of first idea, and of placing in evidence its "systematic solidarity" with other notions and other concepts.[4] It is a question of "closing it" in its constitutive limits without believing that this operation coincides with warranting its end. "What is seized in the *clôture* can continue indefinitely."[5]

The essential of the project consists in the anticipating word. This word constructs its own objective and makes available becoming, bending it to its pursuit. The project appears constitutively logocentric. Everything that is in the "meanwhile" between its original word and the realization of its goal (*telos*) carries out a techno-instrumental function, a secondary function, a simple explication of the idea. The essential, precisely, is in that original potentiality-for-seeing the projected as actually realized: the "meanwhile" is bent to this line. The ideal, in fact, would be the abolition of "meanwhile," the perfect coincidence between the point of the prefiguring-anticipating idea and the line that realizes it, that is, which is logically the same thing, the perfect deduction of the line from that point: *linea est puncti evolutio*. In the project becoming is thought as this *evolutio*. The more the project is powerful the more it will be able to force becoming to *explicatio* or *evolutio*. And if "meanwhile" is reduced to *explicatio* of the idea already implicit in the original project, its secondary, instrumental or merely representative character becomes evident. The project, in this sense, belongs entirely to the epoch of the *logos*, explains one of its essential dimensions, the "fall" of becoming into a chain of "meanwhiles," whose only meaning consists in the mediation which is at work in them between original idea and its incarnation. One should remember what was said at the beginning with regard to the term *project*: in it the fundamental accent falls on freedom from the presupposed, on the predictive-anticipating value of the *pro-*. In the project one pursues an end freely fixed that is to be pursued with as much effectiveness and determination to linearize the distance, the "meanwhile," between its ideation and actual attainment. Now here appears the aporia that closes the project. On one hand, as eliminating or overcoming the presupposed (an abrogation—*Abschaffung* —rather than an overcoming—*Aufhebung*), the project must spill entirely into becoming.[6] It can be understood only as freedom from the presupposed, from every firm foundation (*fundamentum inconcussum*), and therefore its purpose cannot be understood as renewal (*renovatio*) or reintegration of the original order (we shall return on these aspects of the problem). Its teleology is in reality a complex of partial teleologies, spilled in the historical and contingent. The process that leads to this outcome is long and twisted, but its conclusion is predestined: a long process of secularization of the apocalyptical that ends in the total oblivion of its origin, in the definition of multiple objectives arranged in a purely linear time, without conclusion and without return. On the other hand, the project must count as elimination of becoming itself, its reduction to "meanwhile" deprived of any proper sense, a line destined to explicating perfectly its logocentric character, mere practical facticity, superficial, dominated by the plane of the *logos*. But this entails that the very same thinking that founds the project be thought as presupposed. Therefore, the term *project* can be thought of only in this ontotheological sphere, even though it conceals in its very name this systematic solidarity. On one hand, the project posits itself as free productive force, endless constructivity, but, on the other, being continuously forced to reduce becoming itself to mere signifying of its own original *logos*, it returns to an idea of the presupposed: it makes of the original idea the new presupposed—of the thought from which it derives the new foundation.[7]

The more this aporia is manifested, the more secularly the project abandons any pretext to count as incontrovertible prediction. As we have seen, the abandonment of the foundation, of the unchangeable presupposed, is in the fate of the term. In this, the project opens up to becoming. The search for dominating becoming (perfectly precapturing the events) belongs to the initial epistemological dream of technology.[8] The project will be all the more perfect, the more it will recognize the groundlessness of this dream, the absolute possibility of irruption by chance, of the unforeseen, as constitutive of becoming, and this becoming it will want to understand and dominate. Once the project acknowledges to not being episteme, it can happen to it "to be the most powerful form of dominion" (Severino). But its statistical-probabilistic flexion does not overcome the fundamental aporia: the logical development, the *explicatio*, of its original statute. This aporia makes explicit the distancing from any idea of presupposed. On the other hand, it preserves intact the project's will to power. In fact, it leads it to perfection. In order to dominate becoming effectively it is necessary to recognize the arbitrary character of every regularity, it is necessary to construct in probabilistic terms the anticipatory models. We will discover that the most powerful anticipatory forms are, precisely, those that have more clearly abandoned every deterministic illusion. The project appears, thus, finally, as anticipation of chance: the anticipated chance no longer surprises nor irrupts; it is a priori "accounted for" within the grid of the project, which, in its turn, frees itself from any eschatological characteristic to be transformed in techno-experimental apparatus devoted to the effective pursuit of contingent objectives.

Grammatology of the Project

The contemporary philosophy of the project is constituted by the will of taking chance for granted, of controlling-dominating the unpredictable itself. It represents the greatest form of openness to becoming and of abandonment to every presupposition just as it is, at the same time, the greatest form of elimination (*Abschaffung*) of becoming. The project, finally, knows itself and knows with whom it is dealing with. It no longer understands its own thought as new incontrovertible foundation, new immutable. It no longer understands becoming in a deterministic sense and, therefore, available to an absolute prevision. Precisely for this reason, its thought, no longer surprised by chance or by the unforeseeable, dominates becoming now all the more perfectly—precisely for this reason, it can now manage it—rule it, that is, conceive it as simple representative place of its power, mere "meanwhile." Thus, inevitably, the ontoteleological origins of the project reemerge. The free eradication from the presupposed, the greatest openness to becoming, ends up by coinciding with the liquidation of the latter (as groundless as it is disenchanted by every epistemic dream).

Conversely (it is the same movement on the other verse), the presumed dominion of becoming (because it is groundless, knowingly precarious and revocable in doubt, always relative) must constantly return to the autonomous existence of becoming. The project, in the fundamental tone of its "pro," wants constantly that becoming *be* (as we have seen, with *Entwurf* the case is different) and at the same time removing-liquidating becoming, reducing its unpredictability, linearizing it, or, in any case, administering and governing any exception. In the project (and the understanding of technology is projecting) becoming is seen as progress (*Fortschritt*), that is, one wants its liquidation—but, at the same time, because this dominion on becoming may be possible and may be repeated indefinitely (according to the indefinite line that is the time of the project), one wants continuously becoming itself as such.

It is possible to think of opposing the logocentrism of the project along two perspectives, essentially reducible to one another. We could define the first as "grammatological." It sees in the contents of the project (in the projected) not the signifying of the original *logos*, mere image or figuration of its language, but *programs*, systems of conventional signs (*grammata*) endowed of intrinsic rationality, not external and instrumental films of the true word. A programmatology deconstructs the founding links and connections of a still symbolic reading of the relation between project and praxis. Therefore, there would not be project, but only writing program, its pluridimensionality delinearized in opposition to the linear unidimensionality of the project. In such pluridimensionality, the programs are linked together and relate differently according to syntheses and deferments "which prevent that at any moment and in any sense a simple element may be *present* in itself and refer only to itself" (*Positions*, 62).[9] Therefore, it is not a question of substituting to the simplicity and to the presence of the projecting *logos* a more elementary simplicity, that of the program, but of conceiving the latter, always according to Derrida's expression, as a play of differences, a system of signs referring to one another, in continuous transformation, where nothing is simply present or absent. The center of the projecting thought is not replaced by another center, but, instead, by the endless deconstructive work, claiming to produce the plenitude of absolute presence, the play of pro*grammatic* differences.

The second line of response to the projecting logocentrism is rather assimilable to certain Anglo-Saxon analytical reading of Wittgenstein.[10] Apparently, it is opposed to the grammatological one for its strong insistence on factors of habit, custom, training implied by understanding. This line seems to reduce the projecting emphasis of understanding, still evident in its own programmatic deconstruction. One does not understand that by participating, so to speak, in linguistic institutions, the tradition functions here always as presupposed—a secular presupposed, to be sure, represented by concretely happened forms of openness to the world, by linguistic games actually played. What is original is not the thought that projects, but these forms and these games in whose limits (in the limits of whose employ) we understand and project in our turn. It is debatable whether in this line there is "bourgeoisification" of Wittgenstein's dramatics ("When I choose the rule, I don't choose. I follow the rule blindly") in the sense of a paradoxical "blind choosing-deciding."[11] What is certain is the falling of every emphasis or presumed liberation from the term *project*, its fundamental reduction to an intrinsic modality of a historical-relative understanding.

Neither of the two approaches, however, seems to us to exceed that aporia that determines the closure of the project. Meanwhile, they meet on an essential point: the critique of the idea of a unique language representing the world, the absence of simple elements and perfectly present to themselves in the linguistic play. What they affirm positively is the notion of text, never complete, never perfect, of signs relative to one another, never comprehensible in themselves. The project is transformed here, precisely, in a text of pro*grams*, an open system of conventional signs that explain their own reason only in their play of differences. Whether the affinity between analytical and grammatological approaches is philosophically demonstrable, there remains the common deconstructive task of the project's metaphysical system. But this task—and this is the point—turns against the idea of a project still "enchanted" on the firm foundation (*fundamentum inconcussum*) of a Cartesian cogito, not to the project as will of control or rule of the unforeseeable itself. A similar flexion of the project will be necessarily analytical-grammatological, eradicated from any metaphysical assumption, from any general language, "thrown" on the inside of different games. To define the project of chance entails necessarily a conception of becoming as delinearized pluridimensionality and its languages as systems of sign relative to one another. Here we can conclude only what was already explicit in the fate of the term itself. The project will be the more powerful the more programmatically analyzable and analyzed it is. If the project must have value, it can only have value according to this form. Beside, in Derrida, the adherence of grammatological work to this destiny is clear. In his work there are many references to the challenge on the part of the sciences to the imperialism of the *logos*, especially by theoretical mathematics and the sciences of information. Clearly, Derrida was among the first to have sensed in these practices considerable traces of a comprehensive process of deconstruction of all significations dependent on the truth-presence of the *logos*, and, therefore, of truth itself. Contemporary science itself practices that deconstruction pursued by grammatology. The grammatological program is perfectly in agreement with the scientific project that today is expressed as statistical-probabilistic anticipation of chance. This program can be defined in an antimetaphysical sense only on the basis of a naïve and reductive meaning of metaphysics, and not according to the original inspiration which animates it, and which is realized, instead, in all its power, in the secularization and rationalization of the idea of the project.

The State of the Project

The previous linguistic analysis, it is worth repeating it, did not go beyond or overcome the term *project*. It only contested the immediate natural assumption often made of it, trying to show the solidarity of the project with a reinterpreted metaphysical horizon, and, together, the substantial concordance with the programs of techno-scientific rationalization. It is relatively easier, at this point, to attempt a phenomenology of the political project, not only because we dispose of a picture of the limits of the term, but also because this picture already helps us to conclude on the growing harmonization between criteria of the political and criteria of techno-scientific rationality, between reason of political programs and reason of scientific ones. The reference to the political was therefore transparent even in the pages devoted to the philosophy of the project.

The projecting emphasis is the particular tonality of the era of the political. In fact, it corresponds to a decisive break in its history. Albeit slowly and through dramatic contradictions, the era of the political asserts the idea that the forms of power are artificial constructions, whose duration, and ability to resist are directly proportional to the effectiveness with which the forms of power know how to anticipate and govern the unpredictable, the irruption of chance (whose possibility cannot be eliminated). The virtue (*virtus*) of duration against the chance (*tyche*) of the event, a collision renewed incessantly that ends up by admitting only programs, without ever finding the solution.

There is only ambiguity in speaking of project, and of political project, where source and sense of power seem, instead, to be truly ontotheologically founded. Project occurs only there where one may break away from a similar assumption. Therefore, the understanding that the Christian Republic has of itself is essentially antiprojecting, as meaning consists in maintaining the unity and the general ordering of the eon, until its fulfillment, against any *seduction*.[12] To seduce is *to throw* power beyond its foundation, attempting mere ethico-worldly justifications. Any traditional authority has an even more general diabolical vision of the project, namely, a vision of the irrepressible projecting dimension that seems proper of understanding itself.

The project becomes a key term only in an epoch of rationalization and secularization of the political, following a long "meanwhile" of hard struggle in whose center lies the deconstruction of the Christian Republic. Up to its extreme results, which we have already outlined, the term *project* marks the dominion of the calculating intellect, free from assumptions on the complexity of the political—an epoch in which intellectualization of action and political form becomes more and more exhaustive. The same professionalization of politics, which in contemporary "party states" reaches capillary results, belongs entirely to the sense of this process. It is the intrinsic ratio of the projecting calculus that must be asserted, for its own evidence and compelling logic, outside traditional values, not empirically controllable. This is equivalent to affirming that the possibility of being managed by techno-administrative apparatuses, by professionals of the government, is inherent in the project. We shall see to what aporias this possibility gives way. It suffices at the moment to understand the historical-determined meaning of the term *project*, to connect it strictly to what the project is thinking, to its "projected." The project is a project of state, as concrete concept, specific to a determined epoch (Schmitt, *Verfassungsrechtliche Aufsätze*). Project and state are not conceivable separately. On one hand there is the state, not *polis*, not *respublica*, neutralization of the religious war in as much as detheologization of political life, vehicle of secularization, mortal God.[13] On the other, there is the form of the project, critique of every traditional authority, embodying virtue of duration, resistance, capacity of anticipating the events that dominate what is by now secularized becoming, totally extraneous to the eschatological orientation of the Christian Republic's time. The state recognizes its own exceptionality—the exceptionality of a supreme power rationally founded, not limited by traditional laws, that is, free of assumptions (law/*Gesetz*). Even the obedience owed to this extraordinary authority (since such is a completely secularized authority), however absolute, is always reasonable. It is founded on a contract with the sovereign thanks to whom the separate egoistic interests coexist finally in peace.[14] And maybe in this reduction of the idea of peace to the dimension of security and satisfaction of egoistic interests, of the exchange between them, of their almost physically calculable equilibrium, lies the most revolutionary trait of the modern political. It goes together with the idea of a society as artificial body, the loss of any organic characterization, an idea that will find fulfillment in the ratio of political economy. But all this is none other than the projected of the project, the translation of *demos* and *populus* in *societas* of *pax* in equilibrium of intents. Only the liquidation of every traditional organicism, of every symbolic holding between social and political, of every symbolism of the political itself, makes possible the project as calculus, rational will of power, constructive force. The project makes of the social an analyzable artificial body—the new sovereign has value only with respect to such a body. He is, therefore, the strength that projects and reprojects constantly the artificiality of *societas*.

But project and state are also connected by more internal and essential lines, and here are very much a propos the considerations developed in the first part of this study. The radical groundlessness of any claim to interpreting in an ontotheological sense the sovereignty of the state is manifest almost contemporaneously to its origin. Its construction is contingent and ephemeral as any human work, any artifice. The recognition of its condition indeed renders powerful the rationality of the state, and makes a science possible. Paradoxically, a science of this state is possible only by perfectly eradicating and throwing it in becoming. And yet, at the same time, at the very moment that the project of state (in both senses of the genitive) wants becoming to be this way, it also wants its arrest, its block, its suspension, or even its liquidation. It is a question, in fact, of a project of "state." The expression itself would be incomprehensible, if we had not already recognized the aporia that closes the term *project*. *Project* counts as radical openness to becoming and separation from the already unfolded, the "already been" (*già stato*), but at the same time wants *status*, wants to build a situation of equilibrium and synthesis before and against those same forces and those same processes that in violently contradicting themselves have obliged to unfold the already unfolded, to develop the already developed, forcing the "state" into becoming. The problematic character of the state, that is, its problematic nature, even though it unfolds only much later, during and after the crisis of the liberal state, it is already implicit, from this point of view, in its same origins.[15] In the state, a project of relative equilibrium, of profane peace, is articulated along norms that pretend absolute obedience—that want to count perfectly. In the term *state*, a project of ephemeral systematization of contradictions announces itself as synthesis and is organized to last, to be as if it should last eternally. And yet this project moves according to partial teleologies, it knows nothing of the ends to be reached. Its desperate search to be lasting is, literally, nonsensical. To the rationality that unfolds in analyzing and calculating these contradictions, in reconciling forces and means to contingent ends that one wants to pursue, corresponds the nonrationalizable ground of this will-to-last as long as possible whereas no end to duration is any longer recognizable. Once again, the grammatological inflection of the project decenters or disperses the aporia without resolving it. If the historical partiality and relativity of the project is made explicit in its programmatic deconstruction, it is indisputable, however, that this only goes to expand the notion of state, that the different programs aim at the construction of syntheses or "states." It is possible to state that just as the term *project* is in agreement (systematically in agreement) with the form of the modern rational state in the strong sense, so the term *program* concerns the structuring of contemporary democracies (or contemporary standardization of politics) for "competitive polyarchies with large pluralistic dissemination" (*Politica*, 208). This, however, does not overcome that aporia but emphasizes it and dramatizes it, since for a partial "state," for a center of interests *thrown* among the others, any symbolic understanding seems by now absolutely farcical, and, even more obviously, so does the irrational ground of its will to survival, that is, to demand obedience.

The entire Hegelian philosophy of the state develops in the presence of this problem. The method of its solution is indicated in the dialectic synthesis of becoming (*Werden*) and form (*Gestalt*), in the term *state*, whereby the state can be represented as form, as structure in continuous movement, a unified complex of norms and actual power to guarantee its respect on one hand and movement of free subjects on the other, moved by those interests and "appetites" of whom classical political economy offers a disenchanted image.[16] This synthesis (which corresponds, however, to the moment of perhaps widest apperception of the problematic character of the modern state) appears to be more rhetorical harmony than substantial reconciliation. Radically understood, these appetites contain nothing actually concerning the state. The state counts for them until and only as a guarantor of their possible satisfaction. Society, liberated from any organic ties, is resolved in the becoming of complexes contradictory among themselves, of material expectations and questions of power. The development of democratic society exalts the naturalness and rationality of unlimited desire against traditional conceptions that rejected it as greed, lust, sin, by emphasizing precisely its spiritual value, their being, after all, claims to power.[17] But a power that by now can only express the partisan will of partial subjects. This makes even more arcane the possibility of *reconciliation* in the state between becoming and form, of free movement and political structure.

Politics of Myth

It is as if the demythicization of the great traditional political form, operated by the modern state, grasped in its own critical fever its own project, what its own project thinks, namely, the concrete possibility of overcoming becoming, of posing it as "state." The project wants to think this possibility in rational-scientific form. The state that project wants to found will not need to appeal to any myth to legitimize its own sovereignty. The political project, as *Entwurf*, is, in its essence, demythicization (*Entmythisierung*). This is constantly affirmed and constantly contradicted. On one hand, the modern political project pretends to be of value, against any traditional political form, as it is perfectly justifiable in the eyes of pure reason (scrutiny of the solitary mind, *solius mentis inspectio*!). On the other hand, precisely the end that it pursues (placing the state of becoming, reconciling the contradiction, overcoming the conflict) continues to be predicated mythically or, any way, in forms in which the myth plays an essential role. There is a mythology specific to the modern political project, intrinsically contradictory to the logic of the term itself and yet inevitable. It is in the form of the project to want that becoming alone be—and to want at the same time that this becoming can be perfectly discountable or advanceable, namely, surmountable. But let us pause a little longer on this decisive point, returning to the initial explanation of the term *project*. If in *Entwurf* there are echoes of all the violence of the demythicizing break, in the project, as will to power on becoming, anticipatory constructive force, a politics of myth reappear so to speak.[18] The insurmountable differences raised by an exhaustive rationalization of the political project are skipped by the assertion of a will to power that still expresses itself mythically. Or, to put it better, the more intensely the will to make a state (*fare stato*) is expressed in the project, the more the project is project of great political form (and therefore more violent the separation with respect to the past), the greater the function of myth within it. The conditions of a perfect demythicization of the language of the political project would end up by threatening the very same projecting force, namely, with excluding or at least with suspending the concrete possibilities of itself as project of great political form, as an idea of reconciliation between becoming and form (*Werden* and *Gestalt*), however punctual and contingent, or grammatologically declined.

This aporia is at work in a key place for modern political thought, the demythicization of the term *revolution*. From the idea of a change to reform the social cosmos, to bring it back to its supratemporal order, only contingently seductive, the secularization of *re-* (*revolutio, renovatio,* etc.) linearizes the sense of the term, makes it synonymous with radical change or with simple progress.[19] The idea of an original "state" to be reintegrated goes against, in fact, the full openness to becoming inaugurated by the political project. The project that wants to make a state is intrinsically revolutionary, in this demythicized meaning. It conceives its "state" as new construction, as original political form. This state is not a renaissance but creation. While the sacred term *revolution* symbolizes an original justice, whose idea is precisely what legitimizes the concrete revolutionary act, the deconsecrated revolution wants to impose a new law, whose legitimacy consists in the intrinsic force of its coherence and rationality. The fact that the same term indicates two antithetical dimensions is in itself already extraordinary. A simple phenomenology of the modern use of the term *revolution* that would emphasize the mythical-sacred borrowings would still move along outside lines with respect to the essential problem: the inevitable permanence of a mythic foundation in the term, in contradiction with the sense of the political project and its source of legitimacy. The idea of totality, dominant in the old term, remains in the contemporary term, "total revolution."[20] The claim to totality belongs to *any* inflection of the term. What brings together, in substance, the new and artificial creation of the contemporary state and the reintegration of the worldly order as symbol of the cosmic order is the claim of totality by that creation and by this integration. One can speak of revolution only when the change is total, and not in the superficial sense that it grasps all the elements of society in their separateness, but in the sense that it changes the form, that is, the *Gestalt*. This claim is perfectly coherent with revolution as reintegration, perfectly nondeductible for revolution as social change that happens on the line of progress. On this line, nothing total could ever be said. Peace without God is preferable to a war with God, but it will never be affirmed as true peace. Therefore, when we speak of revolution within the sphere of the modern political project, we can speak of it, in principle, only in mythical form—and in a mythical form that by now is necessarily groundless.[21]

Freedom in Utopia

What legitimizes, or seems to ground, the revolutionary claim of the modern political project expresses the power that more radically contests its totality. The deconsecration of the *theatrum europaeum* allows only one thing to stand in common with the different states, everyone of which is equipped with its own exclusive law (*jus*), territory over which theologians have to keep silent (*silete theologi in munere alieno!*), namely, independence, freedom.[22] From that moment on, the raison d'être of every revolutionary project is freedom. The norm that legitimizes revolution, the revolutionary norm of the deconsecrated *theatrum europaeum*, is the absolute will of independence, freedom. This applies to the absolute state with respect to the medieval republic, as well as to the different subjects that slowly emerge on the scene of the single states. In the period of mass democracies this becomes almost commonsense. The idea of revolutionary change is licit in relation to the actual will to freedom exhibited by the project.

A greater difference would not be conceivable with respect to an onto-theological justification of revolution, a deeper separation from the idea of rebirth. But if we analyze more closely the key term *freedom*, we are immediately faced with a contradiction that, once again, can be overcome only in mythological form (and therefore through the reintroduction of elements that belong to the traditional-sacral period of the term). "Freedom is the result of the Art of freeing oneself and separating."[23] Free is he who has succeeded, happily succeeded, to break the bond of the presupposed throwing oneself over (*Entwurf* and project), unboundly (*solutus*), absolutely (*absolutus*). Hence the Cartesian *cogito* as new subject-foundation, hence the modern state, and as absolutely unbound, free, and autonomous—that is, endowed with one's own *nomos*, respecting exclusively one's own law and not a presupposed one, a *Gesetz*. It is of great importance—a decisive and constitutive feature of our culture—how in the term *absolutus*, which points to the project of freedom, we can hear a strong resonance of synthesis, conciliation, totality. But the term points exactly to its opposite. Freedom, the revolution that has freedom as its reason for being, frees from everything, constitutes as part, separates. To free oneself is to tear oneself definitively from any possible idea of totality. Being free is to renounce participation in any totality. It is a definitive critique of an idea of culture as organic complexity of different elements whose meaning is that they partake of and in such a culture.[24]

If freedom, therefore, is the justification for revolution, the revolutionary project will not be able to pretend any totality. In order to do so, it is forced to interpret mythologically the term *solutus, absolutus*, that is, the effect, the concrete result of one's own action. The project that renders into parts, and that coincides with the technical-scientific process of indefinite openness of human actions, is overturned in a project of reintegration of the whole. But it is not at all a question of an ideological overturning. This flexion of the term is the only one capable of rendering it available to express the will of "state," the will that becoming, to which we open radically, is reducible, however, to a progress that can be manipulated and anticipated. If the loosening and separation resulting from the vindication of freedom were to be assumed as such, their strength would explode the will of "state" of the project. Freedom is *de-cision*, a cutting away from the whole. Recognized in this form, freedom secularizes the concept of revolution to the point of rendering it equivalent to an uninterrupted transformation, a negation of "state." The project cannot want this. But it will not be able to draw a happy synthesis between revolution-freedom and revolution-totality, between the decisive eradication affirmed in the modern notion of freedom and its will of state imposed on becoming.

It is precisely this synthesis or this conciliation that constitutes the utopia of the modern political project. Or, better, the utopia appears exactly as the "nowhere" where the two dimensions of the project appear not separate and inseparable. Thus, far from being an almost evasive literary genre, or a mockery, utopia plays a constitutive role for the projecting dimension of the modern political. In it, absoluteness of freedom and totality, programmatic eradication and dissolution on one hand, and will of synthesis and state on the other, they all emerge with plastic evidence, laying bare in this fashion the intrinsically problematic structure of the political project. Separateness and totality dominate together in Utopia.[25] Separateness is even expressed physically as island (*insula*). The freedom of Utopia manifests, as its own a priori condition, the possibility of deciding the relation with the ancient mainland (*Terra firma*) and with its traditional *nomos*. And yet this revolutionary decision, even where it is no longer meant in the mythical sense of rebirth, is conceived as foundation of a new totality. The island is seen as whole, as autonomy. The project that tears definitively from the whole, from the culture of the organic totality, and thus founds the insuperable insularity of the separate, claims to reveal itself and to legitimize itself as project of total state. What is expressed in this claim is the totality of the separate, the impossibility of conceiving other than the separate, the free from the whole: the none-other-than-separate, as insuperable horizon of the project, emerges as new totality.

The freedom of Utopia is, literally, eradication (*Entortung*). But, as Carl Schmitt explains in one of the great books of our century (*Nomos*, 149), this does not stand for any fantastic process, rather for the destiny of the modern state and its law (*jus*). The negative relation to the *topos* that resounds in Utopia is equivalent to the overcoming, to the will to overcome all the founding places of the ancient *nomos*. The same rationalization of the law is an eradication process, whose intellectual universalism accompanies and scans the stages of a planetary market. The free trade that the latter imposes undermines not only traditional public law strictly linked to the idea of national, sovereign state, but also the same international law, rendered ghostly by the lack of proper space and place, simple "sequel of generalizations drawn from previous *cases* of dubious interpretation," simple "inflation of contradictory and empty pacts" (*Nomos*, 212). The becoming of the supranational economic market, of a socioeconomic global era, is asserted in its historico-contingent character as sequel of cases, unforeseeable for the order of the law, neither capable of being anticipated nor governed on the part of the state, on the part of what-has-been (*ciò-che-è-stato*). A general mobilization, opposed to the idea of totality as formed whole, puts an end to the centrality of the family of European states, a centrality guaranteed by the capacity of the political form of each state. The use of the very term *state* appears increasingly untenable. It shapes the passage from the medieval multiverse (*pluriversum*) of the cities that do not recognize any superior entities (*civitates superiorem non recognoscentes*) to the problem of form, of the political-legal structure in whose limits it is finally possible to mitigate the contradictions of this multiverse and the revolutionary process expressed by it. The same term *state*, however, no longer counts with respect to the nontotalizable generality, deprived of space and land, or with respect to contemporary political-economic interstate relations. And even less with respect to the ubiquity of the political (*Politica*, 210), of seats of power and decision making, of the destruction of every founding cultural homogeneity, within every single state.

It may be legitimate to suppose that an awareness of the destiny of the modern state may transpire in utopian form, and that, thereby, it may emphasize its own separateness, its own absolute freedom from the mainland of the European public right (*jus publicum*). In order to be true state it is necessary to sever itself radically from the European state. But the copresence, at times the immediate juxtaposition, of totality and separateness in the utopian project makes it quintessential of the intrinsically problematic form of the political project as such. In this sense, the utopian dimension in the modern political is structural, and therefore in one sense opposed to consolatory literatures and to ideologies that have taken over the term. Utopia, "nowhere," is authentic reconciliation between projecting freedom, as process irremediably turned to the constitution of parts, and will to power imposed on becoming, full dominion over its *cases*, their formalization (equally analogous to that mathematization of language that grammatological work ought finally liberate from the ties of logocentrism and phonologism). The revolutionary project that leads to the modern state is these two dimensions. The content of the utopian form is the same as that of the revolutionary project. One could even assert that, according to its original project, the modern state is conceivable only utopically and that the nowhere expresses the horizon, or the closure of the same state in its actuality. There is no state without revolutionary will to freedom, to eradication, and this resounds powerfully in Utopia. There is no revolutionary project without claim to totality, and this seems perfect only in Utopia. There is no state without the will that becoming has been, or takes on the trace of being, and this will is absolutely transparent in the island of Utopia (decided by the cases of becoming). Caught in their radicalness or at their edge, these elements are finally free to display all those effects that are devastating for the foundation of the state. Freedom and totality, separateness, eradication and political form give way to insoluble knots in their endless transformations, and become according to circumstances that are only from time to time programmable, within a general framework of irreversible deconstruction of the very terms of project and state.

Utopia, mind you, is not a mythological expression at all. In fact, its design is perfectly rational, ever since its origins as a pure product of the Enlightenment. Its rulers are the priests of reason, but of a reason, in fact, grounded on firm foundations, and not made up of contingent measurements and calculations between means and ends. Therein still subsists, without doubt, the symbolic humanist heritage, but by now entirely translated to express the problems of modern political form. The thing being that the search for the solution to this problem (also in a purely intellectual way) does not allow any other language than the language of that heritage, and therefore the mythological return appears inevitable. The eternal return of a politics of myth is necessary in the modern project, every time that one speaks of revolution, freedom and state. Nor is it the case that the project will ever hinder a priori such a return, since with respect to the causality of becoming even return is always possible, namely, it falls within the cases that must be somehow foreseen, anticipated, by defusing its explosive force, in the measure that it is possible for the will-to-state.

To complete the picture of these knots, one could add the extolling of technology, key to any utopia. In certain ways, it would almost seem that the government of Utopia had as its own exclusive end the endless and indefinable progress of scientific research that is realized in technology. As for liberalism, the state seems paradoxically to be legitimized precisely to the extent that it allows for the development of a state-free (*staatsfrei*) economy, free from the political. In the same way, for the utopian project it seems that the state, a sovereign, unitarian organization, could count and stand exclusively as guarantor of the linear, progressive, constructive growth of the sciences. Even here we must proceed beyond the apparent irreconcilability of the two positions. In the liberal state, individual interest, the original egoism, is the foundation from which one would like to determine the organization of the political. In Utopia, instead, this organization is dependent on the general or total human end to expand its dominion over nature. However, it is clear that the conception of time turns out to be identical in both cases, and it is similar to the project as political project: a linear-progressive deconsecrated time, scanned into partial teleologies, open to the irruption of chance (whether this occurs in the form of a contradiction of individual interests or under that of the logic of scientific discovery). This basic identity makes possible the countless exchanges between the two dimensions that characterize the history of the modern political. One could say that there is no antitraditional political project where the value of the development of technology as total human end is not extolled, trying in various ways to combine it with economic considerations. Technology achieves that idea of totality postulated by the revolutionary project. Utopia asserts that political form is conceivable insofar as organically imbued by the exigencies of technology as modern form of totality. But this answer bares, precisely, the contradictions analyzed so far. On one hand, it is equivalent to the assertion that political form is only conceivable there where politics is silenced. This form is entirely depoliticized (as the liberal one). In fact, there is no political problem in Utopia (unless at the level of external relations), since in it the becoming of politics has already been (*stato*) completed. On the other hand, and this is the essential point, technology harks back necessarily to economic production and to its development. The reason for this is that technology is the form that takes on the possibility of corresponding, from case to case, to the unlimited desire issuing from modern revolutionary man, from his rational nature, namely, the possibility of a continuous overcoming of the scarcity opposed to its satisfaction (C. B. Macpherson). This desire is structurally formless (*informe*), immoderate, especially, as we have already seen, whenever it is manifested radically, as desire for power. The idea of erecting the new form of totality on the development of technology, or the new form tout court, clashes inevitably and destructively against these reasons of technology itself, against its structural relation to the formlessness of unlimited desire constitutive of the modern political revolutionary project. In fact, Utopia refuses to acknowledge this desire. The emphasis on the virtue of its inhabitants is not a simple moral *topos*, but corresponds to the exigency of removing the source of a becoming that threatens in every moment the capacity of political form. The heroic grandeur of Utopia consists, therefore, in the fact that this removal occurs not by means of traditional reaction, but within the framework of a full emphasis, overflowing with the will to power of technology (and particularly in its applied value, as condition of the growth of wealth). As if Utopia stared in the face, in a way both perfectly mythological and perfectly disenchanted, the radical aporia of the modern political project: disenchanted in the analysis of its terms, mythological in the claim of its reconciliation.

For a Critique of the Idea of Secularization

In Utopia, the political project thinks the happy place (*eu-topia*: without conflict and without unsatisfied desire) as *ou-topia*, nowhere. Under this aspect, there could be no more radical recognition of the loss of totality and of the spectral character of any idea of true state. At the same time, however, the traits of the radical eradication (*Entortung*) and of the insular freedom of Utopia belong fully to the process of secularization-rationalization of the modern state, as historical-determined concept. And the problem of the incorporation of technology, in its consubstantiality with economic development, in political form, persists as the very content of the term *project*. The political project that prevails in the modern West is a combination of will to power, which is expressed in unlimited desire, in its formless measure, and the will to last and resist as "state." One wants to stay boundlessly to satisfy boundless desires that have exceeded any earthly norm, any definite spatial relation, totally revolutionary, purely intellectual-rational. But from this type of power one can only infer a Utopia-like state. The modern political project, in all its development, confronts this problem, and can be interpreted as the systematic search for its overcoming, namely, the reduction of its own intrinsic utopian capacity.

This process, in Weber's terms, can be designated with the term *rationalization*, even if in this context it takes on a different contour and a different problematic pregnancy. It develops from the liquidation of every symbolic trait in the term *utopia* (to the point of rendering it equivalent to an idea regulating political action, or to an object of transformation; and, beside, the same liquidating outcome is achieved by disembodying it of the effectiveness of the political project), up to the merely grammatological decline of the project, which seems to discount the deconstructive process of the state, reducing its semantic content to a technique for a probabilistic-statistical administration of the subjects that make it up. It remains to be seen to what extent such disenchantment corresponds to an actual solution of the aporetic character of the project, or, to what extent, instead, it expresses ideologically its bourgeois destiny, being limited to an impotent contemplation. The authors, who were the first to analyze the process of rationalization of the terms *revolution/utopia/project*, in the wider context of Western culture, are also those who with greater acuteness have drawn the conclusions at the level of political form. Weber's problem of the relation between bureaucracy and the political, and even more intrinsically, the paradox, in himself, of the professional political person's ethics (formed by an essentially problematic relation between conviction and responsibility), is incomprehensible in another context. The demythicization of political discourse and action seems to frustrate the very form of the political, but this frustration coincides, at best, with the increasing meaninglessness of any authentic projecting comprehension. Even the radical value relativism (*Wertrelativismus*) of Kelsenian democracy is in constant tension with an idea of cultural homogeneity, indispensable in order that the dialectic of interests remains on its feet, on one hand, and with an idea of sovereign function immanent to this same dialectic, of an immanent leader principle (*Führerprinzip*), on the other.[26] The interpretations of these conflicts as late romantic residues or heroic nostalgia belong to the more openly philistine character of contemporary political science.[27] As we have seen, the grammatological outcome of the very notion of state is already entirely interpreted in Schmitt, and we could add that the idea of a shift from a conception of the political that asserts itself as mythical-ideological to a techno-scientific one is, in itself, only a metaphorical generalization of Comte's model. The problem of the conclusive interpretation of the contemporary political is another. Under discussion is not the process of rationalization as such, but the fact that the crisis of its foundations threatens every form of "state" and along two opposed and copresent perspectives. On one hand, such crisis radically opens up to the becoming of unlimited desires. On the other, it prevents the very conceivability of political innovation, that is, by recognizing the relativity and causality of becoming, *or* (even more so, the stronger is that recognition), by criticizing the very sayability of the project as transforming freedom.

As for the aporias intrinsic in the term *project*, on which we have so much insisted by now, this problem is destined to remain such. But the scientific disenchantment, which believes to have resolved the problem by simply keeping quiet or by abstracting only a few simple elements from the whole, is entirely enslaved to it. Slave, first and foremost, and even if unavowed, of the idea-limit of technology as capable of corresponding to the inflation of questions (of which one is forced to deny any transcendental will to power, any political intention economically irreducible), and the naturally progressive conception of time that accompanies technology. But what really count are the contradictions of this servile condition. They attain to that complex situation of the chance project from which we began. The ratio of this extreme version of the project is in the guarantee of the greatest openness to the irruption of the unforeseeable, in the ability to administer or govern the unexpected as unexpected, and not to prevent its emergence, or dispose of it as soon as it emerges, or reduce it to the "already been" (*già stato*). Now, instead, the techno-administrative version of the political, direct heir of the era of depoliticization, can function only in these terms—always more groundless, because foreign by now to any organic idea of state. Only the reduction from the political to any exceptionality, of any authentic causality, allows for the success of techno-administrative calculation. But this implies that this reduction cannot be achieved through this calculation. There must be, therefore, a moment of sovereignty that cannot be rationalized in itself, and that arranges the subjects and responds to circumstance in forms that are compatible with the modalities of calculating comprehension. In other words, even here there must be projecting comprehension, and it does not matter if in necessarily structurally mystified ways, namely, a project that aims at the "state" of the depoliticizing administration. The bourgeois version of the project tries to appear legitimate for its own value relativism, to the extent that it is open to any value, capable of keeping any conflict of value in the depoliticized form of competition.[28] But this relativism presupposes the fundamental value of the will-to-state and, therefore, a project concretely organizing such a will. It functions as a kind of hidden God with reference to the manifest mechanisms of political administration. These mechanisms, which claim to be perfectly demystified, are endlessly compelled to appeal to the actions of such divinity before any case that appears irreducible to the "state" of competition and market.

The relativity of the bourgeois project (as critique of every revolution-ary idea—what we have said so far goes to show, logically, what an awful mess is the expression bourgeois revolution) has the security of eliminating any exception to its own assumptions.[29] The more demystified and open to becoming, the more this guarantee of security must be valid. It is proper of the bourgeois to be legitimized as will to change, without losing secur-ity. Its project knows well that this security can never be guaranteed either a priori or permanently, but for this it wants it all the more. All the more powerful that hidden God (*deus absconditus*) must be that keeps a mere becoming, a ceaseless change, a permanent conflict "in form." But the reason for this will not only is not entirely deducible, but by now it is also contradictory with respect to the techno-administrative logic that the programs, where the project has exploded, exhibit. This logic, in fact, orig-inates from a critique of political form, and precisely insofar as it had to defer necessarily, in its inevitable claim to totality, to the utopian-revolu-tionary terms of the project.

The form in which the bourgeois project can imagine becoming turns out to be, therefore, that of becoming of the always-the-same. A demysti-fied becoming means, for it, a progress without breaks, without jumps, without exceptions, without a hero—a becoming assuaged, assured. But this image of becoming is once again mythical. The ubiquitous complex of the political is at work so that any possibility of innovation may be obliged to appear in the most incredibly utopian projecting-revolutionary form. Utopian, instead, appears to be that same bourgeois project that would like to assuage becoming. Nothing, in fact, can be assuaged where the legal order is totally thrown off by its earthly hinges and the national state has dissolved in the multiverse (*pluriversum*) of the politico-economi-cal planetary relations. Within this framework, the will-to-state abandons any relativistic-neutral claim, and in it the "so-must-be-it" of political force resounds. The metaphor of "play," perhaps structurally effective to describe the system of ubiquity of the political, does not even veil, in the last instance, the reality of this appeal to the *deus absconditus* of force with-out foundation that wants, despite all, the "state" to be. The game implies the acceptance of its rules, it is said. But then, nobody dwells on the nature of these rules. In this game there are no neutral rules. Their premise is, anyway, the reduction of conflict to competition, the value of progress that this reduction must pursue, the security of the distribution of power through any transformation, and one pretends to ignore that among the rules of the political game there is the definition of who holds the cards, that is, the definition of a decisive position. Now, the bourgeois political project consists precisely in removing from the game that set of mecha- nisms and rules that make possible the innovation of this "who," to reach this decisive position. It is a question not of cheating but of the structure of this particular, determinate game in which whoever holds the cards has at his disposal valid moves to conceal its own position, to incorporate the attacker, to reduce him to a condition of business partnership or to mere competitor. To take part in this game (therefore, to accept its rules) always more and more takes on the characteristics of a conservative imperative. On the other hand, refusing to participate turns immediately into revolu- tionary mythology, theoretically and historically meaningless. But the de- mystified emphasis of the bourgeois project is directly proportional to the concealment of its own utopianism and to the specific nature of the rules of its game (the same choice of term is programmatically ideological; it evokes by itself an aura of neutrality entirely nonexistent). A utopianism, if you will, that is entirely negative. It is no longer founded on immutable claims, its state is bent into immanent government programs and manage- ment, and yet this system still pretends to be safe and is organized politi- cally to this end. This is only the extreme conclusion of the intrinsic problematic of the term *project*. Here we recognize the red thread of its history, and it almost seems to describe a circle that closes on itself—an island—a utopia that by now no longer promises even *eu-topia*. The clo- sure of this discourse has nothing to do with the end of the system of which we speak. What is closed can also last indefinitely. But perhaps, for the cognizance of this lasting system, and in order to be active in it, it may make sense to acknowledge the condition and recognize oneself in it. As the ancient saying has it: Destiny leads the way for those who agree to follow.

CHAPTER 5

Catastrophes

Writing to Antonio Valdés, secretary of Charles V, on August 1, 1528, this is how Erasmus explained, against his detractors, the enterprise of the boundary mark (*Termine*): "One time the borders of fields were marked by a special sign; it was a stone protruding from the ground that hereditary laws prescribed to be irremovable. Hence Plato reports the saying: Don't remove what you did not put up. . . . This boundary mark, as is written in the Roman Annals, was the only one that stood up to Jove."[1] Terminus is the God that sanctions boundaries; the feast day of Terminals celebrates their indestructibility. But already in Erasmus the invocation of Terminus sounds by now like a lament, peace complaint (*Querela Pacis*), abandoned and vagrant. Precisely the story of this abandonment, of this eradication, is what Carl Schmitt analyzes in *Der Nomos der Erde*.[2] No divine presence guarantees anymore the power of borders. Everything is freely removable. In perfect agreement with Schmitt, Ernst Jünger speaks in *An der Zeitmauer* of the "geological restlessness" of the present world: "On the ancient earth, man no longer feels safe. He no longer trusts the classical elements . . . behind the invention of machines always more fast there is hidden an impulse to escape," as if the ancient mother, now inhospitable, wanted to belch us out into a fifth element, in pure ether, with no surface, in which no Term could ever be fixed.[3]

Aristotle's architect is a meteorologist with the purpose of tracing according to measurement the limits of the city, of expressing its *nomos*. We are meteorologists in the negative, and because of the impossibility of confiding in the Earth, we seek in that fifth element new, impossible dwellings.

This geological restlessness seems to be at the bottom of contemporary disastrology. It conceives our environment as risk, hazard (*tyche*), in perennial ambush, against whose irruptions, however, programmed responses are possible. An authentic technology of disaster can originate only from the complete abandonment of every trust on the earth.[4] But in this abandon, no doubt, the guilt is revealed for having eradicated what we never placed. Meteorologists, we wait for signs of vengeance, of a punishment that we try in every way not to consider necessary. Speculations on boundaries in the exploitation of resources, on the effects of pollution, just as on the differences by now apparently ungovernable between the great areas of the planet, fall within the framework of such meteorology. The environment has become a hazard because this is how we wanted it.[5] On the other hand, precisely because this hazard is the earth to the extent that we transformed it, it can in some ways belong to us, that is, we can anticipate it—program it, correspond to it. A *science* always more trained in anticipating and calculating disasters develops in complement with our always greater capacity to produce them.

But contemporary disastrology, above all in its black millenarian versions, Club of Rome style, all instrumentally devoted to preventing the latecomers' hope to share in what the North has already greatly enjoyed, is limited to emphasizing the destructive side of catastrophe. Indeed, it does recognize the problem of the discontinuous, but from a strictly medical point of view (*medeor-mediare-medicus*).[6] The discontinuous is, from a medical point of view, pathological irruption to restoring order, precisely as the judge reestablishes the vigor of norm. The great medical symbolism, which for centuries has fluttered around these terms, seems to be irreversibly broken in contemporary culture. For such culture (an event, on the other hand, absolutely exceptional in the history of human societies) the problem of the discontinuous becomes normal. In the most disparate contexts, that critique meanders to any idea of finalized, structural continuity that Foucault has employed to deconstruct the very notion of history.[7] An economist such as Leontief, in confronting the scenario of the next ten years, maintains that methods of long-term forecasting, still founded on the analysis of continuous phenomena, are powerless.[8] They trace relations between income, production, and occupation as if the break, the "transfixion" of one's own spatial-temporal coordinates, were a disastrous exception to be removed or healed at all costs. Not only does such a logic of the "as if" not adhere to life curves, but in the case of the themes Leontief deals with, it also prevents the singling out of which leaps must be produced to attempt effective responses to the complexity of the system. An analogous discourse could be conducted with regard to the analysis of international relations, where the progressive emptying of the bipolar system seems to represent, more generally, the decline of an idea of politics as preservation of a state of equilibrium among equivalent forces. We will return briefly to these themes; for the moment, I want to stress the general emphasis placed in our culture on phenomena of discontinuity as fundamental characters of the very form of the system, phenomena that, in their singularity, it is now possible to grasp with instruments always more formalized. The development of the theory of catastrophes belongs within this picture.

To be sure, even this event, as any other Western one, has its prologue in heaven. In the apocalyptic representations, in fact, the restorative dimension appears inseparable from the destructive one. The messianic aspect, in fact, is only thinkable in the background of the abyss, of *kenosis*, of the self-emptying of God himself.[9] The disorder that prevailed everywhere in the imminence of Advent must have been so horrible, that some pious Jews ended up by wishing openly not to want to assist to the coming of the Messiah. In the Apocalypse, catastrophe and epistrophe end up by forming a single idea: catastrophe is change of order, structural transition.

To this idea two other representations correspond, familiar everywhere in our culture, for which the curve of time reveals its own meaning only in the turning points (apocalypse itself is only the definitive, absolute turning point). It is the apocalyptic time (*chronos apokalipseos*), a dramatic situation par excellence, a heroic act, an ecstatic (*ex-static*) projection of the curve of life, whose meaning, Bloy would say, pierces memorialists, scribes, and bureaucrats "with outcries of apocalyptic vengeance." These are themes deeply dealt even with by Benjamin. It is easy, likewise, to catch some roots in that formidable "time of advent" that ushers Russian culture formed on Dostoyevsky.[10] But, still further, they go back to the iconography of revealing time in its relation with devouring time. Time the devourer is transformed, in this relation, in the positive work of destruction of the multiple, inessential appearances, a work that accomplishes the necessary emptying in order for the *chronos apokalipseos* to manifest itself. In other words, authentic revelation of the sense of time is only possible at the culmination of the dramatic situation. One understands an epoch only when it reveals what its death will be. Both in relation and opposition to this image, the modern space of catastrophe presents itself as that of an apocalypse "without qualities." The turning point that theory analyzes is entirely deprived of value. Neither its form nor the order that is restored by means of the break is superior to the previous system. The modern term of catastrophe both generalizes and secularizes the constructive-destructive symbol of apocalypse, rendering inexpressible, thus, its proper value, that of redemption.

If *every* structural transition or discontinuity, singularly observable, becomes catastrophe, constructively describable, outside every degenerative meaning (but also, as we have seen, of any salvific content), it is nonetheless entirely evident how its idea can assume overall cultural importance in the presence of those "messianic labor pains," of which Cioran, after Jünger, has spoken, namely, in the presence of multiple crises that seem to precipitate inexorably toward changes of phases, general transformations.[11] It is difficult to be completely informed on the variables of these politico-social processes; it is difficult to give statistic consistency to the analysis of these movements. However, it remains that the perception, or the recognition of a break in the continuity of the finalized structures that have maintained the history of these last ten years, is spreading and is being dramatized. "History is on the move," to use Aron's words; great slipups (*dérapages*) have characterized, not so long ago, the events of those structures: the crisis of postwar big government, entirely founded on the classical premise of the reversibility of the processes (that is, on the presumed exceptionality of public intervention which, thanks to its character, did not prime the vicious circles of the monetary crisis); the limits intrinsic to the productive paradigm under the politico-social profile (the decisive passage from assigned priorities with the aim of reaching determinate objectives to comparative objectives, to effects of imitation, undermining the linear equivalency between income and satisfaction); the proliferation of power that makes obsolete the rules of the game, the balance of power established after World War II (with the epochal consequence, already largely foreseen by Schmitt, of a progressive de-Westernization of international politics).[12] These are strictly interrelated processes (it would suffice to think of the relation between crisis of big government, multiplication of contracts of interest within the Western area, and the proliferation of powers) around which, analytically, much has been done, but, once again, we should say, more from the viewpoint of the crisis than from that of the catastrophe—that is, paying greater attention to the contradictions that are generated in the system for the growth of its complexity, and often defining them in destructive-degenerative terms, than in confronting, from within the analysis of the complexity itself, the problem of the form of the transition, of the formally complete representation of the discontinuity, of the transformation. We have at our disposal a large literature on local crises, and, alas, even more numerous complaints on the decline of old equilibriums (willy-nilly, the present complaints addressed to the super powers to define a new, stable *nomos*, join in this impotent choir). We do not have yet a catastrophic reading of these processes, and yet we can perhaps infer their possibility from the fact that: (1) these processes are "informed," and in part, at least, already quantifiable; (2) the phenomenon of discontinuity does not appear in them exogenous or miraculous, but participates intimately in their structure, is produced in the structure itself and does not dissolve it simply from the outside; (3) the critical situation in which these processes find themselves, whereby small variations can by now determine overall changes, is characterized as passage from the quantitative to the qualitative, or, more precisely, from the complex local crises and quantitative transformations to the problem of the qualitative leap. These conditions make at least permissible a catastrophic approach to the process as a whole and to its particular movements, a morphogenetic approach in the place of the one merely critical-dissolutive and/or medical-conservative.

From what we have said so far, there emerges the necessity of distinguishing between the dimension of the catastrophe and that of the crisis. René Thom has particularly insisted on this difference, and one has to believe that one can derive consequences of great importance for the so-called social sciences.[13]

The term *crisis* is suitable to represent intuitively the deregulation of particular apparatuses, the dysfunctions that can strike some points in the system (crisis of the big industry, crisis of Parliament, and so on). It will always take on the aspect of a local phenomenology, strongly emphasizing the supposed degenerative nature of the process. This signals a paradox verifiable in the quasi totality of the critical approaches. On one hand, single functions are taken into consideration; on the other, the discourse tends to develop on very general lines, until ethico-moral or value judgments are implicated. This paradox is perhaps explainable by the fact that it is indeed the impossibility of representing formally the process, in its turning points, through the idea of crisis, which leads to the adoption of general visions of the world. The strongly ideological connotations of the term *crisis* in its current use are developed in direct proportionality to the incapacity of formal representation of the process of transformation of the system. There is no other way than the ideological to make the deregulation of single functions to appear as a general attack on the structure—the local, but often shifty or latent character of the crisis, a comprehensive ebullition of the system.

It is necessary to clarify, therefore, that the sphere of the term *crisis* is to be reduced to the analysis of the processes of complication of determinate functions of an organism (complication that can also leave entirely intact its structure), while the catastrophe points to a phenomenon of evident discontinuity and precisely observable. It is evident how the crises can invade the special spheres, or the diverse functions, to such an extent to prevent compensatory or rebalancing mechanisms in the sphere of the given data, and, therefore, transform the situation in a catastrophic one. But it makes no sense to speak of structural crisis because when the crises arrive at a certain point they are integrated and are surpassed in the catastrophe, which, as we have already indicated, has limited dimensions and precise forms that do not allow the ambiguity inextricably inherent in the term *crisis*. To be coherent, that is, the opposite should occur of what usually is the case in political language and even in that of political theory. While the references to the structurality of the crisis expand the uncontrollable ideological traits of critical analysis to the maximum, the very appearance of the term structure should bring, instead, to the determination of the parameters on whose bases the breaking off of the stability of the previous system proves to be formalizable.

Thus, we can see in the crisis the virtuality of the catastrophe, but we could never analyze it according to the parameters employed for the transitions of structure. It may be that the term *crisis* is destined to remain "a lay term in search of scholarly meaning," given the great variety, the substantial unpredictability of the aspects that can assume episodes of even acute suffering, of determinate functions in the system.[14] The term, in short, reveals itself to be not only relative to the context in which it is used, but also to the nonchronicity or reversibility of the dysfunctions it denounces. Of this term, more than defining forms, it is possible to develop phenomenologies. This is clearly the case with Kahn's *On Escalation*, with its forty-four steps between minor provocation and (nuclear) catastrophe, and with Wiener and Kahn in their attempt to locate twelve general dimensions that would occur in every definition of crisis.[15] The mathematical and formal aspect of these attempts appears weak and in any case not comparable with that of the theory of catastrophes. Furthermore, the original meaning of the term, its original appurtenance to medical semiotics, returns in it, entirely explicit, also because of its primary application in the field of polemology, with the inevitable vitalistic-organic consequences that a similar recovery gives way in political theories and in the interpretation of social phenomena.

Because of these characteristics, a crisis situation can lend itself, instead, to be confronted and resolved within the sphere of a theory of games. In fact, the time of crisis is one of decision. Before a conflict or a determined contradiction, and in a situation of uncertainty, it is necessary to intervene, to decide, to take part. Theory teaches to optimize this conduct, but on condition that the rules of the game remain inviolate for the participants, or that, in the case of social games, the physical and legal sphere, in which the game takes place, remain, in any case, unchanged. Theory assumes explicitly, furthermore, that every participant be perfectly informed on the alternatives that can respond to its moves and that he or she will be able to carry out all the necessary calculations in order to determine its own optimal conduct. The theory of games can be applied to crisis situations, as defined earlier, because in the crisis the stability and continuity of the system is not put into question (unless virtually only). Furthermore, since the crisis is a virtual catastrophe, it is a question, here, of playing it by effecting simple sectorial modifications in the system. The theory of games knows only time-crisis, never *chronos apokalipseos*, and in this rests its extraordinary affinity with an idea (or ideology) of progress as perennial removal of catastrophe, evolution-innovation of the system through crises capable of deluding and enchanting it.

Julien Freund (repeating, on the other hand, the lesson of disenchantment of the masters of modern political science) has called attention to the essential differences between conflict and game, disengaging the term conflict from the field of the analysis of social change and innovation, where a conciliatory sociology (pretending to echo Simmel) tends to confine it.[16] While the game is "defined by rules established in precedence" and, therefore, one can repeat it "any time one wishes," the conflict, while it can entail some ludic elements, "creates its own norms continuously." In it the participants can, strictly speaking, use whatever means, provided they are effective. The element of violence turns out to be impossible to eliminate from the idea of conflict, when radically understood, while it cannot be anticipated in a theory of games. From this, however, does not follow at all a presumed anarchic character of violence. On the contrary, whenever it can be catastrophically represented, as a brush break, an evident and observable discontinuity, its dimension will appear a lot more clearly defined and formally resolved than that of the crisis. If anything, it is the anarchy of the crisis that attempts to remove the morphogenetic order of the catastrophe.

This dimension of the term crisis is best clarified in its application of the problem of government. The preservation of a critical situation, the observance of an anarchic condition of crisis, can function as a powerful factor of rearrangement and compactness of government assets. This can occur either through the institutionalization of procedures to be adopted in the crisis (that is, recourse to provisory dictatorships in the Roman Republic), or by emphasizing the situation of emergency in order to make legally possible a dictatorial way out. The more crises threaten catastrophic results, the more systematic will be the recourse to emergency governments to legalize conservative solutions of the conflict. Paradoxically, these solutions consist precisely in the institutionalization of conflict, and therefore are obliged to be founded on the permanence of crisis. The crisis is preserved (namely, one tends to block the process to its critical elements) in order to prevent a transforming break of government assets. Perennial emergency keeps in form a political system (through various procedures of freezing of the conflict between principal actors, or the progressive dissolution of parliamentarian forms of control, or the inclusion of articles of emergency within constitution itself) on the edge of catastrophe. We are reminded of Weimar, but it does not mean at all that such form is weak, precarious. On the contrary, it can become, in determinate situations, the normal answer to the virtual catastrophic propagation of the crisis. The stability of emergency governments (in the sense of tending to structure themselves on emergencies), a phenomenon that corresponds to the stability reached by the system at the edge of the catastrophic break is, likewise, powerfully reinforced by the effect that stress, panic, anguish, produced by the persisting critical situation, have on the reactions of the public. Disastrology and polemology have been studying empirically such reactions for a long time now.[17] The great majority of the population seems to respond to shock with a lowering of the autonomous capacities to make a decision and a strong increase in the qualities of meekness and obedience. The mass request for strong leadership that physiologically accompanies the development of the critical situation is evidence of this more general behavior. Notice that the greatest compliance does not seem at all correlated to phenomena of spreading of diseases or mental disorders, that is, the capacity of intelligent execution of command is not invalidated at all by greater docility. In England during the Nazi bombings, no anomaly was noticed in the state of mental illness. The same was the case in Hiroshima, in the period after the explosion. In these cases, on the contrary, the capacity for attention is developed, and, precisely, in the direction of the execution of commands, and not in that of autonomous choice, of the autonomous capacity to make decisions.

One of the characteristics of the term *crisis*, which emerges from what we have said, concerns its essential subjectivity. *Crisis* refers always to the apperception of a state, of a subject that is "in crisis" (Thom). He or she notices that his environment has become hazardous, that the *nomos* totters, and tries to correspond to the new situation by modifying its own regulatory mechanisms. The critical situation is reflected in the growing *insecuritas* of the subject, which works in order to overcome it through modifications and rearrangements of the structure. The same *chronos apokalípseos*, on the other hand, takes shapes as definitive consumption of any *insecuritas*, as possible consumption only at the peak of anguish. One could perhaps risk the hypothesis that when the subject feels the necessity of modifying its own mechanisms to correspond to the situation, the process is on the point of going through a break in stability of the system, while, when the critical situation is deemed reformable, greater emphasis will be given to the interventions of a simple modification or rearrangement of the milieu. One reaches a turning point when the milieu is no longer able to be reconstructed in our image and semblance, and its modification passes necessarily through a change of structure in the subject's regulators. This seems by now the case of the de-Westernization of international politics to which we alluded earlier. Western politics meets growing resistance (and can already foresee insuperable knots) in still adapting to itself, to its own interests and to its own culture, the planetary milieu. That is, it has to confront the problem of its own radical change, of its own catastrophe. And yet, its culture barely staggers the first steps on the way to a nondissolutive, nondegenerative interpretation of the term. Western politics is now obliged to confront its own catastrophe, having at its disposal, substantially, only the medical instruments of the theories of crisis and games.

The subjective character of the crisis is not without consequences for the priming of the catastrophe. Nor, however, could it have been otherwise because the subject participates fully in the process, conditioning its modalities of structure and discontinuity. We would like to take into consideration only some hypotheses that seem of some importance in the politico-social field. Confronted with local dysfunctions or with the exigencies of interventions of reorganization that do not entail at all, as such, structural modifications, it is entirely possible that the subjects involved react catastrophically, that is, perceiving these modifications (for the prominence they assume in sectors of their competence) as transitional phases. This perception of the critical situation can be transmitted to other functions in the system, infecting other assets. The subjective character of the crisis makes possible its transmission. But once this contagion is sufficiently generalized, we are indeed confronting a crisis that assumes a general character. The continuous crisis, always drawing closer spatially and temporally, leads effectively near to the boiling point. The subjective apperception of the critical situation, *also* completely localized from the start, not only can be generalized but also can lead the system effectively to the threshold of catastrophe. In fact, nothing obliges that the process schematized here has to be interrupted at the simple exaltation of the elements (even dictatorial ones) of the crisis or emergency government. It can go so far as the explication of active interventions turned to the transformation of crisis into catastrophe. Let it be clear, it is not a question of ideological illusionism. When the apperception of the crisis unfolds in the manner described, it is the situation itself that changes. The apperception is an integral part of its form, and therefore of its own change in the catastrophic sense.

In this picture, the representation of the conflict changes radically. It does not occur any longer among the better known topics, easily recognizable in their values and juxtaposed in a one-dimensional, axial scheme, but in positions intrinsically unstable, sliding into one another, reciprocally short-circuiting. Further: any subject (by deconstructing as such insofar as subjectivity) is always more driven to act in directions always more incompatible among themselves. In this condition, the passage from one direction to another, even an opposite one, can appear suddenly, giving life to unexpected jolts and breaks. Whoever tries to represent conflict still axially remains duly astonished in front of its catastrophic disposition, in the most complete inability to interpret it and, thus, to control it. In order to survive, then, he or she will be obliged to cry at the catastrophe before every conflict, at the same time, as we have seen, stressing objectively the critical character of the situation. The catastrophic character of contemporary social, political, cultural antagonism is the rule, against islands of axial determinism.[18] The parameters that regulate the conditions of stability of our structure have by now assumed values whereby the system finds itself undecided among diverse possible forms, incompatible among themselves.

What condemns technocratic futurology or any political-scientific forecast still confident in the utopia of the progressive fading away of the political is not so much the removal of the conflicting element from the overall process of innovation, as much as the ignorance of the catastrophic character that antagonism has come to assume even from within every subject. And yet, all that has been gathered phenomenologically all these years on social conflict almost points in unison in this direction. From the studies on nationalization of the masses and on the crisis in Weimar, to the analysis on the evolution of political parties (where the paling of any evidence in traditional distinctions among their various forms, corresponds to the growing variety and complexity of the motives that condition the action, motives and objectives normally alternating between them); from the schemes of proliferation of power, already mentioned, and that do not concern only international relations but count inside every single state (for that little that the expression still signifies), to the reproposing with force, despite current prophesying on the death of ideologies, of juxtaposition of values. What seems to mark our experience is not, therefore, the liberal reduction of political conflict to a game, an exchange, a market—to its aestheticization—but the transformation of antagonism in an antideterministic, multidimensional sense, beyond any stable juxtaposition of choices and values.[19] Nor does this picture have anything to do with postmodern redeeming ideologies. The different directions that antagonism assumes do not coexist peacefully amongst each other, if not for some happy exceptions. It is a question of alternatives and contradictions that normally cannot be reconstituted.

Even in the complexity of its relations with the term *crisis*, from what has been said, the term *catastrophe* emerges in its specificity. It results correctly applicable to evident discontinuities alone, to qualitative transformations, changes of state. Differently from simply critical moments, the catastrophe appears formally representable. Powerful formalisms describe the discontinuities that can be represented in the evolution of the system. They assume, in fact, limited forms, their space has definite dimensions that escape the uneliminable ambiguity of the crisis. However great is the number of variables that condition the process, the collapse is quantifiable, the catastrophe assumes regular forms. The growing incompatibility, for the stability of the system, among the values of the different controlling factors, can assume the form of an equation of instability. In a certain sense, the norm of the catastrophe contrasts the anarchy of crisis. The theory analyzes such norms.

It is necessary to differentiate accurately, at this point, the spheres of possible application of this theory. The first sphere, which may be the only one that we have actually attempted, is methodological and linguistic. We propose, so to speak, to contrast to the now-evident consumption of the term *crisis* a more rigorous distinction between a simply critical situation and change of state or catastrophe, in the meaning here often invoked and extraneous to any degenerative or dissolutive meaning. This entails theoretical and political attention to the forms of discontinuity, to the productivity of the discontinuous, to the morphogenesis via catastrophe, which is absent from any "critical critique" consideration. The notion of irreversibility of the process and the critique of every reductionistic methodology accompanies and integrates this approach.[20]

The second order of application should concern the concrete descriptions of sociopolitical situations. But the most important contributions that have appeared to date to this effect still deal with very limited themes. On their limits, even formal ones, Thom has insisted with great precaution. It is not clear up to what point one can go in describing open systems that make impossible the control according to classical procedures or repeatable experiments. What counts for the logic of the living counts infinitely more for the logical of the social. How can one determine, in these systems, the catastrophic leap? What must be given in the structure of the system in order for it to be self-evident? And once one disposes of all necessary information to resolve the equation, will it be possible to foresee the discontinuity, the forms of the transition to the catastrophe? Is it possible to control the process by trusting the regularity of the catastrophic event? Or the length of the code of open systems, the specific complexity and spirituality of the sociopolitical systems, make such an objective only infinitively approximate?

But these are questions at the limit, from a very distant perspective. The question, instead, to which one must answer right away is, whether the term *catastrophe* and its family can effectively reorder our discourse on the sociopolitical processes, allowing us finally to connect, in their interpretation, the discontinuous and the regular, the exception and the norm, the decision and the constitution, or if, on the contrary, we believe insuperable in this field the staggering ambiguity of the term crisis, a term that can be turned to any use even before it can connote according to any meaning, if only with the purpose of rhizomatically repeating would-be postmodern commonplaces, with regard to phenomena of discontinuity, abstract from any serious attempt of formal analysis. Here we will limit ourselves to advance the hypothesis that the methodology that transpires from the theory of catastrophes seems able to confer a precise and clearly representable meaning to that normality of the problem of the discontinuous that we have seen torment the entire contemporary culture. Let this count at least as a call against the too easy liberations, the very bad infinite of "critical critiques" and their perpetual alter ego, the attempt at stabilizing the process in a perennial emergency—an attempt that defines the work of memoirists, scribes, and bureaucrats.

CHAPTER 6

The Language of Power in Canetti

A Scrutiny

"The discursive legitimation of power by law universals" typical of all great revolutionary rhetoric and, more generally, of every "philosophical reading" of political facts"[1] seems to constitute the perennial inexhaustible polemical motive of Elias Canetti's work. Fulvio Papi insists, correctly, that the forms of the destructive intellect "act in a daily shadow zone," that their idols are not traceable so much at the height of great theoretical syntheses, as in the concrete behavior of the "tribe," in their normal and apparently spontaneous circulation ("a destructive spontaneity of discourse circulates which is predisposed to the acceptance of any catastrophe"). This motive, too—the consubstantiality between conceptual confinement and mass behavior—is profoundly Canettian. In contemporary society, the great political rhetoric belongs to the masses and the mass is never innocent or speechless (*in-fante*).

The destructive intellect—those forms of the intellect "that have thought politics as an identity of theory and practice, guaranteed by the figure of a subject . . . who was entitled to the universal" (F. Papi)—has to be understood, first of all, radically, as destruction of the body of the other, of the other as body. Canetti develops this idea, particularly, in his great essay on Kafka. The first product of power seems to be a sort of annihilation of body (*annihilatio corporis*). The body in Kafka is subjected to a desperate *via crucis*, from the impossible struggle for one's recognition, to progressive decay, impotence, absence. The body is condemned to absence from the forms of power. They leave no room for K. For the destructive intellect, there is no Heideggerian "opening of space" (*Freigabe von Orten*), but only procedures of spatialization equivalent to procedures of control-incarceration. The condemned man must feel shame for the body that he still drags behind, or for its own absence of body, interiorizing as guilt the punishment received: "With such a body nothing can be achieved . . . it has no fat whatsoever for creating beneficial warmth."[2] Love requires weight; it's a matter of bodies. The skinny body, instead, is the absent body, the nonbody, or a shameful image of his impotence, a scandalous irruption of death amongst the figures of the living. Naturally, in Canetti's discourse the theme of body-flesh assumes even more general urgency, in connection with his struggle against death, the very idea of death. It seems to me, by contrast, that in Canetti there are none of those three trends of that "mysticism of the body" analyzed by Norman O. Brown in *Life Against Death*, nor that Pauline one of the spiritual body, nor the cabalistic one, nor the alchemical one that reaches its peak in Goethe. These currents transcend the corporeality of the body, transfigure it, or sublimate it, and for which an authentic fullness of life can be reached only through negation, through mystical death. Even the Dionysian body, that no longer denies, apparently *"über"* any form of the destructive intellect, remains actually a transformed-transfigured body, a body initiated to sacred Laughter. If I had to hazard a name to define the conception of the body in Canetti, I would mention only that of Spinoza, except that Spinoza's certainty in its substantial, indestructible productivity has become in Canetti hopelessness and defense, as to say: creatural certainty.

But the *annihilatio corporis* accomplished by power is in its essence philosophical. "The thing that repels me most about philosophers is the *emptying* process of their thinking. The more often and more skillfully they use their basic words, the less remains of the world around them."[3] Philosophical eschatology (different from the Christian one, and from those Jewish trends in which, although never explicitly, Canetti recognizes himself) through the radical putting into question of every sensible experience, of every suffering (*pathein*), aims at overcoming the body. The forms of destructive reason appear, in Canetti, to be proper of philosophical thought. Philosophical discourse is really the weapon of the destruction of the body, of the reduction of the body to powerless otherness. It empties

the body from thought. Therefore there is an intimate connection between philosophy and death. The body as dead is the product of philosophy. Philosophy abandons "man to death as to an invisible blood" (*The
Human Province*, 272), it confers to death supreme power over life, and it
elects death "as the most intimate escort of a whole lifetime" (*The Human
Province*, 271). For philosophy, life is always being-for-death, and authentic only if understood in the figure of its catastrophe. Thought humiliates
the body, just as power condemns K. to the shame of its absolute skinni-
ness and absence of warmth, and, therefore, to the impotence of its struggle. For the body, as for K., "victory is taboo," his liberty seems to consist
only in seeking "salvation in defeat" (*The Conscience of Words*, 75).

The legislator loves the dead body: measurable, calculable, predictable,
anatomizable. Modern science of the state *and* scientific anatomy, state
machine *and* body machine. And neither the politician nor the scientist
can do without the philosophical premise par excellence: no certainty, no
truth, derives from the senses. The body is an inexhaustible source of de-
ceits that have to be suppressed, silenced, relativized, in order to be redis-
covered, if ever, transfigured at the end of the journey of pure reason. The
philosopher, therefore, does not love power out of subjective weaknesses,
even less to gain miserly advantage, but for heartfelt necessity, for rigorous
systematic coherence. In fact, the more his thinking is ascetic, the more it
will seem enchanted by the forms of power. Asceticism of the senses is
heartfelt, immanent fascination with power. The very idea of legislating
contains the idea (utopian, to be sure, but regulated, and very positive) of
the overcoming of the sensitive passions as oscillating, formless contingen-
cies, as infancy to bring to maturity and to educate. The order of philosophical discourse is truly identical to that of the hard matter (*dura res*) of
government and power.

The philosophers Canetti admires are those who, far from covering,
mitigating, or taming, bare this reality together with their love for it. In
them, this same love becomes, however, entirely intellectual. It is no
longer Bacon's almost immediate sympathy for power, but some kind of
very high *amor fati*, all the more profound as it recognizes the artificiality
of forms of government, as it is free from any simple tie (*religio*) with
respect to them. Hobbes is for Canetti the prototype of these philosophers: "I believe that I have found in him the mental root of what I want
to fight against the most" (*The Human Province*, 116). He is the first of the
terrible thinkers who do not mask power, do not share any religion of
power, and who also systematically love it, and want indestructibly to
ground it. (Even Nietzsche, and his connection with the great political

thought of the sixteenth and seventeenth centuries, is a precious indication and is mentioned as one of the "great enemies.") What does Hobbes unmask? Essentially, the "coincidence between effectiveness and legitimacy in sovereign power," whereby it is always the monopoly of force to produce "legitimacy" and not vice versa.[4] "The 'what is right' is transformed first of all—and it's only the first step—in that 'who speaks Justice.'"[5] These thinkers are "terrible," insofar as they unmask this terrible secret of the modern state, of its artificial construction—and because this unmasking-recognition is geometrically grounded. In their method all the power of thought precipitates, abandoning any "decadent utopian fascination" (G. Miglio). In their method, thought is completely destructive, and its constructive power reveals itself to be completely nihilistic.

But how does this system of philosophy, its law-power, speak for Canetti? Around which terms and around which categories is his language concentrated? A fundamental triad seems to sustain its structure: producing-outdoing-surviving.

The dialectic of production dominates the most recent forms of government. Large part of their legitimacy derives from the effectiveness of their power to guarantee normal conditions of development of production. The reverence for economic-productive growth substitutes, and somehow rationalizes and secularizes, the most "raving" (Canetti) among the ancient forms of faith: the religion of power. There is nothing more nonsensical, therefore, than claiming that the universal affirmation of the rules of the economic-productive game (of its natural or objective relations) should or can lead to a universal peace of the markets (*pax mercatorum*), or to the resolution of political relations into exchange relations (according to the precepts of a very light nihilism). Not only is the cult of production an expression of the religion of power, but also in its own womb, from the beginning, "all the individualized forms of the idea of 'peace' are clearly *functional to the war*" (Miglio), reintroducing, in so doing, the dynamic of war and, more generally, the typical categories of destructive reason.

This, first of all, is because producing, the great rhetoric on producing, is indissolubly linked to sacrifice. P. L. Berger has illustrated it in his book, in truly Canettian pages: the "syllogistic dagger" proper of destructive reason consists in connecting the necessity of development with that of sacrifice.[6] In fact, the greater the reverence for growth, the more painful ought to be the sacrifices to bear. The height of the end is directly proportional to the depth of the sacrifice. The number of martyrs (in the literal sense of witnesses of the end) certifies and legitimates in itself the excellence of the end to be reached, and of the effort made in wanting to reach it. (It is important to add, which Canetti does not do, that some of the great economists of this century have been aware of the elective affinity between destructive reason and economic constructivity.)

But it is in its structural relation to the semantic family of outdoing and survival that the dialectics of producing reveals, fully, its own pure will to power. The reverence for economic growth is, in its essence, reverence for outdoing. "Having to grow" expresses the fixed idea of outdoing: "Everything competes, and all people compete in struggle, and the person who outdoes is a never-ending winner."[7] But the continuous outdoing, the constraint to outdo the dialectics of power, feeds on the number of outdoers. The excess of outdoing lays claim to an endless number of vanquished, precisely as the excess of producing founds on sacrifice its own pyramids. To realize the boundlessness of producing, it is necessary to outdo incessantly the obstacles that oppose it. Revolutions, too, are by now conceived in the same way. They have to remove and outdo the enemies of growth, those who do not sacrifice to it, or whose existence is objectively an obstacle to its destined progress.

Producing/outdoing is, finally, survival. One outdoes by producing incessantly, but in such activity one tries to survive to the greatest possible number. This is the recurrent theme in Canetti's *Crowds and Power*.[8] "The true goal of the real power-wielder is as grotesque as it is incredible: he wants to be the *Unique*."[9] The art of the power-wielder is to last, preserving his own power as much as possible. But the logic of this will is paradoxical. Lasting means, in fact, wanting to outdo everyone, wanting to resists longer than anyone, wanting to survive by himself. Stirner's dialectic of the Unique introduces and sums up many of these traits, unmasking indeed the profound plot of the language of the power-wielder, and, therefore, it is very strange that Canetti does not include this author in his gallery of "terribles" (and that, in the same gallery, he blurs somewhat the image of Machiavelli). In the obsession for survival, the nihilism of destructive reason exercises against itself. Whereas in the simple producing/outdoing it manifested its own power over the other body, here it ends by being suffocated in the same vacuum that he has created (or better, produced) around himself. At the peak of the will to power there is the figure of the Unique, or of the survival, which is power of nothing, a power that has annihilated every content, every life within its own power. What Canetti defines as "grotesque" is really the merciless conclusion to the love of law-power for the dead body. Outdated products inhabit his peace.

It ignores every present. It is only in the time that no-longer-is and (perfect equivalent of the first) in the time that is-not-yet.

But for producing-outdoing-surviving it is necessary controlling-governing. In the language of power the government is productive in its more intimate essence. In fact, it is a question of bringing to presence, to illuminate, to prevent any obscuring, any mask. Governing is unveiling. Every subject of political obligation is made transparent in the eyes of power. The ideal consists in the absence of any mediation between subject and power. This is the meaning of the absolute prohibition in the modern state to organize enemy groups within itself. In fact, the enemy will try with every means to avoid pure visibility, to mask or camouflage, to deceive. Within the state only friends will be admitted, or conflicts of interest born on the ground of economic exchange. Those can be mediated, that is, made self-evident in their good reasons, made acceptable to the different parts because finally disclosed, produced. There is a prejudice, or rather a faith, profoundly working in this dialectic, namely, that a thing seen, fully presented in all of its parts, ought to be for this reason accepted and understood—an ancient contemplative prejudice.

The powerful "waits for the right moment" to tear the mask off the face of the rival, thus revealing, finally, the real intentions that move him—intentions that, on the other hand, he already "knows well" (*Crowds and Power*, 377). Unmasking renders harmless. Nudity fixes, freezes, rendering one completely subject to the glance. The obsession of transparence is constitutive of the language of power. Foucault's *Panopticon* has really already been stated in Canetti. But in so doing the dialectic of producing/outdoing/surviving reaches a second grotesque conclusion. Its apparent "projecting" charge (disruptive, transforming) turns into its opposite, in the prohibition of any change, or better, of any change not already programmed, not already anticipated. Therefore, only a change already taken for granted is permissible—and therefore, only an illusory change, a change of scene.

In the ceaseless unmasking of enemies, the typical paranoia of the language of power becomes clear at every level of the political organization. Absolute prohibition of metamorphosis: it deviates from the norm, it is lawlessness, it reveals diabolic capacities. Just like the mask, it hides from the glance and, therefore, "threatens with the secret dammed up behind it" (*Crowds and Power*, 376). "No-one knows what may not burst forth from behind the mask." The language of producing/outdoing/surviving spills into a condition of perennial suspicion. Only if it would come to a universal unmasking, to a total apocalypse, it could be healed from its normal paranoia. As long as there is only one mask, only a virtual meta-morphosis, the language is obliged, instead, to be suspicious and to be afraid.

The mask as such is a sign of enmity, since for power one who avoids the glance is, essentially, an enemy. Perhaps this throws a new light on the unconscious nature of producing. Pressure to produce appears as rever-ence for unmasking much more than religion of growth or of simple devel-opment. One produces because the mask is unbearable—its explicit claim to conceal or, better, to stratify Being, its explicit will to resist in the un-productive. The mask does not produce the face. With respect to the pro-ductive, the mask counts as the pole of the useless—but of a useless that is not educable, that resists its outdoing and, therefore, the end of the survivor.

This resistance magnifies the paranoid traits of the power-wielder's lan-guage: "Plot and conspiracy are for him routine . . . he feels surrounded." Nor will his enemy be happy to attack him alone, but "he will always try to incite against him *a silent* dosage of hatred" (*Crowds and Power*, 469). In this sense, the normal paranoia of the powerful is really all one with the masses, in fact, it is afflicted by a perennial "feeling of persecution" (*Crowds and Power*, 22), "is like a besieged city and, as in many sieges, it has enemies before its walls and enemies within them" (*Crowds and Power*, 23). Just like the masses, the power-wielder can panic in front of forms of resistance, of modes of conduct unproductive for its force. Just as the masses, the power-wielder, then, can crumble. But before being set on fire, he will instigate all his frenzy against the adversary. If the normal dialectic of unmasking proves ineffective, he will try to downgrade the opponent. As in hallucinations, the enemy (and above all the enemy within) is miniaturized, reduced to a minuscule entity, made smaller. It is changed into a little man, later, into an insect, or in a bacillus. The Lilliput effect does not know limits. This degradation to the lowest goes together, however, with the persistent terror for metamorphosis. A new paradox, or grotesque, of power: its language originates from the terror for metamor-phosis, and yet it ends by generating it! If in the miniaturization of the enemy in insect and bacillus is also revealed the latent panic before the immense multitude of others to be annihilated, in its degradation to abor-tion or to "monstrous hybrid figures" (such as those that torment the impervious realism of European painting from Bosch to Hogarth to Kubin) lives the terror for the mask and for metamorphosis, for the in-comprehensible resistance of its unproductiveness.

The summary we have provided in the previous section of Canetti's analysis shows how the investigation on power, on the symbols of power, cannot be disassociated from the one on the formation and behavior of the great contemporary masses. The modern political forms of myth (to employ a Schmittean expression) interact with the extraordinary novelty constituted by the appearance of contemporary free masses (free in every sense: in the economic-productive sense emphasized by classical economy and by Marx; in the politico-institutional sense, in as much as it avoids any corporative guardianship; in that, broadly speaking, cultural sense, as unreligious with respect to ancient faiths). Between these masses and the language of power exist structural analogies (that even the most documented inquiries, for instance those of G. Mosse, can only touch on, not stemming from a precise critique of the language of power as such).

The reverence of power for development finds its own analogue in the necessity on the part of the masses to grow. Never is mass sufficiently mass, and never can the mass be defined in static terms. There is mass only inasmuch as there is mass-in-growth. If the process of development stops, the mass begins immediately to crumble. The more the masses are compact, the more they expand and aggregate, the more they explode. The first signs of internal panic ignite when the masses are at rest. One could say that masses are never in crisis because of explosion, but only because of implosion.

Just like power, the mass loves its own unity, in fact, its own concentrated unity. Large spaces, with nothing in between to divide it, sufficiently large to contain every growth, every development: this is the typical scene of free mass. Likewise, for power is evil all that divides, differentiates, distinguishes, and are good all the terms that correspond to the idea of unity, community, concentration.

But the affinity between this mass and the language of power consists first of all in the fact that "mass needs direction" (the mass thirsts for submission, Le Bon used to say), and the more vital it is (that is, the more in-growth), the stronger, the supreme command it exacts: a command capable of asserting itself on every single member, able to annul it in the universal and absolute equality that must exist within it. Such an imperative is not at all in contradiction with the probable hierarchical structure that the mass can assume in determinate circumstances, since it only appears as functional differentiation within a substantial equality (that rituals emphasize anyway), and since any hierarchical privilege always appears revocable on the basis of the proper and timely intervention of the supreme command (hence its own necessity for the mass). But the legitimacy of command is also dynamic. "The slow crowd is characterized by the remoteness of its goal," and, therefore, command is legitimate for as long as it succeeds in keeping the mass itinerant, in developing toward goals in themselves unreachable, since reaching them would provoke the disintegration of the mass. The mass is always in pilgrimage: "The road is long, the obstacles unknown and dangers threaten them from all sides. No discharge is permitted before the goal has been reached" (*Crowds and Power*, 39). The mass has never stopped growing, just as analogously its goal has never been reached. To organize such an indefinable growth and to repropose it ceaselessly, in different situations, is the task of the supreme command. And in such task the forms of destructive reason are easily recognizable: annihilation of any real present (command, like the mass, is destined to move toward), systematic sacrifice of any difference, polarization and concentration of the masses achieved with the obsession of the threatening enemy (external or within), without accepting its equality, and then masking, transforming itself, and so forth.

In Canetti's discussion of the process of formation of the masses, the refusal of any form of parallelism with the psychical process, as with of any organic hypostatization of relations and functions of concordance, is remarkable. It is precisely to these functions, never interpreted as substance, that Canetti seems to look to.

In this, Canetti's method agrees with Kelsen's observations who, under the clear influence of the philosophies of language of Vaihinger and Mauthner, criticizes Le Bon's *Psychology of the Masses* (and Durkheim's sociological method), as expression of a real and proper *metabasis eis to allo genos* (mythological) assertion of the possibility of "ascending, without abandoning the psychical, through the intermediary level of 'interaction,' to 'super-individuality,' as to a world of the psychical of a more elevated form."[10] For Kelsen, Freud differentiates himself clearly from this tendency, remaining "in the field of individual psychology," and renouncing "the mystical-metaphysical knowledge of a collective soul distinct from its single souls. . . . For Freud only individual souls exist, and his psychology remains in all aspects an individual psychology." For Kelsen, the results of Freud's analyses derive precisely from this coherent methodological formulation "which dissolves the hypostatizations in the most effective manner, armed with all the magic of secular words—God, society and state—in their individual-psychological elements." Canetti's judgment on Freud's mass psychology is essentially the same, even while changing radically the mark. For Canetti, the dissolution of the mass in individual-psychological elements is impossible. Or, better, for Canetti it is an operation that in no way analyzes the peculiar sense of those elements. The problem does not consist in opposing individual psychology and social psychology. One can perfectly agree that this same differentiation falls within the sphere of individual psychology, without having to believe, therefore, that the Freudian reduction is in itself pertinent. The opposition runs between psychology (psychological reduction) and theoretical or ideal-typical consideration, a consideration on the form *or* idea of the masses, on its structure and on its symbolism. Beside, Kelsen too, when in the work quoted earlier, considers (tangentially) the problem of the state, he is careful from dissolving it in the analysis of individual psychology, although he seems to employ some instruments of the latter almost as propaedeutics to every hypostatizing, mythological tendency.

A perfect match to Canetti's study on the composition of the masses is the lesser-known one on Hermann Broch. To the great novelist, Canetti dedicates an essay where he expands the poetics to which he will remain faithful for the rest of his life.[11] The true poet has to be the slave of his time, in fact, its dog (an allusion to Canetti's encounter with Walser's work), and, as a dog, he knows how to follow its traces, interpret them, discover them. This capacity comes to the poet from his peculiar instinct, an "urge for universality," an "eagerness of thought." This urge is characterized by a "hatred for death," and, therefore, for everything that in time gives death, namely, retains it, as is typical of destructive reason, an unavoidable obstacle. The poet is he who shows how, "until there is death, that every *light* (*Licht*) is *a will-of-the-wisp* (*Irrlicht*)." According to Kraus's lesson, aesthetic and ethical dimension, poetics and critique of political language, are found together in Canetti from his earliest works. This is to make clear what should already have been very clear, that the critique of political language cannot do without the symbolical approach that Canetti has tried perhaps with unequaled lucidity, short of resolving it in the sociology of power tout court, or in economic sociology, or in political and institutional history. A return, indeed, to the classical era.

Broch's writings devoted explicitly to politics and to the psychology of the masses date back to the 1940s.[12] For the purposes of this work, we will focus on his "Essay on Mass Hysteria: Contribution to a Psychology of Politics." Broch, too, starts off by acknowledging a "mass instinct that cannot be confronted at the level and with the instruments of individual psychology" (it is well known how Canetti develops his critique of Freud on a similar premise). However, Broch stresses above all one element of Canetti's phenomenology: the sense of exclusion dominant in the process of formation of the masses. The leader himself is legitimate to the extent to which he can promise to overcome this condition. Panic, thus, appears not only as the result of the disintegration of the masses but also as its precondition. Without the panic of exclusion, there are no masses. In order for the process of its formation to begin there must be an *I-only* that confronts a foreign *not-I*, absolutely an enemy. For this reason, the *I-only* must overcome himself in the masses. The ripe masses, in luxuriant development, are an image, therefore, of the total incorporation of the *not-I* in the *I*, which sends its members into ecstasy.

The final pages of *Crowds and Power* seem to express the hope of a possible discharge of the survivor: "Whether there is any way of dealing with the survivor, who has grown to such monstrous stature, is the most important question today; one is tempted to say that it is the only one" (469). Canetti's answer, however, can only appeal to the new historical situation. It is a contingent answer, so to speak. The logic of the language of power, that we have followed so far, is not seriously threatened. The present grandeur of power would render it "more fleeting than ever." The fact (more stated than explained) that "everyone will survive or none" removes from the dialectic of the survivor its uniqueness. The power-wielder could no longer seriously think of remaining Unique. Canetti believes that the normal means of exercising power (the system always finds its point of maximum equilibrium exactly on the edge of the catastrophe) are by now turned against power itself. The threat of death, which is "the coin of power," threatens the survivor. That is why today, perhaps, it is possible to remove from power its usual coin.

But the thread of this argument adds nothing to the dialectics of power. We have already observed its paradoxical or grotesque traits. The logic of power, insofar as it is destructive, is self-destructive. Destructive reason appears fully only when it fulfills itself. It is in reason's view, as such, that the earth does not appear to be nowhere safe (these are terms that recur in another extraordinary work, Jünger's *An der Zeitmauer*). The power-wielder can never stay, like the masses that he leads. He depends on the inexhaustibility of the growth and capacity of sacrifice. Michelstaedter conceives the figure of Persuasion, precisely, in opposition to modern aesthetic philosophies, which, in essence, are philosophies of the modern, free, metropolitan masses. The dissolution of the survivor, therefore, is nothing other than the fulfillment of the survivor. Deep down, he is *ab origine* aware of the utopian character of the Unique. Not the Unique as such, which is of interest in defining the structure of the power-wielder, but the method toward the Unique, the language and the concrete means that are made ready at the level of method.

   When Canetti tries to think the dissolution of the survivor in the same radical manner with which he thought its concrete language, he encounters an insurmountable impasse. This dissolution is not conceivable *in politicis* if not still in terms of overcoming and, therefore, it becomes again a figure of the language of the power-wielder. As we have shown, this language understands the necessity of its own overcoming or, better, to put, in clearly absurd terms (paradoxical, grotesque), its own claim of sole survivor. Canetti, therefore, does not succeed in showing the dissolution of the power-wielder to the extent to which he seems to project it politically. All that one can say politically is that it is necessary that power be more fleeting or insecure (*insecurus*) than ever, and that the coin of death end up by turning itself against him. What Machiavelli knew very well, and Hobbes too, "the great Leviathan is not the Hegelian present god (*numen praesens*) but a mortal god (*deus mortalis*), a machine that breaks down" (*Teoria*).

   Even in Freud's *Massenpsychologie*, a characteristic utopian dissolution of the masses is at work. The task of stable organizations consist for Freud, in fact, in "having the masses acquire those properties that were characteristic of the individual, and that have become extinct in him because of the formation of the masses," that is, "in endowing the masses with the attributes of the individual." Here is clear why individual psychology acquires a primordial (and in the end, destined) character in his analysis of the problem. Now, as we have said, Canetti does not challenge Freud in the name of social psychology, but by showing the different type, and the originality of the form and formation of the masses with respect to the structure of the individual soul. Freud's utopian ideal of this revoking of the masses derives necessarily from its formulation, on whose bases the masses can be dissolved psychologically (that is, they are analyzable). Kelsen, too, is here explicitly critical with respect to Freud: "The 'masses' must achieve certain characteristics of the individual. But how can this be, if it is always and only the case of properties and functions of the individual soul?" That is, how can the masses (in staying as masses) assume the attributes of the individual, "individualize themselves"?

   There is, indeed, a shift here that, as Kelsen states, seems to betray a break within the sphere of Freud's individual-psychological method.

   More lucid on this point, even with respect to Canetti, seems to be Broch's conclusion. If the whole analysis previously developed resulted (and it is difficult to argue against it, given the premises) that the highest priority of a democratic government should be that of preventing the formation of masses, because of their inextricable connection to the dialectic of the Unique, then the impasse of political reasoning would explode in all its obviousness. The formation of the modern free masses not only goes along but also produces in its own development democratic forms of government, those same ones that these masses, in their development, can contest and destroy. The relation, still postulated by many beautiful souls, between socialization and democracy is broken forever. The connection between masses and democracy becomes possible, contingent, anyway, even weaker, as we have indirectly remarked, than that between masses and the destructive reason of power. Democracy in Canetti (and in part even in Broch) should function as prevention against the masses, therefore, as their overcoming. But once again, the language of overcoming cannot be disengaged from the one proper to the masses. Therefore, the masses should want to overcome themselves. This, however, coincides with their fulfillment, which is also their destruction, but not with a new order, beyond the language of the power-wielder, with the panic of discharge, not with the ecstasy of new organisms. Even the great Leviathan, and precisely because of it, is "a machine that breaks down."

Even Bataille recorded similar remarks in his sociological works of the 1930s, on the basis of his experience with the Popular Front, above all in *The Psychological Structure of Fascism* (1933) and *Towards the Real Revolution* (1936), works that illustrate the cultural poverty of the political French left of those years more than do thousands of disciplinary analyses. Against the liberal-progressive simplifications of the democratic game and its revolutionary unmasking (desperately tending to reveal, ultimately, the authoritarian and classist character of formal democracy), Bataille insists on the unavoidably aporetic character of democracy. The anarchic tendencies that the democratic game acknowledges produce, as such, high expectancies for law and order. It is not a question of two opposed dimensions, but of a single process. The anarchic tendency tends to assume the typical order of the masses, which is dissolution of any traditional tie or *religio* (as Simmel was the first to recognize). The contemporary free masses express the anarchic tendencies of the democratic regime, in that they are powerful demands of authority. Siegfried Kracauer, in the Berlin of the 1920s, the Expressionist Berlin, analyzed the same process, anticipating often the best of later critical sociology. He pointed out the forms of the construction of the collective starting with the panic of the defenseless I-only. The massification of the I-only precedes the formation of the collective, of the masses as organized masses, form-mass. One could say, in fact, that massification produces masses, that the mere egalitarian leveling that divides, isolates, determines the different subjects, redeems itself in the will of becoming-mass, of reacting to the panic through the collective. Different individuals, overcoming themselves, thus, in the collective masses, lay claim authoritatively to the satisfaction of their own anarchic tendencies. From this point of view, the politician who obeys to the authoritarian question of the masses does not differ substantially from the one who follows, instead, its anarchic tendencies. We are dealing with the same problem and, often, with the same real historical movement, viewed from both sides. On the other hand, we observed the aporia that looms over any hypothesis of preventing the formation of masses. Unless we want to light candles of hope, we must recognize this, and know that such hypothesis could never give way to forms of "mystical optimism on the necessity and on the possibility of defining political solutions" (Broch). Any attempt at preventing the formation of the masses appears in a very precarious balance between political and nonpolitical, or, indeed, between light and will-o'-the-wisp (*Licht* and *Irrlicht*). And, maybe, the same aporia is compelled to believe, in the end, in that man who, resisting "alone in the face of death . . . does not enter in the collective that would like to set itself up as final purpose" (S. Kracauer).

CHAPTER 7

Law and Justice

On the Theological and Mystical
Dimensions of the Modern Political

Opposition of Mysticism and Asceticism

Perhaps in no other place as in the interpretation of the role of mysticism in the modern political, Weber's spirit of capitalism requires revision and study. A mystical type of religiosity (*eine mystisch gewendete Religiosität*) is in itself entirely reconcilable "with an eminent realistic sense of empirical data" (thanks precisely to its antilogocentric nature; Weber says: thanks to its rejection of dialectical doctrines) and with a rational conduct of life (*rationale Lebensführung*).[1] For Weber, however, mysticism lacks the "positive evaluation of external activity" (*Wertung*), which in Calvinism goes as far as the exigency of a "sanctity of works elevated to system" and that constitutes the fulfillment of mundane duties as supreme ethical norm. Thus, mysticism, in Weber, appears to be entirely inherent to the general process of rationalization and radical disenchantment (*Entzauberung*) of traditional religiosity, but almost as initial dimension of the same process, its immature source. The Weberian interpretation regards the assertion of that absolute transcendence of God before all creatures, in whose framework is located the vocational calling (*Berufsarbeit*), the synthesis of work and *vocatio*, of which mysticism is not yet capable. The transcendence of mysticism is still improper, since what constitutes its essence is the real penetration of the divine in the human soul and this possibility would necessarily devalue human activity.

We are not concerned at this point with the critique of the historical and theoretical foundations of Weber's interpretation of mysticism, but rather in determining, more accurately, on one hand, the reasons of the difference between mysticism and fully unfolded rational conduct and, on the other, why, in such difference, the mystical dimension does not occupy at all the place of a propaedeutic to the reformed effective faith (*fides effi-cax*, according to the interpretation given by Weber). And this still in two senses: in that of the substantial irreducibility of mysticism to Weber's process of secularization, and in that, apparently opposite, of its irreducibility to a simple form of resolution from the mundane to immediate mystical union (*unio mystica*) devaluating mundane activity tout court. We propose the following hypothesis: not only does mysticism function as a permanent form of critique or opposition to reformed ethical norm, but it is also possible to understand this action on political grounds, or better, as political form. The formation of the modern political can be interconnected to a (reinterpreted) dimension of the mystic, and this, probably, throws new light on the entire question of the spirit of capitalism.

Weber opposes mysticism, as world-rejecting, to innerworldly asceticism. However rational the behavior inspired by such a refusal may seem, it will never be able to conceive the world as a duty imposed to the "religious virtuous," nor even the success of one's own work as manifestation of divine blessing.[2] Even mysticism orders and rationalizes, puts into form, but does not give way to that innerworldly asceticism whereby "the certainty of salvation is constantly confirmed by univocal rational actions . . . conform to principles and rules." The typical mystic is not concerned with a systematic conduct to reach an external success, but with a method to free himself from worldly seduction and to reach the perfect union with the divine. This method can certainly function as shaping force of a community (of men living mystically), but these communities will not develop rational actions as such. They will not give life to worldly order founded on practical rationalism. In Weber, the dimension of the mystic is clearly confined either to the role of original method of the process of rationalization, or that of community survival, to the margins of the rationalization and substantially noninfluential for its development. Along these same lines also functions the relation prophecy-clergy (to which we will have to return), where the former ends up by being resolved in the process of systematization and rationalization of religious ethics, as revelation on which rational metaphysics and religious ethics, developed by the clergy, rests. Prophecy appears, thus, as an extraclerical force destined, however, to legitimize the functions of a clergy, of a body of functions, rationally and methodically organized.[3] And, still, the same is the case with the analysis of redemption. In the theme of redemption is expressed the intellectual necessity of responding to the problem of the lasting sense of the world. Redemption is here considered exclusively in relation to its effects on rational behavior turned to the systematic dominion over nature. "The nostalgia of redemption, *however manifested*, has a place in our inquiry to the extent to which it has consequences for the *practical attitude* in life."[4] Just as mysticism, in general, falls into innerworldly asceticism (or becomes simple rejection of the world), so the theme of redemption either signifies organization of a central and positive sense for practical action, or it seems to vanish in a nostalgia beyond reach, so, still, the prophet either develops into an ethical system and in a rational complex of norms, whose actual power is guaranteed by a stable clergy, or it is exhausted by the withdrawal of his own person, since his charisma, very much like that of the sorcerer, is exclusively personal. It is essential to remark that in Weber these relations are organized in an essentially linear, continuous way. That is, this becoming an ethical system is implicit in his treatment of the prophet. Its only value as form of practical orientation in view of unitarian values is contained a priori in the interpretation of redemption. The destiny of rationalization, in the relation between mystic and innerworldly asceticism, seems almost a total mechanism. The pages Weber dedicates to this relation seem to describe a progressive process. But this is possible on condition of reducing mysticism to a rejection of the world or to a primordial and still enchanted form of organization of practical action. It is necessary to withdraw mysticism from this progressive scheme in order to evaluate, at the same time, both the radical opposition to innerworldly mysticism (which in the evolutionary character of that scheme ended up as dialectic overcoming of mysticism itself) and its actuality in the formation of the modern political, or, better, in the definition of the problem of the modern political. To grasp the irreducibility of mysticism does not mean, however, devaluing its importance for political form. On the contrary, it means analyzing it in its structure. This both deepens and complicates the concept of rationalization, since it has to be redefined in the presence of an autonomous mystical dimension with respect to that simply innerworldly of the ascetic.

The method of innerworldly asceticism is in the dominion over the theological, of the systematic explanation of the given of revelation, of the

analysis of his internal relations and coherent deduction of its consequences for practical action. Heidegger's indications on the original solidarity between theological attitude and rational-scientific disposition find
in Weber's concept of asceticism an enlightening precedent.[5] Asceticism
connotes an action that renounces to any immediate empirical enjoyment
in order to rationalize or systematize so much more powerfully the empirical data. Asceticism completely puts into question the seduction of the
immediate empirical, abstracting from it or remaining suspended on it, to
dominate the empirical so much more effectively. But this same method
is also followed by the theological, in its eminently critical disposition with
respect to any immediate-complete participation to the divine, in its recurrent accusation of irrationality with respect to any behavior not pliable or
explainable according to coherence and logic. The given of revelation, or
even the prophetic word, are assumed here as original data, not deducible
as such, but of which one must conduct a systematic analysis according to
the style of discursive reason. The same mystical attitudes that succeed in
passing the scrutiny of theological rationalism, are understood as substantially repetitive and indifferent confirmation of that original word, on
which by now is edified the stable construction of innerworldly asceticism
and of its vocational calling (*Berufsarbeit*).

The theological systematizes that which by its nature irrupts as irrational and unpredictable, organizes this event in rational norms and procedures that, in repeating themselves, tend intrinsically to annul the
possibility of repetition of the event. The theological puts into innerworldly form (since it makes use of discursive language, which belongs to
this dimension) the original word with respect to any syntax. As the state
is the end of the era of heroes, so the theological is the language in which
the word pales until it disappears. Schmitt's problem of political theology
has to be understood in this strong sense. It is not just a question of the
secularization of the theological (according to a scheme that is still Weber's), but of the intrinsic secularity of the very theological project. The
theological "projects" an absolutely silent conservation of the word within
the framework of juridical procedures aimed at excluding any of its new
and powerful interventions, to normalize life according to unitarian ends
rationally pursuable. Weber speaks of this, too, when he analyzes the
method of salvation in the problem of redemption ("the relation to God
became, in a specific way, a form of the relation of subjection judicially
definable"), but in him the exact perception of the insoluble problematic
character of the process is missing. The fact that the intention of the theological tends to the secular, does not mean at all that its integration in the

history of the latter is pacific and can be taken for granted. In so doing, one would proceed along linear, continuous schemes that misunderstand completely the real conflicts. If we limit ourselves to the systematic accord between theological project and innerworldly asceticism (in as much it can explain the spirit of capitalism), we will not be able to determine the real problem, which is the relation between theology and the modern political or, if you will, the "state" of that asceticism. The intrinsic secularity of the theological by no means corresponds to that innerworldly asceticism, nor such asceticism is normally assuaged within the framework of the procedures and mechanisms that make up the modern state and its law (*jus*).

The Knot of Political Theology

Schmitt's famous work *Political Theology*, where the analogical play appears at times forced, has perhaps been quoted a little too much to the detriment of other works of his where the relation between theology and modern state, in its historically determined development, is analyzed in all its tension.[6] It is the problem of political form that dominates (according to this view) the theological, the problem of a form that functions with the purpose of containing the secular, of comprehending its contradictions, so that its destiny may be fulfilled. Such a form is only conceivable theologically, on the basis, that is, of an eschatological conception of historical becoming and of an *auctoritas* that derives legitimacy from being the inflexible guardian of this conception. In the notion of innerworldly asceticism this problem is entirely absent. The ascetic competition of individuals united to consolidate their own vocation and to professing it *in maiorem Dei gloriam* resolves *ipso facto* the problem of political form. If the political form asserts itself, it is as a result of the rational undeducibility of any original consonance (*consonantia*) among the different vocations and for the necessity of recognizing them as contrary interests to be brought to synthesis, to educate as state. Now, the secularization of theological concepts that characterizes this process is likewise a radical detheologizing (*Enttheologisierung*) of public life. The source of sovereign authority changes, the terms of the Christian-medieval law of the people (*jus gentium*) change as well. The secularization is also equivalent to the "*silete theologi in munere alieno.*"[7] But this does not mean at all that the problem of political form disappears, even though one searches for a natural-rational deduction starting from the innerworldly play of egoistic interests. In fact, only now political form becomes really a problem. How can the idea of

state be founded as a new, total organization, as a definitive and comprehensive system of economic contradictions and of confessional civil wars,
if the state is itself aware of not being able to represent the whole, if it
wants to be deducted rationally as mere worldly power? How can the state
pretend to be valued as ultimate end if its own project is radically detached
from the idea of a theologically founded sovereignty? Its form claims to
be absolutely legitimized as agent of the overall process of secularization
that cannot allow, however, in principle, absolute positions.[8] The countless attempts to flex the idea of state (as radically different from that of
polis or *respublica*) toward ethico-religious elements, to identify in the state
a plus, an excess with respect to the immanence of its being nothing other
than power (immanent reduction that made possible both analysis and
rational justification) must prove to be completely irrational. Faced with
these contradictions of the modern political, the eternal return of the
theological problem of political form is inevitable. The state of secularization is intrinsically impotent with respect to the possibility of such a return. Just as, by now, theologically founded political form is powerless to
revolutionize the power of secularization. The theologian keeps putting
into question and in crisis the rationality of the state (or, better, the actuality of such *ratio*), and vice versa. The theologian posits himself in the sense
of the secularization and the problem of his state. The theological dimension is not at all subsumed simply in that of rational politics, and only by
being entirely aware of the conflicting complementariness of the two
terms it is possible to speak of political theology.

The same process of deconstruction of the term state reconstructs incessantly the problem of political form. And this can have no other declension than the theological. Rationally, it is necessary to proceed from the
jus of the single national state to the crisis of such positive law in the epoch
of the universalism of world markets, eradicating every state individuality.[9]
It is necessary to recognize the process of depoliticization, which inaugu-
rates triumphantly political economy and that the postmodern exaltation
of the techno-administrative functions versus humanistic survival finally
seems to bring to a close. And yet, this same process is forced to reveal
itself as will-to-power and will-to-state, a will that, since it is rationally
undeducible from its premises, appears to be increasingly illegitimate. The
theological form is here powerless testimony of that political form (or, so
to speak, of its a priori conditions) of which the modern state is structurally
incapable. The theological form, in short, appears as idea of a well-
founded authority, and this constitutes the insuperable utopia of the modern political. It is the assertion of an ethos made necessary by the same

groundlessness of state force (*kratos*). And the utopianism of such assertion counts, at the same time, as demonstration of the utopianism of the presumed totality of the state.

The method of innerworldly asceticism does not exhaust at all this problematic. No simple deduction of its form can explain the spirit of the modern state. The theological form overflows from the limits of ascetic rationality, centered on the individual notion of *vocatio*. The theological is systematically in sympathy with the great political form in its autonomy with respect to the community of Christians who order rationally, as such, their own existence. Political form attains to the complexity, to the infinite multiplicity of meanings, proper of modern society, completely extraneous to the organicism both of *demos* and *populus* (*Politica*, 189). No founding cultural homogeneity steers this society. What counts in it, what constitutes its supreme value and makes it possible to hold on, can only be the autonomous sovereignty of political form. But this form is theological, in the most pregnant sense of the term *complexio oppositorum*, foreign to any romantic dualism, characterized by precise dogmatism and firm will to decision making, supported by bodies of functionaries strictly dependent on a center.[10] What Roman Catholicism seems to realize, ever since the dissolution of the medieval *respublica christiana*, is that political form is not deducible from the techno-productive development and the factual configuration of interests within itself. According to its view, what the rationalization of innerworldly asceticism does not know or can embrace is precisely political form, as actual recognition of opposites *and* their *complexio*, rational politics *and* charisma.

A similar critique cannot be reduced to a simple reaction. Apart from these specific contents of its project, it asserts the utopian, groundless nature of a state-machine at the disposal of subjects of innerworldly asceticism, of the selfishness of civil society. Only a destiny of depoliticization turns out deducible from these premises. And if the problem of the formation of the modern state is part of the modern state, the arcane of its "state," then this question, which strongly marks its history ever since its origins, belongs to such a spirit, and belongs to it in a radical paradoxical way. It testifies to the utopian character of the idea of state, of its own form, of its own *auctoritas*. It is utopia, in the rigorous sense, since the subject, the *substratum*, the foundation of state sovereignty become unrepresentable. The Leviathan, the Great Definer, cannot be represented. In the era of technical rationalization the subject-state goes without being seen, and this is his fate. Bentham's *Panopticon* is only the extreme, very much reduced, almost pale product of this tragedy that unfolds behind the scenes of the *theatrum europaeum* and yet constitutes its only plot. But the fall of the principle of representation assumes an almost symbolical value: it unrealizes the subject of power, turning the political into utopia. The absolute poverty of representation characterizes the modern search for the state, the will-to-state, in all its forms, and for one radical reason. The different subjects of innerworldly asceticism or the different egoistic interests want the state, to be sure, but as invisible guarantor of their order, invisible hand of their commerce. They want a state as powerful as it is unrepresentable. The subject is transformed in administrative function and technical apparatus, a simple part of the universal machinery. But this transformation corresponds to a more complex process of depoliticization, of loss of political form. The state freed (absolute) from the possibility of representing its own sovereignty, its own subject, cannot lay claim to any totality. Its body is only human, frailty and mortality, *vanitas vanitatum*. The hieroglyphic of sovereignty lays broken, laid to rest.[11] What counts in the ephemeral, whose project is totally secularized, cannot give life to political form, cannot give way to representation. The Roman Church, with respect to this process, bears witness to the form of a royal Christology. It enjoys, as Schmitt says, an "extraordinary monopoly" of the political. But this form lives by now as a ghostly possibility. It appears only in the form of a witnessing, but, through the witnessing, also of the devastating critique of the validity of the claims to totality of the secularized modern state. This same form is now *part*, a partiality that keeps separate from the whole and is always more consciously definite in its mundane impracticability. Political form survives insularly in that part that is the Roman Church—that is, in contradictory conditions with respect to its same essence, is *ab origine* radically antiutopian.

The theological, therefore, is manifested as the space of the full presence of the political, space opposed to the deforming spirit of modern politics. But, likewise, it is clearly distinct from asceticism, which, even requiring political form, is at the same time, intrinsically, powerless to founding it and representing it. We would like to advance the hypothesis here that, precisely, in the insuperable difference constituted by political theology and innerworldly asceticism, the spirit of contemporary socioeconomic formation ought to be investigated. That this spirit is in essence a contradiction is what a similar investigation, historically determined, can easily clarify. A nondialectical contradiction, to be sure, but not a mere juxtaposition of terms. It is a question of a continuous transformation of their connection along historico-contingent lines, projects, truths whose relativism, however, is overregulated by the conflict between detheologization, secularization of the political, and the necessary return of the problem of political form in the same secularized will-to-state.

But the nature of this difference leaves mysticism out of the picture. If this latter dimension is not exhausted in prolegomena to the mature otherworldly asceticism, its relation to the theological will have to be characterized in a different form from that of ascetic vocation (*Berufsarbeit*). We need to analyze the importance of this new difference, evaluate if mysticism constitutes simply another genre with respect to the themes so far dealt with and, therefore, a set of arguments that is indifferent to the relation theology-asceticism, or, if this were not the case, one needs to see what meaning assumes the intervention of mysticism in the problem of political form.

Mythology of Law

While for the ascetic the search for salvation finds confirmation in methodical, rational action, for the mystic "who is in real possession of the well-being of salvation possessed as his own state, it can happen, instead," Weber claims, "that from such a state *lawlessness* [our italics] could stem, namely the feeling . . . of no longer being tied to any rule of action." Once again, Weber's opposition is too reductive. To be sure, for the mystic it is a question of being opposed to the ascetic *nomos*, but insofar as the latter is exclusively "earthly," it is not lawlessness that differentiates mystic behavior but, if anything, its extraneousness to that specific *nomos* on which innerworldly asceticism bases its own fortunes. But let us try to develop, remembering this important warning, Weber's indication. The norms that regulate rational action, as soon as they are conceived in relation to state organism, assume a theological tonality. When personal norm becomes "earthly" *nomos*, when ascetic method becomes legal procedure and rational system of sovereign norms, we have a shift from a simply ascetic dimension to a properly theological one. And it is useless to repeat how this shift in itself has nothing linear or progressive in it. Therefore, there is systematic solidarity between the formation of a rational state law (*jus*) and theology. Weber, too, is aware of it when he speaks of the clergy and of its attitude toward prophecy, and Carl Schmitt reiterates it by distinguishing the legal form assumed by theological *complexio oppositorum* in the Roman Church from every type of charisma of the prophetic type. By now, we have important confirmations of this relation even in other disciplines. René Girard has analyzed, at the light of a quite analogous interpretative scheme, the formation of the modern judicial system.[12] It appears as secularization and rationalization of the dynamics of sacrifice, in its turn "royal way to violence," that is, a force capable of breaking the infinite spiral of vengeance, "by polarizing on the victim the germs of dissent scattered everywhere." By vindicating the absolute monopoly of legitimate vengeance, the state completes the process begun by sacrifice, rationalizing and, in so doing, developing greatly its effectiveness. "Instead of making an effort to stop vengeance, to restrain it, to avoid it, or to deviate it on to a secondary purpose, as in all strictly religious procedures, the legal system *rationalizes* vengeance . . . manipulates it without danger. It turns it into an extremely effective technique of healing and, secondarily, of preventing violence." But this technique reveals the same aporia as the method of innerworldly asceticism in its will toward the state. On one hand, the technique of vengeance appears to abolish any transcendence capable of distinguishing *sub specie aeterni* legitimate and illegitimate violence (it is the same situation analyzed by Schmitt in the crisis of the concept of *justa causa* in the modern war of annihilation). On the other, however, to become legitimate, the same technique must still appeal to the truth of its norms. If the legal procedure is an immanent technique and therefore rational, it could never pretend to exhibit any truth. But if it revealed, thus, its groundlessness, it would not be effective at all; it could not claim absolute recognition and full obedience. The legal procedure, and the judicial systems to which it gives life, are forced to recover continuously a transcendental dimension that, at the light of their rational structure, is senseless but nonetheless remains essential to guarantee its effectiveness. It is not correct to say, "Only a transcendence whatsoever . . . can *deceive* violence permanently." A whatsoever transcendence undermines the bases of the stability of the system, ending up by coinciding, necessarily, as Girard himself recognizes later, with its undoing. Only a theologically founded transcendence can deceive permanently—that is, transcendence capable indeed of founding the notion of legitimate violence distinguishing it absolutely from the illegal and guilty carnal immanence. The rational judicial technique is obliged to yearn nostalgically toward such foundation. It is theological only in its basic idea or utopia. On the other hand, it also means that its foundation is utopian, that the root of its legitimacy is nowhere. According to the same method, the theological reacted on the foundation of the modern sovereign state, revealing its constitutive aporias at the very moment that it bared its own being secularized.

Mysticism and Justice

It is with respect to this systematic affinity between theology and law that the exceptional character of mysticism begins to manifest itself. Law is the ratification of a peace that resolves a conflict by handing over the monopoly of violence to a legitimate power. Viewed in its constitutive elements, law sounds like a complex of violence and power, as *Gewalt*. The roots of this complex are, for Benjamin, in the "mythic manifestation of immediate violence."[13] The theological rationalization of this manifestation is condition of its complete secularization in the system and in the legal-judiciary technique, but, for the reasons just given on the bases of Girard, one can never get rid of these roots. No new laws can be opposed to the golden chain of myth-theology-law, but the image of justice. No new states (always administered violence, always tending to serve and preserve the law), but the halting of that chain (of its eternal repetition) in the pure language of justice (*Gerechtigkeit*), as "principle of every divine finality."[14] But this is precisely the very essence of the mystic: the most radical otherness with respect to every mythic attitude. Justice is the character of the mystic versus theology, which systematizes, orders, and rationalizes that attitude of otherness. The horizon of these similar motives embraces authors as different as decisive for contemporary culture. The conclusion of Wittgenstein's *Tractatus* could be reproposed in the light of these ideas. What is being sought there is the foundation of a just language (*lingua giusta*), a true and proper sphere of pure understanding, other with respect to the violence of law (even though Benjamin already, and Kraus before him, had caught the irruption of law and violence—*Recht-Gewalt*—even in this sphere). This idea is mystic in its essence and therefore the *Tractatus* closes on the mystic, manifesting its own predominant idea.

To the systematic affinity between theology and law we can oppose, therefore, the one between mysticism and justice. And I believe that the sense of *Gerechtigkeit* should not be looked for in the biblical image suggested by Benjamin of "pure divine violence," instantaneous and *not* bloody, "both sign and seal," but in the idea of a language withdrawn from the discursive, from the theological, precisely, and constantly renewing itself to the fount of the "just" word.[15] Analogously, the mystic theme of justice appears in the work of Simone Weil, and in particular in polemics with a quite theological expression by Maritain. Where Maritain (Weber-like!) sees the relation with God as a form of subjection legally definable, for Weil "neither the notion of obligation nor that of law can be proper to God, and infinitively a lot less that of law."[16] It is almost as if Weil wanted to take issue with Weber's reduction of mysticism to powerless lawlessness with respect to the theological-legal notion of the relation with the divine, and wanted to cross it with Benjamin's idea of justice. The theological idea corresponds to the Roman idea of God, corresponding to Roman law, but mystical tradition seeks precisely the abolition of this idea, its total purification. As long as a trace remains, "the union of love is impossible" (Weil).

We will return, more analytically, to Weil's notion of justice. What must be held firm from now on is its irreducibility to law, to the mythical-theological foundation that it is obliged to repeat. To analyze in legal terms the relation to the divine means romanizing Christianity, normalizing it according to the immanence of law.

The loss of the word is at one with wanting becoming to be, and in the form of duration. The romanization of Christianity means, then, full acceptance of innerworldly time. On one hand, legal normalization of the word; on the other hand, eschatological indifference. The norm prevents new irruptions of the justice of the word, and wants time to be duration of equivalent moments, removed of any possible messianic meaning. Benjamin associates the time of redemption to justice. It wrenches even the dead from triumphant law—those total vanquished reduced to pure non-being, of which Weil speaks, and which the nihilism of becoming incessantly produces. Becoming and law are one, even according to the aporia or the paradox that we have already indicated. Laws want becoming incessantly and want it, together, as state. This means that at every moment (at very moment of that eschatologically empty duration) it is possible to preach the possibility of the composition of conflicts according to legal procedures. And exactly this possibility is assumed providentially as sign of a deep sense of becoming. Legal procedure interprets incessantly the simple value of its force according to this mythical form, its *Gewalt*. It presents itself triumphantly as providential progress, as trace of a providential design in history as is. This idolatry of history is consubstantial with the law, whereby it is interpreted, according to more or less secularized versions, as divine pedagogy, destined to progress. Law could not be differently founded. Its system is exclusively on the ground of the contingent and the immanent, of immanent force. But this will to power, since in its essence it is will of state, must try to be legitimized as expression (insofar as it is historically determined) of a divine design. If only chance is, the law cannot count as foundation of state, that is, its claim shows itself to be mere will to power. Instead, if in history one adores the providential design, then any violence has a sense to pursue that end. In de-eschatologized history, a chain of states would express, would indicate, the advent of a total order. And the great political form that lives in the theological, and in the same catholicity of the church of which it is language, bears witness to the possibility of such an event. To be sure, in the church such a process cannot arrive at the "idol of human redemption" since this would imply the refusal of grace.[17] But such idol only expresses the extreme secularization of that (idolatrous) idea of history as divine pedagogy, which the theological hands over to the law to use it as its foundation.

We could define the refusal of this theological-political *complexio*, of this research in history of a unique substance or of a final sense, of a converging tension toward a state of redemption or autoredemption. Redemption does not occur through history, educating duration to its end.[18] This is what the law claims because its space is exactly that of the necessity to persuade to a methodology and to a procedure capable of producing salvation—but for the mystic no methodology, no innerworldly procedure can guarantee salvation. It is not producible, does not belong to progress, to its language destined to connect and reconnect reason and myth, the theological and the political, law and violence, to its syntax made of continuous ambiguities and perennial seductions, to the idolatry of its names. But the right word (the idea of justice) that mysticism remembers is not at all simply preserved in an immediate indifference with respect to history, in an immediate rejection of the world. As critique of the order of the law (critique that aims at deconstructing that order from within), the idea of justice explodes the continuum of its duration and of its return. By rejecting every kind of divine pedagogy (with so much greater decision the more such pedagogy manifests itself in historicist-progressive guise), the idea of justice asserts the possibility of a stoppage of time as mere passage from state to state, the possibility of a messianic instant that breaks up the indifferent chain of homogeneous and empty moments.[19] The antidialectic nature of mysticism insists everywhere on these terms: detachment, leap, decision, in other words, everything that exceeds the norm, the linearizing violence of the law. While the *Recht* has to sacralize every state reached and sacralize its overall movement in as much as progress of mankind in history, justice sees in this time always more secularized idolatry, with procedures always more obligated to exhibit one's immanence (exactly in the sense indicated by Girard with respect to the rationalization of violence). Therefore, the critique of mysticism functions, on one hand, as powerful force from within that deconstruction of the law, of which Schmitt spoke in rigorous legal-institutional terms, and, on the other, as idea of the possible break away from the ground of the law, of the theological, of progress, from their ground as such, as idea of the decision from it. For all these reasons, the opposition of mysticism to political theology cannot be confused with quietist doctrines of abandonment of the profane, or with resigned disillusionments with its vanity.

Decision

Even in Kierkegaard, mysticism exists only for the moment of decision, in opposition to being in history, which justifies providentially the infinite and homogeneous duration, proper of political theology. Decision does not concern particular aspects of history, but is a global commitment to tear oneself as an individual from the continuum of its moments. Commitment sounds here like obligation, bond, *religio* that does not allow accommodation. Commitment makes the person totally responsible, as an individual, to decide, to "cut away" himself from the continuity of the norm, from the eternal repetition of the law. The category of law (and of the theological) is repetition.[20] The category of mysticism is the uniqueness of the moment that decides duration. The individual appears as a step, a decisive threshold. He is the one who did not give up at Thermopylae (if the hordes had been allowed to pass, all would have been lost). Without this category, the idolatry of which we are ill has hopelessly won: "the individual is and remains the anchor which has to stop the pantheistic confusion."[21] Christianity is immersed in this confusion, which has assumed the form of theology and of law, dialecticized with respect to the continuum, organized to last. Precisely the history of this Christianity, or history as the product of this Christianity, is the genre that has to be broken. One can be authentically Christian "only by contrast," deciding the same Christianity, its scandal with respect to the original *vocatio* of Christianity for the individual and of the individual. Christianity calls to the absolute responsibility of the individual. This decision eradicates, constitutes the extraordinary, the exception (*Either/Or*). While the complexity of legal procedure has more power the more it is of the earthly order, the more it is founded on the *justissima tellus* (and its crisis corresponds, in fact, to the necessary dissolution of this foundation), the individual is authentic only in the dimension of the eradication (*Entortung*).[22] The called one cannot be accommodated, cannot be systematized. It is in a hurry to get away. Instead of lasting in the norm, here one exists in the paradox of a perennial state of exception. The individual is no longer comprehensible, is not a part of the *complexio*. Its opposition breaks the theological *complexio*, is not representable within itself.

Kierkegaard's individual refutes point by point the dialectic of political theology. It exceeds it, breaks it, withdrawing itself from the view that claimed to be comprehensive. The mystical relation to God occurs only in the individual, in the extraordinary moment that explodes time from the hinges of duration—a moment that is impossible to incorporate and represent. Any abstract category that turns up to dialecticize the relation forces a relapse into paganism (which Kierkegaard, just like Simone Weil, often tends to assimilate to Judaism). In Christianity, God is placed in relation with man according to the absolute measure of the individual, calling him to the radical responsibility to become "that Single One." It is clear how in this context an innerworldly scheme of redemption cannot even be conceived, for which the profane order could assume the sense of the kingdom's advent. Not only is history not a movement to redemption, but the same possibility of salvation that *calls* in deciding himself is also extraordinary, an exception, a scandal for the genres of history. What differentiates profoundly the two perspectives concerns once again the concept of time, which they subsume. The time of *complexio* and representation corresponds to that of duration, even though providentially characterized. And in it, as its necessary products, the forces must exist, the organisms of asceticism, of the law, of the education of the genre to the sense of history. The time of the individual is the moment that "does not come to terms" with duration, but opens up to the eternity of the word. It is the moment that occurs in time and cuts itself away (*si decide*), together, for eternity, leaping from time to the dimension of the eternal. If this paradox does not count, nothing counts of Christianity, because only such paradox constitutes its essence: "In this life your eternity is decided." To satisfy time is proper to contemporaries, and to preach that "true seriousness" consists in this, but deciding time within time, to satisfy eternity, is proper of the Christian as individual, incoercible to Christianity and to the Church.

Both Löwith and Schmitt have insisted on the fact that this perspective does not mean a simple flight from the world, and on the historico-political dimension assumed, in their turn, by Kierkegaard's categories. "The

force of the era," writes Löwith, "brought Kierkegaard, therefore, to historical speculation despite his polemic against Hegel's historical thinking."[23] The individual does not stop to its immediate antihistorical and
antipolitical meaning. Against the "misfortune of our time" to be nothing
other than time (Kierkegaard), the message of the individual is neither
refusal nor renunciation, but recall, the call of eternity, understanding this
call as force that occurs in time, a perfectly responsible decision of time
within time. On these categories (decision, responsibility, call) should be
focused our attention to discover the essential relation of mysticism "to
the general circumstances of the era" (Löwith), to try to define the decisive
function within these same aporias of the theological-political and of its
nomos. This is partially examined by Löwith, and only indirectly by
Schmitt, but in either interpretation, Kierkegaard occupies a central position in the "knot" of 1848, fatal to European history.[24]

Kierkegaard's mystical eradication (*Entortung*) unfolds with tragic
awareness in the framework of the eradication of European *jus*. The year
1848 dissipates the sacral centrality of Europe. The experience of a fundamental break in the course of history, of an irrevocable decision, of a total
revolution (that is, that does not allow returns or reforms), unites works
as profoundly different as those by Bauer, Tocqueville, Stirner, Kierkegaard, and Marx. The category of decision is produced in this historically
determined context, and so the idea of the leap outside the norm of duration, which is realized in catching the unrepeatable moment. Its call is as
absolutely responsibilizing as instantaneous, and pointing in its purity to
possible justice, the *Gerechtigkeit* that redeems from any *Recht*. Rigorous
historico-political prognoses substantiate these ideas from the setting of
European *Weltpolitik* before the rise of new powers, the United States and
Russia, to the insurmountable aporias of the democratic massification of
the political (in revolutionary theoreticians, as in those of the Restoration).
Kierkegaard reconnects this process to the decadence of Christianity, to
the end of Christian-Romantic civilization. This civilization was founded
on the progressive secularization of the theological-political symbol. Now
this eon is at its end. Secularization has accomplished perfectly the consumption of that symbol, which by now lasts deprived of any authority, as
mere force (*Gewalt*). Reforming it would be absurd, since this destiny is
implicit in the original disposition of the symbol. It is within it that history
as divine pedagogy and law as the force that keeps it in form is posited.
Now, instead, the leap to a new era, a Christianity decided by civilization,
asserts itself. This decision does not enjoy any security. Foretelling, anticipation, assurance belong to time as continuum where the events are connected in a single plot, as equivalent. Since in the individual what occurs

exceeds the continuum, what becomes manifest, here, so to speak, is chance in its purity, irreducible to the chances that make up the world. While the latter are taken for granted in the project that anticipates them and governs them, this one alone is not foreseeable; this alone irrupts with the strength of a radical call. To listen to this *Ruf*, therefore, means accepting the risk, taking a risk fully. "If you do not risk now, you will have an eternity to regret it. . . . But you must also remember that one can make a mistake in taking a risk, and therefore one will have to suffer in time because one made a mistake in taking a risk, and one will have to regret it for all eternity" (*Either/Or*). But while not taking a risk, and being at home in the norm and in its tradition, is always tantamount to a shirking from the call (from the error that risk can bring about), the possibility of error inherent in risk when it authentically cuts itself away from every certainty, opens, anyway, to the call and in the end conquers the dimension of the individual. The value of this dimension goes beyond, in fact, the measure of success, is not measurable at the level of worldly attainment, but uniquely in its desire "to satisfy eternity."

Decision-risk forms, therefore, a sole notion to which certainty in the shadow of the law is opposed. The critique of the European-Christian eon does not emphasize so much the absence of decision in the historical continuum but the loss of a decision in which the individual constitutes and puts himself radically to risk. We find this same dimension, even if deprived of the essentially mystic motive of *Ruf* (on which we shall return) and, consequently, of that relation between individual and eternity, in the most radical conceptions of revolutionary politics produced, precisely, by the "knot" of 1848. What needs to be recognized is the exceptional coherence that mystical formulation confers upon the notions of decision and risk. If the decision must be absolutely risky, it can only turn, in the first and last instance, to the himself of the individual. If one wants to produce absolute exception, it can be produced only in and from the extraordinary thing that the individual is. But the individual can be conceived only within the context of a mysticism of the person. If the concept of revolution must indeed count as total, excluding any reform or any repetition, it can only be understood as excess of duration, moment that in time leaps from time and takes a risk in relation with the eternal. The notions of decision, absolute responsibility, call, and risk do not seem to have any foundation other than that of mysticism, in opposition to the theological.

On the bases of the motives so far considered, it seems possible to distinguish between two perspectives of the mysticism, both of exceptional importance with relation to the modern political as problem. Actually, both move from a refusal of any providential conception of history and from the incurable contrast between law and justice, but this affinity, although strong, remains declined to the negative. On one hand, it gives life to the decisionism of the individual, so to speak, that at any moment sees the possible moment of redemption and exists exclusively for this moment. This motive is prophetic in its essence. The individual, as we have already seen, is the called one, the one who has to serve the word. Not so much and not first of all he who foresees, but he who displays before, who expresses the word.[25] It is for this reason that the prophet embodies the archetype of a redemption in the future. And in fact, the creature, the mere being creatural, can become individual, and the individual must take a risk prophetically. The eradicating tension of this "opening" alarms the people, and above all those people whose greatest idolatry is idolatry of history, of the state, of security. The individual is expelled or sacrificed again and again, but precisely this sacrifice can be eponymous, can give life to new authorities. In this aspect, the figure of the hero is similar to the individual. It appears in a time already deconsecrated, as representative of an unfounded decisionism, of a decision that takes a total risk, but without being called.

On the other hand, the idea of justice and redemption can develop in a gnostic, antiprophetic sense. It is witnessed as necessity. If the same creature is intrinsically fallen, no decision can redeem it. Or, better, only that decision that puts an end to the creature itself, when it cries in reply to the question that God incessantly asks: "Do you want to be created?"— "No, no, no!"[26] The exceptional moment, the paradoxical possibility of the exceptional state is not opposed, therefore, to providential historicism, but to divine providence as necessary order, as equilibrium. Weil's justice is the *diké* of Greek wisdom, equal to necessity, to truth, to sovereignty of sovereignty. "This is how the entire pre-Roman antiquity conceived it" (*The Need for Roots*). It is easy to see how this contrasts profoundly with the God of biblical prophecy. Mysticism appears here as a theory of the immutable, as an asking "what it is." Every wish, every question is understood in the perfect acceptance of providence as unbreakable order. The dimension of the choice concerns the creature that we must deny in ourselves, gift of the original sin.

It would seem elementary, at this point, to place in immediate alternative the two tendencies of mysticism and consider only the former as politically meaningful. What matters, on the contrary, is their reaction. There is no doubt: the form of the decision, of the absolute answer to the perfectly responsibilizing question, this form is mystical. Discontinuity, breakup of the continuum, exception are opposed to tradition, collectivity, law. For the mystic, the possibility of the moment is always. If it has to be form of total revolution, such form can only be found in the mystical dimension of decision. But here lies the problem. This dimension cannot in any way escape the process of secularization. Far from being resolved in the secularization of the theological, it also involves the sphere of mysticism. It appears both as rationalization of the norm and of what exceeds the norm, of duration and of what breaks it, of the *respublica christiana* and of the individual irreducible to it. Thus, the messianic moment is transformed in total revolution, which "betrays itself" necessarily, in political innovation. And, in its turn, we could add, innovation is transformed in a complexity of programs. The problem of the grand political decision comes to be thought mystically, just as that of the grand political form was thought theologically. A profound difference passes between the two dimensions, and yet a common destiny embraces both: the decision, losing every relation with the call that is imposed on it, is deresponsibilized, and rationalizes its own risk, ending up by bending programmatically. Political form, its *nomos*, once lost every *auctoritas*, administers and governs technically the chances in their immanence.

The strength and necessity of the mystical recall lies in that: if grand decision is conceivable, it can only be conceivable (for a thinking that goes to the roots, and does not try to accommodate) in the antitheological form of the extraordinary, instantaneous relation to the divine. The strength and necessity of the theological lies in that: if grand political form is conceivable, it can only be in the antimystical form of the *complexio oppositorum*, of a representative body, of sacral *auctoritas* (this does not exclude, but entails, as we saw, the maximum development of a rational law and of a clergy capable of administering it). The tragedy consists in the fact that neither decision nor political form appears any longer as real possibilities.

On this result reacts, then, that other dimension of mysticism, more gnostic-sapiential than prophetic-heroic. In an author such as Weil one is clearly aware that the rejection of any mystic decisionism derives from the awareness of its inevitable secularization. The form of the decision, however, counts as eradication, as separation. The paradox of the individual is that the act of the most radical separation can constitute the premise of the relation with the eternal. But paradox is not order, is not necessity. In the paradox we ask, obviously, something that is not, we ask the renewal of a miracle. This question can only sound idolatrous and blasphemous in relation to Weil's prayer.[27] What totality can ever be reconstructed through the very voice of separation, which is the premise of nihilism

dominating historical time? How can what is constituted as part "satisfy
the eternal"? To be aware of the paradox and recognizing it does not mean
overcoming it. To exist tragically before it means that its constitutive aporia—in which the time-only-time of secularized decision irrupts—will not
be overcome. And yet, how, in excluding the paradoxical decision of the
individual, is otherness from duration conceivable? How can one break
the time of the law, if from the idea of redemption every messianic expectation is removed and such an idea is equivalent, gnostically, to a pure
contemplation of the necessary pure, and, therefore, of the necessity of
these same chances that today constitute our world, its *Gewalt*? Reciprocally, decision and waiting for God (as methodical exercise of pure attention) seem reducible to the theological, or, better, they seem to denounce
to one another their own impotence with respect of its own destiny (since,
as we have seen, the theological dimension is not at all linearly reducible
to the secular).[28] And, once again, both these perspectives not only expose
the theological and mystical roots of the modern problematic of the political, but they also show how these roots must continuously emerge for the
intrinsic impossibility to resolve this same problematic. If in the political
echoes the theme of the grand decision, it will only be carried out in mystical form. The theme escapes the paradigms of rationalization, and, therefore, in assuming it, the modern political will put into question the very
foundations of its own actual legitimacy. A similar reasoning goes for the
grand political form in its relation to the theological, with the further
complication of the contrast between mysticism and theology and, as we
have had a chance to ascertain, within the same dimension of mysticism.

In both Weber and Schmitt, these motives are not thought radically.
Though in Weber the theme of decision is felt in all its problematic character against the techno-administrative process, and yet, by removing the
mystical foundation, it can maintain itself as suspended, a possibility that
goes perennially weakening without the possibility of ever decreeing its
end. In Schmitt, the declension is in theological terms, and yet as state-
decision, foundation of norm, endowed with exceptional authority. In
Schmitt the original solidarity of decision and justice is removed and inauthentic affinity, proper of completely immanent political decision, between programmatic choice and concrete law takes its place. It is true that
in Schmitt such a choice takes aim at the reform of authority struck by
modern total revolutions, but this, once again, becomes an exclusively
theological notion concerning the problem of the foundation of the state
and its law. How is it possible to maintain the dimension of a radical

choice, there where legal procedure and bureaucratic administration dominate, and the political itself is legitimized as perfectly rational? The removal of the origins (not chronological, to be sure!) of the decision is functional to the attempt to give an answer to this question. But the removal ends up by having to remove the very sense of the question.

On the Possible Unpolitical Completion of the Political

Only in one point this closure seems vulnerable—by deriving, almost from within language itself, the motive of the decision, from its radical formulation in the "knot" of 1848 to Nietzsche, Weber, Schmitt. In *Being and Time*, the contrast with this motive is central, very dense. It is not possible to escape the impression of a contact with the aporias that Heidegger's analysis has so far pointed out. On one hand, there is no "attestation on the part of *Dasein* of an authentic potentiality-for-being" (*Being*, Sec. II, Chap. II) if the foundations of the decision are not given. On the other hand, these foundations can be derived neither from Kierkegaard's category of the individual, nor from Weber's sociological-political typology. All Kierkegaard's and Weber's key notions, none excluded, are already included in Heidegger's analytic of *Dasein*, but in an attempt to refound them, or to finally found them, in such terms as to exclude any mystical and/or political borrowing. It is as if in order to preserve the motive of decision it were necessary to withdraw it in an absolutely pure unpolitical. Better, the immanent political rationalization that the motive undergoes in Weber is not only insufficient but also groundless, since by being preserved in the political, decision must constantly remind itself of the mystical dimension that originates it. Therefore, it is necessary to cross Weber's typology to attest the absolute difference of the decision from any immanent, programmatic flexion, from any determined choice. Hence the impression can arise of a return to Kierkegaard's handling of the theme, precisely when it could not be further from it.

As in Kierkegaard (but it would not be difficult to find similar motives in Weber), decision implies a separation of one's own self from the chatter of They (*Man*), from the dispersal in the impersonal, in the genre. It entails responding to the self of himself, to assume full responsibility. But while in Kierkegaard this is the conditional premise of the call, in Heidegger it appears as the result of appeal (*Anruf*), which summons (*Aufruft*) *Dasein* to its own most potentiality-for-Being. The appeal, which breaks off listening-away (*hinhören*) to the They, which brings *Dasein* back from "this lostness of failing to hear itself," from "the hubbub of the manifold ambiguity which idle talk possesses in its everyday 'newness,'" and that leaves no foothold to "curiosity," comes from conscience. "A close analysis of conscience reveals it as *call*." Bewildered and in its thrownness, from the depths of its lostness, *Dasein* calls, calls forth (*vorrufen*), anxious about its potentiality-for-Being, so that Being-itself can be called to itself and *Dasein* can finally decide for its authentic potentiality-for-Being. The circle of decision is completed in responding to this call, drastically eliminating any mystical-religious dimension. In Kierkegaard, the "who" that calls is only in the first instance *Dasein* from the depths of its lostness. More than an appeal (*Anruf*), his is a cry of anxiety, saturation of the mundane. Once so decided, within the occurred decision, a new anxiety of listening to the call and the anxiety of the question around the "who" that calls, are born. This is inevitable if the sense of the question consists in "satisfying the eternal," namely, in taking care of a dimension of itself irreducible to the historical one. In Heidegger, precisely, this development is interdicted. Since the potentiality-for-Being authentic assigned to *Dasein* does not exceed at all *Dasein* itself, it is not even necessary to pose the question of who calls. *Dasein* itself calls, even though the call is "neither planned nor prepared for nor voluntarily performed, nor have we ever done so." Even though it irrupts against our expectations, it is to be sure not "an extraneous force." "The fact that the call is not something which is explicitly performed *by me*, but that rather 'it' does the calling, does not justify seeking the caller in some entity with a character other than that of *Dasein*." It is Dasein as thrown, bewildered, not-at-home that calls and is summoned to its authentic potentiality-for-Being.

The radical immanence of this notion of decision, which also excludes any compromise with the They, seems as distant from Kierkegaard, as near to Weber. Something calls in me and from me and compels me to total responsibility, even though knowing that who calls is certainly not *Dasein*. We are reminded of Weber's mature man who says, acting according to the ethics of responsibility, "I can do no other, I am not moving from here," and seals political vocation (*Beruf zur Politik*). But every *Beruf*, in the era of rationalization, can answer only the call that irrupts from the full immanence of *Dasein*. And yet, what Heidegger accomplishes, in contrast to Weber, is the complete political emptying of the knot call-decision-vocation (*Anruf-Entschlossenheit-Beruf*). It makes no sense to pose the question of who calls (only *Dasein can* call), even to question the content of the call. "The call does not report events; it calls without uttering anything. The call discourses in the uncanny mode of *keeping silent* . . . in calling the one to whom the appeal is made, it does this only because, in a calling the one to whom the appeal is made . . . *calls* him *back* from this *into its reticence of his existent* potentiality-for-being." The voice of the call cannot reach the one who is called (the "voked," the one who will have *to* profess that for which one is called), mingled as it is with "the public idle talk of the 'they.' " The call calls keeping silent and calls to silence. Therefore, the "what" most proper to the call is silence that suspends radically the idle talk, the information. It reveals the "not-at-home" of *Dasein* and from its depth opens up the anguish of authentic potentiality-for-Being. Therefore, for Heidegger, Weber's *Beruf* belongs still, though desperately, to the "They," to its obvious discursivity and politicity. And this would betray the radical sense of the decision, just as much as its mystical-religious foundation in Kierkegaard. In Weber, the decision rests entirely on the call of *Dasein*, but this call that responsibilizes, aiming at determinate objectives, is, in its essence, political. This, for Heidegger, would resolve the problem in dogmatic terms, and entirely powerless to suspend the discourse of the They. The dimension of authentic decision appears totally unpolitical. Just as it was in Kierkegaard, in a way, only that in him dogmatism was asserted in terms of the who of the call and, as a result, of the end of the call. *Dasein* calls *Dasein* not to redeem it—the dimension of redemption is entirely out of discussion—but to open it up to the anguish of Being-guilty, "*of a primordial Being-guilty.*" (Since *Dasein* finds in the They its own foundation, the matter of dejection always falls within its determination. And, being as potentiality-for-Being, *Dasein* is always either in one or the other possibility, and therefore must always bear "not-having-chosen and not even-being able-to choose the other.") The appeal calls forth this anguish, calls *Dasein* "to be guilty *authentically*—'guilty' in the way in which it is." The call, therefore, does not summon neither to the disenchanted rational of Weber's *Beruf*, nor to the decision of the individual for the moment that redeems satisfying the eternal, but calls to the care of *Dasein* "permeated with nullity."

One could not imagine a clearer reversal of the prophetic dimension (of which, somehow, Weber's political still preserved some memory). But the strength of this reversal can only be acknowledged after having crossed the whole gamut of political theology and its opposition in the mystical theme of decision. Heidegger seems to imply this crossing. His analytics confronts point by point, term by term what we ourselves have tried to do. And term by term, it shows the intrinsic incoherence and contradiction. The play of differences and mirrors between the theological and the

mystical, and within each of these dimensions, fundamental to understanding the modern problem of the political, is here, rigorously judged
as confusion, equivocal, as inner face of the They: in short, as nondecision,
which does not mean that up to now we have not succeeded in founding
political decision, but that such foundation is impossible, that the desire
to find it leads to idle talk. What is the extent of this recognition? That
today only the space of the program is sensibly available, or that idle talk
is inevitable for the political just as the equivocal is for discourse? That,
anyway, the modern political not being able to abandon those terms, is
compelled to repeat them as ideological myth, or that one has to be able
to radically renounce them, as if words that seemed proper of the political
(decision, engagement, responsibility, representation), in their complexity
and diversity, were by now justly sayable only in nonpolitical spheres, better, in the unpolitical?[29]

CHAPTER 8

The Geophilosophy of Europe

Here is the supreme struggle (*agon eschatos*), the labor (*ponos*), and the ultimate confrontation that the soul is called upon to bear: steering the steeds,
which are also its parts, training them for the difficult ascent, preventing
that the wicked one (the spirit of gravity, we could say!) drags us to earth,
negating the joy of contemplating the hyperuranian reality (*ta exo tou ora-
nou*). The memorable *mythos* of the *Phaedrus* (246–247), therefore, teaches
that education (*paideia*) is *agon*, a struggle in the composite structure of the
soul between opposite powers, but also that this *agon* is harmonizing. The
charioteer can assert its own hegemony and establish the connection. He
can mediate the immediate dissonance. The struggle is in its essence an
effort to achieve harmony. No struggle begins without harmony in mind.
It is necessary solely as search for the ways and forms whereby a harmony
can be produced, can be revealed. The meaning of the *agon* consists in the
aletheuein of harmony: in manifesting harmony as its own truth.

And yet, in the struggle, the sides that are distinct offer themselves to
the glance with the greatest neatness, unrelenting. The first moment of
the process consists in determining those distinct sides, in defining them,
in making them *stay* one against the other. The "stay" echoes in the *stasis*,
in the war between kinsmen, since the two opposite principles belong eternally to the soul. Furthermore, they are both effort, impulse, appetite,

innate nostalgia, and without the innate, and, therefore, necessarily *a-logos*, speechless, impulse of the thoroughbred—for how else could the charioteer steer them up there toward the "native country"? The last moment (the *agon eschatos*) consists in demonstrating the connection. In between: the adventure, the great trip, utterly dangerous (*periculosum maxime*), where only the *logos* can guide us. This is the art of placing into communication, of informing, of establishing relations, of connecting what opinion deems impossible to reconcile.

At the same instant when the Two emerges (and the root of *dyo* is the same of the verb that speaks the fear, *deido*, of the term that points to the frightful, the bewildering, *deinos*)—the *wonder* of the Two, which makes uneasy and afraid—also emerges the search for its origin, of its inner relations and of its very end, that is, the questioning on that power that makes of twos, *one* Two. To question the difference entails questioning the identity. To wonder at the manifold initiates the memory of the One. Will it be possible not only to get to know what is absolutely distinct, but also to remember, in fact, why and how the split occurred? It is clear, in fact, that if we were capable of the *logos* of separation, we would understand it unitarily, and the harmony between the One and the many would be thus established. Of the One, there cannot be simple and immediate intuition. The One is, here, always, the unity of harmony, the unity of the harmonic construct that is the product of the *agon eschatos*.

These are the fundamental aporias of European philosophy, inextricably connected to the *historein*, to the cultural and political roots of European history, to the historical *Dasein* of Europe. These roots could not even be conceived without a geographic definition, without the determination of the European borders.[1] Only a full *anamnesis* of the past, one that establishes the truth of the past and therefore a critique with respect to the "many and ridiculous *logoi*" that are narrated around it, will be able to heal the city from its ills, guaranteeing it a future life. The discourse of Hecateus, historian and geographer, would result incomprehensible without the work of a sage that preceded him by a century, Epimenides the Cretan, the cleanser of Athens.[2] In order to make the city obedient to justice, it is necessary to get to know its true origin, to risk the travel in the long sleep of the past.

Between the sage and the historian, there are the great upheavals of the sixth century, the irrepressible looming of the awful problem of difference, of the distinction between powers and their respective *timai* (in which terms, within which boundaries do they have value?), a problem that in its turn, imposes that of the search for their specific identity, of the reason of their present difference, and of the possibility of its overcoming. Let us look, with Mazzarino's help, to the writings of the seventh and eighth centuries. The indistinct rules. The power of limiting has not asserted itself yet. The archipelagos of the Homeric "white-haired Aegean" form crowns of bridges. The cities are ports, passages.

In the manifold Ionia, East and West meet immediately, almost without having to meet. To meet entails, in fact, the split already. Hesiod, enthusiastic worshiper of the Asiatic Hecate, foreign to the Homeric Olympus, knows Asia and Europe as the name of two little Oceanides, belonging to the family of Ocean and Thetis, sacred family (*hieron genos*), destined to nourish the youth of men together with Lord Apollo and the rivers. Asia is the iridescent whole of the Greek Ionian cities, with, at most, the strongly Hellenized lineages of the Lydians and Phrygians.

The awful problem matures slowly, digs with method. First of all, it emerges from the contrast between the irreducible archipelago of the cities, the *poleis*, that never, not even in the moments of greatest danger, succeed in harmonizing, and the powerful reign of the Lydians that had been able to resist the invasion of the Cimmerians and to stop on the Halys (the day of the famous eclipse foretold by Thales) the Median army. Already Mimnermus, a poet from Smyrna, had questioned the reasons of the conflict that had opposed the Asia of Gyges to Greek Ionia, and thought that he could locate it in the ancient violence of the colonization of Colophon by the Pylians. Greek hubris at the origin of the division. Looms here the great historiographic-geographic scheme of uninterrupted events of wrongs and vengeance, violence that call for violence, of an ancient war that is also the only firm connection between East and West.

But in order that this scheme may acquire its full meaning, may empower our language and our thinking, it is necessary to arrive at the decisive years, to the *Achsenzeit*, when the "true" Asia sweeps away its Hellenizing screens, where the Greeks reflected themselves, and subjects to itself with different chains from those used by the Lydians, the cities of Ionia, undisputed spiritual leaders of all Hellas. The fatal distinction now becomes clear after the defeat of the Lydians by the hand of Cyrus. The problem of the division imposes itself once and for all with the domination of the Persian Empire. On the other side of the sea, the ancient *mare nostrum* for the Greeks, there is now the absolutely distinct. The unity is decided for all time. One must think, know this multiple "unheard-of." But in order to think it, it will be necessary first of all to know ourselves. The appearance of the other forces the return to oneself. To this laborious task, difficult more than any other, maybe impossible, the gods force the Greek. Without knowing one's identity, it will be impossible to confront the other. All the sages repeat it, and this is the fruit of their *sophia*. But on the pediment of Delphi there is an enigma. If the cities of trade and travels must now turn into themselves, to remember and to identify themselves in front of the Great King who advances, they will find necessarily in their very own soul that division that they had to learn to know. The external conflict (*polemos*) is connected to the inner civil war (*stasis*). And this harmony is the *polis*, a figure that the East never knew and will never know.

But the entire Greek nation and, therefore, the same idea of the West, is the result of these decisive years, in which the conscience of the inevitable war with the immense empire of the Great King asserts itself, and at the same time the conscience that in order to deal with this war, it is necessary to assume an impossible task, to know oneself. The contrast entails the analysis, the precise distinction of the parts, the measurement of their boundaries, the investigation of their internal structure. And it entails likewise the harmony, the search on the forms of the possible connection of the distinct. The first form of connection is the war. The first voice of the togetherness (*cum*) resounds in the *polemos*. Historical, geographical, political, and philosophical anamnesis in one. As will always be the case for the West.[3]

Forty years before Herodotus's *Histories*, this drama, the action whereby the destinies of Asia and Europe are in opposition, is expressed in Aeschylus's *Persians*. Half a century of laborious elaboration of the idea, the idea (*eidos*) of the polis and of the entire Greek world, produce this epochal work, of which the twenty-five-year-old Pericles assumed the sponsorship of the chorus (*khoregia*). At this point we are not interested to situate *The Persians* politically (the disproportionate emphasis on the Persian defeat and on Athens as savior of Hellas is doubtlessly a sign of the will to direct Athens' politics against the ex-ally Sparta), nor to enumerate those key ideas on the Greek daimon that we find in Herodotus (poetry is always more philosophical than history!). Of Aeschylus's play we are only interested in a single scene: the Queen's dream. For a long time now, Atossa is prey to turmoil, nightmares, and omens of misfortune, but this night the dream that visited her seems to her clear and terrifying. She dreamed of two women, imposing in their stature and of incomparable beauty. But there was *stasis* between them that the Great King Xerxes could not mitigate. He yokes them both to a chariot, but one accepts the rein, tame, in fact, "proud of that harness," while the other rebels to it, taking the harness apart, breaking the yoke, and throwing Xerxes from the chariot. The woman who in Persian dress follows the king is Asia "rich in people ... divine herd." The woman dressed in Doric is untamable *Eleutheria*, Greek freedom, subject to none. But the tragedy does not limit itself to oppose them immediately. It confronts face to face the enigma of their *stasis*, and, therefore, of their same relation. Asia and Europe not only appear both beautiful and divine but also are really "blood sisters, of the same lineage." They inhabit different lands, but their source is one.

On the stage (*skene*) of Europe, an image of similar tension will never appear again.[4] Only the absolutely distinct appears inseparable. Only of the agonists of a mortal *stasis*, one can predicate the oneness of the lineage (*genos*). (We can never emphasize it enough. Here, the *polemos*, par excellence, between Greeks and barbarians is indicated with the term of civil war, *stasis!*) The opposites, to be recognized as such, to be such in actuality (*actu*), have to manifest more profound harmony. The perfect characterization of the opposite is the most powerful harmony.

But will the horse that does not tolerate any yoke be able to recognize this harmony? To be sure, no harmony could produce the empire of One alone, as unlimited indistinct, where the opposing views could not be expressed. But neither Athens' simple victory, nor Athena's staff on the Persian arch, will be able to resolve the enigma. Its liberty counts by itself as immediate assertion of its own being-part. And the forms of *hubris* are two: delirious violence, but also inhospitable separation. The Greek description of Asia expresses always the sense of the boundless: boundless lands, boundless armies, boundless power of the king, or the sense of confusion, of the formless, of what, in short, has not yet met the power of the limiting. But what succeeded in the task of defining itself in its own limits—this victorious Hercules—how could he not produce, not evoke the problem of the boundless that he embraces? The form, the *kosmos*, was it not perhaps the boundless? And having seen and known the form, shall not one, at once, *sola mente*, intuit also the formless wounding, the *periechon*? Every statue, every Greek temple expresses it, that is, they bring to intuition what they are not.

Therefore, the boundless and the limiting must be harmonized. Both are constitutive principles of *physis* and *kosmos*. If there were no harmony between them, nothing would appear (there would be no *physis*, to be sure, that is, no birth.) Thus Philolaus, thus Plato's *Timaeus*, of which the Pythagorean Timaeus is the direct source. The problem is inseparable from the immense trauma that produced the revelation of true Asia, first of all to science, to Ionic physiology, to the weapons of their critical spirit. It is necessary to awaken the mind to this harmony. Sleeping are those who ignore it. Sleeping, to be sure, are the peaceful subjects of Asia. They live oblivious of the "great changes in all things (*metabolai ton panton*)." Their mind is left in immobility; they do not count on their own strength; they are not autonomous.[5] But sleeping could also be the troubled inhabitants of Europe, if they limited themselves to extol their own freedom, their own power to tear themselves from any yoke, to throw any king from his command, without understanding the common *logos*. Those who in opposing powers, in the game of the *polemos*, perceive only dissonances, or only the voice of manifest harmony, namely of the simple connection, and not the one also of their invisible unity; they also would be living "as idiots," as if there was a "private" wisdom.

This is the aporia that the mind must unfold (*diaporein*: and in this consists the *askesis*, the exercise of philosophy). In the term *eleutheria*, by which the Greek characterizes himself, it will be necessary to hear the timbre of *lyein*, from *lysis*, the force that in detaching us from the formless herd makes autonomy possible, but together with it, in perfect simultaneity, also that of *philia* (friendship), of *philotes*.[6] It is Empedocles's *vicissitudo*, where, mind you, the principle demiurge-poet of genesis is *Neikos* (only *polemos* characterizes, manifests, expresses, gives form), and that of *apokatastasis*, of the return to unity, is *Philia* (31 DK, B 16). We could say that *Neikos*, that mortal enmity that "cuts itself away," divides forever from Asia, gives form, gives birth to the Greek (and on the wonderful, terrifying spectacle of his liberty hinges the entire speculation of the fifth century). But if his frank speech, his *parresia*, forgets the common *logos*, and if *logos* will not found on this common ground (*xynon*) his own *nomos*, freedom will turn into the most violent hubris, condemning the *polis* to ruin.[7] This is Sophocles's drama, of whose epilogue the martyr, the witness, will be Plato. But then the Doric horse needs a yoke indeed! It is right that Neikos rebels to the formless rule of Asia, but woe if her freedom transforms in *anomia*, in lawlessness. Her indomitable nature requires a despot, but the only despot that will be able to persuade her is the "*despotes nomos*" (Herodotus VII, 102), the despot that is the law of the city. *Eleutheria*, according to its true root, is connection. But connection is harmony of the really opposites, just as the most acute and the most grave, male and female, are. As Asia and Europe. Those are the opposites that Heris herself, the goddess of discord that Homer wished would perish (*Iliad* 18:107), unleashes. Heris and Dike, Discord and Justice, are the same. The violent difference and the cosmic order form the most beautiful harmony. *Polemos* generates the multiplicity of the distinct, and in being distinguished, in the perfection of the act that distinguishes them, the many are connected. The common *logos* contains such harmony, and this is the place where the *nomos* of the city has its real, solid roots.

It is impossible, therefore, to separate in the thinking of that part that is Europe (the form of judgment, which is the form of European thought, which reflects perfectly that original crisis, whereby Europe exists, ek-sists, distinguishing itself from abstract, immediate unity) the manifest harmony (which is the connection deriving from the accord amongst the many, and therefore a simple compound) from the *aphanes*, the harmony that does not appear or, better, that appears only to the eyes of the mind, whose light, *phaos*, is precisely the object of the sage's intuition, *sophos*. The *logos* of the sage says that there is only one process from the many to the one and from the one to the many. The harmony appears, indeed, *palintropos*, it unfolds in many forms, but always remaining one in itself. It always returns to itself. Harmony between Apollon, as *a-pollà*, the orphic *apocatas* of the many into the One, and Dionysus torn to pieces by the Titans. Thus, the *logos* would recognize the violence of opposition and, at the same time, he would know how to overcome it—almost consoling, we would dare say, Atossa's own despair, as well as the defeat of the Great King.

Therefore, the sense of the first *agon* would be to prevent that our form, our being-part, is dissolved in the indistinct. But the greatest *agon* would consist in expressing the harmony between *apeiron* and *peras*, between the One and the determination of the many, between identity and difference. Through the first *agon* we shake the yoke of Asia, but the decisive battle, to which the Muse invites us, is in knowing how to connect to that despot which is the law, before which we are all equal, as we are before the *logos* for the *logos*. The freedom whereby everyone, any individual, can speak frankly, counts only insofar as it is harmonized with the equality of everyone else. Autonomy and isonomy either form *a* harmony, or they simply do not exist.

The always living origin of our philosophy, therefore, is paradoxical. It asserts, on the one hand, that only on the strength of difference and of its transformations (*metabolai*) the mind is awakened, frees itself of the slavery of the immediate, and that the only *logos* is that of opposites. On the other hand, our philosophy also asserts that the difference of opposites remains incomprehensible, as such. In fact, as soon as they are understood as opposites they cease to be such in order to belong to a unique *genos*, as the divine women of Atossa's dream. If there is a *logos* that connects opposites, it is necessary that they be ontologically one, that the thought that predicates their harmony is the same as their being, just as we are free in the *polis* on the strength of being sons of this earth, of its people, of its *ethos*. But what can the discourse of the truly common assert to the multiplicity of beings? Nothing else than difference. Beings are one in their reciprocal difference. In this they are equal, the ones contending against the others. The original *cum*, the *xynon* of the divine and eternal *logos*, coincides with the perfect singularity of each being. The opposites harmonize in being all perfectly single and, therefore, not other from themselves. If, then, from the frightful Two, unity is necessarily produced, at the moment that the Two are comprehended by the eye of the *logos*, the unity of the *logos*, in its turn, can signify only the original community of difference, the being one of the multiple in its difference.

The decision whereby Europe stays (*stasis!*) with respect to Asia cannot produce, therefore, any *absolutum*. It is precisely by asserting my difference from the other that I am with him. The other is my inseparable *cum*. My freedom from him is my friendship with him. To be able to give him hospitality he must be a stranger (*hostis*). No harmony will ever be abstract overcoming of difference, and never a difference will be a negation of harmony. Since the connection that it expresses is much more than the connection between opposites, it counts as the very opposition common to everyone. European thought, which originates in Ionic Asia, and that moves the very same Irremovable (ancient laws, myths and traditional rites), is always nourished by the problem of how to save the irreducible singularity of beings from the horror of barbarian emptiness (*horror vacui barbaro!*), by conceiving it as the very force of connection, the very principle of harmony (*aphanes*, the nonappearing, the most powerful). The same force that individualizes, that makes stay and therefore opposes, is that of *philia*, which makes inseparable.

But here a path opens up to which Greek thought only hints at (namely, that it neither says nor keeps from saying). Explicitly, this path has confronted the enigma of harmony as if it were the problem of the middle, of *metaxy*, of the "pontifex" between opposites. In these terms, the Greek thought has already constructed harmony with the first Pythagorism. But, then, harmony is nothing but the number on whose basis the distance that separates the limit and the boundless, the acute and the grave, is articulated. Still not differently in the *Timaeus*, harmony is the *logos* that mixes the without-parts (*ameres*) and the distinct (*meriston*). Its research is reduced to that of a determined number, near the opposites, that allows simply to *rhythm* the distance that separates them, their in-between. But if harmony is this number, which determines this *rhythm* (*arithmos-rythmos*), it will participate essentially to the nature of the multiple, it will belong to the sequence of numbers.[8] Harmony, so to speak, becomes entified (*entificata*). It appears sensibly and musically, and its hidden power is lost. And since the possible harmonic middles are infinite, the connection of the multiple that will appear from time to time (thanks to the determination of one of these middles), will only turn out to be a simple artifice, convention, deal, the result of an arbitrary decision. I believe that the idea of peace, as occasional cessation of conflict, as nothing other than not-war, temporary pause, of our idea of peace as mere *pactum*, could be derived from this intrinsic aporia of the Pythagorean-Platonic idea of harmony.[9] Peace as *pactum* is intrinsically turned to the determination of a middle term, but no middle can really connect opposites, since, simply, the middle belongs to their very same nature, it is determined as they are. What is absolutely distinct harmonizes in no-thing (*ni-ente*). No golden number fills in, by "entifying" it, their in-between. They are harmonized in being such, absolutely distinct, and, therefore, in postulating the existence of the other. If an apparent number covered their distance, in that number the essentiality of their distinction would be denied, and, therefore, no harmony of opposites would take place. To cover the distance by the production of a *metaxy* is the hubris of Xerxes, who purports to yoke two horses, or the two shores of the Hellespont. But in order to be saved, the difference will have to be understood. In other words, it will have to be understood that difference is the common (*to xynón*), that what is absolutely distinct always needs the other, and the distance from the other, in order to be saved as distinct. If Europe succeeded in this sense to remember its own distinction, it would also succeed, perhaps, to express from its *metabolai* an idea of harmony foreign to any fascination with conciliation or synthesis, as well as to any assimilative arrogance. The place of *cum* is *atopos*, "no-where," as elusive and absurd as *exaiphnes*, Plato's moment. But just as for the latter, only the connection of numbers is conceivable, so it is for that nowhereness (*atopia*) that illuminates and defines the space of opposites, in the multiple forms of their contradiction.

CHAPTER 9

Weber and the Politician as Tragic Hero

Weber's Phenomenology

If by phenomenology we mean essentially that attitude or mode of thinking that puts the vision of essences before a formal definition of the valid criteria of knowledge, Max Weber is a great phenomenologist (even though his knowledge of Husserl's philosophy may have been minimal), and any attempt to reduce his approach to a methodology of the sciences of culture is destined to be misunderstood. How imperative is in him the "return to the thing" is demonstrated by his two important lectures on the future of the scientist and politician.[1] These lectures actually make up a single study, since Weber's problem consists not in abstracting two "types" from the historical material at his disposal but in determining the form of their conflict. The very existence of this conflict is the source of Weber's thought, whose necessity originates, in a Hegelian way, when the oppositions "gain independence;" when, in fact, "the highest division" is reached and the two (*Ent-zweiung*) confront each other in their own irreducible individuality.[2] But here Hegel's influence on Weber ends, namely, with the assertion of the necessity of conflict, of its being a "factor" of life. No "higher fullness of life" is possible for Weber, no synthesis is reachable as actual development of division itself. Synthesis, then, can only be thought as beyond division: a scientific and philosophical empti-ness. Hegel's *Phenomenology of Mind* and its grandiose program—to show the *Aufhebung* concretely, the possibility to reposit the division in the Ab-solute, will have to be, therefore, "disenchanted" and abandoned. The conflict from which the necessity for philosophy arises cannot be resolved according to the terms in which it really manifests itself, but only by mysti-fying its characters, by ignoring the individualities of which it consists or by being consoled in the formalism of what "has to" be. If we can call tragic the awareness of the impossibility of resolving the conflict that is at the heart of life itself—an impossibility whose traits and sense only the most valiant research can define and make self-evident—then, Weber's phenomenology reveals itself as definitely tragic. The "types" that Weber singles out do not reify in an abstract separateness, but, in fact, they con-flict with one another in the form of their insurmountable contradiction. They are not organized in well-ordered hierarchies but generate, pre-cisely, the order of their own conflict. This order is the object of science, and not a description limited to juxtaposing elements empirically. But it is an order that excludes the possibility of a unifying law, capable of satisfy-ing and reconciling opposites.

From this point of view, every dualism would also represent a solution of the conflict: to subside in a dead separateness or indifference.[3] There-fore, any interpretation of Weber's work that is based on the notion of dualism, even when it is able to grasp sharply its distinct aspects, is com-pletely wrong when considered as a whole. The relentless criticism that Weber moved to any "emanatist" logic (which derives historical facts from an *idea* of their connection and development, to the point of asserting their synthesis in a "universal history"),[4] his sharp refusal of "any intuitive representation, that penetrates empathically in the inside of the process," not only are worth infinitely more that the actual "aversion of the positiv-ist" with respect to every idealism, but they also acquire the opposite meaning.[5] Weber's *will to knowledge* asserts itself "only through the unbi-ased analysis of meanings that are present from time to time and through the rigorous analysis of the processes that are thereby linked and put to-gether" (*Lo storicismo*, 335). And above all, Weber's approach asserts itself as *groundless will*, or better, as expression of that supremacy of the will that is a philosophical problem and a problem of *value*, and that will never be smuggled as a given attitude because of its natural self-evidence. The will to knowledge in the exact terms of scientific reason cannot be reduced to a "cold inquiry into being" (as Troeltsch would like), for the simple and basic reason that, as Weber was entirely aware, its very own principles, and its very logico-historical origin, are grounded in decision and choice. And here there is conflict, since the *vocation* of pure research, which forbids any idea of organic development, just as it relinquishes any claim to delve into the lived experience of a historical individual, in order to provide a complete explanation, is not simply *other*, extraneous and indifferent to the world of values, but it is a form of this very same world, one of the forms of its making in unsurmountable conflict with the other forms— and, therefore, in unavoidable *communication* with them. Science *must* pursue objectivity through the principles of logical consistency and by means of empirical statements—but it is a question, precisely, of a *duty* that, as such, is not so different from the duty of affirming one's own ideal, which is the purpose of the man of action.[6] The two forms of duty clash, and they clash tragically for Weber (they give life to an *Entzweiung*, precisely). But it is because of their *difference* that each can express its own essence. In order to "return to the thing," it is necessary, therefore, to place the very thing in its conflict with respect to the others. The dimension of decision that follows clearly from the vocation and the assertion of duty is not, therefore, considered at all in an extrinsic and unmediated way with respect to the pure and value-free research of the determining connections that drives scientific enterprise.

Science is always organized according to *values*. Without recognizing this *fact*, science would betray its own fundamental systematic assumption. But there is more: precisely the rationality of modern science becomes the *value* that permeates the vital worlds of the modern. Even the ideals that are opposed to such rationality are determined by it. Every discourse on the order or hierarchy of values cannot fail to acknowledge that science is directly involved in their *drama*. No choice or decision of value would be conceivable in the modern unless with respect to and in relation to the idea-ideal of scientific rationality. And none has helped us to understand this fatal tangle better than Weber.

Weber's struggle against any religion of science, any salvific consideration of its value, is, therefore, as hard as the one he leads against any impressionistic philosophy of life. It is the *basso continuo* of his work. In rejecting every prejudice, science rejects this rationalistic prejudice as well. The rational forms of scientific understanding must never be misunderstood by being transformed in a *faith*, namely, that of the prevalence of rational calculation in human action. The scientist suffers (*pathos!*) an authentic vocation for its own activity but, unlike the religious man and also, as we shall see, the politician, he cannot point to it as *the* value to put before all others, taking it out from their sum total. This is, in fact, how one could define a *Wertordnung*, a hierarchy of values that precisely the actual historico-sociological predicament shows to be impracticable. The deeper the scientific understanding (and the more *evident* the connections that scientific analysis grasps among the facts), the more science will abstain from proclaiming itself as model for an entire life, that is, from believing that life could overcome its own confrontational conflicting character if only it were allowed to conform entirely to the model of scientific rationality. Neither must science lose its "form" in the unforeseeable flux of vital values, nor can these values "save themselves" in the rigor with which science attempts to explain connections and link facts to motives. Science must never abdicate to the search for objectivity (even in the explicit awareness of being founded on a historically conditioned idea of truth: science is relative as to the origin, but not relativistic as to its method and with respect to the reality it aims to comprehend). The types science constructs or the laws it expresses (connections that are likely to remain completely hidden to those who actually act) represent only statistical possibilities or "uniformities." Without this construction any authentic interpretation would be impossible and only *Schwärmerei* (the empty exaltation of sympathetic intuition) would remain. However, once again it is important to recognize the *contrast* between the form of types and laws and the "dark area" in which real action moves, its "relative unreality" with respect to action.[7]

Science is called on to formulate *judgments* on the lived experience (without indulging in any psychologism), on the bases of recognizing obvious regularities, not to judge values, and still less put them in a hierarchical order that would only reinforce science's supremacy. However, science's radical rejection of any teleological perspective, of any idea of development-progress capable of "comprehending" the inexhaustible creation of new values, remains in incurable conflict with the value-driven perspective that constitutes the essential character of human actions, and that this science takes on as its own object. The end of the conflict could be envisioned only if science would offer itself as *the* form of life. If, in other words, beside comprehending the lived experience according to types and laws science also meant to guide life according to its own method and its own ends (which consist in the attainment of the evidence of the connections with which an action develops—evidence that will never be anything more than a causal *hypothesis* "particularly evident" [*Economy and Society*, 9]). Then, what would cease to be is not the conflict, but science itself! The more powerful the scientific interpretation is, the more rigorously it defines its own limitations. Real behaviors, and the motives that move them, are always infinitively more vast and complex than the causal explanation that we can provide for them. That is why the living always returns, ceaselessly, to "resuscitate" the dead.[8] But the dead can give an answer (never *the* answer) only to those who know how to question them according to rite. Otherwise one can only obtain from them a confused and incomprehensible noise. And then, perhaps, that answer will be a sign for the destination of the living, but, certainly, not a prophecy.

A Hierarchy of Values

What can be stated scientifically is the *fact* of Western techno-scientific rationalization (*Rationalisierung*) as the fundamental structure of modern life and a determining factor of its *Weltanschauung*, whose originality derives, equally factually, from a *comparison* with other civilizations and cultures. This is the historical origin and this is the content, at the same time, of *sociology*. But these considerations must remain absolutely value-free (*wertfrei*), that is, they cannot be made into value judgments. The comparative analysis is rigorously distinct from any attempt to construct a hierarchical order, a *Wertrangordnung*. Its nonevaluative character must be *valued* by science first of all with respect to science itself. Here lies its value. Is it possible to assert it, without negating other values at the same time? Can the pure and universal nature of the nonevaluative character of the scientific mind be asserted without at the same time stating the inferiority of those values that cannot claim a similar purity and universality? Leo Strauss's critique of Weber is well known: the comparison would not be possible without the definition of an order that establishes a hierarchy of values.[9] There is no comparison without a yardstick to judge it. But Weber knows full well that every age offers a hierarchy of dominant values that are expressed materially in "rules of preference" (to say it with Scheler). Otherwise, how could we explain his work on the *spirit* of capitalism? His understanding of a historically relative ordering does not imply any metaphysics. In other words, orders are *posited* by conflicting individualities that never appear as their *repository*. Here lies Weber's abyssal difference with Scheler's philosophy—and, on the other hand, his deep connection with Nietzsche's.[10] If every value has value insofar as *positum*, and this is all that science states, science can certainly develop the richest comparison among values, but it will have to renounce to choose one over another, on pain of losing any critical distance and the loss of its vocation. Science can, and in fact, it must, trace the idea-form (*Gestaltheit*) of values, and on whose bases the "goods" of an era orient and order themselves reciprocally, however, without maintaining the authority of one over another. But in so doing are we not asserting, once again, the superiority of nonevaluative science over any other method? This would be the case, if the imperative of nonevaluation did not mean the acknowledgment of the limits of scientific rationality, its impotence as a method for the resolution of the confrontational character of life. Such an imperative constitutes the essential condition for the construction of types necessary to master the historical material, but who are nonetheless incapable to orient action.

This is the *tragic* stamp of *Wertfreiheit*, of being free from value that escapes Strauss and Scheler, Weber's greatest critics, and that, instead, it is possible to intuit in Jaspers and in Löwith.[11] Science holds its own inalienable individuality. It does not choose among values in the conflict but, on the other hand, it is not situated at all in an abstract beyond. A critical distance does not imply detachment or separation. We could say that science lives in the world of values without belonging to them. Value-driven action is its object, its *problem*, but not in a contemplative sense. Science's form, in the very moment that interprets this action, *can* also interact in it and transform it. In fact, it is destined to do so.

That is why the relation between social science and social action cannot be reduced to deterministic-naturalistic paradigms. Science is a form of action and its individuality is defined in historical opposition with respect to other actions. *Pathos* for science and titanic will-to-know, both the trademarks of Weber's work, are generated from this opposition. Far from dissolving that *pathos*, Weber's "I want" introduces the firm scientific will to be free from the "tyranny of values" in the context of their struggle, which only dissolves any claim to conceive science in a metaphysical and salvific perspective.[12] Even the scientist decides, but he decides to understand the struggle of values without taking part in it for anyone, in the exercise and within the limits of his own research. However, in already undertaking a research he has *decided*, and therefore his relation to other vocations is a priori, original. A relation without confusion, absolute distinction without separation.

This point of view has to be asserted. No valuable insight could otherwise take place. The scientist can understand the spirit of an era or a culture not because he intuitively identifies with it or because he contemplates it as an object naturalistically given, but because the same logical rigor that must be expressed in its interpretation intertwines constituently with the different forms of action oriented to value. The scholar is called to define himself *absolutely* in relation to the man of action. He will never neutralize the latter's energy and will always have to know how to resist from succumbing to it. Science degenerates in ideology when it surrenders to the power of action or, conversely, when it conceives its critical distance as a blessed autonomy and not in function of a *confrontation* with the other, which must be focused, above all, precisely on the comparison between the two. In Weber's case it is not a question of "wisdom," if for wisdom one understands the search for an irenic balance between values in conflict. But the drama does not unfold between the figures of a scientific asceticism and of a dancing dervish![13] On one hand, the *askesis*, or the exercise of science, is always *in-situation* and is defined in its difference from other forms of action; on the other hand, it does not deal at all with the presumed irrationality of value-oriented action. The values' lack of foundation is not at all equivalent to mere arbitrariness.[14] Science can grasp an order and a sense only to the extent to which values are immanent to their development. That is why the ideal types are not reducible to fictions, nominal *ficta*, functional to the order of *discourse* alone.[15] They describe, to be sure, case-limits, but cases where the concrete figures that empirical experience gathers are recognized according to their final possibility. They bring a certain order and clarity in the darkness of actual action not from outside but, by suspending any occasional consideration, shedding light on long-lasting forms.

The problem, therefore, does not consist in defining the *quidditas* of science, but the *relation* between scientific action and action according to values. Every problem is "relative" not because it is treated "in a relative way," but because it posits the question of the relationship among absolutely distinct things, in which each conditions the other precisely on the strength of its distinction. Among the powers that determine the life of an era, the reciprocal differing tends to develop (statistic regularity, not absolute Law!) in the form of a struggle. But the contestants appear to Weber, I would say, more as *hostes* than as *enemies* (*inimici*). The battle cannot assume the destruction of the adversary as its end. The tragic form of the relation excludes necessarily such solution. Nor the distinction that science wants to represent could attain any evidence if in the end the research would reach either an indifferent unity or, which is the same, the termination of the conflict. The antinomy has no other choice than that of being clearly understood. Authentic social science does not overcome the antinomy, nor does it indicate which values could overcome the latter. It shows its necessity, though. Social science must tend to clarify the sense of human action, and this is possible because the action's compelling motives are far from being irrational or arbitrary. For Weber, values that shape the motives are not at all purely "founded on nothing," as Strauss, Scheler, and also, in part, Troeltsch have claimed.[16] *Some* of them (and only some, as we will see) are manifested in the form of "so I will, so I command" (*sic volo, sic jubeo*), but this will-that-commands is always, in its turn, conditioned, its sense can never be expressed in an unrelated way to the context of other values and other visions of the world. Even less unconditioned is the process triggered by the *sic volo*, where the original relative liberty must necessarily come to an agreement and compromise with all the other factors that favor or hinder the "project." The idea of liberty becomes pure illusion when it is a question of acting, of embodying the end that is willed. Phenomenologically, only the reciprocal conditioning of motives is then registered. Anyhow, the liberty of acting could be made manifest in no other way than by contradicting itself. Liberty is such because it wants to realize its world—and manifest itself by "misplacing" its own pure idea, precisely, by actually trying to realize it. Thus the conflict that we have followed between science and its material, human action (of which science is a part, a part-in-conflict), and the contrast between a nonevaluative approach and the inalienable assumption of value (the ideal of scientific rationality, which founds it), find their outcome and their exemplary dimension within the contradiction between scientific vocation and that limit-form of action that is the political act.

We could say that the modern *civitas* is defined by their polarity. To the pure type of scientist, devoted exclusively to the research of the "truths" (since he knows that *Veritas* cannot be grasped within the limits of his discourse), absolutely free of any prejudice and precomprehension, disenchanted with respect to the *idola tribus*, capable of separating perfectly fact and value, one cannot simply oppose a general and generic idea of action according to values, of social action on the basis of particular motives and interests, often confused and obscure for the same subjects that are their bearers. Here is not even question of a real opposition, since the undefinable zone of daily empirical action, conditioned by every kind of drive and opinion, is not constituted in any way by its own idea-form (*Gestaltheit*) with respect to the disposition-vocation of science, nor does it differ knowingly from it. Both the scientist and the politician are detached from its territory. They separate *starting from* this *common* exodus. The unity of the modern *civitas* is represented, then, by the *stasis*, by the brotherly enmity between the city of science and the city of politics. On one hand, we have the elaboration of a priori forms, which find application only in the world of experience but in themselves are pure and disinterested. On the

other hand, we have the will to understand the overflow of life and prede-
termine it, forcing it in the *value* of one's own project, with the effects that
inevitably will repeat themselves even if albeit in always new forms. Science can only deceive itself that its own purity can be transformed in an
ethico-political model—actually, in a depoliticized project, aimed at the
elimination of the very same possibilities of conflict (Voltaire used to say
that the Amsterdam Stock Exchange is never at war with itself—precisely
the opposite position taken by Weber!).[17] Yet politics cannot renounce to
putting into question the abstract autonomy of scientific research every
time that it seems convenient to the pursuit of its own ends, which means,
to the realization of its values.

Therefore, it is *stasis*, because the two dimensions are not only originally connected (the history of the spirit of modern science runs along that
of the modern political), but they are also continuously *perplexed*. A highly
political perspective is reborn from the very form of scientific research,
just as political praxis necessarily claims to "becoming true" scientifically.
The distinction between types, once again, is truly interesting when it
allows us to see its living contradictoriness. They contradict each other in
the reciprocal attempt to give form to life, to react radically to every irrational vitalism. And, in the end, the accusation that they move to each
other is also mutual, that is, of not being able to realize such an end:
science, because it would be simply renouncing any power on real action;
politics, because its control on such action would prove to be a mere contingent device, in fact, nothing else than an infinite chasing after the unforeseeable development.

The analogy with Augustine's two cities, which is tempting perhaps,
also to the point of accounting for the depth of the term *Beruf*, in the sense
bestowed upon it by Weber, ends here—but for a reason that makes the
conflicting even stronger. They are both godless. In fact, the scale of values that they establish presupposes God's death.[18] Scientific research *ex-*
cludes any teleological consideration of nature thereby excluding that
science itself (as if its truth could transcend the forms of knowledge), will
ever constitute a way to God, just as the modern political asserts its own
rigorous autonomy from any metaphysical or religious foundation. As the
a priori forms of the experience of nature are immanent to the subject, so
the criteria of praxis are justified on the basis of their own internal coherence and for the relationship that they are able to establish between means
and ends. It is from the structure of the techno-scientific-political apparatus and its parts that the conflicts must be brought to light. They all belong

to the era of the "image of the world"—that is, of the world as representation, but far from exhausting itself in this finding, it is from here that
Weber's authentic scientific reflection begins.[19] Science counts only as *an
analysis* of the differences shaping this era—comparable differences, whose
distances can be measured, but never idealistically made into a synthesis.
Politics and science share the era's destiny: secularization of fundamental
theological ideas, overturning of their values. But opposite is their way of
following it. Science has value (and enjoys actual *auctoritas*) to the extent
that it does *not* seem to take part in the conflict between values. Politics
defines and redefines constantly the scale of values, attempting to attribute
to those it promotes the highest possible degree of universality. Of course,
in the era of generalized "loss of values" (*Entwertung*) these scales of values
will be subject to continuous shifts, to ever-new interpretations. The values of which we speak have always been "estimated" already, even if one
will try to conceal it in every way. And yet, the fact remains that political
action must be oriented according to values, partake in their conflict, consider the values of the adversary as negative, or, at least, subordinate them
to one's own vision. There is an inner, insurmountable *aggressiveness* in
the definition of any hierarchy of values—namely, in making politics.[20]

An Impossible Harmony

That type of politics can only be rational with respect to value, which
means that we are still dealing with *rationality*! The conflict is not at all
determined between an abstract rationality aiming for a purpose and an
irrational drive toward an end, but between the calculation of eligible
means to realize a project and the pure form of having-to be, in pursuit of
its own end, without any consideration of its price. But the form of duty
is *purely rational*! The original contradiction is, again, the one between
techno-scientific rationality and politics on one hand and the merely empirical dimension in which real action for the most part unfolds on the
other. Only on these bases, the decisive difference between the two powers
emerges at the center of Weber's phenomenology. Politics can only be an
action according to imperatives. It is not necessary that it generated from
being driven by absolute duty, but it cannot certainly disregard the conviction in the same values it asserts and the need to make them convincing.
The more the form of politics will be able to orient itself with respect to
its purpose (on the basis of the means at its disposal and the consequences
of its acts), the more it will be rational. We could say that the form of

political action is characterized, in fact, by the attempt to combine, as much as possible, the ethics of conviction with the ethics of responsibility. The reflection on this impossible harmony is at the center of Weber's essay, and not the definition, intrinsically "in crisis" of the reciprocal autonomy of the two ethics. Scientific knowledge does not know this internal conflict precisely because of its claim to "pure knowledge," which has to do with the world of being, not of duty.[21] Science does not intervene in the conflict of values in order to guide them, unless in the sense of their disenchantment. And yet, it does not possess any means to decree the irrationality of the political, not only because acting according to values is a *fact*, and to affirm its irrationality would transform immediately scientific knowledge into sole judge and supreme value, but also because acting according to one's own conviction does not exclude (in fact, in some ways, it implies, politically), the rational pursuit of purpose. Why should conviction blind us with respect to the rational calculation of means or turn to a realistically impossible end, to an *adynaton* in Aristotle's sense?

It is entirely evident that Weber introduces the figure of the modern politician in the development of the bureaucratic-rational form that dominates every economical and institutional structure of the modern. With similar realism, he aims however at defining its specificity and individuality. The professional politician originates from the modern division of labor destined to dominate all fields. How could the politician contradict its rationality without being reduced to a perfect will to *impotence*? And at the same time, he would equally reduce himself to a will to impotence if he limited himself to an organizational capacity, or entrepreneurial dimension, and would deal with his fundamental "means" (the modern party, the parliamentarian institutions, and so on) as business. Political action is *called on* (precisely in the sense of "vocation") to break what Raymond Aron calls "the net of determinism" through a *decision*, whose consequences are in large part unforeseeable—but that the politician must always try to calculate. He does not derive the sense of his action from the degree of realization of his own purpose, but this does not entail in any way that he should pursue it anyway and despite it all. Therefore, not only are the means always to be rationally utilized, but also the very purpose rests on an objective knowledge and ought to be the fruit of a reasonable choice, aware of its risks. In other words, the real and true political decision always takes place, for Weber, within the techno-bureaucratic-rational dimension of the modern political. It is always in dialogue with structures and authorities devoted to the rational analysis of the situation, to define the validity of the process on the basis of historical knowledge, to elaborate reliable statistics that may help establish how many and that are the possibilities to reach the appointed goal.[22]

A politician who claims to be able to do without this knowledge and expertise, namely, to be abstractly separated from the scholar, will be purely and simply a man of the *phrase*, and he will never be able to reach the true power of the demagogic *word*. He will stop at the platonic *kolacheia*, the *adulation* of the masses, in its most plebeian drives.

However, the difference remains and is radical. The politician is not called on to understand the facts, and even less he is led to reflect on the past. Inevitably, such disposition leads to evaluate continuity as fundamental, as well as privilege regularity and conservation in human actions. The politician cannot afford not to pay attention to the inertia of social behaviors, but only with the purpose of grasping their criticality, understanding where and how the *continuum* they seem to trace can be broken. The vocation of the politician is the transformation and promotion of new values—a purpose that will be much more effectively pursued, the more it is rationally organized and founded on the knowledge of circumstances, but that remains absolutely distinct from that of the scientist. Otherwise, what sense would have Weber's invectives *versus* the unpolitical pacifists *and* unpolitical revolutionaries? They do not place their will of transformation *in-situation*. They conceive the political project as abstractly free. In short: they do not *know*. Their action is destined to be as pathetically impotent as that of the intellectual who pretends to direct the political process on the basis of regularities that he has derived from historical material. To define in ideal-typical terms the two forms of *making* (making politics, making science) is precisely the task of scientific sociology, called on to repel any unprofessional confusion. But one needs to be aware that such a process leads to the individualization of *extreme* cases, and even more, of pure *possibilities*. Their study allows us to define clearly the terms of our language rather than describe real experiences. The balance between the two dimensions is difficult and every time is "to be reconquered" with respect to the situations of fact.

The impossibility of reducing Weber's political to the groundlessness of decision is made even more obvious by the relation that must be posited between the will of transformation that animates the action and the overall *Weltanschauung* of the age. In the supremacy of the innovating-transforming act over pure contemplation of the fact, more than one simple distinction is expressed between the scholar and the man of praxis: the *philosophy of praxis* is expressed as horizon of the age. That is, the *fact* that there is no knowledge that is not action, interpretation that is not transformation—

that every comprehension of the situation intervenes in it and modifies it
ipso facto. In Weber's phenomenology the sense of Marxist *philosophy*
emerges without being thematized, and for this reason is even more
meaningful.[23]

The idea of the nonevaluative character of science has nothing to do
with reasserting the supremacy of theorizing (*theorein*)! If anything, it
means the rise to value of a dominant scientific method in the contemporary world-system. Science is successful—but because this is the immanent
end to its original project—because it exists, in all its articulations, to dominate the world. If Weber does not explicitly develop this perspective,
those who will later (from Schmitt to Heidegger) do not follow a different
line. Not only does Weber recognize first and more deeply than anyone
the transforming-innovative power of contemporary science, but far from
separating it from the political one, he also seems rather interested in understanding how the latter loses in effectiveness and realism when it ignores the criteria of scientific rationality. Politics becomes then avant-
gardism, or exhibition of blind hopes. It ceases to be what it is, and is
reduced to a sign of the times. By innovating, the politician will also be
entrepreneur, capable of organizing better the *factors* at his disposal, clarity
in his objectives, economic calculation of the means, etc. But it is on the
nature of the ends that he will distinguish himself absolutely, since the
end of the entrepreneur is the development of his own enterprise through
continuous organizational transformations and product transformations—a goal that is open to risk, and yet reducible to a quantitative
method of calculation.[24]

The purpose pursued by the politician, instead, is that of the realization
of values not economically exchangeable (although *posited* by the subject
itself, as we saw). The entrepreneur also can feel his own work as a mission
and conceive his own enterprise as an instrument for the promotion of
universal goods (safety, occupation, well-being, and so forth), but he will
never be the one to define them as values to which every mean and every
calculation is to be subordinated, least of all will he be the one to be able
to *convince* to them. Even if role of economics in political choices turned
out to be more and more determinant (which is, however, an aspect of the
general techno-scientific apparatus), that would not imply the blurring of
distinction between the politician and the entrepreneur. The pursuit of an
economic goal becomes a political value only when it succeeds to represent
itself as *transcending* the economic horizon. And political action—and political vocation—will once again accomplish this metamorphosis. Also the
innovative entrepreneur is called on constantly to decide, but his decision

does not take place among alternative values, rather among different organizations with the same purpose. When this form of innovative action asserts itself as orientation of political action, as a necessary consequence the conflict among values will be reduced to a competition among business rivals. And yet, even to persuade someone that the end consists in the overcoming of the conflict among values, in its subsumption within techno-economic rationality and the form of the relation characteristic of the market, will be tantamount to "making politics" once again. In short, the depoliticization process can only take place as a political project.

But even more constitutive of political form is precisely its relation to the intellectual vocation rather than to the entrepreneurial one. The politician that would "devalorize" such a relation could not operate disenchantedly and would compromise, thus, any possibility of success. Since the values toward which political action is oriented are relative historically, they cannot contradict abstractly the *Weltanschauung* of an age that is marked tragically, for Weber, by the devaluation (*Entwertung*) of any transcendental position of value. The *actual* politician (a much more pertinent attribute than "authentic") activates the conflict among values without remaining "enchanted." He is convinced of them as much as he is convinced of their relativity. To be sure, he is essentially responsible for the pursuit of his own ends—just as, we could say, the scientific project is characterized today in terms more and more purely self-referential. But he could not operate coherently if he did not recognize the historical limitations of his project, or, better, if he did not conceive his own action in the very form of the project, which implies predetermination of his final "discovery." The politician operates by experiment, constructs experiments tending to demonstrate the objective possibility of the ends. At the same time he must also show himself to be disenchanted with respect to the feasibility of the latter. The actual politician knows "that history is truly the tragedy of a humanity that makes its own history, but does not know the history it makes."[25] He knows as none else the law of the heterogenesis of ends. And yet for him his work is nothing but "the tireless effort of acting with clarity" so as not to be betrayed by the consequences of the actions undertaken. This knowledge can come to him only from the scholar, from the scientist of the spirit. And little matters whether the scholar is *in* him or beside him.

The politician appears now already as a centaurlike figure.[26] And the centaur symbolizes the art of keeping united two natures in their distinction. But of which two natures do we speak? There are possible misunderstandings here, made inevitable by the problematic greatness of Weber's work. The space of political action is constituted by an undefinable tension between two polarities. On one hand, politics finds its real extreme in the bureaucratic routine, in conservative rationality, in the technique of administration. On the other hand, in the uprooting drive of permanent revolution, in the claim that its own act could completely achieve the kingdom of liberty. But without organizational ability one does not preserve the essential instruments with which the fight for power unfolds in the modern—and without the assertion of noninterchangeable values one could not even begin this fight. Weber's politician is at the exact opposite of any irrational dimension. His form originates from the necessity of balancing and tempering the two tendencies, leaving their energy active without letting it be transformed into a ripping, seductive force with respect to the end. The composition occurs, then, between scientific rationality, which is simply directed to its end, and that other rationality whereby the purpose is defined with evidence in terms of value and that is realizable only through a conflict between values. It is important to understand that the political is *delirious* (*delira*) from its own boundaries, and, therefore, its autonomy cannot even be defined, when its nature is transformed in pure bureaucratic practice or, on the contrary, in pure, unambiguous, intractable affirmation of value. Both positions constitute rather what is *beyond* the political and its boundaries. But that is why, it is obvious, the political affects them, and its rationality must take *care* of them. The two tendencies constitute for the political praxis a constant danger of transgression, but also, at the same time, the domains on which sovereignty can be extended. From these dangers, in short, politics can derive energy and motives to transform and strengthen itself. A sort of positive *environmental challenge*. Never simple *enemies*.

The politician differentiates himself from the entrepreneur not so much because the latter is a pure hedonist, a selfish bourgeois (in the reductive and, in the end, entirely wrong sense of the term), or because the latter is absolutely incapable of conceiving profit as a mean and not as an end subordinated to high politics, but because the politician lives in and of the conflicts of value and his vocation consists in transforming the overall orientation of human actions, while for the entrepreneur rationality will always have supremacy over the end, and the conflict among values will always tend to be seen as a *tyranny* of values.[27] For analogous reasons the politician will also differentiate himself from the diplomat, who remains at the *service* of the strategy he wants to preserve and constitutes an integral part of that bureaucratic structure also essential to the rational development of "making politics." Similarly, and in fact with even greater force, the politician *divides himself* from the simple parliamentarian, who is devoted to functions of criticism and control and defends his own con- stitutionally guaranteed sphere—just as he *divides* himself from the oppo- site and complementary figure of the officer tied to the party program and to the parliamentarian, namely, the demagogue, *ape* of the authentic will to power who looks for power without responsibility, and does not intend to transform the mass tendencies on the bases of his own convictions, but to adjust to them, to "present them again," not to represent them. The demagogue, therefore, is always in the end a conservative, and his activity is tied to an indissoluble way to the strengthening of the bureaucracy in ways analogous to military discipline.

There is no political vocation if one does not sense the supremacy of politics, and senses it as *responsibility*. Political action is oriented according to values, of which the politician must be able to argue the supremacy (an argument that is never scientific), to appearing convinced in a way that his conviction does not look like a negation of the others (in which case, then, he would become an ideologue, religiously enchanted with his own vision and, therefore, in the end, ineffective). But, then, what does conviction mean? What does responsibility mean? How is the discourse *between* these two ethics arranged? How to reread the (perhaps too famous) page that deals with them?

The Gods Are in Conflict

The *responsible* will to power appears to be the demon-character of the politician. What does this mean? First of all, that it cannot be question of an irresponsible will to power, as an end in itself. The politician does not act to assert himself, for his own power, for empty ambition, but for the victory of his own hierarchy of values. He is responsible for what he is convinced of. Therefore, he cannot be ambiguous about his own "thing" (*Sache*). His vocation calls him to those values that are his business (*Sache*) to bring to victory. Since he senses deeply this responsibility, he will calcu- late, measure, organize in the most effective way possible the suitable means to pursue such a purpose. To be sure, this does not shelter him from being compromised by diabolical powers. Disenchanted as to the possibility of realizing his own end just as he had projected it, he is simi- larly disenchanted on the possibility of pursuing it with ethically justifiable means. But this does not entail at all that all means are good, as many hurried readers of Weber's *Politics as Vocation* still claim. A compromise is necessary with diabolical powers—but subjugation to them is disastrous for politics, since it would dissolve every distinction between means and ends, and would overthrow the hierarchical order. Whenever the ends are reached with violent means, which because of their very arrogance become autonomous and independent from any rationality, sooner or later that same violence will turn into a self-destructive energy, as if the antibodies created to defend the will to life and power of an organism were to develop such strength to feel compelled to attack their host, trying to substitute themselves to it.

But the idea of responsibility also acquires in Weber another, and deeper, meaning. The actual politician, who *knows* the scientific ground-lessness of one's order of values, is, in an entirely peculiar way responsible also for those values that he contradicts—in the sense that he is called to answer to them, to *correspond to them*. The essential factor of his disen-chantment is the awareness of the irreducible conflict of values, and that these do not constitute the pieces of a puzzle waiting to be resolved.[28] There is no predetermined design for the unity of the world, or, at least, there is not one for politics, or for a "godless" science. But as the scientist compares these values and does not restrict himself at all to the description of their contradictoriness, so the politician is called on to respond, on the basis of his own motives and his own ends, to the *problem* that the oppo-nent constitutes. A *skandalon* that cannot be circumvented, but that is nec-essary so that the individuality of a historically determined political action can emerge. The belief in one's own values and the responsibility with respect to one's own "thing," do not contradict at all either the polytheis-tic dimension in which the conflict unfolds (and is destined to continue to unfold), or the substantial polytheism that the professional politician must profess. Responsibility means *knowing* "that every existence has its own god, and that the gods are in conflict."[29] Scientific reflection will make an effort to establish comparatively the relations among the respective "goods," the dominions of each one. To be sure, this is not the purpose of the politician, which will remain that of asserting his own god. But this assertion will be effective only if he will represent an authentic *response* to the question of the *other*—and therefore if he will be able to know it and, so to speak, to traverse it.

The tone of Weber's polytheism, therefore, clearly detaches itself both from a relative, agnostic and, in the end, indifferent consideration of the values in conflict—since they are always arranged according to the point of view of each of the opponents, and the space to which they give life is never homogeneous in all its points—and from the idea that polytheism itself can constitute a simple passage toward a rigorously monotheistic order. The *convinced responsible* politician appoints polytheism as a stable scene of his actions. But the scene is *tragic*. On one hand, no *religio civilis* (neither the one founded on the agreement operated by the law, nor the one that appeals to ethnic homogeneity, by tradition or costume) can superorder the conflict, maintaining it in its proper order. On the other hand—and this is the aspect of the problem that allows us to speak of tragedy in the proper sense—the politician, the very moment in which he chooses his own way and is called to live it with coherence but all the way, ready to deal with the consequences, even those unexpected and unforeseeable, is responsible for the other ways as well, not only in the sense just indicated of having to recognize them and having to correspond to them, but also in the sense of feeling guilty not to be able to share them. To decide for a god is to fail the other gods. To decide is absolutely necessary—but it is also absolutely to commit sin with respect to those values that we cannot choose, that we can even know intimately, but that cannot convince us. This limit is insurmountable: an absolute limit on the way to an authentic satisfaction, which could only be conceived as perfect reciprocity and sharing. In other words, political action not only cannot promise such satisfaction, but also cannot even think it. This means that political action can no longer be conceived as a search for *happiness*, but because of this renunciation, the responsible politician cannot stop to feel the pain and the guilt.

In Weber, therefore, responsibility is linked indissolubly to another term, "feeling guilty" (*Schuldig-sein*), a key term, as is well known, of Heidegger's analytic.[30] In the same act in which I take residence (*ethos!*), in my "good" (*timé*), I exclude myself from the others. Nor can I assert it without placing myself *against* them. There is no value (*Wert*) that is not *converted*, that does not turn against, that does not become (*werden!*), according to this polemical "conversion." An irenic agreement between authentic positions of value (and not vacuous skepticism!) is a priori impossible. However, there is an abyssal difference among those who assume radically the responsibility to resist in their own "good," recognizing its partiality as a factor and element of conflict among the gods, and those who turn it into an absolute, seeing in the other *timai*, in other "goods" only demons and superstitions.[31] The former will feel responsible with respect to that which opposes him, as well as responsible for the insurmountable limit of not being able to accept it. The latter will feel responsible or guilty only for not having succeeded in vanquishing his own opponent, understood *sic et simpliciter* in the form of absolute enemy. The first will always see in his opponent the *hospes*, perhaps, in the form of a radical impossibility or absence. The second will fight precisely so that such form may no longer be manifest or is suppressed.

The polytheism of Weber the "Romanist," therefore, has an absolutely non-Roman tone. It contradicts the very idea of a *pax deorum*, founded on the supremacy of the power cult of Rome. The conflict always reemerges. No politics can overcome it, but only interpret it. And no *civitas* can claim that its own values are called to exercise *imperium sine fine*. Having recognized such an *imperium*, the Roman was free to roam (*dis-correre*) among his gods. The great works of late Latinity (Macrobius's *Saturnalia*, for instance) show the extreme richness that such roaming discourse could attain. But here the gods had become pawns of a wonderful game of glass beads.[32] Here, in fact, their values were transformed in mere signs, evanescent reflexes of a will to power by now in decline. Weber's polytheism exacts, instead, decision—and a decision so much more painful as it must occur among the values of which he recognizes, disenchantedly, their relativity. The conflict among the divine "goods" (*timai*) compels one to choose. Even the illusion to be able to avoid it is a choice: *Wille*, will to impotence. But the decision is also a deciding for one's own being (ontologically not psychologically) responsible or guilty.

It was a great Catholic, Donoso Cortés, who declared himself the enemy of the One God, "winner of everything that is varied . . . of everything that is particular . . . winner of everything that is born and dies . . . armed of a sole attribute, omnipotence."[33] Weber's tragic polytheism could have shared this position. It is not in opposition to a monotheism that attempts to conceive "the joint inclusion in my salvation of *all* the *possible finite* people and of my salvation in that of all the people,"[34] but to the monotheism that rejects the idea of a multiplicity as *essential* to the very idea of culture. In Scheler, this monotheistic position establishes the possibility of a hierarchy of values, which is relative, as far as specific contents are concerned, to the imperatives through which, from time to time, it is embodied, and yet universal for its informing principles. For Weber, on the contrary, this outcome remains forbidden. The scientist is called on to disenchant it and the politician not to be deceived by it. And yet polytheism can never take on the aspect of a quiet coexistence. It is manifested as the totality of relations among responsible decisions, above all, with respect to one's own god.

Macrobius's gods are essentially interchangeable signs; not so those who give life to the *drama* of the conflict among values. Each one of them invests fully with responsibility. But for none it would be right to assert the *nothingness* of the other or to regard oneself as the power (the *omnipotence!*) capable of resolving the conflict definitely. Perhaps Weber would have accepted Scheler's definition: "Strife is tragic whenever the judgment of the Godhead is the *only* just solution that can be presented" (*Formalism*, 590), that is, a form of the essential strife, which is played out among types and fields of values as well as duties, all legitimate in themselves, towards whom only the idea of God could represent "a possible solution" (*Formalism*, 591). A limit-idea that, somehow, transpires from the pathos of guilt that the consciousness of the limits of our "good" continuously arouses— but for Weber a truly unutterable limit-idea. Only the value that such limit-idea indicates, and not the values that struggle on the tragic scene of polytheism, is absolutely other from the world of facts. Only to this value is applicable, and it is applicable in absolute, Wittgenstein's famous proposition in the *Tractatus:* "If there is any value that does have value, it must lie outside the whole sphere of what happens and is the case."[35] But the values that conflict by converting into one another, and against one another, are the *facts* of the world, its events, and, as such, they are understandable and interpretable.

But how to decide in and for them? The idea of decision acquires a semantic breadth that transcends the limits of sociological investigation and, as we shall see, the interpretation of political action. However, it also comprehends them, since the politician is a key figure of the conflict among values and his decisions contribute precisely in a determining way to characterize the form of conflict itself. From what has already been said, it should have emerged clearly that the criticism often directed at Weber that he understood the decision in nihilistic terms, as founded on nothing, or, on the purely arbitrary "I want" (which is, however, a completely different criticism), turns out to be completely misleading. First of all, the decision, in order to be politically effective will have to be situated in the historically determined dimension of the conflict of values. Any innovation rests on this ground and it is intrinsically conditioned by it. In order to be constituent, the decision will have first to be constituted and be aware of this situation. No decision is mere property of the subject that assumes it. Furthermore, and it is important to reiterate it, the decision is in itself also the rational calculation of the means. One does not decide rationally and only later look for the instruments capable of realizing the end, but the project is *in-one* in both dimensions, lest it is empty daydreaming (little matters if reactionary, conservative or revolutionary).

The tactic, in other words, is not an appendix to the strategy, but constitutes its essential factor. Finally, the search for legitimization, and the practice necessary to obtain it, are however immanent to the assertion of any purpose, end, value. If value, in fact, is not, but has value, and has value if it actually directs to social action, it will enter in relation with the forms of the latter in a necessarily interactive way. Political innovation is always more transformation than innovation. When it claims to establish an absolute *Novitas*, often, under the facade of order that it applies or imposes on the social process, the latter remains almost unchanged. Under this aspect, also, I believe that one can compare Weber's polytheism and decisionism to Scheler's acknowledgment that the order of values is essentially tied to forms of *ethos*, as they are historically carried out. Beside, is Weber's political action not the most convincing demonstration of decision's ethical determination (where *ethos* has precisely the meaning that Scheler attributes to it, not ethico-moral, but historico-social)? Values are never mere signs; the conflict is never nominalistic. Ideas are always confronting each other in the *ethos* of a culture or in the relationship among cultures. The decision is always a commensuration between arbitrary will and such an *ethos*. It is not a leaping *out* of the historical process, but *beyond* the situation that it has reached.

The Form of Political Decision

This is the form of the *political* decision. Not of the decision tout court. Here is the source of many misunderstandings on Weber's position. The *political* decision cannot in any way be interpreted in an almost Kierkegaardian light, even though the philosopher-sociologist Max Weber knows very well that there is also the pure decision as leap that breaks any historico-dialectic continuum. But it is a question of two forms of the decision—and these, yes, for him cannot be absolutely comparable. The actual politician decides on the basis of *responsibility and conviction*, in the terms and within the limits that we have examined. Their interweaving is not a happy "case," but the norm of political action as such. To this end, one must disenchant Weber's language. There is nothing heroic in the search for this composition. But in order that it may take place it is necessary that the term "responsibility" acquire all the depth that we have indicated (otherwise the purpose becomes mere rationality), and that the term "conviction" expresses an unconditional adherence to a "good" that neither abolishes nor claims to overcome the polytheism of values. As paradoxical as this condition may appear, it does not share, however, that of an ethics of conviction, which obeys purely to one's own "I must," answering exclusively to one's own faith and claiming that only in following it, whatever it may cost, there is salvation.

This form of the decision, absolutely unconcerned of its effects, without care for the consequences of its acts, transcends the type of the professional politician. Its vocation is not the political one, which does not entail that it cannot produce devastating effects on the scene of social action. All the "cases" that constitute the world support and condition each other reciprocally. But precisely for this reason it is necessary to know how to differentiate them: political vocation is clearly characterized by his *having to* put together responsibility and conviction, and, in order to imagine the realization of such agreement, it is necessary to conjugate its terms in the forms that we have followed. Political vocation, therefore, is not in opposition to a pure ethic of conviction, which is entirely other with respect to political dimension, but to the translations that conviction can assume in the properly political arena—translations that are also, inevitably, betrayals of the pure, unconditional nature of conviction itself. Weber's language, on this issue, as it has often been remarked, is not entirely clear. The slightly rhetorical insistence on the distinction between the two ethics hides the fundamental fact that they have to, somehow, come together to justify political vocation, which does not have as adversary pure conviction as such, but that decision that affirms and plans conviction's practical translatability. Such decision demands that faith be the resolution of the conflict, and that the idea of an omnipotent god must count as foundation of political omnipotence.

The heroism of the politician does not consist, then, in harmonizing this latter form of conviction, which is totally irresponsible, with the ethic of responsibility. This would not form a centaur but an iron horse! We would not be facing a tragic conflict, but a pure and simple contradiction. In this sense, Weber's discourse must be clarified. The absolute faith in the unique and exclusive character of one's own value every time it aims at "becoming true," practically and historically, cannot tolerate any compromise with a political action directed responsibly to its purpose and expression of a convinced adherence to its own "thing"—and vice versa. Here there can only be the *aut-aut*. But the relation that can intervene between this political action and a pure ethic of conviction—an ethic, that is, conscious that its kingdom is not of this world—is completely different. Indeed, this appears in Weber as the absolutely extreme relation—asserted in and for the radical impossibility that the two ethics will ever meet. Instead, between the politician who "heroically" bears in himself the responsibility and conviction, awareness and innocence, and the absolute faith that claims to impose its own hierarchy of values on the social order (and translate its own legitimacy in legality), the relation can only be that of an open hostility, of a showdown *on the field*. The actual politician has nothing to say versus pure conviction, but contradicts, instead, with the greatest decision, the politically irresponsible forms in which the ethics of conviction can unfold.

And the scholar can share in the action without betraying his own duty to nonevaluative approach. In fact, he does not condemn at all, nor does he place in a superior or inferior position on a presumed universal scale of values, the contents of an ethics of pure conviction, but he can demonstrate the absolute incoherence and unreality of a praxis that claims to be completely informed by it. Furthermore, he can demonstrate logically how such praxis ends up suppressing the polytheism of values (whatever its meaning may be). If we call "ideological" the political positions that confuse absoluteness of conviction (and nonconviction tout court!) and responsibility, since they advance the claim of being global explanations, emancipated from the concrete experience that they interpret on the basis of occult meanings, then a scientific critique of ideology should appear immanent to the actual political action.[36]

But the understanding between the two figures, however contained, will always remain extremely improbable. The appeal to responsibility will never be able to subject to itself the deterministically incalculable decision, which is only predictable, broadly speaking, on the bases of historical regularities. In the political decision, which is such only to the extent that it imposes itself to its own bureaucratic machinery by breaking its procedural "naturalism," one will always find ideological or mythological motifs. If nothing else, political decision will always express the exigency to postulate a universal recognition. The utilization of this expectation is essential precisely for the purpose of obtaining the necessary consensus. And this is entirely independent of the contents of the decision and the interests that support it. Even the most disenchanted critic of the political and the most skeptical of experts in political affairs must recognize that the instrumental use of that expectation is of one nature with the praxis. But there is no doubt that he who has the vocation for politics will be aware of the instrumental dimension of that expectation for universal recognition that stems from the limited value of the end that he pursues. At any moment he can say, "Paris is worth a mass," but because he is truly convinced of the value of Paris! On the other hand, the real scholar can disenchant or "scientify" any social relation, by interpreting its senses and motives, but he will never be able to teach the politician the complete rationalization of the ideological-mythological dimension—this would entail pointing out self-destruction as the politician's goal. The demythicization of the political can be only relative and functional to the effectiveness of the decision, which is actualized in the age of the techno-bureaucratic rule. But the theatre of the political remains open to the assertion of a purely demagogic-ideological power that uses, at least for a while, the power of the techno-bureaucratic machinery. The scholar must consider such a possibility as real. Weber's political must fight it. Two duties absolutely distinct, but absolutely not in contradiction.

Limits of Political Action

We have now at our disposal, perhaps, all the elements to understand the concluding image of this essay: the politician as hero.[37] Even this emphatic term is to be understood with phenomenological sobriety. In short, it has nothing to do with any kind of superman.[38] First of all, as we have said, the politician is no hero in so far as he may jump out of every conditioning. He is not unchained arbitrariness, pure "I will," or irresponsibly obedient to his "voice." This has nothing to do with the complexity of the political, let alone with heroism. Hero is not he who accomplishes himself in extremis, but he who tolerates the tension of opposites. *Hic labor, hic opus est.* He does not rush to make a decision under the illusion of resolving the contradiction. On the contrary, he chooses to save the terms of contradiction within himself. This is the *"dran,"* the making of the hero. He is will to *know*, but he also *knows* that the decision that he assumes responds essentially to the imperative that dominates any rationality directed toward a purpose. He is aware that his end arises out of a combination of situations, facts, and that he has his roots in them; at the same time, he wants to change them. He is convinced of his and in his own "good," but he is aware of his responsibility for only one, and in not being able to share it together with the others. His obedience to "One only" does not entail any blind faith in the omnipotence of the One. A hero is he who fights till the end for one's own convictions, without ever thinking that his struggle is either salvific or his politics messianic.

With this we have also indicated what are the powers with which the politician hero will enter into relations, to subject them to himself, to render them functional to the pursuit of his own ends. On one hand, the force of the bureaucratic machinery, a conserving force, organized rationality of

given factors; on the other, the energy of the demagogic word, inseparable
from charismatic power, but also essential for any will to power. We can
also add disenchantment and realism, which, if taken at face value, would
compromise every effective action—in fact, decision itself. With these
powers the politician hero is *in-situation*, with them he is constantly at war,
in *polemos*, according to all the meanings that the term can take on. Together they determine the space of modern social action in as much as it
is confrontational (having in itself the contradiction as motor of development, not a pathological factor). The hero does not detach himself from
such a scene, does not act out any solos. He pretends, instead, to be the
protagonist.

But social action, that is, action that must represent itself in historically
determined situations, with reference to traditions and values that socially
matter, which orient or are capable of orienting, is not any possible action,
not even any possible thinking. Neither political action, praxis, is the supreme end, the reconciliation and the synthesis of any form of social action. Political activity distinguishes itself from other practical activities, or,
better, *poietic*, just as all of them, praxis and *poiesis*, from the authentic
dimension of conviction—and this is the most difficult and highest point
of Weber's thinking and of the lived experience of the man Weber. The
poietic activities, however, have always as their end the satisfaction of
needs or of sensitive interests, such as to allow a calculation of their relative utility. It is obvious that political action can be reduced to this calculation at any moment. But the politician who orients his own action to
increasing pleasure, measurable on the part of individuals (and this can be
calculated only by the mean of property, by identifying, that is, being
happy with being property owner), renounces, both in the eyes of Weber,
and of Scheler, to any great politics, to any autonomy of his ends, to any
project that is not mere extrapolation from the situation of facts.[39] If the
aim of the politician is to increase individual well-being, his goal becomes
equal to that of the private individual. Any legitimate distinction between
the two dimensions ceases, and also, therefore, any legitimacy on the part
of the politician to ask the individual for any sacrifice (whether it is taxes
or wars, nothing changes logically.)

Political activity, therefore, is not social because the ends that it pursues
are not conceivable outside of social relations. Its peculiarity consists in
wanting to pursue an idea that is unrealizable a priori without arranging
the fundamental orientations of society, that is, without transforming
them in one's own image. Naturally, even in this case, the distinction is

interesting to the extent that it shows the possible interweaving. The innovative entrepreneur will also try to create his own demand. He will not, to
be sure, restrict himself to satisfy the actual. And yet, he must orient himself to the satisfaction of individually enjoyable goods, and thanks to the
awareness of the limitations of his project, he can calculate its success.
The politician, instead, is such if he aims at an end that transcends the
"eudemonic" calculation, without however denying its value in any way.
Once again, only one figure reappears capable of carrying on high the
strength, the energy of opposites, without being overcome by their weight:
the hero.

But the hero cannot compose in himself the contradiction of social action that does not want just to orient itself, but acts according to the imperative call that absolutely transcends any arbitrary will. This form of
conviction does not partake in any way of the law (*nomos*) that regulates the
different forms of social action and distributes the parts in their polemical
direction. It is a question of *another law*, for which a criticism of the ideology does not count, because it has nothing ideological, the demythicization does not count either because it has nothing mythical, the *Entwertung*
does not count because his values are neither ethically measurable nor are
they values that claim to be politically relevant. At such high level, Weber
sketches his two cities. On one hand is the city of man, of the interweaving
between rationality to purpose and rationality according to values, between responsibility and conviction, conservation and innovation, innocence and guilt, always on the point of falling in the steel cage of techno-
bureaucratic monotheism or in the empty exaltation of ideologies. And
what about the other? The city of God? How could the scholar make even
an allusion to that? Has he perhaps experience in social action oriented
purely and disinterestedly to be "enjoyed in God" (*frui Deo*)? Does he
receive from his historical material the testimony of a political expression
of loving your enemy, of showing the other cheek—and of being able to
do it happily, in the spirit of the Gospel?

Two laws—the existence of two laws, this is all the scholar has to assert
in trying to make the politician aware.[40] There is the law in which both fit
in, law that is the order of the conflict; and there is another, an absolutely
Other, that we feel for its absence infinitely more than we could ever describe, which has no roots in any political system, impervious to any
worldly authority. Radical is the separation that Weber traces between this
law and the continuous ideological betrayals-distortions to which it gives
life: pacifisms, moral solidarisms, consolatory flights from the reality of
the conflict and responsibility of the decision that will always have the

strength as its fundamental mean, and, therefore, will always have to compromise itself with demonic powers. Those who are in politics and do not
understand this are "children." But those who really obey, in the flame of
pure conviction, to the God-Love, are not children—or not in this sense.
The conviction of the hero politician is in incurable contrast to this flame.
He can stand the collapse of all his hopes, he can attempt the impossible
(but with the means of politics and to reach the possible), but, as a politician, he will never be able to obey to the "absolute ethical and acosmic
demands of the Sermon on the Mount," or he will be able to exploit them
only. But it is not a question of a negative contrast. The politician can
conceive of the law of God-Love simply as the Stranger. And together
with the scholar he can clarify rigorously all the consequences that all
those who declare themselves to be their faithful ought to draw: reject not
only war, but also every form of political or economic struggle that can
harvest more victims and produce more suffering than any military confrontation; not only subvert that scale of values that sees political, military,
economic power, and the same individual well-being as top priority, but
also undermine *every* worldly scale of values, even the one founded on
values of *Kultur*, of science and art, perhaps versus (as was the case in
Weber's time and in Mitteleuropa, but not only then and there) those of
the techno-economic *Zivilisation*.[41] The purebred politician, or the
scholar, can only insist on clarity and coherence. But the Sermon on the
Mount hovers above them, inaccessible.

However, that Word has resounded; even if never realized, it has given
meaning, it has oriented conduct and conflicts. Could not this Word constitute, precisely, that Impossible that is always necessary to maintain if
one wishes to reach the possible? The manner in which the Sermon on
the Mount is articulated appears precisely to differentiate between what
belongs to the law, even in its practico-political value ("as it was said unto
you"), from what constitutes its own divine, supernatural ("but I say unto
you"). Therefore, the latter ought to be understood as the complement of
the former, but if this were the case, the second assertion, thanks to his
connection to the first, would express a powerful judgment on social action
and on the dimension of the political, if for no other reason than as eschatological reserve on their every asset. But this is a perspective that Weber
does not follow, stuck, it seems to me, on a strongly Marcionite reading
of the evangelical text, which in Germany at the time had formidable theological precedents (suffice it to think of Harnack).[42]

Even within this perspective Weber's phenomenology remains tragic (a
tragedy without even the help of a deus ex machina!): no privileged point

of view, no principle can judge the conflict of values to which the political belongs. His solution is contingently immanent to its development, which is to say that there is no solution, or that it is *the impossible*. But did not a complete realization of the project seem impossible too—and "judged" as such rationally? And yet it is this scope that gives a sense to social action. And impossible did not appear also a perfect harmony among the dimensions that converge-conflict in the political praxis? And yet this attempt at perfect harmony constitutes the value that Weber defines as heroic. Thus, what is impossible is to free the political from the ideological once and for all. But a convinced and responsible politician will always have to attempt to break the knot. How, then, to eliminate the impossible? And that voice that resounds superhumanly in the Sermon on the Mount will it not constitute, then, the revelation of the same Impossible in itself, of what remains beyond all the measures of our capacities and our possibilities and our power, and yet, *in-one*, thrust in them? A revelation that the measure of our possibilities is nothing with respect to the infinite potentiality of the Impossible. Or that the measure of our responsibilities and our convictions, disenchanted about their insurmountable relativity, and just as firm in its resistance against any relativism, seems a dismal strip of land with respect to the power of holiness, to its capacity of donating beyond reciprocation, to love the enemy, to resist evil by showing the other cheek, without the pretense to gain any Kingdom *here*.

It is important to reach this edge of Weber's phenomenology if we wish to understand its vast and dramatic character. The type of ethics of conviction takes us to explain an aspect of the political, but also to the overcoming of the entire ethical situation. The ethics of conviction takes place between the figure of the politician, of the political *Beruf* (that can always be transformed in revolutionary or conservative utopianism, in ideology, enthusiasm, *Schwärmerei*), and that of the saint, whose conviction is pure *obedience*, beyond any measure of *ethos*.[43] Between the energy of the hero, strictly correlated to socially realizable values (founding hero, eponymous hero, great statesman), and the *homo religiosus* perfectly represented by the saint, no hierarchy is possible, since they are situated on distinct ontological planes. The hero is imperative will, a superabundant affirmation of himself. The saint is opening and gift of himself to the superabundance of Grace. The hero, as we have seen, has nothing to do with the fanatic. He pursues with intelligence and disenchantment, as well as with dedication and conviction, his own "thing," but his kingdom is of this world and his values are of this world. The saint is witness in himself of a peace that is absolutely impossible for the hero. And yet great politics and great mysticism are, without being able in any way to organize themselves in hierarchical order, the powers that we can trust versus the reduction of the political to the administrative-bureaucratic or the disfiguring of conviction in ideology, versus the depoliticization or fanaticism, versus the conception of the conflict as a game that can be resolved or the skeptical exercise with an end in itself. At the "witches' dance"—which interweaves deresponsibilized will to power and power of the techno-bureaucratic system, progressive ideologies and techno-scientific religion, political messianism and mere rationality to the purpose—neither the real politician nor the saint will take part.[44] But the first will oppose it with political means—that is, fighting what he esteems evil with evil; the other, instead, by witnessing how evil can exhaust his own energy without leaving an impression, how evil's power is powerless with respect to perfect conviction, which is faith, *gratia*, in the possibility of the impossible.

Both are equally legitimate spheres of duty forming together an essential axiological dissimilarity, which in a strict sense is not to be traced between an ethics of conviction and an ethics of responsibility. As a result, the political hero will never be able to "comprehend" the saint, and vice versa—never, in any sense of the term. And yet the two characters provide the extreme image of what Nietzsche called "stellar friendship." Their orbits are such that make their reunion in the infinite believable. They both represent their own law in a pure way, developing their ratio with absolute coherence. Both know how to give of themselves, in complete devotion to their god. But, above all, both are founded on a radical anti-idolatrous aspiration. And the highest idolatry is that of the Self: the belief (implicit in the techno-scientific project), "that the power of man is so great to allow him to be really what he wants to be" (Hannah Arendt). Man has no power over his own will. He can only foresee that the result of his actions, his *facts*, *do not* constitute the act (*energeia*) of his project. The politician will fight with interworldly means to reduce the difference. Whoever operates according to a pure faith knows that this is also impossible without grace and prays that the Seducer will not win out (demonic is precisely the pitiless and desperate accusation moved to the impotence of the will). Orbits that can be imagined united only in the infinite, but that will never clash, namely, a city of man powerful enough against idolatry and ideology, all animated by its having-to-be (which is embodied in actual political praxis), capable of being defined in its own insurmountable limits in imitation of the *civitas dei*, finally free of the will to realize itself historically, to realize legally one's own legitimacy. If they could recognize themselves in this ideal-typical picture, both those who orient their actions according to the essence of the political, and those who orient themselves according to holiness, they ought to conclude that the only possible reconciliation of their persons can be found in the idea of God.

The Two Cities

The existence of the two cities is the guarantee against the affirmation of a monism of identity, of any theologico-political short circuit. Precisely, the *nonjudgeable* inequality that they form makes it possible for historical existence to remain open to its ultimate goal. The political decision does not decide the end of history. The leap of faith does not decide the forms of political action. But both dimensions together maintain existence in its transcending form, as the transcendent. If someone follows with coherence "the demon that holds the threads of *his* life," and follows it till the ultimate consequences, he will be able to see his life as an experiment, whose sense and value move beyond all the *personae* in which it was manifested. In Weber's political passion this sign is very clear, without excluding and in fact implying the firmest adherence to one's own cause. But Weber the scholar also shows a similar form (*facies*): elusive of academic categories, alien from any commonplace, expression of a knowledge as great as it is always risky, form that is born of the most painful experience, but that does not surrender to the flow of life, not even for a moment.[45]

The cause to which political vocation obeys cannot be *simplex et unum*. The responsibility excludes it: the politician orients himself according to values *and* according to facts. If he were to follow the imperative alone we would have an illusory politics. On the contrary, if he would only operate within the limits of the facts, we would have nothing more than a reasonable politics of balance, a bureaucratic administration. Yet, the politician's ability to innovate must maintain its own readability, without falling into occasionalism. Weber's cause was the affirmation of a national policy of power, of a German *Machtstaat* at the center of a network of political relations with other Mitteleuropean states, conceived (illusorily) with a defensive function, and particularly against Russia.[46] This did not prevent him, as is well known, to move the harshest criticism both politically and socially to the Wilhelmine Reich after Bismarck's resignation. For Weber, in fact, cultural prestige and the prestige of German power, in their indissoluble connection, depended on the assertion of a strong parliament, and this would have avoided becoming a *discutidora* assembly only if centered on a strong alliance between entrepreneurial bourgeoisie and realist socialism. This cause had to change after the defeat of Versailles, and none more than Weber attacked the "grief-stricken souls" on one hand and violent revanchism on the other. If the tragic hero is he who, in his defeat, in the catastrophe, asserts his own value, looking for the sense of his own destiny and "working" all his mourning, then this Weber of the definitive decline of all hopes is the classical example of the politician hero. A power politic was no longer feasible and, for Germany and for Europe, it would have been inauspicious for decisive political forces to cultivate demagogically that dream of power. But equally irresponsible would have been a Germany reduced to a small state, without influence on the destinies of the world, and disarmed in every sense. The antinationalism of the revolutionaries, the pacifist ideology with its ethics immediately reversed in responsibility, the utopianism of the left, would have been the best ally of those who aimed at avenging Versailles. The political passion of the scholar continued to resound against any cheap solution, to tear "all the veils from the world of desires"—only to be always less and less heard.[47]

The conference that "for your own expressed wish I am about to give will necessarily disappoint you." Perhaps the authentic politician was beginning to appear to Weber a stranger *in* this world, as much as the saint. Whether he was confronting the reform of Wilhelmine Reich, or whether he was proposing, in the evidence of the defeat, a way out for the very fragile Weimar democracy, the main preoccupation of Weber the politician and scholar was the state, the *reason* of the state, whose power is essential also for the economic development of a nation. And between state and nation Weber establishes an essential link. It is not the state of Hegel's *Philosophy of Right*, or the ethical state, or the romantic-sentimental state founded on the idea of an organic community. It is the great rational ploy that holds the monopoly of the exercise of legitimate power. No preestablished harmony, no promise of an end to conflict, but power actually capable to impose laws on it and direct it. There is no political form, for Weber, without the state, without that great rational enterprise that the modern state is called on to be. Every proposal is in function of this purpose: once the Reich collapsed, both the strengthening of the role of parliament first, and that of the government then ("democracy with a head"), had to aim at the maximum possible consolidation of the state form's authority, even in a stormy changing situation. The absolute centrality of the state for Weber's conception of politics entails the progressive disappearance of the more properly charismatic and traditional forms of power in favor of the one founded on legality. Legality and legitimacy coincide, and legality becomes the way the bureaucratic machinery functions, oiling every wheel of the enterprise-state.[48] Even great politics, which is foreign policy, which is the will to play a role in the world, must be founded on this state form. When Weber speaks of international relations, he always refers to relations among states—in fact: among nation-states. Where this form is lacking, what other one could be conceived legitimately to be the bearer of the exercise of violence? If it is always force that decides in the last instance the establishment of international balances, this force always finds its foundation in the reality of the ordering of the state. What happens when this foundation is shaky, in crisis? Weber could only be opened to this question, not traverse it. But there is no doubt that his entire discourse on the political is situated, almost naturally, within the framework of state power.[49]

Quid tum? What happens to the political when the power of *Gestell* (to employ Heidegger's expression), of the techno-economic system, is planted globally and grows its intolerance with respect to every national regulation? What happens when the rationality of purpose is transformed in the decisive orientation of social action denying recognition to any value or rationality outside itself? Is it possible to believe that such rationality of purpose has in itself the possibility of self-regulation, that it is completely emancipated from being at the service of the political? This is, precisely, the present *faith* of the West. I doubt that Weber would have shared it. On the basis of his fundamental ideas, he would have certainly and harshly criticized it—but not gone beyond it. These ideas, in fact, would not have allowed him to venture past the state form.

And yet, I do not even doubt that such a task would represent today, for Weber, the essential content of political action, since he, with disenchantment, would have been the first to recognize the decline of that great product of the European spirit. The state never was, for him, a Nietzschean "icy monster," because it was always animated by the tragedy of the political. I am afraid the icy monster would have been rather, in his eyes, the world-system, which today it is so fashionable to idolize. But no idol can freeze the energy of the conviction and the supreme appeal of the single person toward the recognition of one's own liberty as *his* liberty, liberty that would never be if it were donated, if it depended on the will of another. The world-system of which today we speak and prophesy seems to promise the illumination of our life. But in the *Lichtwesen*, in conceiving the substantial as simple bright light, Hegel already understood that individual self-consciousness would have been eventually considered to be something negative or transitory.[50] The individual would have been represented only in the form of a ceaseless destruction. Liberty would have been conceivable only as the kingdom of the liberators and as the subjection of the liberated. The strongest and most odious of caste system would have seemed capable of organizing a completed whole. But the whole is only the universal liberty of individuals who conflict in their convictions and correspond with one another, obeying their own responsibility. This political vocation is more necessary today when confronting the unresolved and, perhaps, irresolvable problem of the "Law of the Earth" than it was in the age marked by the work of Max Weber. But what appears to us necessary is always also highly improbable. The tone of Weber's talks is marked by such an anguished awareness. It is pronounced at the height of night and knows how feeble it is the light it sends out as guidance for practical action. And yet, *he has to*. In honor of his god—and without hope of salvation.

NOTES

INTRODUCTION: ON MASSIMO CACCIARI'S DISENCHANTED ACTIVISM

1. Raniero Panzieri (1921–1964) was on the editorial staff of Einaudi publishing house in Turin and never held a university position. See Raniero Panzieri, *La ripresa del marxismo-leninismo in Italia, Scritti 1956–1960, Lotte operaie nello sviluppo capitalistico*, and *L'alternativa socialista. Scritti scelti (1944–1956)*. The most influential book produced by the Neomarxist school was Mario Tronti's (b. 1931) *Operai e capitale*. It is virtually impossible to understand Italy's 1968 movement and many events that followed without referring to this work. See also Mario Tronti, *Hegel politico, Sull'autonomia del politico*, and *Il politico; Soggetti, crisi, potere*, ed. Antonio De Martinis and Alessandro Piazzi; and *La politica al tramonto*. For a survey of that period of Italian history see Robert Lumley, *States of Emergency: Cultures of Revolt in Italy from 1968 to 1978*.

2. For Antonio Negri (b. 1933) in the 1970s, see *Descartes politico, o della ragionevole ideologia, Zyklus und Krise bei Marx, Crisi dello Stato-piano, Proletari e stato, La forma stato, Il dominio e il sabotaggio*, and *Marx oltre Marx; Dall'operaio massa all'operaio sociale*, ed. Paolo Pozzi and Roberta Tomassini; *Il comunismo e la guerra*; and *L'anomalia selvaggia*, French trans. *L'anomalie sauvage*, introduction by Gilles Deleuze.

3. To place *Krisis* in its proper context, see also Aldo G. Gargani, *Il sapere senza fondamenti*; Pier Aldo Rovatti, Roberta Tomassini, and Amedeo Vigorelli, *Bisogni e teoria marxista*; Salvatore Veca, *Saggio sul programma scientifico di Marx*; and *Crisi della ragione*, ed. Aldo G. Gargani.

4. Franco Fortini, "Gli ultimi Cainiti," in *Questioni di frontiera*, 91–106.

5. Antonio Negri, "Simplex sigillum veri. Per la discussione di *Krisis* e di *Bisogni e teoria marxista*." As far as Negri's accusation of mysticism is concerned, Cacciari has thoroughly investigated the political dimension of mysticism. See his "Law and Justice," Chapter 7 of this volume.

6. The first seminal anthology of Carl Schmitt's essays to appear in Italy was *Le categorie del "politico,"* ed. Gianfranco Miglio and Pierangelo Schiera. Miglio was a conservative political theorist who joined the separatist Northern League in the 1990s, hoping to forge it into a federalist force. The League's

anti-intellectualism, however, had no room for the sophistication of Miglio's theories. He was soon expelled from the party and publicly vilified by the people that he had tried to counsel. When Miglio died, Cacciari eulogized him in *La Repubblica* on August 20, 2001. Political differences notwithstanding, there were similarities between Cacciari's and Miglio's federalist agendas. Cacciari also owed Miglio his discovery of Schmitt. American political scientists have often wondered why Schmitt (1888–1985), despite his anti-Semitism and his well-known association with the Nazi regime, has found sympathetic readers in the European Left (see Mark Lilla, "The Enemy of Liberalism"). The reason is that Schmitt is to political science what Heidegger is to philosophy and, as much as Heidegger, he holds the key to the understanding of many things that went wrong in the twentieth century and could go even worse in the twenty-first. Like a modern Talleyrand, before associating himself with the fate of Nazi Germany, Schmitt was the most prominent constitutional jurist of the Weimar Republic. To the recollection of the Jewish theologian Jacob Taubes (who visited Schmitt in the 1970s and had a correspondence with him), Pinchas Rosen, then the Israeli Secretary of Justice, checked out Schmitt's *Verfassungslehre* at the library of Jerusalem's University in 1949 when he was drafting the Constitution of the State of Israel. See Jacob Taubes, *In divergente accordo*, 30–31. Carl Schmitt's complete bibliography in English is too large for the purposes of this introduction. See *The Concept of the Political, Political Theology, Land and Sea, Legality and Legitimacy*, and *Theory of the Partisan*. See also Chantal Mouffe, ed., *The Challenge of Carl Schmitt*; Gopal Balakrishnan, *The Enemy: An Intellectual Portrait of Carl Schmitt*, and Raphael Gross, *Carl Schmitt and the Jews: The "Jewish Question," the Holocaust, and German Legal Theory*.

7. We refer here to Hugo von Hofmannsthal, *Der Turm. Ein Trauerspiel in Fünf Aufzügen. Erste Fassung*, in *Sämtliche Werke. Kritische Ausgabe* XVI.1—*Dramen 14.1*, 43; *The Tower: A Tragedy in Five Acts—First Version*, in *Selected Plays and Libretti*, 3:230; and *La Torre*, 33. Hamburger's translation is based on the first version of the play, while Bortoli Cappelletto's translation is based on the third version. The King's line, however, remains the same in all three versions.

8. Cacciari was definitely influenced by Schmitt's decisionism in 1978, when Italian politics came to an unprecedented stalemate and it seemed that the terrorists were the only political forces capable of action. However, Cacciari's attention to Schmitt goes beyond "Cainism" (see note 4) or what has been called "Leftist Schmittism" (Jacob Taubes, Joachim Schickel, and Chantal Mouffe, among others, but one should go back to Albert Salomon's *The Tyranny of Progress*, published in 1955 and heavily influenced by Schmitt's ideas about political theology). Although Cacciari was perfectly aware of how

dangerous Schmitt could be if taken at face value (see his 1991 essay "Carl Schmitt e lo stato"), he needed Schmitt's criticism of liberalism's "impotence" in order to stifle the political timidity of the Italian Left. On the other hand, Cacciari's use of Schmitt was not just instrumental. Several pages of *Icone della legge* (Icons of the Law), *Dell'inizio* (On Beginning), *Geo-filosofia dell'Europa* (The Geophilosophy of Europe), "Filosofia e teologia," and *L'arcipelago* (The Archipelago) are deeply indebted to Schmitt's *Der Nomos der Erde*. Recently, Giorgio Agamben has argued that the category of "exceptional state" (widely adopted by Schmitt) suits the unending war against terrorism and the liquidation of democracy very well. See Giorgio Agamben, *State of Exception*.

9. Marcello Veneziani, "Cacciari, aristocratico conservatore," *Il Giornale*, April 24, 2001. Cacciari's overcoming (not rejection) of Marxism stems from his refusal of the notion that a "just" transformation of society (revolutionary or otherwise) would or should abolish the basic social antagonism. It is true, however, as Veneziani points out, that Cacciari has occasionally appropriated Joseph de Maistre's infamous quote, "Man is too wicked to be free." For this taste of negative anthropology, see M. Cacciari and Gianfranco Bettin, *Duemilauno. Politica e futuro*, 24.

10. Cacciari derives his use of the term *impolitico* from Mann's title *Betrachtungen eines Unpolitischen*. Although the current English edition translates *Unpolitische* as *nonpolitical*, the translator and I have preferred *unpolitical*, which is closer both to German and Italian, and it is also used by Mark Lilla when he quotes "Thomas Mann's *Reflections of an Unpolitical Man*" in his article "The Lure of Syracuse," 83.

11. Following Cacciari's steps, political philosopher Roberto Esposito has devoted much attention to the category of the "unpolitical" in Romano Guardini, Hermann Broch, Elias Canetti, Simone Weil, Georges Bataille, Ernst Jünger, Walter Benjamin, and Hannah Arendt. Esposito has also connected the unpolitical with community theory. See Roberto Esposito, *La pluralità irrappresentabile, Categorie dell'impolitico, Nove pensieri sulla politica, Oltre la politica, Communitas, Nichilismo e politica, Immunitas, Bíos. Biopolitica e filosofia*, and *Terza persona. Politica della vita e filosofia dell'impersonale*.

12. Cacciari has always been a fine critic of Musil. See the third chapter of *Krisis*, some brief passages in *Walther Rathenau e il suo ambiente*, the Musil chapter in *Dallo Steinhof* (English translation "Wonders and Marvels" in *Posthumous People*), "L'attenzione profana di Robert Musil" (German translation in *Zeit ohne Kronos*, English translation in *Posthumous People*), and "L'uomo senza qualità di Musil," in *Il romanzo* vol. 5, ed. Franco Moretti.

13. Slavoj Žižek, *The Sublime Object of Ideology*, 2.

14. When Cacciari was in his first and second term as mayor of Venice, the deputy mayor was the sociologist and novelist Gianfranco Bettin. Cacciari

and Bettin have collaborated in *Petrolkimiko* and *Duemilauno*. See also Gian-franco Bettin, *L'erede*, a true crime story in which the author analyzes the rapid social transformation of the Veneto region in recent years.

15. See also the English translation, "Eupalinos or Architecture." A good selection of Cacciari's essays on urbanism is *Architecture and Nihilism*. See also Francesco Dal Co, *Figures of Architecture and Thought*, and Manfredo Tafuri (1935–1994), *Teoria e storia dell'architettura, Architecture and Utopia, La sfera e il labirinto*, and with Francesco Dal Co, *Architettura contemporanea*.

16. I have discussed the notion of compossibility and pure possibility, with references to Cacciari, in the last section of my *L'esperienza dell'istante*, 201–227. A few pages of the same section are also dedicated to an "ethics of indeci-sion" as a possible criticism of the modern emphasis on decision (not necessarily Cacciari's emphasis).

17. The collaboration between Cacciari and Luigi Nono (1924–1990) in-cludes four vocal-instrumental compositions: *Io, frammento del Prometeo* (Io, Fragment from Prometheus, 1981), *Das Atmende Klarsein* (The Breathing Being-Clear, 1980–1983), *Prometeo. Tragedia dell'ascolto* (Prometheus: A Trag-edy of Listening, 1984), and *Guai ai gelidi mostri* (Woe to the Icy Monsters, 1983–1988). Cacciari has collected his and Nono's discussions and notebooks in *Verso Prometeo*. Some of Cacciari's writings on Nono are also included in *Nono*, ed. by Enzo Restagno, and *Migranten* by Edmond Jabès, Massimo Cac-ciari, and Luigi Nono. See also Luigi Nono, *Texte, Écrits*, and *Scritti e colloqui*.

18. Luigi Nono in *Verso Prometeo*, 30, my translation. Nono's "hegemonic sound-transmission" refers to the linear transmission of sound in the concert hall and at the opera.

19. Cacciari refers to Simone Weil's play *Venise sauvée*, based on Pierre Antoine de la Place's *Venise sauvée* and Thomas Otway's *Venice Preserved*. See also "L'Espagne et Venise," Cacciari's introduction to César Vichard de Saint-Réal, *Conjuration des Espagnols contre la république de Venise en 1618*.

20. Joseph Brodsky, *Fondamenta degli incurabili*, 41. Beauty may not be one of time's possessions, but time does have an effect on beauty. Leopardi called it "grace." Beauty reveals itself in an instant, but grace exists only in succes-sion, in a sequence of parts: "Therefore grace usually consists in motion. We shall then say that beauty is in the moment, and grace in time" [Perciò la grazia ordinariamente consiste nel movimento: e diremo così, la bellezza è nell'istante, la grazia nel tempo]. Giacomo Leopardi, note of August 4–9, 1820, *Zibaldone di pensieri*, 1:189. It would be interesting to compare Leop-ardi's notion of grace with Schiller's—the "movable beauty" Schiller intro-duces in *On Dignity and Grace* (1793). Here, however, the difference between beauty and grace accounts for different politics of beauty, as it is discussed in the next note.

21. A personal recollection: In 1977 I was in Mestre, attending a jazz workshop as a music critic. After the concert, in the open discussion that followed, a worker from the Porto Marghera plant came to the microphone and delivered a long speech on his idea of beauty. As a revolutionary communist, he was supposed to desire the destruction of Porto Marghera in the name of the radical transformation of society (the reader probably remembers that Porto Marghera was the place where the "destruction of labor" became a catchphrase at the end of the 1960s), but he admitted to being paralyzed by the plant's uncanny beauty at night when thousands of lamps would fill it with light. To a certain extent, his dilemma was Jaffier's dilemma. In its double incarnation, as archipelago or oil refinery, Venice is just too fragmented, too ungraspable to become the symbol of anything that is as clearly defined as bildungsroman or the revolution. It would be giving the managers of the Marghera plant too much credit to say that in their longtime disregard for workers' safety and the ecology of the city, they exploited the same contradictory beauty that paralyzed that sensitive, jazz-loving worker. But exploitation it was. Just as the Venetian Council was not moved by the motivation behind Jaffier's repentance, the refinery's managers were not impressed by the aesthetic feelings of their employees, and they proceeded to pollute the environment even more. Which only proves Cacciari's point and ours: beauty is a complex political factor precisely because it is antipolitical, because it wants to "save the world" (as Dostoyevsky's Prince Mishkin has it, "only beauty will save the world") and therefore it can and it will be manipulated by purely political forces. As long as it is conceived as eternal, beauty has nothing to offer the unpolitical. But grace does. Grace is beauty within decay; it is beauty accepting its own mortality.

22. Mark Lilla, "The Politics of God," 18.

1. IMPRACTICABLE UTOPIAS: HOFMANNSTHAL, LUKÁCS, BENJAMIN

1. Richard Alewyn's *Über Hugo von Hofmannsthal* is responsible, among other books, for this gentlemanly, mannered version of Hofmannsthal. [Trans.: Loris was Hofmannsthal's pseudonym when at sixteen he published his first poems and was accepted at the Café Griensteidl, where famous Viennese literati such as Arthur Schnitzler and Hermann Bahr were habitués. The term "Romània" is obviously derived from Ernst Robert Curtius's *European Literature and the Latin Middle Ages*.]

2. Hermann Bahr, "Studien zur Kritik der Moderne" (1894), in Helmut A. Fiechtner, *Hugo von Hofmannsthal. Der Dichter im Spiegel der Freunde*, 43 (henceforth cited as *Dichter* and not to be confused with Hofmannsthal's essay "Der Dichter und Unsere Zeit," for which see note 5). Peter Szondi, *Das lyrische Drama des Fin de siècle*, ed. Henriette Beese, 160–180, is essential on the young Hofmannsthal.

3. This is also Freud's problem. See his essay "On Transience" (1915), one of his most hermetic writings, in Sigmund Freud, *Writings on Art and Literature*. From this essay and its correlate, "The Uncanny" (1919), it is possible to work out the relation Freud-Hofmannsthal-Schnitzler. See Adriano Pagnin, "*Das Unheimliche*, la ripetizione, la morte," in *La critica freudiana*, ed. Franco Rella. [Trans.: Cacciari alludes indirectly to Hofmannsthal's famous poem "On Transitoriness" (1892–1894) where the poet laments the passing of time while affirming the reality of the past. See Hofmannsthal's "Tercets on Transitoriness," in *Great Poems from Goethe to Brecht*, ed. Walter Schweppe.]

4. Olga Schnitzler, *Hofmannsthal und Schnitzler*, in *Dichter*, 207–230. See also Freud's essay "The Uncanny."

5. Hugo von Hofmannsthal, "Der Dichter und unsere Zeit." [Trans.: Here and elsewhere Cacciari refers to Hofmannsthal's writings collected in the Italian anthology *Viaggi e saggi*, ed. Leone Traverso, henceforth cited as *Viaggi*. Unless noted, here and elsewhere the translation is mine.] One is reminded of Benjamin's *Angelus Novus*: "Even the dead will not be safe from the enemy if he wins." See "Theses on the Philosophy of History" VI, in Walter Benjamin's *Illuminations*.

6. Hugo von Hofmannsthal, *Das Buch der Freunde*. [Ed.: Cacciari refers to the Italian translation, *Il libro degli amici*, henceforth cited as *Amici*.]

7. Ernst Robert Curtius, "To the Memory of Hofmannsthal," in *Essays on European Literature* (henceforeth cited as *Essays*).

8. Hugo von Hofmannsthal, "Österreich im Spiegel seiner Dichtung," in *Viaggi*.

9. Ernst Robert Curtius, "George, Hofmannsthal, and Calderón," *Essays*, 146.

10. Hugo von Hofmannsthal, *Christinas Heimreise* (1910) in *Lustspiele*, 1:257. "In the name of God! Always travel happy, Sir. You seem to be one of those who is destined to always be traveling." Arthur Schnitzler's *Casanovas Heimfahrt* (*Casanova's Return*) is in many ways the conclusion of the desperate journey of adventure. On *Christinas Heimreise*, see Erich Rösch, *Komödien Hofmannsthals*. On the relationship between Hofmannsthal and Venice, see also the description of the Carnival, with the quotation by Jacob Böhme: "Thus every figure turns covetously to the other / imbuing the other with yearning pleasure/bringing the other to life / so that eternity is an uninterrupted magic" (*Amici*, 106).

11. Rudolf Goldschmit, *Hugo von Hofmannsthal*, 65. Harry Kessler, Walther Rathenau's greatest biographer and close friend, was also very close to Hofmannsthal. The most important documentation on Weimar's aristocratic and upper-middle-class society is in Kessler's *Diaries*. See Harry Kessler, *Tagebücher 1918–1937*.

12. On "The Great Theater of the World" and "Ceremony," see Hugo von Hofmannsthal, "Appunti e diari" (*Amici*, 195, 51). [Ed.: *El gran teatro del mundo* is also the title of one of Calderón de la Barca's most celebrated *autos sacramentales*, or sacred representations.]

13. [Ed.: Hofmannsthal's *The Tower*, which is the main subject of this essay, is based on Pedro Calderón de la Barca's *Life Is a Dream* (*La vida es sueño*, 1635). In 1902–1904, Hofmannsthal attempted a verse translation of Calderón's drama. Between 1918 and 1925 he wrote the first version of *The Tower*. Between 1925 and 1927 he wrote two more versions, with major changes in the fourth and fifth acts. The reader who is not familiar with Calderón's *Life Is a Dream* and Hofmannsthal's *The Tower* may need some elucidation about their main plots. In Calderón's play, Sigismund has been confined in a tower by his father, King Basilius of Poland. Wary of the prophecy about his son leading an insurrection against him and turning into a cruel tyrant, Basilius, who is old and has no other sons, is about to hand down the power to Astolfo, duke of Moscow. However, he wants to put his son to the test first. He commands that Sigismund be drugged, brought to court by his guardian Clotaldo, and dressed in princely garb. If Sigismund wakes up and behaves cruelly, he will be sent back to the Tower forever. When Sigismund finds out the truth about himself, he becomes furious and kills one of his servants, but he is not even sure whether he is dreaming or is awake. He is brought back to the Tower, but now the people of Poland know that the king has an heir and they do not want to be ruled by Astolfo, who is a foreigner. A soldier frees Sigismund, and war erupts. Basilius, who is captured, finally yields (in the words of Sigismund, both he and his father are now "disenchanted," or awaken to the awareness that life is a dream, and that dreams are a dream). Sigismund will be the new king of Poland, but the soldier who betrayed Basilius in order to free him will be sent to the Tower because "once the cause of treason's past, there's no need to keep the traitor." In Hofmannsthal's play (version of 1925), only the first act follows Calderón's plot. Sigismund is twenty-two years old and has never left the Tower, and yet the rebellion against the king is under way. Julian, the Tower's governor and Sigismund's guardian, advises King Basilius to meet his son and grant him pardon in order to quench the revolt. The king brings Sigismund to court and wants to know from him if Julian is the secret mind behind the rebellion. Sigismund does not understand, calls his father "Satan" and tries to kill him. Julian, who is indeed the head of the revolt, brings Sigismund back to the Tower and makes clear his intention to make a new ruler out of Sigismund. But Sigismund thinks that he is still dreaming and wants no part in Julian's scheme. Soon Julian finds out that his right-hand man, Olivier, has taken over and leads the rebellion in the name of the dispossessed. Olivier kills Julian, but in the chaos that engulfs the

country Olivier is killed as well, and the Gypsy woman who is pregnant by Olivier poisons Sigismund. In the end, Sigismund, who wanted to become a "just" king, a founder and not an owner, dies in the arms of the Children's King, the ultimate utopian redeemer. In the version of 1927, the "life is a dream" theme, the Gypsy woman and the Children's King have disappeared. Olivier, no longer just another would-be tyrant, is much more cold and dispassionate, a mixture of revolutionary character and faceless bureaucrat. After killing Julian, Olivier recognizes that Sigismund is too pure and "unpolitical" to serve his political purposes and arranges his death. Sigismund goes voluntarily to his sacrifice and dies saying: "Bear witness. I was here, even though nobody knew me.'"]

14. On *Semiramis*, see *Essays*, 195–197.

15. Egon Schwarz, *Hofmannsthal und Calderón*, 16 (henceforth cited as *Hofmannsthal*).

16. Published in Hugo von Hofmannsthal, *Dramen*, vol. 3. At the end of September 1902, Hofmannsthal went to Rome to write *Life Is a Dream*, but fifteen days after his arrival, "he switched" to another subject, Thomas Otway's *Venice preserved*. See "Appunti e diari" (*Amici*, 131).

17. Hugo von Hofmannsthal, *Briefe 1900–1909*, 56.

18. See Hofmannsthal's letter of November 15, 1920, in Hugo von Hofmannsthal and Richard Beer Hofmann, *Briefwechsel*.

19. Carl Jacob Burckhardt, *Zu Hugo von Hofmannsthal*. [Ed.: Cacciari refers to the Italian translation, *Ricordi di Hofmannsthal*, henceforth cited as *Ricordi*.]

20. See Schnitzler's letter of February 16, 1925 in Hugo von Hofmannsthal and Arthur Schnitzler, *Briefwechsel*.

21. See the letter to Schnitzler of February 16, 1925 (*Briefwechsel*).

22. [Ed.: "Wozu Dichter in dürftiger Zeit?" (What are poets for in a destitute time?) is a quote from Friedrich Hölderlin's *Brot und Wein* (Bread and Wine).]

23. For Hofmannsthal, even this endless analysis of the subject matter, of the language of tradition (language cannot be invented) is secretly Freudian. See Sigmund Freud, "Analysis Terminable and Interminable" (1937). Franco Rella has devoted numerous pages to the Freudian concept of endless analysis (*unendliche Analyse*).

24. See *Hofmannsthal*, Chapter 5. The trochaic version stops at Act IV.

25. On *The Letter of Lord Chandos*, I refer the reader to my *Krisis*.

26. Calderón de la Barca, *Life Is a Dream*. [Trans.: I have slightly modified the translation.]

27. Walter Benjamin, *The Origin of German Tragic Drama*, 81, henceforth cited as *Origin*. [Trans.: I have slightly modified the translation here.] On the theoretical and philosophical structure of Benjamin's work, see my "Di alcuni motivi in Walter Benjamin."

28. Karl Löwith, in his seminal essays on the Christian tradition in *Zur Kritik der christlichen Überlieferung*, deems the importance of the *Trauerspiel* for Christianity very slight.

29. The devaluation (*Abwertung*) of the king (of kingship) also comprehends the fundamental devaluation of the earthly world on the whole. This tendency of Hofmannsthal's analysis is present ever since the rewriting of 1902. See Lothar Wittmann, *Sprachthematik und dramatische Form im Werke Hofmannsthals*, 94 (henceforth cited as *Sprachthematik*).

30. *The Tower*, in Hugo von Hofmannsthal's *Selected Plays and Libretti*, vol. 3. [Trans.: *The Tower* is translated by M. Hamburger. All quotations and references are to this edition.]

31. Gerhart Pickerodt, *Hofmannsthals Dramen*, 251 (henceforth cited as *Dramen*).

32. Leo Spitzer, *Classical and Christian Ideas of World Harmony*, 32.

33. On Hofmannsthal's nonoriginality (which is equivalent to a critique of the modern, of the anti-avant-garde in all the "great Viennese [writers] of language") also insisted Walter Benjamin in his 1926 review of the first version of the *Tower*. See his *Gesammelte Schriften*, 3:30 (henceforth cited as *Schriften*).

34. Franz Grillparzer, *Family Strife in Habsburg*.

35. Rudolph would like to be *pontifex*, rainbow, symbol. On the traditional strata of these ideas, see René Guénon, *Le roi du monde*. [Trans.: Cacciari quotes from the Italian translation, *Il Re del mondo*, henceforth cited as *Re*.]

36. On John Dee, see Frances Yates, *The Theatre of the World*. This quotation from Grillparzer shows, however, how Yates is completely wrong when she claims that Dee was rejected in the nineteenth century as a "ridiculous charlatan." See Frances Yates, *The Rosicrucian Enlightenment*, xxiii.

37. For Hugo von Hofmannsthal on Grillparzer, see "Grillparzers politisches Vermächtnis," in *Gesammelte Werke, Prose*, vol. 3.

38. Rudolf Kassner also falls in Hofmannsthal's Stifterian mask. See his collection of articles on Hofmannsthal in *Dichter*, 242–251, and Thomas Mann, "In memoriam," *Neue Freie Presse*, July 21, 1929, in *Dichter*.

39. Walter Benjamin, "Hugo von Hofmannsthal's 'Turm,'" a review of the second version now in *Gesammelte Schriften*, 3:98–102.

40. Georg Simmel, "On the Concept and Tragedy of Culture" and "The Conflict in Modern Culture," in *The Conflict in Modern Culture and Other Essays* (henceforth cited as *Culture*). On this issue, see my introduction to Simmel, *Saggi di estetica*.

41. Walter Benjamin insists on a similar concept in *The Origin of German Tragic Drama* and in his two reviews of *The Tower*.

42. In the "Notes" to *Oedipus* and *Antigones* (1804). I have called attention to the absolute centrality of Friedrich Hölderlin's writings in my "*Entsagung*" [Resignation].

43. György Lukács, *Soul and Form*, 158 (henceforth cited as *Soul*). [Trans.: Cacciari quotes only from the last chapter "The Metaphysics of Tragedy," 152–174, to which he refers specifically later in the essay. I have used Anna Bostok's translation in every instance except here, where Bostok does not translate the phrase in question but uses a paraphrase.]

44. But the categorical imperative of this ethics consists in the death drive of any new action. In these instances, the "culture" of the young Lukács has indeed close affinity with Heidegger's. See, for instance, Lucien Goldmann, *Lukács and Heidegger*. In Max Scheler, too, the tragic is conceived as antinaturalism, as representation of the dynamics of values (*Werte*) and their conflict. The essence of the tragic hero consists in having to realize values to the end in conflict with normal morality, with the naturalism of existing social relations, that is, in being the bearer of a paradoxical ethics. See Max Scheler's *Zum Phänomen des Tragischen* now in *Gesammelte Werke* (1915), later with the title of *Vom Umsturz der Werte* (1919).

45. The critique of modern drama had already been developed by Lukács in his monumental youthful work *History of the Development of Modern Drama* (in Hungarian, 1911). See Laura Boella, *Il giovane Lukács*.

46. See Lucien Goldmann, *The Hidden God*.

47. Hence the relation between *tragédie classique* and "metaphysics" in the Heideggerian sense of the term.

48. Georg Wilhelm Friedrich Hegel, *Aesthetics*. But this difference that Hegel marks beyond any romantic nostalgia (*Sehnsucht*), as well as beyond any classical Jacobinism, determines his general attitude (with respect to romanticism) toward European civilization as being necessarily Christian. The impossibility of the tragic is the necessity of the theological Christian, of Christendom as theology.

49. A very clear red thread links the tragic utopia of the young Lukács to the realistic utopia of the later Lukács. The dialectic concept of totality supports them both.

50. *Il giovane Lukács* (see n. 69), Laura Boella points out the importance of Paul Ernst for Lukács. But Boella does not analyze Ernst by himself.

51. Paul Ernst, "Bühne und Theater," in *Ein Credo*, 116.

52. Paul Ernst, "Vom Weg meiner Dichtung" (1912), "Tragödie und Erlösungdrama" (1917), and "Die Erlösungsdichtung" (1916), in ibid.

53. Paul Ernst, "Kierkegaard" (1910), in ibid., 198.

54. Walter Benjamin, "Hugo von Hofmannsthal" and "Der Turm," in *Schriften*, 3:32.

55. *Neue Deutsche Beiträge* 2, no. 3 (August 1927): 89–110.

56. Franz Rosenzweig is a determining presence in Benjamin's essay. Rosenzweig's importance for Benjamin's *The Origin of German Tragic Drama* is

clear from his brief article "Bücher, die lebendig geblieben sind," in *Die literarische Welt*, May 17, 1929, where besides Alois Riegl and Alfred G. Meyer's *Eisenbauten* he also quotes György Lukács's *History and Class Consciousness* and Franz Rosenzweig's *Stern der Erlösung*. This volume was published in Frankfurt in 1921 with Kaufmann. There the tragic is seen as dissolution of idealistic dialectics and as representation of *Dasein* as "anxiety before death" (7). Very close is the relationship between Rosenzweig, the last teachings of Hermann Cohen and Martin Buber. The paradoxical ethical element in Rosenzweig is instead less present than in Lukács's *Soul and Form*. With respect to this philosophy of German Hebraism, one cannot ignore the relationship between Buber and Hofmannsthal. See Hugo von Hofmannsthal and Martin Buber, "Briefwechsel."

57. The focus on the *Trauerspiel* in general philosophical terms had already been brought by Wilhelm Dilthey in "Leibniz und sein Zeitalter," in *Gesammelte Schriften*, vol. 3. On Daniel Casper von Lohenstein and his entirely secularized political tragedies, see Ladislao Mittner, *Storia della letteratura tedesca. Dai primordi pagani all'età barocca*, 848–900.

58. On the allegorical character of the German Baroque, see the repertory of Manfred Windfuhr, *Die Barocke Bildlichkeit und ihre Kritiker*.

59. Here another aspect of Benjamin's relation with Rosenzweig becomes evident. In the light of Scholem's own work on Hebrew mysticism, an examination of the correspondence with Gershom Scholem would be seminal in dealing with the problem mentioned here. See Walter Benjamin, *Briefe*, 2 vols. (henceforth cited as *Briefe*).

60. The anxiety before the Jewish diaspora or, better, anxiety itself as diaspora, forms a large part of the allegorical nature of Hofmannsthal's *Trauerspiel*. The nobles of the kingdom around Basilius and Sigismund are repeatedly characterized by their anti-Semitism (particularly in the great scene of Ignatius's convent). Even the reference to Poland of the seventeenth century takes on, in this light, a meaning that is certainly not a mannerism. Poland was the theater of some of the greatest pogroms of the era, and where the apocalyptic-messianic tendencies took root more deeply.

61. The following quotations are from the fundamental work of Henri de Lubac, *Histoire et esprit*. By the same author, see the monumental work *Exégèse médiévale*, 4 vols. See also Erich Auerbach, *Studi su Dante*, and especially "Figura."

62. Walter Benjamin, "Goethe's Elective Affinities" in *Selected Writings*, 1:297–319. On Goethe and his extraneousness to romanticism, Benjamin had already written some very important remarks in "The Concept of Criticism in German Romanticism" (116–125).

63. Quoted in Helmut A. Fiechtner, "Hugo von Hofmannsthals Leben-Werk" (*Dichter*, 23).

64. This is a paraphrase of an expression used by Benjamin in his essay "Goethe's *Elective Affinities*."

65. On this question in seventeenth-century political philosophy, see Alessandro Biral, "La genesi dell'opposizione tra 'pubblico' e 'civile'," and Claudio Pacchiani, "Spinoza e l'assolutismo politico," in Alessandro Biral et al., *Per una storia del moderno concetto di politica*. On Thomas Hobbes, see Mario Tronti, "Hobbes e Cromwell," in Alessandro Piazzi, Mario Segatori, and Mario Tronti, *Stato e rivoluzione in Inghilterra*.

66. René Guénon, *Symboles fondamentaux de la science sacrée*. [Ed.: Cacciari quotes from the Italian translation, *Simboli della scienza sacra*, 22.]

67. The pilgrimage is Hermann Hesse's utopia. For him, the symbolism of tradition lives essentially in the idea of the possible sublimation of the journeying and of adventure in *Morgenlandfahrt* [*The Journey to the East*]. This resistance of the traditional nostalgic aspect of the symbol differentiates clearly Hesse from Benjamin's disenchantment of the *Trauerspiel*, and therefore also from the *outcome* of Hofmannsthal's work. In Hofmannsthal the notion of Orient is always an allegorical figure, as in *The Woman Without a Shadow*. It is never Paradise, never supreme land, center of the world, or its symbol, as in Hesse. Hesse's inauthenticity consists also in his articulating these traditional symbolic elements with the ideas of rational European humanism. His *Magister Ludi* is a typical example of this.

68. Robert Klein, *La forme et l'intelligible*. [Ed.: Cacciari quotes from the Italian translation of the chapter "L'immaginazione come veste dell'anima in Marsilio Ficino e Giordano Bruno," in *La forma e l'intelligibile*, 49–67.]

69. Étienne Gilson, *Les métamorphoses de la cité de Dieu*. [Ed.: Cacciari quotes from the Italian translation, *La città di Dio e i suoi problemi*.]

70. St. Augustine, quoted in *La città di Dio*, 68.

71. Max Weber, *Gesammelte Aufsätze zur Religionssoziologie*, 2:363–386.

72. See *Origin*. Also Frances Yates, *The Rosicrucian Enlightenment*, Chapter 1, and *The Theatre of the World*.

73. Carl Schmitt, *Politische Theologie* (henceforth cited as *Theologie*). In *Origin*, Benjamin makes great use of Schmitt.

74. This is what happens in Schmitt. See his *Die Diktatur*. See also Christian Graf von Krockow's *Die Entscheidung*, who criticizes, in fact, the process of absolutization (*Verabsolutierung*) of decision as a process that restores in the end the absolute positivity of the norm (the "absolute positivity").

75. Walter Benjamin, "Hugo von Hofmannsthal, Der Turm," *Die Literarische Welt*, July 9, 1926; *Schriften*, 31.

76. Walter Benjamin, "Hugo von Hofmannsthal's Der Turm," *Die Literarische Welt*, March 2, 1928; *Schriften*, 99.

77. One may recall the children's song at the end of Act V in the first version, "Powerful! The lark is powerful!"

78. [Ed.: T. S. Eliot, in a short note on Hofmannsthal's play, observes that if *The Tower* cannot be called a success, "it is at least a failure grander and more impressive than many successes," and that the latter part, with the Gypsy woman and the Children's King, "becomes so phantasmagoric that one can only imagine its representation in terms of a dream-film such as Jean Cocteau might devise." If *The Tower* is unplayable, it is because the author wished to exceed the limits of theater: "He seems to have loaded this play," T. S. Eliot observes, "with all the burden of his feelings about the catastrophe of the Europe to which he belonged." It is true, however, that the play expresses not only the author's sufferings, "but also his ultimate Christian hope." And Eliot concludes: "I find it interesting to compare the message of *The Tower*, so far as I have succeeded in grasping it, with that of the masterly essay which Paul Valéry wrote in 1919, called "La Crise de l'esprit". . . . Perhaps the hope of the one and the despair of the other were each in its own realm justified." Eliot, "A Note on 'The Tower,' " in Hugo von Hofmannsthal, *Selected Plays and Libretti*, lxxiv. Eliot makes no mention of the third version. It would be interesting to know what he would have made of it.]

79. See Ernst Bloch, *Zwischenwelten in der Philosophiegeschichte*, and above all the stupendous pages on utopias in the Renaissance.

80. In this respect, *The Tower* has deep affinities with Hofmannsthal's *The Difficult Man*.

81. See Martin Heidegger's "Language in the Poem: A discussion on Georg Trakl's Poetic Work," in *On the Way to Language*. See my "La Vienna di Wittgenstein."

82. On the complexity of the power of martyrdom in Sigismund see Grete Schäder, "Hofmannsthals Weg zur Tragödie," *Deutsche Vierteljahrsschrift*, and William Henry Rey, "Tragik und Verklärung in *Turm*," in *Hugo von Hofmannsthal*, ed. Sybille Bauer.

83. One may recall Heidegger's "The question is the godliness of thinking" ("Das Fragen ist die Frömmigkeit des Denkens").

84. In Ludwig Wittgenstein's *Tractatus Logico-Philosophicus* and at the end of Musil's *Man Without Qualities*, the presence of the mystic is the same. See my *Krisis*. Even in the first version the Children's King tells Sigismund, "I ask you nothing but that which you cannot say."

85. Chandos is present at the massacre of the poisoned rats in his cell, just as Sigismund remembers the slain pig.

86. Feigning peace is proper to the political, but in order that this mask be effective it is necessary that the political know that it cannot have true peace. The true radical, allegorical character of the political consists in its total absence of tragedy as well as in its theological symbolism. The very same political theology is the mask of the theological.

87. See Pierre Yves Petillon, "Hofmannsthal: le règne du silence." On this
issue the relation between Hofmannsthal and Schnitzler, and Freud, becomes
even clearer.

88. Harry Kessler, "Tagebücher" (*Dichter*, 284).

89. On the figure of Simon the Jew, see *Sprachthematik*, 242, and notes 91,
100, and 101. Simon is a baptized Jew, a typical figure in Poland and in Eastern
Europe after 1648, the year of Chmielnicki's great pogroms. The role of the
Jews among the Polish nobility is clearly indicated in the dialogue between
Basilius and his followers, while they visit Ignatius. Many Jews were adminis-
trators and collectors and they were especially employed in these roles against
the Cossacks. After the Cossack rebellion, headed in fact by Chmielnicki, who
destroyed entire Jewish communities, the Jews were subjected to Polish persecution for many decades. In this context, the most important mystical-messi-
anic trends of the modern diaspora are developed. The first version of *The
Tower* is particularly attentive to these trends.

90. It may be worthwhile here to research the sense of Joseph Roth's metaphor in his novel *Das Falsche Gewicht*.

2. NIETZSCHE AND THE UNPOLITICAL

1. Ulrich von Wilamowitz-Möllendorf, "Gli intellettuali tedeschi e il loro
presunto magistero di violenza" (1918), in *Cultura classica e crisi tedesca*, ed.
Luciano Canfora, 82.

2. Friedrich Nietzsche, *Frammenti Postumi 1888–1889*, 3:3:410 [Ed.: Cacciari quotes from the Italian critical edition of Nietzsche's *Werke*.] Generally,
as concerns passages on Nietzsche's critique of the political in Wilhelmine
Germany, see Giorgio Pasqualotto, "Nietzsche: considerazioni attuali"
(henceforth cited as *Nietzsche*). and Roberto Escobar, *Nietzsche e la filosofia politica del 19. secolo*. The opposition, clearly, is far from being simply political. It
extends to the notion of scientific work, to its academic organization, to its
historical *koiné*. It is shocking to realize how Nietzsche's critique has no effect
on Wilhelmine *Kultur*, at any level. The stories that have circulated on this
presumed relationship stem from superficial thematic comparisons, such as in
Roy Pascal, *From Naturalism to Expressionism*.

3. On the "Decline of the West," there were books such as those by Rainer
Thiel, *Die Generation ohne Männer*; by Ernst Niekisch and Edgar Salin of the
Tat group; and, naturally, Ernst Jünger's books *Der Kampf als inneres Erlebnis*
and *Die totale Mobilmachung*. On this historical period, see Anton M. Koktanek, *Oswald Spengler in seiner Zeit*; Christian Graf von Krockow, *Die Entscheidung*; Herman Lebovics, *Social Conservatism and the Middle Classes in Germany
1914–1933*. See also Thomas Mann, *Reflections of a Nonpolitical Man*. On this
seminal text see Alberto Asor Rosa, *Thomas Mann o dell'ambiguità borghese*.
[Trans.: For the translator's choice of "unpolitical" over "nonpolitical," see
the introduction, note 10.]

4. Thomas Mann is obviously indebted to György Lukács's interpretation of Theodor Storm in *Soul and Form*.

5. But Meinecke continues by saying: "This is how I felt then. . . . I still had not understood completely the demonism of the old power politics and the more recent demonisms of nationalism, surging up from the depths of the XIX century" (*Erlebtes 1862–1901*, 307). [Trans.: Cacciari quotes from the Italian translation, *Esperienze 1862–1919*, 306. The translation is mine.]

6. Karl Löwith, *From Hegel to Nietzsche*, 175.

7. On this point, see Sergio Moravia, "Morale come dominio. Per una rilettura della *Genealogia*," introduction to the Italian edition of Friedrich Nietzsche's *Genealogy of Morals*.

8. Carl Schmitt, "Weiterentwicklung des totalen Staats in Deutschland," in *Verfassungsrechtliche Aufsätze aus den Jahren 1924–1954*.

9. Schmitt, "Staat als konkreter, an eine geschichtliche Epoche gebundener Begriff," in ibid.

10. This is essentially Max Weber's line of interpretation in *Wirtschaft und Gesellschaft*, Eng. trans. *Economy and Society*, 3 vols. See also Schmitt, *Verfassungsrechtliche Aufsätze*, 384.

11. It is interesting to recall on this point that Friedrich Naumann regarded Social Democratic ideology as the great heresy of the Protestant church ("die grosse Häresie der evangelischen Kirche").

12. Friedrich Nietzsche, *Human, All Too Human*, vol. 1.

13. [Trans.: All the quotes here are from the Hollingdale edition of *Human, All Too Human*. Cacciari quotes mostly from volume 1, section 8, "A Glance at the State."]

14. The critical discussion of these concepts, so far dominant as self-evident, has finally begun, even in the "constructions" of Marxism. See Salvatore Veca, *Saggio sul programma scientifico di Marx*.

15. Friedrich Nietzsche, *Twilight of the Idols*, no. 43. Negri is completely mistaken when he quotes Nietzsche as a reactionary critic of democracy. The definition is literally wrong. See Antonio Negri, *La forma stato*, 277.

16. This passage should be read together with "Of passing by," in *Thus Spoke Zarathustra*, Part III. See also my *Metropolis*.

17. Friedrich Nietzsche, *Daybreak*, book III, no. 206. We are reminded of Kurt Tucholsky's desperate passage: "When the buglers of life take a rest to shake their instruments to get rid of the spit."

18. From Heinrich Heine's "Jan Steen," in *The Poetry and Prose of Heinrich Heine*, 636. [Trans.: The prose piece is translated by Frederic Ewen.]

3. WEBER AND THE CRITIQUE OF SOCIALIST REASON

1. On this aspect of *Der Sozialismus*, see Antonino Bruno's "Politica e valori in Max Weber," introduction to Max Weber, *Scritti Politici*.

2. Weber's position is always ruthlessly critical not only of socialist-Prussian myths (certainly not limited to the overtly reactionary circles of the Moeller van der Bruck type), but also of projects of radical socialization, put forward, for instance, in the works of Walther Rathenau (not entirely exempt from Prussian influence). In this respect, Werner Sombart's theoretical career absolutely departs from Weber's magisterial authority.

3. Wolfgang J. Mommsen, *Max Weber und die deutsche Politik*, 69.

4. Hans Maier, "Max Weber und die deutsche politische Wissenschaft," in Bernhard Pfister, Karl Engisch, and Johannes Winckelmann, *Max Weber*, 177.

5. Joseph A. Schumpeter, "Max Webers Werk," in *Dogmengeschichte und biographische Aufsätze*. Schumpeter's idea of Weber is entirely focused on the category of resignation, whose content consists in the impossibility of reconciling the political objective of the party with the normative authority proper to science. The antisocialist bent of this critique is self-evident.

6. At least two essays by Joseph Schumpeter, written in the 1920s on the question of socialism, should be remembered here: "Sozialistische Möglichkeiten von Heute" and "Der Sozialismus in England und bei Uns," now in *Aufsätze zur ökonomischen Theorie*.

7. Included in *Gesammelte Aufsätze zur Wissenschaftlehre*, it is now available in a good Italian translation by A. Roversi ("Sulla teoria dell'utilità marginale e la 'legge fondamentale della psicofisica'") [Trans.: All translations into English here are mine.].

8. The usage of such a category refers back to the epistemological debate within neo-Kantianism (particularly in Hans Vaihinger), rather than to Edmund Husserl's *Investigations*.

9. Böhm-Bawerk, as is well known, makes no distinction between Marx, Marxism, and Ricardism. On this point I refer the reader to the first chapter of my *Krisis*.

10. On these issues, and on the historical and theoretical framework in general as analyzed in this chapter, see Roberto Racinaro's important introduction to the Italian edition of Hans Kelsen's *Sozialismus und Staat* (henceforth cited as *Socialismo*), which ought to be complemented, perhaps, with an analysis of Friedrich Naumann's work on social democracy, especially *Das Schiksal des Marxismus* (1908), in *Werke*, vol. 4—works that obviously have influenced even Weber's *Kreis*.

11. Werner Sombart, *Why Is There No Socialism in the United States?* See Adolf Sturmthal, "Werner Sombart und der Amerikanische Sozialismus," in *Geschichte und Gesellschaft*.

12. Werner Sombart's work on socialism, in his entire research and many revisions, contain only a few references to the United States. See *Sozialismus*

und soziale Bewegung im 19. Jahrhundert, also *Sozialismus und soziale Bewegung,* and finally the two volumes of *Der proletarische Sozialismus.* There are some references in Walther Pollack, "Werner Sombart und der Sozialismus."

13. There are some indications, submerged by Stalinist orthodoxy, in Werner Krause, *Werner Sombarts Weg vom Kathedersozialismus zum Faschismus.*

14. See Karl Löwenstein, *Max Weber staatspolitische Auffassungen in der Sicht unserer Zeit.* Still interesting on the relation between Weber's notion of *Demokratisierung* and the elaboration of the Weimar Constitution is Jacob P. Mayer, *Max Weber and German Politics.*

15. I have called attention many times to the importance of Carl Schmitt's critique to understand Weimar's theoretical and political debate, for instance, in "Trasformazioni dello Stato e progetto politico."

16. Therefore, even tendencies toward the establishment of dictatorial nationalist forms can find fertile ground in the aporetic nature of democratization. The myth that democracy has essentially an exogenous enemy—that the relation friend/enemy in democracy is comparable to that of sovereign states—is the focus of Weber's critique as well as Schmitt's.

17. In developing this critique, the recent studies of Biagio De Giovanni seem to me of great importance; his influence is obvious on the more historical works of Giacomo Marramao and Roberto Racinaro.

18. For Schumpeter on Weimar, see "Das Soziale Antlitz des deutschen Reiches," in *Aufsätze zur Soziologie,* and "Die Wirtschaftstheorie der Gegenwart in Deutschland," in *Dogmengeschichte.*

19. Joseph A. Schumpeter, *Capitalism, Socialism, and Democracy.* See especially his 1949 lecture "The March Into Socialism," which concludes the volume. On the obsolescence of the entrepreneurial function and on the destruction of the institutional framework of capitalist society, see 131–139.

20. I owe this fitting expression to Gianni Vattimo, with whom I have also had a lively discussion on what follows.

21. Max Weber, *The Theory of Social and Economic Organization.* See also Remo Bodei and Franco Cassano, *Hegel e Weber,* 203–204.

22. This is Max Scheler's formula. See *Socialismo,* lxxv.

23. Robert Musil, *The Man Without Qualities.* This is Musil's meditation on nihilism and activism, which concludes the novel.

4. PROJECT

1. See the beautiful analysis that Fritz Mauthner gives of these terms in his *Wörterbuch der Philosophie 1910–1911.*

2. Here and elsewhere the reference is to paragraphs 31 and 32 of Martin Heidegger, *Being and Time.*

3. I believe that this relation can be theoretically and rigorously founded, as I try to show in this paper and in "Law and Justice" (Chapter 7 of the present volume). Useful also in this regard is von Krochow's *Die Entscheidung*.

4. Jacques Derrida, *De la Grammatologie*, 25. I refer to this work throughout this chapter. The thematic transposition to other genres seems to me entirely appropriate and conforming to the spirit of Derrida's program.

5. Jacques Derrida, *Positions* (Ital. trans. *Posizioni*), 51.

6. On this distinction between *Abschaffung* and *Aufhebung*, see Franz Rosenzweig's critique to *Philosophia* in the introduction to *Der Stern der Erlösung*.

7. Within this perspective, the logico-philosophical problem of the subject intersects with that of the foundations of politics, as was shown by the debate around the book by Antonio Negri, *Descartes politico o della ragionevole ideologia*. On this problem, from a different perspective, see Antonio Pavan, *All'origine del progetto borghese*; Pavan engages in controversy with Negri, in my view, with good reason. See also the important study by Salvatore Natoli, *Soggetto e fondamento*.

8. Emanuele Severino, *Legge e caso*, 29.

9. The notion of delinearized multidimensionality is discussed in *De la Grammatologie*.

10. For example, in Peter Winch, *The Idea of a Social Science and Its Relation to Philosophy*, widely discussed in Karl-Otto Apel's important essay "Analytic Philosophy of Language and the *Geisteswissenschaften*," in *Selected Essays*, vol. 1. On the present German debate on these issues, see the useful summary by Franco Volpi, "La rinascita della filosofia pratica in Germania," in *Filosofia pratica e scienza politica*, ed. Claudio Pacchiani.

11. Ludwig Wittgenstein, *Philosophical Investigations* (Ital. trans. *Ricerche filosofiche*), 114.

12. Carl Schmitt, *Der Nomos der Erde*, 25.

13. Giovanni Sartori, *La politica*, 189 (henceforth cited as *Politica*).

14. By developing these elements, it is possible to critique Schmitt's interpretation of Hobbes. See Leo Strauss, *Hobbes politische Wissenschaft*, 167–169.

15. On this point, I would like to refer to my *Dialettica e critica del Politico. Saggio su Hegel*.

16. See Hermann Heller, *Hegel und der nationale Machtstaatsgedanke in Deutschland*, a very important book for the reconstruction of the German philosophical-political debate of the period, contemporary with Friedrich Meinecke's research on *Staatsräson* and with those of Franz Rosenzweig on Hegel.

17. Crawford B. Macpherson, *Democratic Theory*.

18. Carl Schmitt, "Die Politische Theorie des Mythus," in *Positionen und Begriffen in Kampf mit Weimar-Genf-Versaillles*.

19. Karl Griewank, *Der neuzeitliche Revolutionsbegriff.* See also Claudio Cesa's important introduction to the Italian translation, *Il concetto di rivoluzione nell'età moderna*, the entry "Rivoluzione" by Salvatore Veca in *Enciclopedia Einaudi*, vol. 12, and Pierangelo Schiera et al., *Il concetto di rivoluzione nel pensiero politico moderno.*

20. Eugen Rosenstock, *Die europäischen Revolutionen*, 91, where Rosenstock quotes Lukács's *History and Class Consciousness* as a typical contemporary manifestation of this "universal claim" (*Universalanspruch*) of the idea of revolution.

21. For a completely different point of view from mine, an important critique of this aspect of secularization can be found in Augusto Del Noce, *L'epoca della secolarizzazione*, and in another work by Del Noce, though limited to the Italian sphere, *Il suicidio della rivoluzione.*

22. [Ed.: *"Silete, theologi, in munere alieno!"*—Keep silent, theologians, where there you do not belong!—is a quote from natural law theorist Alberico Gentili (1552–1608), *De jure belli libri tres* I, XII, published in 1612. In *Der Nomos der Erde*, Carl Schmitt often points out that Gentili's exhortation signaled the beginning of the end of European religious wars and the birth of international law.]

23. Emanuele Severino, *Destino della necessità*, 268.

24. This idea of culture can be found also in Ludwig Wittgenstein in his *Culture and Value*. On the modern notion of freedom, see Hans Freyer, "Die Idee der Freiheit in technischer Zeitalter," in *Festschrift für Carl Schmitt.*

25. The extensive literature on utopia is almost entirely useless for our purposes, either because utopia is immediately resolved in the productive principle of prevision-anticipation (Mannheim) or because it is abstracted from the concrete of the modern political as problem, as state-problem. On the motives of totality and separateness some useful material in Jean Servier, *Histoire de l'utopie*, and in Gilles Lapouge, *Utopie et civilisation.*

26. Hans Kelsen, *Von Wesen und Wert der Demokratie*, 101.

27. They are even present in Niklas Luhmann, as Giacomo Marramao has clearly shown in his article in *Il Centauro*, 1.

28. See Wolfram Bauer, *Wertrelativismus und Weltbestimmheit im Kampf um die Weimarer Demokratie.*

29. Wolfgang Schluchter, *Entscheidung für den sozialen Rechtstaat*, 150.

5. CATASTROPHES

1. See Desiderius Erasmus, *The Complaint of Peace.*

2. On this important work I refer the reader to my essays "Project" and "Law and Justice" [Chapters 4 and 7 of this volume.]

3. Ernst Jünger, *An der Zeitmauer* (Ital. trans. *Al muro del tempo*), 155.

4. Diana H. Manning, *Disaster Technology.*

5. Ian Burton, Robert W. Kates, and Gilbert F. White, *The Environment as Hazard*.

6. Émile Benveniste, *Le vocabulaire des institutions indo-européennes*.

7. Michel Foucault, *The Archaeology of Knowledge*.

8. Wassily Leontief, *The Future of the World Economy*.

9. Gershom Scholem, "Zum Verständnis des messianischen Idee im Judentum," and, generally, in the essays collected in the three volumes of *Judaica*.

10. Laura Satta Boschian, *Tempo d'avvento*.

11. Emile Michel Cioran, *Écartèlement*.

12. Raymond Aron, in *L'Europe des crises*.

13. René Thom, "Crisi e catastrofe," in *La crisi del concetto di crisi*, ed. Marco D'Eramo.

14. John A. Robinson, "The Concept of Crisis in Decision-making."

15. Herman Kahn, *On Escalation: Metaphors and Scenarios*; Herman Kahn and Norbert Wiener, *Crisis and Arms Control*.

16. Julien Freund, "Dalla crisi al conflitto," in *La crisi*.

17. Douglas C. Dacy and Howard Kunreuther, *The Economics of Natural Disaster*.

18. Jean-François Lyotard, *La condition postmoderne*.

19. "Aestheticization" is Carl Schmitt's definition in *Politische Romantik*.

20. René Thom, *Parabole e Catastrofi. Intervista a cura di G. Giorello and S. Morini*.

6. THE LANGUAGE OF POWER IN CANETTI

1. Fulvio Papi, "Crisi della politica e critica dell'intelletto distruttivo."

2. Franz Kafka, *Diaries*, November 22, 1911, quoted in Elias Canetti's "Kafka's Other Trial: The Letters to Felice," in *The Conscience of Words*, 74.

3. Elias Canetti, *The Human Province*, 126.

4. Gianfranco Miglio, "Guerra, pace, diritto," in Umberto Curi, ed., *Della Guerra*.

5. Gianfranco Pasquino, "Teoria della giustizia e della dottrina in Hobbes" (henceforth cited as *Teoria*).

6. Peter L. Berger, *Pyramids of Sacrifice*.

7. Elias Canetti, "Hitler, According to Speer," *The Conscience of Words*, 150.

8. [Trans.: Despite the translation of "mass" as "crowds," I have preferred to translate all instances of "mass" as "masses" or just "mass."]

9. Elias Canetti, "Power and Survival," *The Conscience of Words*, 22.

10. Hans Kelsen, "Der Begriff des Staates und die Sozialpsychologie" (Ital. trans. *La democrazia*), 419.

11. Elias Canetti, "Hermann Broch," *The Conscience of Words*, 1–13.

12. Hermann Broch, *Erkennen und Handeln*.

7. LAW AND JUSTICE: ON THE THEOLOGICAL AND MYSTICAL DIMENSIONS OF THE MODERN POLITICAL

1. Max Weber, *The Protestant Ethic and the Spirit of Capitalism*. The history of the discussion on Weber's theses is summarized in *Seminar: Religion und gesellschaftliche Entwicklung*, ed. Constans Seyfarth and Walter M. Sprondel.

2. Max Weber, *Economia e società*, 1:537–538.

3. For the prophetic type in Weber, see ibid., 1:445. These issues raise difficult questions of biblical exegesis, which Weber deals with in his writings on the sociology of religion, and, in particular, "Die Entstehung des jüdischer Pariavolkes," in *Gesammelte Aufsätze zur Religionssoziologie*, vol. 3.

4. Weber, *Economia e società* 1:524.

5. Martin Heidegger, *Phänomenologie und Theologie*. On this question I refer the reader to my paper "Die Christenheit oder Europa." See also Giorgio Penzo, *Pensare heideggeriano e problematica teologica*.

6. The first collections of essays on Schmitt to appear in Italy are the volumes edited by Gianfranco Miglio and Pierangelo Schiera (*Le categorie del "politico." Saggi di teoria politica*) and by Giuseppe Duso (*La Politica oltre lo Stato: Carl Schmitt*). Very useful for our purposes has proved to be the other volume edited by Giuseppe Duso, *Weber: razionalità e politica*, which contains essays by Pietro Rossi, Remo Bodei, Giacomo Marramao and others.

7. [Ed.: See "Project," note 22.]

8. These theses can be found in Ernst Troeltsch, *The Absoluteness of Christianity and the History of Religions*.

9. In this sense, Carl Schmitt's theses dismiss the historicist-organicist ones, last and bloodless heirs of the *Magnus Homo*, still traceable in Friedrich Meinecke and in Rudolph Smend. They differ clearly, likewise, from those of the conservative revolution from Moeller van der Bruck to Oswald Spengler. Schmitt has a place within the panorama of the German right, liberal and not, only at the price of unprecedented simplifications of the complexity of his thought.

10. Carl Schmitt, *Roman Catholicism and Political Form*.

11. Schmitt himself invites us to read the formation of the modern state according to this point of view (indeed, of the crisis which its formation commands), in Shakespeare's tragedy. See his *Hamlet oder Hekuba*. In a certain way, Ernst H. Kantorowicz's *The King's Two Bodies* is a development of these intuitions. Both these works are partially translated into Italian in two important issues of *Il Calibano*, 4 (1979) and 5 (1980).

12. René Girard, *Violence and the Sacred*.

13. Walter Benjamin, "Critique of Violence," in *Writings*, vol. 1.

14. A separate chapter on the theme of *Gerechtigkeit* should be devoted to Nietzsche, even under the profile of the history of legal thought. The work of

Roberto Escobar (*Nietzsche e la filosofia politica del 19. secolo*) is the only one along these lines at present.

15. On this see Giulio Schiavoni, *Walter Benjamin*, 176–181.

16. Simone Weil, *The Need for Roots* (Ital. trans. *La prima radice*), 295.

17. Augusto Del Noce, "Simone Weil interprete del mondo di oggi," in *L'epoca della secolarizzazione*, 141.

18. These points are well clarified by Fabrizio Desideri, *Walter Benjamin. Il tempo, le forme*, 97. In particular, Desideri sees in it the reasons for Benjamin's (and Schölem's) critique to Ernst Bloch's *Geist der Utopie*, 104–110.

19. I would like to refer here to papers by various authors that I collected in *Crucialità del tempo* that best could clarify the conception of time that decision necessarily implies.

20. One of the essential books by Søren Kierkegaard, and perhaps the least studied, is devoted precisely to the notion of repetition. See *Repetition*.

21. Søren Kierkegaard, *Either/Or*, vol. 1 (Ital. trans. *Diario*), 630.

22. See *Nomos*. This thesis is further developed by Carl Schmitt at the conceptual level in "Nehmen-Teilen-Weiden," in *Verfassungsrechtliche Aufsätze*.

23. Karl Löwith, "Kierkegaard: 'quel Singolo,'" in *Studi kierkegaardiani*, 199.

24. Carl Schmitt, *Donoso Cortés in gesamteuropäischer Interpretation*. In the fourth and last essay, which gives the title to the short but precious collection, Schmitt develops on historico-legal grounds the typically Löwithian theme of the relation between Kierkegaard, the Left Hegelians, and Nietzsche.

25. On the interpretation of the biblical prophet, see Gerhard von Rad, *Theologie des Alten Testament*, 2 vols.

26. Simone Weil, *La connaissance surnaturelle*.

27. See Weil's interpretation of the Lord's Prayer in *Attente de Dieu*. She shows how (against what many recent theses would like to imply) even the Christian prayer can be pronounced according to necessity (*kata to kreon*).

28. The theme of *attention* refers back with particular intensity to the spirituality of the Orthodox Church, but there is no doubt that some moments of contemporary mysticism are related to it, precisely where the vein of discourse seems to be exhausted, namely, in the last part of Musil's *The Man Without Qualities*. See my article, "L'attenzione profana di Musil."

29. The ideological moment can emerge even within a displaced decisionism with respect to any political vocation (the *Unheimlichkeit* of Heidegger's choice of choice), when it seems to found a *Mitsein* of public character (as if the power of "They"—*Man*—counted for the metropolitan *Gesellschaft* alone). This ideological flexion is clear in Jünger (and it is perhaps the distinctive trait of his entire work), and not even Heidegger is entirely exempt from it. I

have alluded to the Nietzschean origins of this process of unpoliticization, rigorously distinguishable from that of depoliticization in my "L'impolitico nietzschiano," included in the Italian translation of Friedrich Nietzsche, *Il libro del filosofo* [Ed.: "Nietzsche and the Unpolitical," Chapter 2 of this volume].

8. THE GEOPHILOSOPHY OF EUROPE

1. This chapter's historical background is entirely based on the extraordinary study of Santo Mazzarino, especially, *Fra Oriente e Occidente* and his *Il pensiero storico classico*. How many useless studies on the ancient conception of time and space would have been avoided by philosophical research if it had seriously come to terms with the greatest works of historiography!

2. Hecateus seems to use *mythos* to designate its own truthful discourse, and *logos* the deceitful and oblivious discourse of the masses. Here I cannot even get into the problem that this relation raises. I refer to my *Dell'inizio*, Book II, Part I, Section 1.

3. At the eve of the *Achsenzeit*, do not the Greeks conceive the One as the indistinct? In Hesiod's theology, Giorgio Colli reminds us, One is only Chaos, the Open without form. The *logos* requires distinction. To the one empire, and therefore, formless and indistinct, one opposes the productive, revealing *logos*. After the Persian War, the *logos* will have to count also as *logos* of the One. In order to triumph, one has to assimilate it.

4. This is also the case from the point of view of the dramatic representation alone: "As if he were an archaic poet like Homer, Aeschylus, shows here not to know the 'barbarian' of nationalist propaganda, of oratory, of historiography. The fight between the Achaeans and the Trojans, the Hellenes and the Persians (between 'us' and 'others') is played in the epic and in the tragedy in a dimension of relations much more complex and difficult, in which the easy polarization of the figure of the 'enemy' is lacking." See Monica Centanni, introduction to Aeschylus, *I Persiani*, 106. We believe that this dimension can be defined only within the sphere of the philosophical problematic that we are dealing with.

5. Hippocrates, "De aeribus, aquis, locis," in *Testi di medicina greca*, 248–251.

6. The ambiguity belongs constitutively to our own same language. The Latin *libertas*, the Greek *eleutheria* (perhaps belonging to the same root), define the condition of legitimate members of a community, a condition that assigns us to a people, its laws, and its rites. The condition of free makes us social, companions, friends. Even more evident is the link in the Germanic languages, where from the same root derive expressions that designate freedom, friendship, and peace.

7. It is precisely *parresia*, take note, the trait that in the eyes of the Greeks most distinguishes them from barbarians. The exile feels the loss of *parresia* as the loss of the greatest good (Euripides, *The Phoenicians*, 391).

8. Plotinus, in one of his most important and most difficult treatises (*Enneads* VI, 3 [34]), understands perfectly this limitation of Pythagorism by positing the difference between *ousiodes arithmos*, a purely intelligible number, and number as *monadikos*, that is, consisting of unity.

9. That Plato is very much aware of this is proved by the ambiguity in his works on the issue of the soul. In the *Phaedo*, he expressly opposes the Pythagorean idea of harmony as compound, which he then reintroduces in the *Timaeus*.

9. WEBER AND THE POLITICIAN AS TRAGIC HERO

1. The two lectures, *Wissenschaft als Beruf* and *Politik als Beruf*, were given in Munich in November 1917 and January 1919, respectively. They were meant for students of every political persuasion who had requested them in the first place. The reaction these talks created, however, was both upsetting and disappointing. Weber's positions on the German situation and on the limitations of science and politics were irrevocable. The talks contained no concrete indication of a practical "line" or a political "program" to follow. All quotations not indicated in the text are from *Politik als Beruf* [Ed. English translations of both essays in *From Max Weber: Essays in Sociology*].

2. These are the words with which Hegel introduces his philosophical system in *The Difference Between Fichte's and Schelling's System of Philosophy*.

3. This is true both for the supposed dualism between being and duty, between ethics of conviction and ethics of responsibility, as we will see, and, even more, between science and politics. It is not a question of dualism but of polarities! In his moving necrology for Weber, Troeltsch showed that he had understood this aspect of the scholar and the man by concluding with the final words from *Julius Caesar*: "The elements so mixed in him, that Nature might stand up and say to all the world, 'This was a man!' " (Ernst Troeltsch, *Deutscher Geist und Westeuropa*, 264).

4. See Gaetano Calabrò, "Il rifiuto della 'storia universale' e il politeismo dei valori," in Pietro Rossi, ed., *Max Weber e l'analisi del mondo moderno*. But it is fair to state that Weber's extraordinary comparative approach and his search for the connective tissue show that the rejection of metaphysical universal histories results in something other than a collection of specialized inquiries, or a sort of philosophical agnosticism around the overall sense of the materials analyzed. See, for instance, Domenico Conte, *Storicismo e storia universale*, 111.

5. Ernst Troeltsch, *Lo storicismo e i suoi problemi*, 2:336–337.

6. Talcott Parsons's sociology seems to show scientific interest only in the empirical side of Weber's thought. See the heated discussion around his

paper "Value-freedom and Objectivity" at the Heidelberg Conference for the centenary of Weber's birth, now in Otto Stammer, ed. *Max Weber and Sociology Today*.

7. Max Weber, *Economy and Society: An Outline of Interpretive Sociology*, 1:17.

8. Raymond Aron, "Max Weber et Michael Polanyi," 161.

9. Leo Strauss's critique can be found in particular in Chapter 2 of his *Natural Right and History*.

10. See Max Scheler, *Formalism in Ethics and Nonformal Ethics of Values*. On the Weber-Nietzsche relation, I refer the reader to two recent contributions: Wolfgang Schluchter, *Unversöhnte Moderne*, and Giuseppe Antonio Di Marco, *Studi su Max Weber*.

11. Scheler's philosophy can be seen as a confrontation with Weber's science. The place where this hand-to-hand combat takes place with great energy is in an essay of 1922 (in Italian translation, "L'esclusione della filosofia in Max Weber," in Max Scheler, *Lo spirito del capitalismo*). See also Karl Jaspers, *Max Weber. Politiker, Forscher, Philosoph*, published in the *Grenzsituazion* of 1932, at the edge of night; and Karl Löwith, "Max Weber e il disincanto del mondo" (a paper given in Italy for the 1965 "Archivio di Filosofia" Conference, subsequently included in *Dio, uomo e mondo da Cartesio a Nietzsche* and *Gott, Mensch und Welt in der Metaphysik von Descartes bis zu Nietzsche*). See also "Max Webers Stellung zur Wissenschaft" in *Zur Kritik der christichen Überlieferung*.

12. The decision, for Weber, rests exclusively with "the individually *free resolution*, with the *fiat* of the will." Scheler, "L'esclusione," 148. As is well known, the expression "tyranny of values" belongs to Carl Schmitt, "Die Tyrannei der Werte," in *Säkularisation und Utopie*.

13. Scheler, "L'esclusione," 147.

14. This is Troeltsch's criticism of Weber. In Weber, we find the "sharpest" expression of this "forced and arbitrary isolation of judgments of value," that confines them to a "groundless and illogical point of view of an arbitrary choice and reference." *Lo storicismo e i suoi problemi*, 1:130.

15. This, versus Scheler, was also understood, among others, by Herbert Marcuse in his paper, "Industrialization and Capitalism in Weber" to the already mentioned Heidelberg Conference: "Formal theory, with its abstract concepts, attains what a psuedo-empirical sociology, hostile to theory, strives for in vain, i.e. the true definition of reality." See *Max Weber and Sociology Today*, 134.

16. Troeltsch, however, adds that the interpretation of action in Weber is also based on a specific form of psychic *causality*, the "waiting chance" (*Erwartungschance*). Every acting, therefore, is "founded" on *chances* we believe we have in order to achieve our end. Acting is an attentive waiting (*ad-tendere*) that calculates the possibility that our waiting has an end.

17. This is the connection between science's positivist religion, the idea of progress, economic free enterprise and the ultimate consequences of liberal political philosophy characterized by Carl Schmitt in *Der Begriff des Politischen*.

18. See Karl Löwith, "Max Weber e il disincanto del mondo," 173.

19. There is no doubt that Weber would have been at home philosophically in Heidegger's "Age of the World Picture." But, at the same time, he would have scientifically detached himself with respect to anything that in it still appears in the style of a philosophy of history, of a global explanation founded on the idea.

20. This is the fundamental criticism that Schmitt moves to every philosophy of values, drawing to an extreme, but not distorting, to be sure, Weber's position.

21. Raymond Aron has particularly insisted on this distinction, not only in the essay already cited but also in "Introduction á la philosophie de l'histoire," his important preface to Weber's two lectures (in English translation, *Introduction to the Philosophy of History*). However, we should remember that for Weber this distinction does not have at all the meaning of underestimating the having-to-be, but exactly the opposite: "I cannot tolerate that problems of a universal importance and of the greatest universal significance, which are in a certain way supreme problems, capable of moving the human soul, be reduced here to a techno-economic question of 'productivity' and transformed in subjects for discussion within the sphere of a *specialized* discipline such as political economy" (Max Weber, *Gesammelte Aufsätze zur Soziologie und Sozialpolitik*, 419).

22. Raymond Aron, who is also among the few specialists to have understood the tragic tone of Weber's sociology, errs in opposing to the decision that promotes new values the reasonable one, and to the conflict of values the possibility of their comparison, their nonincoherence. These developments are entirely implicit in Weber's conception.

23. Joseph A. Schumpeter, in his "Marx the Prophet" (in *Capitalism, Socialism and Democracy*), has also well understood that Weber's criticism of Marx cannot be leveled to a supposed unambiguous materialistic explanation of social processes on Marx's part. But Weber's relation to Marx is to be interpreted at the level of the epochal philosophical meaning that Marxism has for Giovanni Gentile, first, and for Heidegger after the collapse of nineteenth-century liberalism, a collapse prophesied precisely by Max Weber.

24. On the figure of the entrepreneur, it would be possible to establish a strong connection between Weber and Schumpeter. Years ago, I called attention to this in *Pensiero negativo e razionalizzazione*, but I do not think that my suggestion was picked up by the specialists.

25. Raymond Aron, "Max Weber: Lo studioso ed il politico," 21 [Ed. English trans. in *Introduction to the philosophy of history*].

26. There is no point in reminding the reader how the Machiavelli-Weber analogy is a *topos* of the critical literature on Weber. Beyond the more properly political aspects, it is striking the close sympathy expressed by the Machiavellian idea of *virtus* and the Weberian idea of *responsibility*. In the absence of such ethos any authentic political act that can be directed to the constitution of a *Machtstaat* is impossible for either.

27. I think it is possible, in order to clarify affinities and differences between the politician and the entrepreneur (and the diplomat, the parliamentarian, and the demagogue), to compare Max Weber's voice with that of Max Scheler in *Vorbilder und Führer*.

28. Isaiah Berlin. *The Crooked Timber of Mankind*, 281 (of the Italian translation).

29. Aron, "Max Weber: Lo studioso e il politico," 37.

30. It is a guilt not subjectively ascribable, a guilt without culpability ascribable to this single person and that entirely invests it with a responsibility (according to the dual sense that the expression has in German and in Germanic languages in general). Guilty is the voice that calls the nothingness of *Dasein* to be for its possibility, tearing itself from the inauthenticity of "*Man*" (see Martin Heidegger, *Being and Time*, par. 285).

31. In his ruthless essay on the "tyranny of values," which is essentially a critique of the materialistic values of Max Scheler, Schmitt does not explore (but perhaps because it excludes it a priori) such a possibility, which emerges from Weber's position.

32. I am referring, naturally, to Hermann Hesse's novel *Magister Ludi*, the great allegory of the parting of European humanism from any utopia of pre-established harmony between values and culture, just as from the idea of the past and of the historical tradition as superpersonal power, and yet fully relivable by the subject. In my view, Georg Simmel's conception of historical time is very close to Weber. Like the author of *Probleme der Geschichtsphilosophie*, Weber shares the critique to any claim to grasp the *in-itself* of the historical material through the forms of empathy or *Einfühlung* (however "worked"), as well as he shares the idea of the types as ideal constructs capable of leading, yes, to an experience of the other, but precisely insofar as *other* (*Fremderfahrung*).

33. Juan Donoso Cortés, *Letter to Cardinal Fornari on the Errors of Our Time*.

34. Max Scheler, *Formalism in Ethics and Nonformal Ethics of Values*, 671 (of the Italian translation).

35. Ludwig Wittgenstein, *Tractatus Logico-Philosophicus*, 6.41.

36. Hannah Arendt, *The Origins of Totalitarianism*, 641 (of the Italian translation).

37. In Weber, the characterization of "hero" introduces aspects that recall closely Hegel's and Schelling's remarks on the tragic. See Peter Szondi, *La poetica di Hegel e Schelling* and *An Essay on the Tragic*.

38. Just so, there is no superman in Nietzsche's *Übermensch*. I take the liberty of referring the reader to what I have written on the subject in *L'arcipelago* and in *Della cosa ultima*.

39. Max Weber, "Der Nationalstaat und die Volkswirtschaftspolitik," in *Gesammelte politische Schriften*, 14.

40. Max Weber, "Zwischen zwei Gesetzen," in *Gesammelte politische Schriften*, 139–142.

41. I am not implying that Weber did not realize the greatness of certain expressions of *Kultur* (suffices it to think of his appreciation for Stefan George), but he certainly rejected with the greatest harshness any mingling with the political sphere, just as with any salvific-messianic fancy. A perfect Weberian, in this sense was Robert Musil.

42. [Ed.: Marcion of Sinope (c. 140) was a heretic who made a distinction between the creator God of the Old Testament and the redeemer God of Jesus Christ. Adolf von Harnack (1851–1930), theologian and historian of the church, promoted social gospel and defended Marcion from the accusation of Gnosticism].

43. On the figure of the saint, see Max Scheler, *Formalism in Ethics*, 594, which tops the hierarchy of absolutely legitimate and absolutely unreconcilable types of value.

44. "One day talking to Max Weber about the perspectives for the future a question emerged: when will the witches' dance end that humanity has staged in capitalist countries from the beginning of the nineteenth century? He replied: when the last ton of iron will be fused with the last ton of carbon." Werner Sombart, *Der moderne Kapitalismus*, 853 (of the Italian translation).

45. See Otto Hintze's essays on Weber collected in *The Historical Essays of Otto Hintze*.

46. See Raymond Aron's paper at the Heidelberg conference for Weber's centenary, "Max Weber and Power-Politics," in *Max Weber and Sociology Today*.

47. Karl Löwith, *Mein Leben in Deutschland vor und nach 1933*, 37 (of the Italian translation).

48. Carl Schmitt, *Legalität und Legitimität*. [Ed.: Cacciari refers to the Italian translation "Legalità e legittimità" included in *Le categorie del politico*, 218, but also 284 and 292.]

49. See Anthony Giddens, *The Consequences of Modernity*.

50. I am referring to that extraordinary page from Hegel's *Phenomenology of Mind* that introduces the section on *Natural Religion*. It seems that for many of our contemporaries these are considered the last words of Hegel's philosophy of history, and not, precisely, that origin that matters only insofar as it *passes away*!

Works Cited

Agamben, Giorgio. 2005. *State of Exception*. Trans. Kevin Attell. Chicago: University of Chicago Press.

Alewyn, Richard. 1963. *Über Hugo von Hofmannsthal*. Göttingen: Vandenhoeck und Ruprecht.

Apel, Karl-Otto. 1994. "Analytic Philosophy of Language and the *Geisteswissenschaften*." In *Selected Essays*, vol. 1. Ed. Eduardo Mendieta. Atlantic Highlands, N.J.: Humanities Press.

Arendt, Hannah. 1951. *The Origins of Totalitarianism*. New York: Harcourt, Brace.

Aron, Raymond. 1971. "Max Weber and Power-Politics." In *Max Weber and Sociology Today*. Ed. Otto Stammer. Trans. Kathleen Morris. New York: Harper & Row.

———. 1976a. *Introduction to the Philosophy of History: An Essay on the Limits of Historical Objectivity*. Trans. George J. Irwin. Westport, Conn.: Greenwood Press.

———. 1976b. *L'Europe des crises*. Brussels: Brujlant.

———. 1992. "Max Weber e Michael Polanyi." In *La politica, la guerra, la storia*. Trans. Angelo Panebianco. Bologna: il Mulino.

Asor Rosa, Alberto. 1971. *Thomas Mann o dell'ambiguità borghese*. Bari: De Donato.

Auerbach, Erich. 1963. *Studi su Dante*. Trans. Maria Luisa De Pieri Bonino and Dante Della Terza. Milan: Feltrinelli.

Bahr, Hermann. 1963. "Studien zur Kritik der Moderne." In *Hugo von Hofmannsthal. Der Dichter im Spiegel der Freunde*. Ed. Helmut A. Fiechtner. Bern: Francke.

Barcellona, Pietro. 1984. *I soggetti e le norme*. Milan: Giuffrè.

Bauer, Wolfram. 1968. *Wertrelativismus und Weltbestimmheit im Kampf um die Weimarer Demokratie*. Berlin: Duncker & Humblot.

Benjamin, Walter. 1926. "Hugo von Hofmannsthal, Der Turm." *Die Literarische Welt*, July 9.

———. 1928. "Hugo von Hofmannsthals Der Turm." *Die Literarische Welt*, March 2.

———. 1929. "Bücher, die lebendig geblieben sind." *Die Literarische Welt*, May 17.

———. 1955. *Schriften*. Frankfurt: Suhrkamp.

———. 1966. *Briefe*. 2 vols. Frankfurt: Suhrkamp.

———. 1969. "Theses on the Philosophy of History." In *Illuminations*. Ed. Hannah Arendt, 253–264. New York: Schocken Books.

———. 1972. *Gesammelte Schriften*, vol. 3. Ed. Rolf Tiedemann and Hermann Schweppenhäuser. Frankfurt: Fischer.

———. 1996. *Selected Writings*, vol. 1, *1913–1926*. Ed. Marcus Bullock and Michael W. Jennings. Cambridge, Mass.: Harvard University Press.

———. 1997. *The Origin of German Tragic Drama*. Trans. John Osborne. London: NLB.

Benveniste, Émile. 1969. *Le vocabulaire des institutions indo-européennes*. Paris: Minuit.

Berger, Peter L. 1974. *Pyramids of Sacrifice: Political Ethics and Social Change*. New York: Basic Books.

Berlin, Isaiah. 1991. *The Crooked Timber of Mankind: Chapters in the History of Ideas*. Ed. Henry Hardy. New York: Knopf, 1991.

Bettin, Gianfranco. 1993. *L'erede. Pietro Maso, una storia dal vero*. Milan: Feltrinelli.

———. 1998. *Petrolkimiko. Le voci e le storie di un crimine di pace*. Milan: Baldini & Castoldi.

Biral, Alessandro, et al. 1977. *Per una storia del moderno concetto di politica*. Padua: Cleup.

Bloch, Ernst. 1977. *Zwischenwelten in der Philosophiegeschichte*. Frankfurt: Suhrkamp.

Bodei, Remo, and Franco Cassano. 1977. *Hegel e Weber*. Bari: De Donato.

Boella, Laura. 1977. *Il giovane Lukács*. Bari: De Donato.

Broch, Hermann. 1955. *Erkennen und handeln*. Ed. Hannah Arendt. Zürich: Rhein Verlag.

Brodsky, Joseph. 1991. *Fondamenta degli incurabili*. Trans. Gilberto Forti. Milan: Adelphi.

Bruno, Antonino. 1970. "Politica e valori in Max Weber." In Max Weber, *Scritti politici*. Catania: Giannotta.

Burckhardt, Carl Jacob. 1948. *Erinnerungen an Hofmannsthal und Briefe des Dichters*. Munich: Rinn.

———. 1974. *Zu Hugo von Hofmannsthal*. Frankfurt: Fischer.

Burton, Ian, Robert W. Kates, and Gilbert F. White. 1978. *The Environment as Hazard*. New York: Oxford University Press.

Calabrò, Gaetano. 1981. "Il rifiuto della 'storia universale' e il politeismo dei valori." In *Max Weber e l'analisi del mondo moderno*. Ed. Pietro Rossi. Turin: Einaudi.

Calderón de la Barca, Pedro. 1970. *Life Is a Dream*. Trans. Edwin Honig. New York: Hill & Wang.

Calvino, Italo. 1974. *Invisible Cities*. Trans. William Weaver. New York: Harcourt, Brace, and Jovanovich.

Canetti, Elias. 1962. *Crowds and Power*. Trans. Carol Stewart. New York: Viking Press.

———. 1978. *The Human Province*. Trans. Joachim Neugroschel. New York: Seabury Press.

———. 1979. *The Conscience of Words*. Trans. Joachim Neugroschel. New York: Seabury Press.

Carrera, Alessandro. 1995. *L'esperienza dell'istante. Metafisica, tempo, scrittura*. Milan: Lanfranchi.

Centanni, Monica, ed. 1991. *Eschilo, I Persiani*. Translated and with an introduction. Milan: Feltrinelli.

Cioran, Emile Michel. 1979. *Écartèlement*. Paris: Gallimard.

Conte, Domenico. 2000. *Storicismo e storia universale*. Naples: Liguori.

Curtius, Ernst Robert. 1953. *European Literature and the Latin Middle Ages*. Trans. Willard R. Trask. New York: Pantheon Books.

———. 1973. *Essays on European Literature*. Trans. Michael Kowal. Princeton: Princeton University Press.

Dacy, Douglas C., and Howard Kunreuther. 1969. *The Economics of Natural Disaster: Implications for Federal Policy*. New York: Free Press.

Dal Co, Francesco. 1990. *Figures of Architecture and Thought: German Architecture Culture, 1880–1920*. New York: Rizzoli.

Dal Co, Francesco, and Manfredo Tafuri. 1988. *Architettura contemporanea*. Milan: Electa.

Del Noce, Augusto. 1970. "Simone Weil interprete del mondo di oggi." In *L'epoca della secolarizzazione*. Milan: Giuffrè.

———. 1978. *Il suicidio della rivoluzione*. Milan: Rusconi.

Derrida, Jacques. 1967. *De la Grammatologie*. Paris: Éditions de Minuit.

———. *Positions*. 1972. Paris: Editions de Minuit.

Desideri, Fabrizio. 1980. *Walter Benjamin. Il tempo, le forme*. Rome: Editori Riuniti.

Dilthey, Wilhelm. 1959. "Leibniz und sein Zeitalter." In *Gesammelte Schriften*, vol. 3, *Studien zur Geschichte des deutschen Geistes*. Ed. Karlfried Grunder and Frithjof Rodi. Stuttgart: Teubner.

Di Marco, Giuseppe Antonio. 2003. *Studi su Max Weber*. Naples: Liguori.

Donoso Cortés, Juan. 1964. "Lettera al cardinale Fornari sugli errori del nostro tempo." In *Il potere cristiano*. Ed. Lucrezia Cipriani Panunzio. Brescia: Morcelliana.

———. 2000. *Selected Works of Juan Donoso Cortés*. Ed. Jeffrey P. Johnson. Westport, Conn.: Greenwood Press.

Duso, Giuseppe. 1980. *Weber: razionalità e politica*. Venice: Arsenale.

———. 1981. *La Politica oltre lo Stato: Carl Schmitt*. Venice: Arsenale.

Erasmus, Desiderius. 1917. *The Complaint of Peace: Translated from the "Querela Pacis."* Chicago: Open Court.

Ernst, Paul. 1935. *Ein Credo*. Munich: A. Langen, G. Müller.

———. 1963. "Hugo von Hofmannsthal Leben-Werk." In *Hugo von Hofmannsthal. Der Dichter im Spiegel der Freunde*. Ed. Helmut A. Fiechtner. Bern: Francke.

Escobar, Roberto. 1978. *Nietzsche e la filosofia politica del 19. secolo*. Milan: Il formichiere.

Esposito, Roberto. 1987. *La pluralità irrappresentabile. Il pensiero politico di Hannah Arendt*. Urbino: Quattro Venti.

———. 1988. *Categorie dell'impolitico*. Bologna: il Mulino.

———. 1993. *Nove pensieri sulla politica*. Bologna: il Mulino.

———, ed. 1996. *Oltre la politica. Antologia del pensiero impolitico*. Milan: Bruno Mondadori.

———. 1998. *Communitas. Origine e destino della comunità*. Turin: Einaudi.

Esposito, Roberto, Claudio Galli, and Vincenzo Vitiello, eds. 2000. *Nichilismo e politica*. Rome: Laterza.

———. 2002. *Immunitas. Protezione e negazione della vita.* Turin: Einaudi.

———. 2004. *Bíos. Biopolitica e filosofia*. Turin: Einaudi.

———. 2007. *Terza persona. Politica della vita e filosofia dell'impersonale*. Turin: Einaudi.

Forsthoff, Ernst, et al. 1967. *Säkularisation und Utopie. Ebracher Studien, Ernst Forsthoff zum 65. Geburtstag*. Stuttgart: Kohlhammer.

Fortini, Franco. 1977. *Questioni di frontiera. Scritti di politica e letteratura 1965–1977*. Turin: Einaudi.

Foucault, Michel. 1972. *The Archaeology of Knowledge*. Trans. A. M. Sheridan Smith. New York: Pantheon Books.

Freud, Sigmund. 1968. "Analysis Terminable and Interminable." In *The Standard Edition of the Complete Psychological Works of Sigmund Freud*, vol. 23, *Moses and Monotheism*. Ed. James Strachey et al. London: Hogarth Press, 1968.

———. 1997. *Writings on Art and Literature*. Stanford: Stanford University Press.

Freund, Julien. 1980. "Dalla crisi al conflitto." In *La crisi del concetto di crisi*. Ed. Marco D'Eramo. Rome: Lerici.

Freyer, Hans. 1959. "Die Idee der Freiheit in technischer Zeitalter." In *Festschrift für Carl Schmitt*. Ed. Hans Barion, Ernst Forsthoff, and Werner Weber. Berlin: Duncker & Humblot.

Gargani, Aldo G. 1975. *Il sapere senza fondamenti*. Turin: Einaudi.

———. 1979. *Crisi della ragione*. Turin: Einaudi.

Giddens, Anthony. 1991. *The Consequences of Modernity*. Cambridge, Mass.: Polity Press.

Gilson, Étienne. 1952. *Les métamorphoses de la cité de Dieu*. Paris: Vrin.

Giordano, Aldo, and Francesco Tomatis, eds. 1992. *Cristianesimo ed Europa. La sfida della mondialità*. Rome: Città Nuova.

Girard, René. *Violence and the Sacred*. Trans. Patrick Gregory. Baltimore: Johns Hopkins University Press, 1977.

Goldmann, Lucien. 1964. *The Hidden God: A Study of Tragic Vision in the Pensées of Pascal and the Tragedies of Racine*. Trans. Philip Tody. London: Routledge and Kegan Paul.

———. 1977. *Lukács and Heidegger: Towards a New Philosophy*. New York: Routledge and Kegan Paul.

Goldschmit, Rudolf. 1968. *Hugo von Hofmannsthal*. Hannover: Friedrich.

Griewank, Karl. 1969. *Der neuzeitliche Revolutionsbegriff. Entstehung und Entwicklung*. Frankfurt: Europäische Verlag.

Grillparzer, Franz. 1940. *Family Strife in Habsburg*. Trans. Arthur Burkhard. Yarmouth Port, Mass.: Register Press.

Gross, Raphael. 2007. *Carl Schmitt and the Jews: The "Jewish Question," the Holocaust, and German Legal Theory*. Madison: University of Wisconsin Press.

Guénon, René. 1958. *Le roi du monde*. Paris: Gallimard.

———. 1965. *Symboles fondamentaux de la science sacrée*. Paris: Gallimard.

Hegel, Georg Wilhelm Friedrich. 1977. *The Difference Between Fichte's and Schelling's System of Philosophy*. Trans. H. S. Harris and Walter Cerf. Albany: SUNY Press.

———. 1979. *Phenomenology of Spirit*. Trans. A. V. Miller. New York: Oxford University Press.

———. 1991. *Elements of the Philosophy of Right*. Ed. Allen W. Wood. Cambridge: Cambridge University Press, 1991.

———. 1975. *Aesthetics*. Trans. Thomas M. Knox. Oxford: Clarendon Press.

Heidegger, Martin. 1962. *Being and Time*. Trans. John Macquarrie and Edward Robinson. New York: Harper & Row.

———. 1970. *Phänomenologie und Theologie*. Frankfurt: Klostermann.

———. 1971. "Language in the Poem: A discussion on Georg Trakl's Poetic Work." In *On the Way to Language*. Trans. Peter D. Hertz. New York: Harper & Row.

———. 2002. "Age of the World Picture." In *Off the Beaten Track*. Ed. Julian Young and Kenneth Haynes. Cambridge: Cambridge University Press.

Heine, Heinrich. 1948. "Memoirs of Herr Von Schnabelewopski." In *The Poetry and Prose of Heinrich Heine*. Ed. Frederic Ewen. New York: Citadel Press.

Heller, Hermann. 1921. *Hegel und der nationale Machtstaatsgedanke in Deutschland. Ein Beitrag zur politischen Geistesgeschichte*. Leipzig: Teubner.

Hesse, Hermann. 1949. *Magister Ludi*. Trans. Mervyn Savill. New York: Holt.

———. 1957. *The Journey to the East*. Trans. Hilda Rosner. New York: Noonday.

Hintze, Otto. 1975. *The Historical Essays of Otto Hintze*. Ed. Felix Gilbert and Robert M. Berdahl. New York: Oxford University Press.

———. 1990. *Storia, sociologia, istituzioni*. Ed. Giuseppe di Costanzo. Naples: Morano.

Hofmannsthal, Hugo von. 1922. *Das Buch der Freunde. Tagebuch-Aufzeichnungen*. Leipzig: Insel.

————. 1932. *Andreas oder die Vereigniten. Fragmente eines Romans.* Berlin: Fischer.

————. 1937. *Briefe 1900–1909.* Berlin: S. Fisher.

————. 1947. *Christinas Heimreise.* In *Gesammelte Werke in Einzelausgabe,* vol. 2, *Lustspiele.* Ed. Herbert Steiner. Stockholm: Bermann-Fischer.

————. 1952. "Grillparzers politisches Vermächtnis." In *Gesammelte Werke. Prose,* vol. 3. Ed. Herbert Steiner. Frankfurt: Fischer.

————. 1957. *Dramen,* vol. 3. Ed. Herbert Steiner. Frankfurt: Fischer.

————. 1958. *Viaggi e saggi.* Ed. Leone Traverso. Florence: Vallecchi.

————. 1963a. *Il libro degli amici.* Trans. Gabriella Bemporad. Florence: Vallecchi.

————. 1963b. *The Tower.* In *Selected Plays and Libretti,* vol. 3. Ed. Michael Hamburger. New York: Pantheon Books.

————. 1978. *La Torre.* Trans. Silvia Bortoli Cappelletto. Milan: Adelphi.

————. 1990. *Sämtliche Werke. Kritische Ausgabe,* vol. 16, *Dramen.* Ed. Werner Bellman. Munich: Fischer.

Hofmannsthal, Hugo von, and Martin Buber. 1962. "Briefwechsel." *Neue Rundschau,* 1962.

Hofmannsthal, Hugo von, and Richard Beer Hofmann. 1972. *Briefwechsel.* Frankfurt: Fischer.

Hofmannsthal, Hugo von, and Arthur Schnitzler. 1964. *Briefwechsel.* Frankfurt: Fischer.

Jaspers, Karl. 1948. *Max Weber. Politiker, Forscher, Philosoph.* Bremen: Storm.

Jünger, Ernst. 1959. *An der Zeitmauer.* Stuttgart: Klett-Cotta.

————. 1980. *Sämtliche Werke,* vol. 7, *Essays 1: Betrachtungen zur Zeit.* Stuttgart: Klett-Cotta.

Kahn, Herman. 1965. *On Escalation: Metaphors and Scenarios.* New York: Praeger.

Kahn, Herman, and Norbert Wiener. 1962. *Crisis and Arms Control.* Croton-on-Hudson, N.Y.: Hudson Institute.

Kant, Immanuel. 1997. *Critique of Practical Reason.* Ed. Mary J. Gregor. Cambridge: Cambridge University Press.

————. 2000. *Critique of the Power of Judgment.* Ed. Paul Guyer. Cambridge: Cambridge University Press.

Kantorowicz, Ernst H. 1957. *The King's Two Bodies: A Study in Medieval Political Theology.* Princeton: Princeton University Press.

Kelsen, Hans. 1929. "Der Begriff des Staates und die Sozialpsychologie." In *Vom Wesen und Wert der Demokratie.* Tübingen: Mohr.

———. 1975. *Sozialismus und Staat. Eine Untersuchung der politischen Theorie des Marxismus.* Mesenheim am Glam: Hain.

———. *Socialismo e stato. Una ricerca sulla teoria politica del marxismo.* Ed. Roberto Racinaro. Bari: De Donato.

Kessler, Harry. 1961. *Tagebücher 1918–1937.* Frankfurt: Insel.

———. 1963. "Tagebücher." In *Hugo von Hofmannsthal. Der Dichter im Spiegel der Freunde.* Ed. Helmut A. Fiechtner. Bern: Francke.

Kierkegaard, Søren. 1941. *Repetition: An Essay in Experimental Psychology.* Trans. Walter Lowrie. Princeton: Princeton University Press.

———. 1959. *Either/Or*, vol. 1. Princeton: Princeton University Press.

Klein, Robert. 1970. *La forme et l'intelligible.* Paris: Gallimard.

Koktanek, Anton M. 1968. *Oswald Spengler in seiner Zeit.* Munich: Beck.

Krause, Werner. 1962. *Werner Sombarts Weg vom Kathedersozialismus zum Faschismus.* Berlin: Rutten und Leoning.

Krockow, Christian von. 1958. *Die Entscheidung. Eine Untersuchung über Ernst Jünger, Carl Schmitt, Martin Heidegger.* Stuttgart: Enke.

Lami, Alessandro, ed. 1983. *Testi di medicina greca.* Milan: Rizzoli.

Lapouge, Gilles. 1978. *Utopie et civilisation.* Paris: Flammarion.

Lebovics, Herman. 1969. *Social Conservatism and the Middle Classes in Germany, 1914–1933.* Princeton: Princeton University Press.

Leontief, Wassily. 1977. *The Future of the World Economy: A United Nations Study.* New York: Oxford University Press.

Leopardi, Giacomo. 1991. *Zibaldone di pensieri.* 3 vols. Ed. Giuseppe Pacella. Milan: Garzanti.

Lilla, Mark. 1997. "The Enemy of Liberalism." *New York Review of Books*, May 15.

———. 2001. "The Lure of Syracuse." *New York Review of Books*, September 20.

———. 2007. "The Politics of God." *New York Times Review of Books*, August 19.

Loos, Adolf. 1981. *Das Andere. Festschrift per i sessant'anni di Adolf Loos.* Milan: Electa, 1981.

Löwenstein, Karl. 1965. *Max Weber staatspolitische Auffassungen in der Sicht unserer Zeit.* Frankfurt: Athenäum Verlag.

Löwith, Karl. 1957. "Kierkegaard: 'quel Singolo.'" In *Studi kierkegaardiani. Con un inedito di Soren Kierkegaard.* Ed. Cornelio Fabro. Brescia: Morcelliana.

———. 1964. *From Hegel to Nietzsche: The Revolution in Nineteenth-century Thought.* Trans. David A. Green. New York: Anchor Books.

———. 1966a. "Max Webers Stellung zur Wissenschaft." In *Zur Kritik der christlichen Überlieferung*. Stuttgart: Kohlhammer.

———. 1966b. "Max Weber e il disincanto del mondo." In *Dio, uomo e mondo da Cartesio a Nietzsche*. Trans. A. L. Kunkler Giavotto. Naples: Morano.

———. 1986. *Mein Leben in Deutschland vor und nach 1933*. Stuttgart: Metzler.

Lubac, Henri de. 1950. *Histoire et Esprit. L'intelligence de l'Écriture d'après Origène*. Paris: Aubier.

———. 1959–1964. *Exégèse Medièvale*. 4 vols. Paris: Aubier.

Lukács, György. 1978. *A modern dráma fejlodésének története*. Budapest: Magveto.

———. 1971. *History and Class Consciousness: Studies in Marxist Dialectics*. Trans. Rodney Livingstone. London: Merlin Press.

———. 1974. *Soul and Form*. Trans. Anna Bostok. London: Merlin Press.

———. 1983. *Diario (1910–1911)*. Ed. Gabriella Caramore. Milan: Adelphi.

Lumley, Robert. 1990. *States of Emergency: Cultures of Revolt in Italy from 1968 to 1978*. New York: Verso.

Lyotard, Jean-François. 1984. *Postmodern Condition: A Report on Knowledge*. Trans. Geoff Bennington and Brian Massumi. Minneapolis: University of Minnesota Press.

Macpherson, Crawford B. 1973. *Democratic Theory: Essays in Retrieval*. Oxford: Clarendon Press.

Macrobius, Ambrosius Aurelius Theodosius. 1969. *The Saturnalia*. Trans. Percival Vaughan Davies. New York: Columbia University Press.

Maier, Hans. 1966. "Max Weber und die deutsche politische Wissenschaft." In *Max Weber. Gedächtnisschrift der Ludwig-Maximilians-Universität, München, zur 100. Wiederkehr seines Geburtstages 1964*. Ed. Karl Engisch, Bernhard Pfister, and Johannes Winckelmann. 1966. Berlin: Duncker & Humblot.

Mann, Thomas. 1929. "In memoriam." *Neue Freie Presse*, July 21, 1929.

———. 1983. *Reflections of a Nonpolitical Man*. Trans. Walter D. Morris. New York: Ungar, 1983.

Manning, Diana H. 1976. *Disaster Technology: An Annotated Bibliography*. Oxford: Pergamon.

Marcuse, Herbert. 1971. "Industrialization and Capitalism in Weber." In *Max Weber and Sociology Today*. Ed. Otto Stammer. Trans. Kathleen Morris. New York: Harper & Row.

Marramao, Giacomo. 1981. "Niklas Luhmann." *Il Centauro* 1, no. 1.

Mauthner, Fritz. 1980. *Wörterbuch der Philosophie 1910–1911*. Zürich: Diogenes.

Mayer, Jacob P. 1940. *Max Weber and German Politics: A Study in Political Sociology*. London: Faber & Faber.

Mazzarino, Santo. 1947. *Fra Oriente e Occidente*. Florence: La Nuova Italia.

———. 1965–1966. *Il pensiero storico classico*. 3 vols. Bari: Laterza.

Meinecke, Friedrich. 1941. *Erlebtes 1862–1901*. Leipzig: Koehler und Amerlang.

Meyer, Alfred Gotthold. 1907. *Eisenbauten, ihre Geschichte und Ästhetik*. Esslingen: Neff.

Miglio, Gianfranco. "Guerra, pace, diritto." In *Della Guerra*. Ed. Umberto Curi. Venice: Arsenale.

Mittner, Ladislao. 1977. *Storia della letteratura tedesca. Dai primordi pagani all'età barocca*. Turin: Einaudi.

Mommsen, Wolfgang J. 1959. *Max Weber und die deutsche Politik*. Tübingen: Mohr.

Moretti, Franco, ed. 2003. *Il romanzo*, vol. 5, *Lezioni*. Turin: Einaudi.

Mouffe, Chantal, ed. 1999. *The Challenge of Carl Schmitt*. New York: Verso.

Musil, Robert. 1996. *The Man Without Qualities*. 2 vols. Trans. Sophie Wilkins. New York: Vintage.

Nancy, Jean-Luc. 1991. *The Inoperative Community*. Ed. Peter Connor. Minneapolis: University of Minnesota Press.

Natoli, Salvatore. 1979. *Soggetto e fondamento. Studi su Aristotele e Cartesio*. Padua: Antenore.

Naumann, Friedrich. 1964. *Das Schiksal des Marxismus*. In *Werke*, vol. 4. Cologne: Westdeutschen Verlag.

Negri, Antonio. 1970. *Descartes politico, o della ragionevole ideologia*. Milan: Feltrinelli.

———. 1972. *Zyklus und Krise bei Marx*. Berlin: Merve.

———. 1975. *Crisi dello Stato-piano. Comunismo e organizzazione rivoluzionaria*. Milan: Feltrinelli.

———. 1976a. *Proletari e stato. Per una discussione su autonomia operaia e compromesso storico*. Milan: Feltrinelli.

———. 1976b. "Simplex sigillum veri. Per la discussione di *Krisis* e di *Bisogni e teoria marxista*." *aut aut* 158:180–195.

———. 1977. *La forma stato. Per la critica dell'economia politica della Costituzione*. Milan: Feltrinelli.

———. 1979a. *Il dominio e il sabotaggio. Sul metodo marxista della trasformazione sociale*. Milan: Feltrinelli.

————. 1979b. *Marx oltre Marx. Quaderno di lavoro sui Grundrisse*. Milan: Feltrinelli.

————. 1979c. *Dall'operaio massa all'operaio sociale. Intervista sull'operaismo*. Ed. Paolo Pozzi and Roberta Tomassini. Milan: Multiphla.

————. 1980. *Il comunismo e la guerra*. Milan: Feltrinelli.

————. 1981. *L'anomalia selvaggia. Saggio su potere e potenza in Baruch Spinoza*. Milan: Feltrinelli.

Negri, Antonio, and Michael Hardt. 2001. *Empire*. Cambridge, Mass: Harvard University Press.

————. 2004. *Multitude: War and Democracy in the Age of Empire*. New York: Penguin.

Nietzsche, Friedrich. 1974. *Frammenti Postumi 1888–1889*. In *Opere*, vol. 3. Ed. Giorgio Colli and Mazzino Montinari. Milan: Adelphi.

————. 1977a. *Genealogia della morale*. Ed. Ferruccio Masini. Rome: Newton Compton.

————. 1977b. *Twilight of the Idols*. Trans. Reginald John Hollingdale. Harmondsworth: Penguin.

————. 1978. *Il libro del filosofo*. Ed. Marina Beer and Maurizio Ciampa. Rome: Savelli.

————. 1996. *Human, All Too Human*. 2 vols. Trans. Reginald John Hollingdale. Cambridge: Cambridge University Press.

————. 1997. *Daybreak*. Trans. Reginald John Hollingdale. Cambridge: Cambridge University Press.

Nono, Luigi. 1975. *Texte. Studien zu seiner Musik*. Ed. Jürg Stenzl. Zürich: Atlantis.

————. 1993. *Écrits*. Ed. Laurent Feneyrou. Paris: C. Bourgois.

————. 2001. *Scritti e colloqui*. Ed. Angela Ida De Benedictis and Veniero Rizzardi. Milan: Ricordi.

Pacchiani, Claudio. 1977. "Spinoza e l'assolutismo politico." In *Per una storia del moderno concetto di politica*. Ed. Alessandro Biral et al. Padua: Cleup.

————, ed. 1980. *Filosofia pratica e scienza politica*. Abano: Francisci.

Pagnin, Adriano. 1977. "*Das Unheimliche*, la ripetizione, la morte." In *La critica freudiana*. Ed. Franco Rella. Milan: Feltrinelli.

Panzieri, Raniero. 1972. *La ripresa del marxismo-leninismo in Italia*. Milan: Sapere.

————. 1973. *Scritti 1956–1960*. Milan: Lampugnani Nigri.

————. 1976. *Lotte operaie nello sviluppo capitalistico*. Turin: Einaudi.

————. 1982. *L'alternativa socialista. Scritti scelti (1944–1956)* Turin: Einaudi.

Papi, Fulvio. 1981. "Crisi della politica e critica dell'intelletto distruttivo." *Materiali filosofici* 6.

Parsons, Talcott. 1971. "Value-freedom and Objectivity." In *Max Weber and Sociology Today*. Ed. Otto Stammer. Trans. Kathleen Morris. New York: Harper & Row.

Pascal, Roy. 1973. *From Naturalism to Expressionism: German Literature and Society 1880–1918*. London: Weidenfeld and Nicolson.

Pasqualotto, Giangiorgio. 1975–1976. "Nietzsche: considerazioni attuali." *Nuova corrente* 68–69.

Pasquino, Gianfranco. 1981. "Teoria della giustizia e della dottrina in Hobbes." *Materiali filosofici* 6.

Pavan, Antonio. 1979. *All'origine del progetto borghese. Il giovane Descartes*. Brescia: Morcelliana.

Penzo, Giorgio. 1970. *Pensare heideggeriano e problematica teologica*. Brescia: Queriniana.

———, ed. 1985. *Il Potere. Saggi di filosofia sociale e politica*. Rome: Città Nuova Editrice.

Petillon, Pierre Yves. 1975. "Hofmannsthal: le règne du silence." *Critique* 339–340.

Pickerodt, Gerhart. 1968. *Hofmannsthals Dramen*. Stuttgart: Metzler.

Pollack, Walther. 1967. "Werner Sombart und der Sozialismus." In *Humanitas ethnica. Menschenwürde, Recht und Gemeinschaft. Festschrift für Theodor Veiter*. Ed. Franz Hyeronimus Riedl. Vienna: Braumüller.

Rad, Gerhard von. 1962–1965. *Theologie des Alten Testament*. 2 vols. Munich: Kaiser.

Restagno, Enzo, ed. 1987. *Nono*. Turin: EDT.

Rey, William Henry. 1968. "Tragik und Verklärung in *Turm*." In *Hugo von Hofmannsthal*. Ed. Sybille Bauer. Darmstadt: Wissenschaftliche Buchgesellschaft.

Robinson, John A. 1962. "The Concept of Crisis in Decision-Making." National Institute of Social & Behavioral Sciences Symposium 11.

Rösch, Erich. 1963. *Komödien Hofmannsthals*. Marburg: Elwert.

Rosenstock, Eugen. 1931. *Die europäischen Revolutionen*. Jena: Diederichs Verlag.

Rosenzweig, Franz. 1921, 1930. *Der Stern der Erlösung*. Frankfurt: Kaufmann.

Rossi, Paolo, ed. 1995. *La filosofia*, vol. 2. Turin: Utet.

Roth, Joseph. 1965. *Das falsche Gewicht*. Frankfurt: Suhrkamp.

Rovatti, Pier Aldo, Roberta Tomassini, and Amedeo Vigorelli. 1976. *Bisogni e teoria marxista*. Milan: Mazzotta.

Salomon, Albert. 1955. *The Tyranny of Progress: Reflections on the Origin of Sociology*. New York: Noonday Press.

Sartori, Giovanni. 1979. *La politica*. Milan: Sugar.

Satta Boschian, Laura. 1981. *Tempo d'avvento. Alle origini culturali, religiose e sociali della prima rivoluzione russa*. Naples: ESI.

Schäder, Grete. 1949. "Hofmannsthals Weg zur Tragödie." *Deutsche Vierteljahrsschrift* 23, nos. 2–3.

Scheler, Max. 1957. *Vorbilder und Führer. Schriften aud dem Nachlass*. Bern: Francke.

———. 1973. *Formalism in Ethics and Non-formal Ethics of Values: A New Attempt Toward the Foundation of an Ethical Personalism*. Trans. Manfred S. Frings and Roger L. Funk. Evanston, Ill.: Northwestern University Press.

———. 1988. "L'esclusione della filosofia in Max Weber." In *Lo spirito del capitalismo e altri saggi*. Ed. Roberto Racinaro. Naples: Guida.

———. 1997. *Gesammelte Werke in 16 Bänden*. Ed. Manfred S. Frings. Bonn: Bouvier.

Schiavoni, Giulio. 1980. *Walter Benjamin. Sopravvivere alla cultura*. Palermo: Sellerio.

Schiera, Pierangelo, et al. 1979. *Il concetto di rivoluzione nel pensiero politico moderno. Dalla sovranità del monarca allo stato sovrano*. Bari: De Donato.

Schluchter, Wolfgang. 1968. *Entscheidung für den sozialen Rechstaat. Hermann Heller und die staatstheoretische Diskussion in der Weimarer Republik*. Cologne: Kiepenheuer & Witsch.

———. 1996. *Unversöhnte Moderne*. Frankfurt: Suhrkamp.

Schmitt, Carl 1921. *Die Diktatur. Von den Anfängen des modernen Souveränitätsgedanken bis zum proletarischen Klassenkampf*. Munich: Duncker & Humblot.

———. 1928. *Verfassungslehre*. Munich: Duncker & Humblot.

———. 1940. "Die Politische Theorie des Mythus." In *Positionen und Begriffen in Kampf mit Weimar Genf-Versailles*. Hamburg: Hanseatische Verlagsanstalt.

———. 1950. *Donoso Cortés in gesamteuropäischer Interpretation*. Cologne: Greven.

———. 1956. *Hamlet oder Hekuba. Der Einbruch der Zeit in das Spiel*. Düsseldorf: Diederichs.

———. 1958. *Verfassungsrechtliche Aufsätze aus den Jahren 1924–1954. Materialen zu einer Verfassungslehre*. Munich: Duncker & Humblot.

———. 1968. *Politische Romantik*. Munich: Duncker & Humblot.

————. 1972. *Le categorie del "politico." Saggi di teoria politica*. Ed. Gianfranco Miglio and Pierangelo Schiera. Bologna: il Mulino.

————. 1976. *The Concept of the Political*. Trans. George Schwab. New Brunswick, N.J.: Rutgers University Press.

————. 1985. *Political Theology: Four Chapters on the Concept of Sovereignty*. Trans. George Schwab. Cambridge, Mass.: MIT Press.

————. 1996a. *Roman Catholicism and Political Form*. Trans. G. L. Ulmen. Westport, Conn.: Greenwood Press.

————. 1996b. *The Tyranny of Values*. Trans. Simona Draghici. Washington, D.C.: Plutarch Press.

————. 1997. *Land and Sea*. Trans. Simona Draghici. Washington, D.C.: Plutarch Press.

————. 2003. *The Nomos of the Earth in the International Law of the Jus Publicum Europaeum*. Trans. G. L. Ulmen. New York: Telos Press.

————. 2004. *Legality and Legitimacy*. Trans. Jeffrey Seitzer. Durham, N.C.: Duke University Press.

————. 2007. *Theory of the Partisan: Intermediate Commentary on the Concept of the Political*. Trans. G. L. Ulmen. New York: Telos Press.

Schnitzler, Arthur. 1918. *Casanovas Heimfahrt*. Berlin: Fischer.

Schnitzler, Olga. "Hofmannsthal und Schnitzler." In *Hugo von Hofmannsthal. Der Dichter im Spiegel der Freunde*. Ed. Helmut A. Fiechtner. Bern: Francke.

Scholem, Gershom. 1977. "Zum Verständnis des messianischen Idee im Judentum." In *Judaica*, 3 vols. Frankfurt: Suhrkamp.

Schumpeter, Joseph A. 1952. *Aufsätze zur ökonomischen Theorie*. Tübingen: Mohr.

————. 1953. *Aufsätze zur Soziologie*. Tübingen: Mohr.

————. 1954. *Dogmengeschichte und biographische Aufsätze*. Tübingen: Mohr.

————. 1976. *Capitalism, Socialism, and Democracy*. London: Allen & Unwin.

Schwarz, Egon. 1962. *Hofmannsthal und Calderón*. The Hague: Mouton.

Schweppe, Walter, ed. 1979. *Great Poems from Goethe to Brecht*. Calcutta: Writers Workshop.

Servier, Jean. 1967. *Histoire de l'utopie*. Paris: Gallimard.

Severino, Emanuele. 1979. *Legge e caso*. Milan: Adelphi.

————. 1980. *Destino della necessità*. Milan: Adelphi.

Seyfarth, Constans, and Walter M. Sprondel, eds. 1973. *Seminar: Religion und gesellschaftliche Entwicklung. Studien zur Protestantismus-Kapitalismus-These Max Webers*. Frankfurt: Suhrkamp.

Simmel, Georg. 1907. *Die Probleme der Geschichtsphilosophie. Eine erkenntin-stheorische Studie.* Leipzig: Duncker & Humblot, 1907.

———. 1968. *The Conflict in Modern Culture and Other Essays.* Trans. K. Peter Etzkorn. New York: Teachers College Press.

Sombart, Werner. 1901. *Sozialismus und soziale Bewegung im 19. Jahrhund-ert.* Jena: G. Fischer.

———. 1902. *Der moderne Kapitalismus.* Leipzig: Duncker & Humblot.

———. 1920. *Sozialismus und soziale Bewegung.* Jena: G. Fischer.

———. 1935. *Der proletarische Sozialismus.* Berlin-Charlottenburg: Buch-holz & Weisswange.

———. 1976. *Why Is There No Socialism in the United States?* Ed. C. T. Husbands. London: Macmillan, 1976.

Spitzer, Leo. 1963. *Classical and Christian Ideas of World Harmony: Prole-gomena to an Interpretation of the Word "Stimmung."* Baltimore: Johns Hopkins University Press.

Strauss, Leo. 1953. *Natural Right and History.* Chicago: University of Chi-cago Press.

———. 1965. *Hobbes politische Wissenschaft.* Neuwied-Berlin: Luchterhand.

Sturmthal, Adolf. 1974. "Werner Sombart und der Amerikanische Sozia-lismus." In *Geschichte und Gesellschaft. Festschrift für Karl. R. Stadler.* Vi-enna: Europa Verlag.

Szondi, Peter. 1975. *Das lyrische Drama des Fin de siècle.* Ed. Henriette Beese. Frankfurt: Suhrkamp.

———. 1974a. "Hegels Lehre von Dichtung." In *Geschichtsphilosophie I.* Frankfurt: Suhrkamp.

———. 1974b. "Schelling Gattungspoetik." In *Geschichtsphilosophie II.* Frankfurt: Suhrkamp.

———. 2002. *An Essay on the Tragic.* Trans. Paul Fleming. Stanford: Stan-ford University Press.

Tafuri, Manfredo. 1968. *Teoria e storia dell'architettura.* Bari: Laterza.

———. 1976. *Architecture and Utopia: Design and Capitalist Development.* Cambridge, Mass.: MIT Press.

———. 1980. *La sfera e il labirinto. Avanguardie e architettura da Piranesi agli anni '70.* Turin: Einaudi.

Taubes, Jacob. 1996. *In divergente accordo. Scritti su Carl Schmitt.* Ed. Elet-tra Stimilli. Macerata: Quodlibet.

Thiel, Rainer. 1932. *Die Generation ohne Männer.* Berlin: Neff.

Thom, René. 1980. *Parabole e catastrofi. Intervista a cura di Giulio Giorello e Simona Morini.* Milan: Il Saggiatore.

———. 1980. "Crisi e catastrofe." In *La crisi del concetto di crisi*. Ed. Marco D'Eramo. Rome: Lerici.

Troeltsch, Ernst. 1925. *Deutscher Geist und Westeuropa*. Tübingen: Mohr.

———. 1972. *The Absoluteness of Christianity and the History of Religions*. Trans. David Reid. London: SCM Press.

———. 1985–1989. *Lo storicismo e i suoi problemi*. 3 vols. Ed. Giuseppe Cantillo and Fulvio Tessitore. Naples: Guida.

Tronti, Mario. 1966. *Operai e capitale*. Turin: Einaudi.

———. 1975. *Hegel politico*. Rome: Istituto della Enciclopedia Italiana.

———. 1977a. *Sull'autonomia del politico*. Milan: Feltrinelli.

———. 1977b. "Hobbes e Cromwell." In *Stato e rivoluzione in Inghilterra*. Ed. Alessandro Piazzi, Mario Segatori, and Mario Tronti. 1977. Milan: il Saggiatore.

———. 1979. *Il politico*. Milan: Feltrinelli.

———. 1980. *Soggetti, crisi, potere*. Ed. Antonio De Martinis and Alessandro Piazzi. Bologna: Cappelli.

———. 1998. *La politica al tramonto*. Turin: Einaudi.

Veca, Salvatore. 1977a. *Saggio sul programma scientifico di Marx*. Milan: il Saggiatore.

———. 1977b. "Rivoluzione." In *Enciclopedia Einaudi*, vol. 12. Turin: Einaudi.

Veneziani, Marcello. 2001. "Cacciari, aristocratico conservatore." *Il Giornale*, April 24.

Vichard de Saint-Réal, César. 1999. *Conjuration des espagnols contre la république de Venise en 1618*. Toulouse: Ombres.

Weber, Max. 1920. *Gesammelte Aufsätze zur Religionssoziologie*, vol. 2, *Induismus und Buddhismus*. Tübingen: Mohr.

———. 1921. *Gesammelte politische Schriften*. München: Drei Masken.

———. 1922. *Gesammelte Aufsätze zur Wissenschaftslehre*. Tübingen: Mohr.

———. 1923. "Die Entstehung des jüdischer Pariavolkes." In *Gesammelte Aufsätze zur Religionssoziologie*, vol. 3, *Das Antike Judentum*. Tübingen: Mohr.

———. 1924. *Gesammelte Aufsätze zur Soziologie und Sozialpolitik*. Ed. Marianne Weber. Tübingen: Mohr.

———. 1930. *The Protestant Ethic and the Spirit of Capitalism*. Trans. Talcott Parsons. New York: Scribner.

———. *From Max Weber: Essays in Sociology*. Ed. H. H. Gerth and C. Wright Mills. New York: Oxford University Press.

———. 1947. *The Theory of Social and Economic Organization*. Trans. A. M. Henderson and Talcott Parsons. New York: Oxford University Press.

————. 1958. *Gesammelte politische Schriften*. Ed. Johannes Winckelmann. Tübingen: Mohr.

————. 1959. *Le savant et le politique*. Trans. Julien Freund. Paris: Plon.

————. 1968. *Economy and Society: An Outline of Interpretive Sociology*. 3 vols. Ed. Günther Roth and Claus Wittich. New York: Bedminster Press.

————. 1970. *Scritti politici*. Trans. Paolo Manganaro. Catania: Giannotta.

————. 1978. "Sulla teoria dell'utilità marginale e la legge fondamentale della psicofisica." Trans. Antonio Roversi. *Rivista internazionale di scienze economiche e commerciali* 5.

————. 1979. *Sul socialismo reale*. Rome: Savelli.

————. 1992. *Max Weber-Gesamtausgabe*, vol. 17, *Schriften und Reden*. Ed. Wolfgang J. Mommsen and Wolfgang Schluchter. Tübingen: Mohr.

Weil, Simone. 1950a. *Attente de Dieu*. Paris: Éditions du Vieux Colombier.

————. 1950b. *La connaissance surnaturelle*. Paris: Gallimard.

————. 1952. *The Need for Roots: Prelude to a Declaration of Duties Towards Mankind*. Trans. Arthur Wills. London: Routledge & Kegan Paul.

————. 1955. *Venise sauvée*. Paris: Gallimard.

Wilamowitz-Möllendorf, Ulrich von. 1977. "Gli intellettuali tedeschi e il loro presunto magistero di violenza." In *Cultura classica e crisi tedesca. Gli scritti politici di Wilamowitz 1914–1931*. Ed. Luciano Canfora. Bari: De Donato, 1977.

Winch, Peter. 1958. *The Idea of a Social Science and Its Relation to Philosophy*. New York: Humanities Press.

Windfuhr, Manfred. 1966. *Die Barocke Bildlichkeit und ihre Kritiker. Stilhalungen in der deutschen Literatur des 17. und 18. Jahrhunderts*. Stuttgart: Metzler.

Wittgenstein, Ludwig. 1961. *Tractatus logico-philosophicus*. Trans. D. F. Pears and B. F. McGuinness. London: Routledge and Kegan Paul.

————. 1968. *Philosophical Investigations*. Trans. G. E. M. Anscombe. Oxford: Blackwell.

————. 1998. *Culture and Value: A Selection from the Posthumous Remains*. Ed. Georg H. von Wright and Heikki Nyman. Chicago: University of Chicago Press, 1980.

Wittmann, Lothar. 1966. *Sprachthematik und dramatische Form im Werke Hofmannsthals*. Stuttgart: Kohlhammer.

Yates, Frances. 1969. *The Theatre of the World*. London: Routledge and Kegan Paul.

————. 1972. *The Rosicrucian Enlightenment*. London: Routledge and Kegan Paul.

Žižek, Slavoj. 1989. *The Sublime Object of Ideology*. London: Verso.

Selected Works of Massimo Cacciari

BOOKS

1969a. Ed. *Ciclo capitalistico e lotte operaie. Montedison, Pirelli, Fiat, 1968.* Padua: Marsilio.

1969b. Ed. *Che fare. Il '69–'70. Classe operaia e capitale di fronte ai contratti.* Padua: Marsilio.

1969c. Ed. Nicolai Hartmann, *L'estetica. Pagine scelte.* Padua: Liviana.

1970. Ed. Georg Simmel, *Saggi di estetica.* Padua: Liviana.

1972a. With Manfredo Tafuri and Francesco Dal Co. *De la vanguardia a la metrópoli. Critica radical a la arquitectura.* Barcelona: Gustavo Gili.

1972b. Ed. Eugen Fink, *La filosofia di Nietzsche.* Padua: Liviana.

1972c. Ed. György Lukács, *Kommunismus, 1920–1921.* Padua: Liviana.

1973a. *Dopo l'autunno caldo. Ristrutturazione e analisi di classe.* Padua: Marsilio.

1973b. *Metropolis. Saggio sulla grande città di Sombart, Endell, Scheffler e Simmel.* Rome: Officina Edizioni.

1973c. *Qualifikation und Klassenbewusstsein.* Frankfurt: Verlag Neue Kritik.

1973d. With Sergio Bologna. *Zusammensetzung der Arbeiterklasse und Organisationsfrage.* Trans. Volker Hunecke. Berlin: Merve.

1975a. With Franco Amendolagine. *Oikos. Da Loos a Wittgenstein.* Rome: Officina Edizioni.

1975b. With Paolo Perulli. *Piano economico e composizione di classe. Il dibattito sull'industrializzazione e lo scontro politico durante la NEP.* Milan: Feltrinelli.

1976. *Krisis. Saggio sulla crisi del pensiero negativo da Nietzsche a Wittgenstein.* Milan: Feltrinelli.

1977. *Pensiero negativo e razionalizzazione.* Padua: Marsilio.

1978a. With Giancarlo Buonfino and Francesco Dal Co. *Avanguardia, dada, Weimar.* Venice: Arsenale.

1978b. *Dialettica e critica del Politico. Saggio su Hegel.* Milan: Feltrinelli.

1979. *Walther Rathenau e il suo ambiente. Con un'antologia di scritti e discorsi politici 1919–1921.* Bari: De Donato.

1980a. Ed. *Crucialità del tempo. Saggi sulla concezione nietzschiana del tempo.* Naples: Liguori.

1980b. *Dallo Steinhof. Prospettive viennesi del primo Novecento.* Milan: Adelphi.

1982a. *Krisis. Ensayo sobre la crisis del pensamiento negativo de Nietzsche a Wittgenstein.* Trans. Romeo Medina. Mexico City: Siglo XXI.

1982b. Ed. *Il concetto di sinistra*. Milan: Bompiani.

1984. Ed. Luigi Nono, *Verso Prometeo*. Milan: Ricordi.

1985. *Icone della Legge*. Milan: Adelphi.

1986a. *L'Angelo necessario*. Milan: Adelphi.

1986b. *Zeit ohne Kronos*. Ed. and trans. Reinhard Kacianka. Klagenfurt: Ritter.

1987a. Ed. *Le forme del fare*. Naples: Liguori.

1989a. *Drama y Duelo*. Ed. and trans. Francisco Jarauta. Madrid: Tecnos.

1989b. *Hombres póstumos. La cultura vienesa del primer novecientos*. Trans. Francisco Jarauta. Barcelona: Peninsula.

1990a. *Dell'Inizio*. Milan: Adelphi.

1990b. *Icônes de la loi*. Trans. Marilène Raiola. Paris: Bourgois.

1992a. *L'Angelo necessario*. 3rd ed., with *"Paralipomeni."* Milan: Adelphi.

1992b. *Drân. Méridiens de la décision dans la pensée contemporaine*. Trans. Michel Valensi. Paris: Éditions de l'Éclat.

1993. *Architecture and Nichilism: On the Philosophy of Modern Achitecture*. Trans. Stephen Sartarelli. New Haven: Yale University Press.

1994a. *Desde Nietzsche. Tiempo, arte, política*. Trans. Monica B. Cragnolini and Ana Paternostro. Buenos Aires: Biblos.

1994b. *Geo-filosofia dell'Europa*. Milan: Adelphi.

1994c. *The Necessary Angel*. Trans. Miguel E. Vatter. Albany: SUNY Press.

1995a. *Adolf Loos e il suo angelo. Das Andere e altri scritti*. Milan: Electa.

1995b. With Carlo Maria Martini. *Dialogo sulla solidarietà*. Rome: Edizioni Lavoro.

1995c. *Grossstadt. Baukunst. Nihilismus*. Trans. Reinhard Kacianka. Klagenfurt: Ritter.

1995d. With Edmond Jabès and Luigi Nono. *Migranten*. Ed. and trans. Nils Röller. Berlin: Merve.

1996a. *Déclinaisons de l'Europe*. French translation by Michel Valensi. Combas: Éditions de l'Éclat.

1996b. *Posthumous People: Vienna at the Turning Point*. Trans. Rodger Friedman. Stanford: Stanford University Press.

1997a. *Arcipelago*. Milan: Adelphi.

1997b. With Carlo Maria Martini. *Diálogo sobre la solidaridad*. Trans. Sabina Morello. Barcelona: Herder.

1997c. With Bruno Forte and Vincenzo Vitiello. *Filosofia e cristianesimo. Dialogo sull'inizio e la fine della storia*. Naples: Parresia Edizioni.

1998. *Der Archipel Europa*. Trans. Günter Memmert. Cologne: DuMont.

2000a. With Massimo Donà. *Arte Tragedia Tecnica*. Milan: Cortina.

2000b. *Le Dieu qui danse*. Trans. Marilène Raiola. Paris: Grasset.

2000c. With Sergio Romano et al. *Dopo 2000 anni di cristianesimo*. Milan: Mondadori.

2001a. With Maurice Bellet and Carlo Molari. *Il Cristianesimo sta morendo?* Città di Castello: l'altrapagina.

2001b. *Dell'Inizio*. Rev. ed. Milan: Adelphi.

2001c. *Duemilauno. Politica e futuro. Colloquio con Gianfranco Bettin*. Milan: Feltrinelli.

2002a. *Icone della Legge*. Rev. ed. Milan: Adelphi.

2002b. *Sulla responsabilità individuale. Conversazione con Paolo Bettiolo*. Sotto il Monte: Servitium.

2002c. With Antonio Maria Baggio and Vannino Chiti. *La politica come servizio alla speranza*. Florence: Polistampa.

2002d. *Wohnen. Denken*. Trans. Reinhard Kacianka. Klagenfurt: Ritter.

2003a. *Geo-filosofia dell'Europa*. Rev. ed. Milan: Adelphi.

2003b. *La lotta con Platone. Michelstaedter e Nietzsche*. Rome: Sossella.

2004a. With Aldo Bonomi and Giuseppe De Rita. *Che fine ha fatto la borghesia? Dialogo sulla nuova classe dirigente in Italia*. Turin: Einaudi.

2004b. *La città*. Rimini: Pazzini Editore.

2004c. *Della cosa ultima*. Milan: Adelphi, 2004.

2004d. *Il dolore dell'altro. Una lettura dell'Ecuba di Euripide e del libro di Giobbe*. Caserta: Edizioni Saletta dell'Uva.

2004e. *Soledad acogedora. De Leopardi a Celan*. Trans. Carolina del Olmo and César Rendueles. Madrid: Abada Editores.

2005a. *Magis amicus Leopardi. Due saggi*. Caserta: Edizioni Saletta dell'Uva.

2005b. *Paraíso y naufragio. Musil y El hombre sin atributos*. Trans. J. Pérez Ugena. Madrid: Abada Editores.

2006a. With Enzo Bianchi. *L'incredulità del credente*. Milan: Alboversorio.

2006b. With Luciano Canfora, Gianfranco Ravasi, and Gustavo Zagrebelsky. *La legge sovrana. Nomos Basileus*. Ed. Ivano Dionigi. Milan: Rizzoli.

2006c. With Domenico Jervolino and Aldo Masullo. *Scienza e coscienza tra parola e silenzio. Atti del Convegno del Centro per la Filosofia Italiana (Monte Compatri, 2–4 maggio 2002)*. Ed. Pietro Ciaravolo, Rome: Aracne.

2007a. With Raimon Panikkar and Jean Léonard Touadi. *Il problema dell'altro. Dallo scontro al dialogo tra le culture*. Città di Castello: l'altrapagina.

2007b. With Biagio De Giovanni, Giuseppe Galasso, et al. *Sul partito democratico. Opinioni a confronto*. Ed. Roberto Racinaro, Michele Salvati, and Pietro Scoppola. Naples: Guida.

2007c. *Tre icone*. Milan: Adelphi.

2007d. With Mario Tronti. *Teologia e politica al crocevia della storia*. Milan: Alboversorio.

2007e. *Anni decisivi*. Caserta: Edizioni Saletta dell'Uva.

2007f. Ed. *Sofocle, Antigone*. Turin: Einaudi.

2007g. *Europa o la filosofía*. Trans. Francisco Campillo. Madrid: Machado Libros.

ARTICLES CITED IN THIS VOLUME

1969. "Sulla genesi del pensiero negativo." *Contropiano. Materiali marxisti* 2, no. 1: 131–200.

1971. "*Entsagung*." *Contropiano. Materiali marxisti* 4, no. 2: 411–444.

1975. "Di alcuni motivi in Walter Benjamin." *Nuova Corrente* 67: 209–243.

1977a. "Razionalità' e 'Irrazionalità' nella critica del Politico in Deleuze e Foucault." *aut aut* 161: 119–133.

1977b. "La Vienna di Wittgenstein." *Nuova Corrente* 72–73: 59–106.

1978a. "Die Christenheit oder Europa." *Nuova Corrente* 76–77: 216–241.

1978b. "Eupalinos o l'architettura." *Nuova Corrente* 76–77: 422–442.

1978c. "L'impolitico nietzschiano." In Friedrich Nietzsche, *Il libro del filosofo*, 103–120.

1978d. "Intransitabili utopie." In Hugo von Hofmannstahl, *La torre*, 155–226.

1978e. "Trasformazioni dello Stato e progetto politico." *Critica marxista* 16, no. 5: 27–61.

1979. "Weber e la critica della ragione socialista." In Max Weber, *Sul socialismo reale*, 81–108.

1980. "Eupalinos or Architecture." Trans. Stephen Sartarelli. *Oppositions: A Journal for Ideas and Criticism in Architecture* 21: 169–181.

1981a. "L'attenzione profana di Robert Musil." *Metaphorein* 7: 65–73.

1981b. "Catastrofi." *Laboratorio Politico* 5–6: 145–161.

1981c. "Diritto e giustizia. Saggio sulle dimensioni teologica e mistica del moderno Politico." *Il Centauro. Rivista di filosofia e teoria politica* 1, no. 2: 58–88.

1981d. "Progetto." *Laboratorio Politico* 2:88–119.

1981e. "Sull'inesistenza dell'estetica nietzscheana." *Humanitas. Rivista bimestrale di cultura* 1:149–162.

1982a. "Il linguaggio del potere in Canetti. Uno spoglio." *Laboratorio Politico* 4:185–197.

1982b. "Salvezza che cade." *Il Centauro. Rivista di filosofia e teoria politica* 6:70–101.

1983. "Metafisica della gioventù." In György Lukács, *Diario (1910–1911)*, 69–148.

1984. "Misura e dismisura della democrazia." *Democrazia e diritto. Rivista critica di diritto e giurisprudenza* 24, no. 6: 159–165.

1989. "Venezia possibile." *Micromega. Le ragioni della sinistra* 1:217–240.

1991. "Carl Schmitt e lo stato." *La rivista dei libri* 9:12–15.

1992. "Geo-Filosofia dell'Europa." *Paradosso. Quadrimestrale di filosofia* 1, no. 2: 175–184.

1995. "Filosofia e teologia." In Paolo Rossi, ed., *La filosofia*, 365–421.

1998. "Nota." Gianfranco Bettin, *Petrolkimiko. Le voci e le storie di un crimine di pace*. Milan: Baldini & Castoldi, 178–189.

1999. "L'Espagne et Venise." In César Vichard de Saint-Réal, *Conjuration des Espagnols contre la république de Venise en 1618*. Toulouse: Ombres, 9–21.

2001. "Miglio, la lezione di un eretico." *La Repubblica*, August 20.

2003. "Robert Musil, *L'uomo senza qualità*, 1930–43." In Franco Moretti, ed., *Il romanzo*, vol. 5. *Lezioni*. Turin: Einaudi, 5:491–537.

2006. "Introduzione." In Max Weber, *La scienza come professione. La politica come professione*. Milan: Mondadori, v–lx.